China's One Belt One Road Initiative and Private International Law

China's One Belt One Road Initiative and Private International Law explores possible challenges to the success of the OBOR arising from the situational interface of diversity of laws, with the focus primarily on issues associated with private international law. It shows the latest state of knowledge on the topic and will be of interest to researchers, academics, policymakers, and students interested in private international law issues pertaining to the OBOR routes as well as private international law in general, Asian studies, and the politics of international trade.

Poomintr Sooksripaisarnkit is a Lecturer in Maritime Law with the Australian Maritime College, University of Tasmania, Australia.

Sai Ramani Garimella is a Senior Assistant Professor at the Faculty of Legal Studies, South Asian University, New Delhi, India.

Routledge Research in International Law

Available:

The Rule of Unwritten International Law
Customary Law, General Principles, and World Order
Peter G. Staubach

State Interest and the Sources of International Law
Doctrine, Morality, and Non-Treaty Law
Markus P. Beham

Demilitarisation and International Law in Context
The Åland Islands
Sia Spiliopoulou Åkermark and Saila Heinikoski

International Criminal Law and Sexual Violence against Women
The Interpretation of Gender in the Contemporary International Criminal Trial
Daniela Nadj

Unilateral Acts
A History of a Legal Doctrine
Betina Appel Kuzmarov

Regional Developmentalism Through Law
The Use of Law to Support the Effective Establishment of an African Economic Community
Jonathan Bashi Rudahindwa

China's One Belt One Road Initiative and Private International Law
Poomintr Sooksripaisarnkit and Sai Ramani Garimella

For a full list of titles in this series, visit www.routledge.com/Routledge-Research-in-International-Law/book-series/INTNLLAW

China's One Belt One Road Initiative and Private International Law

Edited by
Poomintr Sooksripaisarnkit
and Sai Ramani Garimella

Routledge
Taylor & Francis Group
LONDON AND NEW YORK

First published 2018
by Routledge

2 Park Square, Milton Park, Abingdon, Oxfordshire OX14 4RN
52 Vanderbilt Avenue, New York, NY 10017

Routledge is an imprint of the Taylor & Francis Group, an informa business

First issued in paperback 2020

British Library Cataloguing-in-Publication Data
A catalogue record for this book is available from the British Library

Library of Congress Cataloging-in-Publication Data
A catalog record for this book has been requested

ISBN: 978-1-138-56382-7 (hbk)
ISBN: 978-0-367-59044-4 (pbk)

Typeset in Galliard
by Apex CoVantage, LLC

Contents

Editors and contributors

About the editors

Dr Poomintr Sooksripaisarnkit LLB (Thammasat), LLM (International Commercial Law) (Leicester), PhD (Leicester) is a Lecturer in Maritime Law with the Australian Maritime College, University of Tasmania. Prior to joining the Australian Maritime College, he was an Assistant Professor with the School of Law, City University of Hong Kong, where he was also the Associate Director of the Hong Kong Centre for Maritime and Transportation Law. His research interests lie in the fields of insurance law (marine and non-marine), admiralty and maritime law (excluding the law of the sea and regulations), carriage of goods by sea, international sales of goods carried by sea, private international law (commercial conflict of laws), and aspects of international arbitration (relevant to conflict of laws). He is an Accredited Mediator by both the Centre for Effective Dispute Resolution (CEDR) and the Hong Kong Mediation Accreditation Association Limited (HKMAAL). He is a Member of the Chartered Institute of Arbitrators (CIArb) and the London Court of International Arbitration (LCIA). He is also a Supporting Member of the London Maritime Arbitrators Association (LMAA). He was an Executive Committee Member of the Hong Kong Maritime Law Association (HKMLA) and is still involved in activities of the Hong Kong Insurance Law Association Limited (HILA), where he used to sit on the Executive Committee. In Australia, he is a Member of the Maritime Law Association of Australia and New Zealand (MLAANZ) and an Associate Member of the Australian Insurance Law Association (AILA). His recent publications include chapter contributions on 'The Hague Convention on Choice of Court Agreements – Should the European Union's Footsteps Be Followed?' in Sai Ramani Garimella and Stellina Jolly (eds), *Private International Law: South Asian States' Practice* (Springer Nature Pte Ltd 2017) and 'Bills of Lading', 'Marine Insurance', and 'Jurisdiction and Applicable Law' in Justice Barma and Mary Thomson (eds), *Maritime Law and Practice in Hong Kong* (Sweet & Maxwell Asia 2015). He is working on a book entitled *Marine Insurance – Comparative Common Law Perspectives* (under contract with Springer Nature Pte Ltd until early 2022). His academic activities can be followed from his website www.poomintr.com or his Twitter @pom_maritime.

Dr Sai Ramani Garimella works as a Senior Assistant Professor at the Faculty of Legal Studies, South Asian University, New Delhi, India. She was trained at the International Chamber of Commerce (ICC) summer programme in International Commercial Arbitration. Her research interests are in legal theory and in private law as represented in private international law, international commercial arbitration, international dispute settlement, and comparative constitutional law. Her recent research work includes co-editing a collection of research papers, *Private International Law: South Asian States' Practice* (Springer Nature Pte Ltd 2017). She also authored the country report on the law of international arbitration in India in this collection. She has written a textbook on private international law for undergraduate courses in Indian universities entitled *Private International Law* (Central Law Publications 2014) and served as the subject-expert for the UGC-NME e-lecture database on private international law, a programme sponsored by the Government of India. Her research work has appeared in the volumes of the *AALCO Journal of International Law*, published by the Asian-African Legal Consultative Organization, and the *Journal of the Indian Law Institute*. Her recent research on Seat-centric Arbitration and India is available in the latest volume of *Young Arbitration Review*. She also served on the editorial board of the *Journal of Law and Conflict Resolution*.

About the contributors

Banu Bozkurt was born in Germany and raised in Turkey. She graduated from the University of Galatasaray (a bilingual French/Turkish university) Law School. She obtained her postgraduate degree in European Union Law from Izmir University of Economics. She completed her PhD degree in the field of Air and Maritime Law from Yeditepe University with her thesis entitled 'Legal Responsibility of Air Transporter in case of the Death and Bodily Injury of the Passenger under Turkish and International Law'.

She is working at Akdeniz University as an Assistant Professor teaching and researching on maritime law, insurance law, and air law.

She has participated in many international conferences including the International Congress of Maritime Arbitrators (ICMA) XIX (Hong Kong) and XX (Copenhagen), the Comité Maritime International (CMI) 2015 Conference at Istanbul, and the ETL 50 years of Maritime Law in Motion. She is a member of the Turkish Maritime Law Association and an arbitrator of the International Arbitration Chamber of Paris (CAIP). She is a writer and co-writer of many books and articles on carriage of goods and persons by sea, maritime law, carriage of goods and persons by air, aviation law, and insurance law.

Kittiwat Chunchaemsai is an Assistant Professor within the Faculty of Law, Thammasat University. He received his LLB degree with the Second Class Honours also from the Faculty of Law, Thammasat University. He then passed the Thai Bar Examination and became qualified in Thailand. He received his LLM degree in International Trade Regulation from the Faculty of Law, Thammasat University and another LLM degree in International Economic Law with Merit from the London School of Economics and Political Science. In 2012, he also attended the Summer Courses on Private International Law organised by the Hague Academy of Private International Law. He obtained his PhD from Durham University in the United Kingdom in 2015. His teaching and research interests lie in Private International Law (Conflict of Laws), International Business and International Trade Laws, International Financial Law, Juristic Acts and Contracts, and European Law.

Béligh Elbati is an Associate Professor at the Graduate School of Law and Politics – Osaka University, where he teaches, *inter alia*, Japanese law, comparative law, and private international law. He is a holder of the Master's in Law Degree in Common Law Studies obtained in Tunisia. Since 2008, he has been established in Japan, where he continued his advanced studies in the field of Private International Law. In addition to another Master's degree in the Legal Studies in 2011, he earned his Doctor of Law Degree in 2014 from the Graduate School of Law, Kyoto University. His thesis was on the theme of the liberalization of the recognition and enforcement of foreign judgments. He is the author of a number of scientific articles and case notes notably in the field of private international law (international jurisdiction, the recognition and enforcement of foreign judgments, and choice of law). His research, which is based on extensive comparative research, focuses on the development of private international law at a national level, especially in some Asian and Arab countries. Part of his research is focused on the development of private international in Tunisia and other Arab countries in order to make it accessible to foreign lawyers and scholars. List of publications, which is regularly updated, is available at https://papers.ssrn.com/sol3/cf_dev/AbsByAuth.cfm?per_id=1567139.

Pengyuan Fu is a PhD candidate in the Law School of Wuhan University, class of 2019. He is mainly engaged in research on private international law and cyberspace law. He worked as one of the editors of *Chinese Yearbook of Private International Law and Comparative Law* (2016). He worked at the banking and finance department of King & Wood Mallesons from April 2014 to September 2015. He received his Bachelor of Laws degree and Bachelor of Economics degree from Wuhan University in 2012 and his LLM degree from University of California, Los Angeles in 2013.

Rishi Gulati is a Barrister at the Victorian Bar, Australia, where he primarily practices in public and private international law, having represented clients at various international fora. In 2017–2018, he has been a Visiting Lecturer in Public International Law at King's College University, London, where he is also a Dickson Poon Scholar of Law. He is on the Panel of Counsel of the Federation of International Civil Servants. He is an Affiliate Member of the International Criminal Law Bar Association and is an Oxford International Organizations Rapporteur. Previously, he has been a judge's associate at the Federal Court of Australia, and between 2011 and 2014, he worked as an international lawyer for the Australian Attorney-General's Department and also internationally in various capacities. He completed a Bachelor of Laws with Honours from the Australian National University in 2008, and undertook an Advanced Masters in Public International Law from Leiden University in 2009–2010. He has been a Laureate Research Fellow at the University of New South Wales, where he undertook research on national security law as well as lecturing in public international law. He has published various articles and book chapters on International Organisations Law, the Law of Nationality and Citizenship, International Terrorism, and Private International Law. Additionally, he is presently working on a major project on the right to a fair trial in international law and another project on international institutional law.

Yujun Guo is the Professor of Law and Doctoral Supervisor of Wuhan University Institute of International Law, the Director of Wuhan University Art Law Center, the Vice-President and Secretary-General of China Society of Private International Law, the Secretary-General of HAN Depei Jurisprudence Foundation of Wuhan University, the Specialist of Legal Committee in Cultural Relic Academy China, a member of International Law Association, the Associate Member of International Academy of Comparative Law, the Deputy Secretary-General of the Standing Committee of People's Congress of Hubei Province, and a member of the 12th People's Congress of Hubei Province, China.

She was awarded the Prize of Hubei Province Young and Middle-Aged Outstanding Jurist in 2010. She has been researching and teaching conflict of laws, international civil procedure law, international commercial arbitration law, art and cultural heritage law, and cultural industry law for many years. She has published many books and papers in China and overseas. Her leading treatise is *The Law of International Loan*. Her papers include *Trends of Private International Law in the 21st Century*, *Changing Private International Law in China*, *The Practice and Legislation on Proof of Foreign Law in China*, *Personal Status in Chinese Private International Law Reform*, *On the Legitimacy Crisis in Investment Treaty Arbitration and Its Remedies*, and *Who Owns the Rat Head and Rabbit Head of Yuanmingyuan*.

She received her Doctor of Law from Wuhan University in 1993. She studied at Hokkaido University, Japan. She was the Chinese member of the working group for the Hague Conference on Private International Law's project on *Principles of Choice of Law in International Commercial Contracts.* She was a visiting scholar at Harvard-Yenching Institute in the US, Osnabrück University and Max Planck Institute of Comparative and International Private Law, Germany, and so forth.

Zhengxin Huo was born on 5 November 1976, in Anhui Province, China. He received his PhD from Wuhan University in June 2005. He is currently a Professor of Law and Vice Dean of Faculty of International Law at China University of Political Science and Law (CUPL). He is an observer of the UNESCO, an Associate Member of the International Academy of Comparative Law, a member of the Standing Committee of China Society of Private International Law, and an Associate Member of the Centre for Private International Law at the Law School of the University of Aberdeen, the United Kingdom. He is also a practicing lawyer of the PRC.

His principal areas of teaching and research include private international law, comparative law, and international cultural property law, and he has published extensively in these areas. His recent works in English are published in *International & Comparative Law Quarterly*, *American Journal of Comparative Law*, *Hong Kong Law Journal*, *Asian-Pacific Law and Policy Journal*, *Journal of East Asia and International Law*, *International Journal of Cultural Policy*, and other prominent journals. He has also published two monographs and more than fifty articles and review essays in Chinese. He has won various awards for academic and teaching achievements in China. He attended the Summer Course of Private International Law at the Hague Academy of International Law in 2004 and has been a visiting scholar at Minnesota Law School (2007) and Seoul National University School of Law, Republic of Korea (2009–2010). He may be contacted at zhengxinh@cupl.edu.cn or huozhengxin@hotmail.com.

Thomas John joined the Permanent Bureau of the Hague Conference on Private International Law in 2014 and works as a Principal Legal Officer. The primary focus of his work is international litigation and commercial work, including the Hague Convention of 30 June 2005 on Choice of Court Agreements, the Hague Principles on Choice of Law in International Commercial Contracts, and the Conference's Judgments Project. A dual Australian/German national, he has over ten years of professional experience in private practice, public service, and academia. His interests include private international law, international procedural, commercial arbitration, banking and financial law and advocacy. He also has a strong interest in constitutional law, with a particular focus on federal systems. With undergraduate and postgraduate qualifications in both common and civil law jurisdictions, he has a strong comparative approach to his work.

Prior to joining the Permanent Bureau of the Hague Conference on Private International Law, he headed the Private International Law Section of the Australian Attorney-General's Department, Australia's designated National Organ to the Hague Conference on Private International Law and its Central Authority for the Hague Service, Evidence and Apostille Conventions. In charge of this area, he was Australia's expert for these three Conventions and several key Hague Conference projects, including the Judgments Project and the Choice of Law Principles. Drawing on his experiences with these Conventions and projects, he initiated and oversaw several significant private international and commercial law reform projects.

In previous roles, he acted as a lawyer to the Australian Government, the Australian Federal Parliament, and the Queensland Government. He also worked as in house legal advisor to a German bank. He has held several teaching positions including at the University of Queensland and the University of New England.

He is admitted as a Barrister of the Australian High Court and Federal Court as well as in the state of Queensland. He is a member of the Chartered Institute of Arbitrators. He has published widely, co-authoring *The Future of Australian Federalism: Comparative and Interdisciplinary Perspectives* with Cambridge University Press and *Australian Constitutional Law: Commentary and Materials* with Oxford University Press. Other publications, also covering private international law, include book chapters, articles, and research papers and commentaries on proposed legislation for the Australian Federal Parliament.

Ivana Kunda is an Associate Professor and the Head of the International and European Private Law Department at the Faculty of Law of the University of Rijeka and Vice Dean for Science and Director of the Doctoral Study Program at the same Faculty. She received her LLM in EU law from the University of Rijeka and her SJD from the University of Zagreb. Throughout her academic career, she received many scholarships and awards including the Fulbright Research Fellow Scholarship in 2010 for the research at the Columbia University, the *Gewerblicher Rechtsschutz und Urheberrecht* scholarship in 2007, 2008, and 2014 for the research at the Max Planck Institute for Innovation and Competition, the *Deutsche Stiftung für internationale rechtliche Zusammenarbeit* scholarship in 2002 for research at the University of Hamburg and the Max Planck Institute for Comparative and International Private Law, and the University of Rijeka Foundation Award for the year of 2008. She participated as a researcher in various domestic and EU scientific projects, ranging from restructuring of knowledge-based companies and cross-border financial transactions to EU family law, enforcement of foreign judgments and access to justice in the context of business and human rights in the EU. Within these and other projects, she was invited to train judges and legal practitioners on topics on EU law in Germany, Italy, Spain, Finland, Lithuania, Romania, and Croatia. She authored a monograph on overriding mandatory provisions written in English and papers and book chapters published in Croatia and abroad. Two most recent from 2017 are chapters in books "Secondary Liability of Internet Service Providers" and "Cross-Border Litigation in Europe" published with Hart and Springer, respectively. She edited several books on EU legal topics, the latest one being *EU Competition and State Aid Rules: Public and Private Enforcement* published with Springer in 2017. She had been invited to teach the European Private International Law graduate course at the University of Navarra in 2010, where she spent a semester there as a guest professor. Since 2012, she has been teaching the European Private Law and Intellectual Property Law course within the graduate program of the Intellectual Property Summer Institute of the Michigan State University. She was elected as a member of the Scientific Committee for State Administration, Judiciary and Rule of Law of the Croatian Academy of Science and Art and as a member of the editorial board of the Santander Art and Culture Law Review (for Intellectual Property and Internet law). Since the foundation of the Centre for Private International Law at the University of Aberdeen, she acts as its associate member. She is a member of the International Law Association (currently a member of the Committee on Intellectual Property and Private International Law) and International Association for the Advancement of Teaching and Research in Intellectual Property. She is also the Deputy President of the Croatian Comparative Law Association.

King Fung Tsang is an Assistant Professor in the Faculty of Law at The Chinese University of Hong Kong. His main research areas are comparative private international law and company law. He has published in a number of leading international journals, including *the Journal of Private International Law*, *Texas International Law Journal*, and *Columbia Journal of Asian Law*.

Prior to joining academia, he practised as a corporate finance lawyer at two leading international law firms, working in their New York, London, Hong Kong, Beijing, and Shanghai offices. He is admitted to practice in the State of New York, England and Wales, and Hong Kong. He was awarded his LLB and PCLL at the University of Hong Kong. He also holds degrees from Georgetown University (SJD), Columbia University (LLM., JD) and University College London (LLM).

Man Yip is an Associate Professor of Law at the Singapore Management University. Before joining academia, she worked as a dispute lawyer at WongPartnership LLP, practising mainly in the area of international commercial arbitration. She researches in equity, contract, restitution, remedies, and private international law. She has published in leading peer-reviewed journals including *International & Comparative Law Quarterly*, *Cambridge Law Journal*, *Legal Studies*, *Lloyd's Maritime and Commercial Law*

Quarterly, *Conveyancer and Property Lawyer*, *Journal of Equity*, *Journal of Business Law*, *Restitution Law Review*, *Singapore Journal of Legal Studies*, and *Singapore Academy of Law Journal*. Her work has been cited by the Singapore Court of Appeal, Singapore High Court, and the High Court of England and Wales as well as treatises on various areas of private law. She has also acted as an expert witness on Singapore commercial law and private international law in an international commercial arbitration matter. In 2016, she was appointed the DS Lee Foundation Fellow in recognition of her research on issues of Asian business law. She is presently the Deputy Director of the Centre for Cross-Border Commercial Law in Asia, Singapore Management University.

Bruno Zeller PhD (Law) is a Professor in Transnational Commercial Law at The University of Western Australia, Perth. His teaching interests include international trade law, conflict of laws, international arbitration, and maritime law. His research contributes to the understanding of uniform international laws, which have developed under the auspices of the United Nations, especially the United Nations Convention on Contracts for the International Sales of Goods. In addition, he has also published on alternative dispute resolution mechanisms and free trade agreements. He is an Adjunct Professor at Murdoch University, Perth, and an Adjunct Professor at Sir Zelman Cowan Centre, Victoria University, Melbourne. He is also a visiting professor at La Trobe University, Melbourne, and Humboldt University of Berlin. He is also a fellow of The Australian Institute for Commercial Arbitration and listed as an Arbitrator with the Maritime Law Association of Australia and New Zealand (MLAANZ).

Foreword

China's Belt and Road Initiative (BRI) (also known as One Belt One Road or OBOR) is an ambitious undertaking. It aspires to enhance trade and investment among more than sixty countries along land and sea routes spanning Asia, Africa, and Europe. Some have criticised the project as being too vague. But the boldness and scale of the idea is such that it will inevitably take time to know and understand precisely what will be involved, and how and what will have to be implemented, if the enterprise is to be successful. Now, then, is the time to engage in spirited debate on how the BRI's objectives can best be achieved.

China's One Belt One Road Initiative and Private International Law co-edited by Poomintr Sooksripaisarnkit and Sai Ramani Garimella is part of that ongoing discussion. The book offers ideas on what it will take for the BRI to deliver on its promise. The book does this by examining private international law issues that are likely to arise in connection with the anticipated increase in commercial dealings among those engaging in business along the Belt and Road. The chapters in the book, each written by a specialist contributor, consider possible answers to the familiar questions of the conflict of laws in the novel context of the BRI. Those questions are: (1) How will courts in relevant countries resolve conflicting jurisdictional claims? (2) Where a court asserts jurisdiction, will it apply foreign law to the cross-border dispute before it, and (if so) what foreign law, and how will it ascertain the content of that law? (3) Will a judgment of a court in one country be recognised and enforced in another Belt and Road country? The book, however, does not just confine itself to the familiar. It also explores the degree to which the commercial laws and dispute resolution practices of Belt and Road countries may be harmonised, so as to provide certainty and promote efficiency within the BRI.

Certain themes pervade the book and it might be useful to signal just two as matters to watch out for as emerging trends in the BRI. The first theme is the importance of the work of the Hague Conference on Private International Law and the United Nations Commission on International Trade Law (UNCITRAL). The Hague Conference, through its conventions on legal cooperation (especially the 1961 Apostille Convention, the 1965 Service Abroad Convention, the 1970 Evidence Abroad Convention, and the

2005 Choice of Court Agreements Conventions) and its Regional Officer Asia Pacific (ROAP) on the one hand, and UNCITRAL through its 1958 New York Convention, its various Model Laws, and its Regional Center Asia Pacific (RCAP) on the other, are both bound to play major roles in the harmonisation of commercial laws and dispute resolution practices along the Belt and Road. The second theme is the rise of international commercial courts, especially (within the Asia Pacific) the Singapore International Commercial Court (SICC). Litigation of disputes before international courts will offer an alternative to international commercial arbitration and mediation as modes of resolving cross-border disputes and will hopefully help to bring down the cost of dispute resolution altogether along the Belt and Road.

There is, therefore, much excitement to look forward to in the near future. This book is a harbinger of what is to come.

Anselmo Reyes
1 January 2018

Preface

An idea to create the 'One Belt One Road' (OBOR), since President Xi Jinping of the People's Republic of China proclaimed it in 2013, has sparked much interest among international community. Many conferences – both in the People's Republic of China and overseas – were organised to debate on different aspects of this idea. Gigantic and ambitious as this project is, it in fact gives rise to much ambiguity and uncertainty. During the course of 2016, the Law Society of Hong Kong established the Belt and Road Committee and, in doing so, it called for advisers on aspects involving conflict of law issues relevant to the Belt and Road. This pointed to the fact that, within the context of the One Belt One Road, private international law is indeed much of a concern. So far, emphasis has been put on building or developing infrastructures along countries within the OBOR routes. It must be reminded, however, that having adequate and efficient infrastructures is only the first step in support of the very ultimate goal of the OBOR project, that is, to create seamless international trade system from the People's Republic of China to significant parts of the world – Eastern Europe and Africa. In fact, such smooth trade system must be supported by well-harmonised legal infrastructures. Yet, readers would appreciate, upon examining what different chapters in this book have revealed, such uniform legal mechanism simply does not exist. It will take time for a real harmonisation of international commercial laws and dispute resolutions to happen. It is with hope that all thought-provoking chapters in this book will stimulate and generate further discussions towards such efforts in harmonisation of law, at least within the OBOR participating countries, if not throughout the world.

To this end, the editors would like to thank anonymous reviewers who were supportive of the initial proposal for this edited collection. The editors would also like to thank all contributors who accepted our invitation to contribute despite their busy schedule. Their tolerance of our chaser e-mails is much appreciated. The editors extend their special gratitude to Professor Anselmo Reyes, who contributed a valuable foreword for this book. Without support from a very efficient team of the publisher, Routledge, this book would not come to light. The editors would like to thank the team, especially Brianna Ascher, Mary Del Plato, Siobhán Poole, and Nicola Sharpe, for their enthusiasm and guidance to see this project through.

Poomintr Sooksripaisarnkit
Sai Ramani Garimella
18 January 2018

Acknowledgements

Dr Sooksripaisarnkit would like to acknowledge spiritual support from his father, Mr Chaiporn Sooksripaisarnkit, and his mother, Mrs Apira Sooksripaisarnkit. He would also like to acknowledge all his former students in private international law class at the School of Law, City University of Hong Kong, for their active participation in class, which stirred his enthusiasm on the subject.

Dr Garimella acknowledges the inspirational support of her parents, Mr Krishna Murthy Garimella and Mrs Parvati Garimella. She would also like to acknowledge the support of family at home. She would like to take this opportunity to acknowledge the engaged conversations with the students at the Faculty of Legal Studies, South Asian University, and especially MZ Ashraful, and Parthiban B for research assistance.

1 The role of private international law in the context of the One Belt One Road initiative

Poomintr Sooksripaisarnkit, Sai Ramani Garimella

Introduction

So one would ask: why is private international law much of a concern in China's One Belt One Road (OBOR) initiative? Indeed, it is a theme of this book that private international law should be a prime focus for this initiative to succeed. Yet academic discourses so far reveal blatant ignorance regarding this crucial branch of law. At the same time, the Chinese government, who initiated this gigantic project, has focused its mind only on building infrastructure in support of this initiative. This chapter will start in the first part by explaining what is, exactly, the OBOR. Then, in the second part, it will explain a branch of law called 'private international law' or 'conflict of laws' and what it entails and why it is crucial to the success of the OBOR. Then, in the third part, the authors will summarise the concerns brought up in each chapter of this book, all of which call for the immediate attention of the Chinese government, governments of other countries and those involved in the OBOR.

One Belt One Road initiative – what is it?

The OBOR is seen as 'an ambitious economic diplomacy initiative', and for President Xi Jinping, this initiative is supposed to be 'his one and only major foreign policy initiative during his administration'.[1] President Xi mentioned the idea to build the 'Silk Road Economic Belt' and the '21st-century Maritime Silk Road' during his visit to Central Asia and Southeast Asia in October 2013.[2] These two projects are collectively known as the OBOR. However, an academic commentator maintained that the idea of building the OBOR

1 Lim Tai Wei, 'Introduction' in Lim Tai Wei et al. (eds), *China's One Belt One Road Initiative* (Imperial College Press 2016), 3.

2 'Vision and Actions on Jointly Building Silk Road Economic Belt and 21st-century Maritime Silk Road Issued by the National Development and Reform Commission, Ministry of Foreign Affairs, and Ministry of Commerce of the People's Republic of China, with State Council authorisation' (*Xinhua*, 28 March 2015) <news.xinhuanet.com/English/china/2015-03/28/c_134105858.htm> accessed 26 August 2017.

could be traced back at least to October 2011 in Warsaw during the meeting of '22 heads of government from Central and Eastern Europe (CEE)' during which the then Prime Minister Wen Jiabao of China broke the news that China had been consulting with academics since 2010 on the thought of developing economically closer ties between countries along the old Silk Road.[3] The pioneering of the Silk Road happened in 138 BC when Zhang Qian, an official during the Han Dynasty, received an order from Emperor Wudi to travel to where is now Tajikistan to form a coalition against the Xiongnu, a tribe dominating China's north and northwest borders who, from time to time, posed dangers to the security of China.[4] Subsequently, Zhang Qian was ordered to make another expedition in 115 BC. It was recorded that after he arrived at Wusun 'at the southern part of Issyk Kul Lake in southeast Uzbekistan', he sent his subordinates to foster relationships with 'Dayueshi, Afghanistan, Iran, India, and other native states which led to the trade between Han China and Persia'.[5] Areas which came to be known as the Silk Road during those periods stretched from Changan (or, in modern days, Xi'An) to Istanbul. The Silk Road consisted of three major parts: '(1) Eastern section beginning in Changan, and running along the northern and southern borders of the Talamakan Desert to the Pamir Mountains; (2) Central Asian section crossing the Pamirs and the Central Asian region of Samarkand and (3) Western section that runs through Persia to the Mediterranean'.[6] The ancient Maritime Silk Road was developed later during the third century, and the maritime trade of China was further enhanced during the Tang Dynasty (618–907). Its route started at Guangzhou and Quanzhou before proceeding through the Malay Archipelago and then through the Persian Gulf.[7]

To reinvent this history in the twenty-first century, over 60 countries are included in the OBOR project. These countries span across Southeast Asia, South Asia, Central Asia, Northeast Asia, Central and Eastern Europe, Africa, Australasia and the Middle East.[8]

Southeast Asia	Brunei, Cambodia, Indonesia, Laos, Malaysia, Myanmar, Philippines, Singapore, Thailand, Timor-Leste, Vietnam
South Asia	Bangladesh, Bhutan, India, Maldives, Nepal, Pakistan, Sri Lanka

3 Henry Chan Hin Lee, 'The One Belt One Road Initiative – Who's Going to Pay for It? in Lim Tai Wei (n 1), 169–170.

4 TAN Ta Sen, 'Introduction of the Overland Silk Road and Maritime Silk Road' in Lim Tai Wei (n 1), 21–22.

5 *Ibid.*, 22.

6 *Ibid.*

7 *Ibid.*, 27.

8 See The Hong Kong Trade and Development Council, 'Belt and Road: Country Profile' <http://beltandroad.hktdc.com/en/country-profiles> accessed 27 August 2017.

Central Asia	Afghanistan, Armenia, Azerbaijan, Georgia, Kazakhstan, Kyrgyzstan, Tajikistan, Turkmenistan, Uzbekistan
Northeast Asia	Mongolia, Republic of Korea
Central and Eastern Europe	Albania, Belarus, Bosnia and Herzegovina, Bulgaria, Croatia, Czech Republic, Estonia, Hungary, Latvia, Lithuania, Macedonia, Moldova, Montenegro, Poland, Romania, Russia, Serbia, Slovenia, Turkey, Ukraine
Africa	Ethiopia, South Africa
Australasia	New Zealand
Middle East	Bahrain, Egypt, Iran, Iraq, Israel, Jordan, Kuwait, Lebanon, Oman, Palestine, Qatar, Saudi Arabia, Syria, United Arab Emirates, Yemen

As explained by the National Development and Reform Commission:

> The Silk Road Economic Belt focuses on bringing together China, Central Asia, Russia, and Europe (the Baltic); linking China with the Persian Gulf and the Mediterranean Sea through Central Asia and West Asia; and connecting China with Southeast Asia, South Asia, and the Indian Ocean. The 21st-Century Maritime Silk Road is designed to go from China's coast to Europe through the South China Sea and the Indian Ocean in one route, and from China's coast through the South China Sea to the South Pacific in the other.[9]

To support the success of this OBOR project, six international economic cooperation corridors have been created: 'the New Eurasia Land Bridge; China-Mongolia-Russia; China-Central Asia-West Asia; China-Indochina Peninsula; China-Pakistan; and Bangladesh-China-India-Myanmar'.[10] These six international economic cooperation corridors are explained as follows:

1 The New Eurasia Land Bridge Economic Corridor

The New Eurasia Land Bridge, also known as the Second Eurasia Land Bridge, is an international railway line running from Lianyungang in China's Jiangsu province through Alashankou in Xinjiang to Rotterdam in Holland. The China section of the line comprises the Lanzhou-Lianyungang Railway and the Lanzhou-Xinjiang Railway and stretches through eastern, central and western China. After exiting Chinese

9 'Full Text: Vision and Actions on Jointly Building Belt and Road' *(Xinhua)* <news.xinhuanet.com/English/china/2015–03/28/c_13410858_2.htm> accessed 27 August 2017.

10 The Hog Kong Trade and Development Council, 'The Belt and Road Initiative' <http://beltandroad.hktdc.com/sites/default/files/imported/beltandroadbasics/hktdc_1X0K715S_en.pdf> accessed 28 August 2017.

territory, the new land bridge passes through Kazakhstan, Russia, Belarus and Poland, reaching a number of coastal ports in Europe. Capitalising on the New Eurasia Land Bridge, China has opened an international freight rail route linking Chongqing to Diusburg (Germany), a direct freight train running between Wuhan and Mêlník and Pardubice (Czech Republic), a freight rail route from Chengdu to Łódź (Poland) and a freight rail route from Zhengzhou to Hamburg (Germany). All these new rail routes offer rail-to-rail freight transport as well as the convenience of 'one declaration, one inspection, one cargo release' for any cargo transported.

2 The China-Mongolia-Russia Economic Corridor

Linked by land, China, Mongolia and Russia have long established various economic ties and co-operation by way of frontier trade and cross-border co-operation. In September 2014, when the three country's heads of state met for the first time at the Shanghai Co-operation Organisation (SCO) Dushanbe Summit, agreement was reached on forging tripartite co-operation on the basis of China-Russia, China-Mongolia and Russia-Mongolia bilateral ties. At the same meeting, the principles, directions and key areas of trilateral co-operation were defined. The three heads of state also agreed to bring together the building of China's Silk Road Economic Belt, the renovation of Russia's Eurasia Land Bridge and the proposed development of Mongolia's Steppe Road. This commitment will strengthen rail and highway connectivity and construction, advance customs clearance and transport facilitation, promote cross-national co-operation in transportation and help establish the China-Russia-Mongolia Economic Corridor. In July 2015, the three leaders held the second meeting in the Russian city of Ufa. The second summit saw the official adoption of the *Mid-term Roadmap for Development of Trilateral Co-operation between China, Russia and Mongolia.*

3 China-Central Asia-West Asia Economic Corridor

The China-Central Asia-West Asia Economic Corridor runs from Xinjiang in China and exits the country via Alashankou to join the railway networks of Central Asia and West Asia before reaching the Mediterranean coast and the Arabian Peninsula. The corridor mainly covers five countries in Central Asia (Kazakhstan, Kyrgyzstan, Tajikistan, Uzbekistan and Turkmenistan) as well as Iran and Turkey in West Asia.

At the third China-Central Asia Co-operation Forum held in Shandong in June 2015, a commitment to 'jointly building the Silk Road Economic Belt' was incorporated into a joint declaration signed by China and the five Central Asian countries. Prior to that, China had signed bilateral agreements on the building of the Silk Road Economic Belt with Tajikistan, Kazakhstan and Kyrgyzstan. China had concluded a co-operation document with Uzbekistan on the building of the Silk Road Economic Belt. This was aimed at further deepening and expanding mutually beneficial co-operation in such areas as trade, investment, finance, transport and communication. The national development strategies of the five Central-Asian countries – including Kazakhstan's 'Road to Brightness', Tajikistan's 'Energy, Transport and Food' (a three-pronged strategy aimed at revitalising the country) and Turkmenistan's 'Strong and Happy Era' – all share common ground with the establishment of the Silk Road Economic Belt.

4 China-Indochina Peninsula Economic Corridor

During the Fifth Leaders Meeting on Greater Mekong Sub-regional Economic Co-operation held in Bangkok in December 2014, Chinese Premier Li Keqiang put forward three suggestions with regard to deepening the relations between China and the five countries in the Indochina Peninsula. The suggestions were (1) jointly planning and building an extensive transportation network as well as number of industrial co-operation projects, (2) creating a new mode of co-operation for fund-raising and (3) promoting sustainable and coordinated socio-economic development. Currently, the countries along the Greater Mekong River are engaged in building nine cross-national highways, connecting east and west and linking north to south. A number of these construction projects have already been completed. Guangxi, for example, has already finished work on an expressway leading to the Friendship Gate and the port of Dongxing at the China-Vietnam border. The province has also opened an international rail line, running from Nanning to Hanoi, as well as introducing air routes to several major Southeast Asian cities.

5 China-Pakistan Economic Corridor

The concept of the China-Pakistan Economic Corridor was first raised by Premier Li Keqiang during his visit to Pakistan in May 2013. At the time, the objective was to build an economic corridor running from Kashgar, Xinjiang, in the north, to Pakistan's Gwadar Port in the south. At present, the two governments have mapped out a provisional long-term plan for building highways, railways, oil and natural gas pipelines and optic fibre networks stretching from Kashgar to Gwadar Port. According to a joint declaration issued by China and Pakistan in Islamabad in April 2015, the two countries will proactively advance key cooperation projects, including Phase II of the upgrade and renovation of the Karakoram Highway (the Thakot-Havelian section), an expressway at the east bay of Gwadar Port, a new international airport, an expressway from Karachi to Lahore (the Multan-Sukkur section), the Lahore rail transport orange line, the Haier-Ruba economic zone and the China-Pakistan cross-national optic fibre network.

6 Bangladesh-China-India-Myanmar-Economic Corridor

In a series of meetings during Premier Li Keqiang's visit to India in May 2013, China and India jointly proposed the building of the Bangladesh-China-India-Myanmar Economic Corridor. In December 2013, the Bangladesh-China-India-Myanmar Economic Corridor Joint Working Group convened its first meeting in Kunming. Official representatives

> from the four countries conducted in-depth discussions with regard to the development prospects, priority areas of cooperation and cooperation mechanisms for the economic corridor. They also reached extensive consensus on cooperation in such areas as transportation infrastructure, investment and commercial circulation and people-to-people connectivity. The four parties signed meeting minutes and agreed the Bangladesh-China-India-Myanmar Economic Corridor joint study programme, establishing a mechanism for promoting cooperation among the four governments.[11]

Behind the massive OBOR plan lie three policy drivers. First, China is faced with an oversupply of domestic products.[12] Some of these products are needed overseas, especially to build up infrastructure in support of the OBOR project, including materials for buildings infrastructure and equipment used in railway networks.[13] Second, this project will enhance China's influence in other parts of the world.[14] As a policy to counter the Asian financial crisis which happened in 1997, China has developed expertise in constructing cost-saving basic infrastructure. China's capacity to offer construction of such cost-saving infrastructure and to provide necessary financing fits the needs of many developing countries involved in the OBOR project – many of which are 'either unrated or rated below investment grade'.[15] Third, the OBOR provides a chance for China to demonstrate its financial strengths by providing alternative financing sources.[16]

To enable many of these developing countries to build infrastructure to support the OBOR plan, China made funds available through different channels. The first channel is through the Asian Infrastructure Investment Bank (AIIB) which started operating on 16 January 2016.[17] Per Article 4 of the Articles of Agreement, the bank has the authorised capital stock of US$100 billion.[18] As of 17 June 2017, it consisted of 37 regional members (including countries such as Australia, China, Hong Kong, India, New Zealand, Singapore and Thailand), and 19 non-regional members (including countries such as the United Kingdom, France, Germany, Denmark, Austria, the Netherlands, Norway and Switzerland).[19] These members contributed

11 *Ibid.*
12 Lim (n 1), 3.
13 Chan (n 3), 173.
14 Lim (n 1), 3.
15 Chan (n 3), 172.
16 Lim (n 1), 3.
17 See Asian Infrastructure Investment Bank, 'Introduction' <www.aiib.org/en/about-aiib/index.html> accessed 27 August 2017.
18 Asian Infrastructure Investment Bank, 'Asian Infrastructure Investment Bank: Articles of Agreement' <www.aiib.org/en/about-aiib/basic-documents/_download/articles-of-agreement/basic_document_english-bank_articles_of_agreement.pdf> accessed 27 August 2017.
19 Asian Infrastructure Investment Bank, 'Members and Prospective Members of the Bank' <www.aiib.org/en/about-aiib/governance/members-of-bank/index.html> accessed 27 August 2017.

funds by way of subscriptions. They also have voting power proportionate to their subscription. The scope of the work of the AIIB is to provide funds for 'sound and sustainable projects in energy and power, transportation and telecommunications, rural infrastructure and agriculture development, water supply and sanitation, environmental protection, and urban development and logistics'.[20] To date, the AIIB has approved funding for a variety of projects such as Gujarat Rural Roads in India, Natural Gas Infrastructure in Bangladesh, Railway System Preparation in Oman, Duqm Port Commercial Terminal and Operational Zone in Oman and National Motorway M-4 in Pakistan.[21] As Chan observed:

> AIIB will surely face a steep learning curve ahead; how long will the management take to overcome hurdles and become a leading MDB will serve as an acid test of China's soft power. In a certain sense, the success or failure of AIIB will also determine the fate of the OBOR.[22]

The second source of funding, according to Chan, is the 'New Development Bank (NDB)' or known as the 'BRICS Development Bank' as the setting up of it was by Brazil, Russia, India, China and South Africa.[23] The five countries that founded the NDB each hold equal share of 20% each. It has the authorised capital of US$100 billion.[24] The NDB has just become fully operational in 2016.[25] Its stated purpose is to 'mobilise resources for infrastructure and sustainable development projects in BRICS and other emerging economics and developing countries, complementing the existing efforts of multilateral and regional financial institutions for global growth and development'.[26] So far, it has financed projects relating to renewable energy in India, China, South Africa, Brazil and Russia and has financed a project for upgrading major district roads in India.[27] However, the NDB has its own challenge:

> An immediate challenge to NDB is the credit rating it can get from international rating agencies. Based on the current credit rating of Moody's, China's sovereign rating is AA3 while India is BAA3 (the lowest

20 Asian Infrastructure Investment Bank, 'Introduction' <www.aiib.org/en/about-aiib/who-we-are/our-work/index.html> accessed 27 August 2017.

21 Asian Infrastructure Investment Bank, 'Approved Projects' <www.aiib.org/en/projects/approved/index.html> accessed 27 August 2017.

22 Chan (n 3), 184.

23 *Ibid.*

24 New Development Bank, 'NDB Factsheet' <www.ndb.int/wp-content/uploads/2017/05/factheet-1.jpg> accessed 27 August 2017.

25 New Development Bank, 'About Us' <www.ndb.int/about-us/essence/history/> accessed 28 August 2017.

26 *Ibid.*

27 New Development Bank, 'List of All Projects' <www.ndb.int/projects/list-of-all-projects/> accessed 28 August 2017.

> investment grade assignment). Brazil's current rating is also BAA3 but are facing reviews and there is a very high likelihood of a downgrade in the immediate future, any downgrade will move Brazil to speculative grade assignment. South Africa's current rating is BAA2 and Russia's current rating is BA1, which are both speculative grade . . . Initial rating on NDB might not be high and it cannot afford the luxury of AIIB to forego international bond market and turn to domestic market for funding.[28]

To date, the NDB received AAA credit rating from only two Chinese rating firms – China Chengxin International Credit Rating Co. Ltd and China Lianhe Credit Rating Co. Ltd.[29] Therefore, Chan predicted that at least at the initial stage the NDB will have a role only among countries forming its members.[30]

Another source of funding set up specifically for the purpose of the OBOR project is the 'Silk Road Fund' for which the Chinese government put up US$40 billion.[31] The shareholders are China Foreign Exchange Reserve (SAFE) (65%), China Exim Bank (15%), China Investment Corporation (15%) and China Development Bank (5%).[32] It was only in May 2017 that the Chinese government announced an injection of an additional US$14.5 billion into the Silk Road Fund, citing likely greater demands of funds.[33] So far, the Fund has invested in the '1.65-billion-dollar Karot hydropower project in Pakistan'.[34] This hydropower project will generate '3.213 billion kw-hours each year' and will be put into operation in the year 2020.[35] There was also a report that the Fund would cooperate with Russian financial institutions on electricity and energy development projects. The Fund also signed an agreement with a natural gas company in Russia to buy a '9.9 percent stake of the Yamal LNG – a liquefied natural gas project at Sabetta, north-east of the Yamal Peninsula of Russia'.[36] The Fund has also been looking for investment

28 Chan (n 3), 185–186.

29 New Development Bank, 'Credit Ratings' <www.ndb.int/investor-relations/credit-ratings/> accessed 28 August 2017.

30 Chan (n 3), 186.

31 *Ibid.*

32 *Ibid.*

33 'China Boosts Silk Road Fund's Capital to Meet Enormous Funding Demand: Official' (*Xinhua* 14 May 2017) <http://news.xinhuanet.com/english/2017-05/14/c_136282392.htm> accessed 28 August 2017.

34 'Commentary: Silk Road Fund's 1st Investment Makes China's Words into Practice' (*Xinhua* 21 April 2015) <http://news.xinhuanet.com/english/2015-04/21/c_134170737.htm> accessed 28 August 2017.

35 'Silk Road Fund to Invest in Hydropower Project in Pakistan' (*Xinhua* 21 April 2015) <http://news.xinhuanet.com/english/2015-04/21/c_134167500.htm> accessed 28 August 2017.

36 China Daily, 'China's $40b Silk Road Fund Signs MoU with Russian firms' (3 September 2015) <www.chinadaily.com.cn/china/2015-09/03/content_21785297.htm> accessed 28 August 2015.

opportunities in the European Investment Fund, which is part of the European Investment Bank.[37] The head of the Silk Road Fund revealed that the Fund had spent US$6 billion in 15 projects, plus US$2 billion in projects with Kazakhstan.[38]

Aside from these, the Export-Import Bank of China initiated the 'China-Central and Eastern Europe Investment Corporation Fund' at US$435 million to finance two energy projects in Poland.[39] The Industrial and Commercial Bank of China also established the 'Sino-CEE Financial Holdings' in Latvia to handle funds for investments in Central and Eastern European countries: 'The fund aims to raise €10 billion and mobilise £50 billion in bank loans'.[40] Apart from these, there are also residual funding sources from major Chinese commercial banks and the state-owned enterprises (SOEs).[41] However, the crucial point is China admitted that it does not have sufficient funding for all OBOR-related projects. It advised countries along the OBOR initiative to 'work with capital markets, set up dedicated financial agencies of their own and try to make use of local currencies, including the yuan'.[42] Moreover, there has been a warning sign that the OBOR might ultimately create chaos for the global financial system because lending is being made to countries with financial risks.[43]

As can be observed, the focus of the OBOR project so far has been on building up infrastructure. In fact, this infrastructure will in turn support cross-border trade and more efficient movement of goods. The whole idea of the Silk Road Economic Belt, by focusing on the rail network, is because carriage by rail is faster than carriage by sea: 'The idea is . . . to fill up the rail cargo with higher value-added items . . . and time-sensitive product . . . like smartphones so that feasibility is dependent on value-addedness of products rather than volume'.[44] It is expected that increase in cross-border trade will stimulate the activities of private parties – companies and international corporations. It is with such enhanced commercial relationships between these firms

37 South China Morning Post, 'China's Silk Road Fund "Seeking Investment Projects in Europe"' (22 March 2017) <www.scmp.com/news/china/diplomacy-defence/article/2081067/chinas-silk-road-fund-seeking-investment-projects> accessed 28 August 2017.

38 South China Morning Post, 'Who Will Pay for China's New Silk Road?' (11 May 2017) <www.scmp.com/news/china/diplomacy-defence/article/2093672/who-will-pay-chinas-new-silk-road> accessed 28 August 2017.

39 *Ibid.*

40 *Ibid.*

41 Chan (n 3), 188–190.

42 South China Morning Post (n 38).

43 Karen Gilchrist, 'China's "Belt and Road" Initiative Could Be the Next Risk to the Global Financial System' (*CNBC* 24 August 2017) <www.cnbc.com/2017/08/24/chinas-belt-and-road-initiative-could-be-the-next-risk-to-the-global-financial-system.html> (accessed 28 August 2017).

44 Lim (n 1), 5.

that private international law will come into play. Regrettably, discourses so far have not moved much beyond the step of creating infrastructure.

What is private international law? And why is it important to the OBOR?

The name 'private international law' is indeed misleading. It is misleading because, different from public international law which is 'a supranational law that exists independently of the legal systems and legislatures of each nation', private international law is 'part of the municipal or domestic national law of each country (or law area within a country, in the case of federations) and subject to unilateral changes by its legislature'.[45] Thus, while public international law is more or less the same everywhere, private international law rules are 'differ from country to country'.[46] It sits within the 'private law' of a national legal system.[47] In the context of the domestic legal system, the private law 'deals with the relationships between private persons or organisations'.[48] Private international law also touches upon such kinds of relationships, with an addition that such relationships contain a 'foreign element'.[49] The foreign element is understood as 'a contact with some system of law other than that of the "forum", that is the country whose courts are seised of the case'.[50] For example, X, a company registered in Hong Kong agreed to sell steel coils to Y, also a company registered in Hong Kong. In such a scenario, the transaction is purely domestic and to be governed by the Sale of Goods Ordinance (Cap. 26) of Hong Kong. In a different scenario, X, a company registered in Hong Kong, agreed to sell steel coils to Z, a company in India. The transaction in this scenario involved a foreign element. Suppose the steel coils arrived in Z's office in India in a damaged condition. Several questions arise: Which court should adjudicate the dispute between X and Z? A court in Hong Kong or a court in India? In the absence of agreed choice of law by X and Z, should the law of Hong Kong or the law of India govern this transaction? At this juncture, further problems can arise. Assuming the case is brought before the court in Hong Kong, the court, in referring to the private international law rules of Hong Kong, may determine that the law of India governs this contract. Differently, if the case is before the court in India, the court, in referring to the Indian private international law rules, may determine that the law of Hong Kong governs this contract. Assuming further that while Z is registered in India, it also operates a factory in

45 Martin Davies and others, *Nygh's Conflict of Laws in Australia* (9th edn, LexisNexis Butterworths 2014), para 1.4.

46 David McClean and Kisch Beevers, *The Conflict of Laws* (6th edn, Sweet & Maxwell 2009), para 1–002.

47 *Ibid.*

48 Clive Turner and John Trone, *Australian Commercial Law* (30th edn, Lawbook Co. 2015), para 1.720.

49 McClean and Beevers (n 46), para 1–002.

50 *Ibid.*

Thailand. Suppose X obtained a judgment against Z in a court in India, can X enforce this Indian judgment in Thailand? These questions fall into the domain of private international law, or sometimes known as 'conflict of laws'.

But it is not correct to understand that the private international law deals only with cases involving parties from two different countries. In countries with federal systems such as Australia or the United States where laws may be different in each state or province, there are also problems of conflict of laws at the inter-state level. Likewise, Hong Kong and Macau are treated as the Special Administrative Regions (SARs) of the People's Republic of China, with different laws and legal systems. For the purpose of the Hong Kong conflict of laws, the law of the People's Republic of China is considered 'foreign' before the Hong Kong courts: '[T]he direct application of Mainland law based on submissions by counsel to a judiciary educated and experienced in a very different legal tradition appears unattractive'.[51] The same can be said for Macau. The effect of this is that judges in Hong Kong are not taken to know the laws of the People's Republic of China or the laws of Macau and hence these must be pleaded and proved before the courts.[52] Likewise, for the English conflict of laws rules, 'Scotland and Northern Ireland are for most but not all purposes as much foreign countries as France or Germany'.[53]

Different from the law of contract or the law of torts, private international law is 'not a separate branch of law. . . [i]t is all pervading'.[54] Private international law always addresses three issues:

jurisdiction: whether the local court – or 'forum' – has the power to hear and determine the case, or whether the contacts the case has with another state or country limit or otherwise restrain the forum court's power or willingness to decide the case;

recognition and enforcement of foreign judgments: where the case has proceeded to judgment in the other state or country, whether that judgment can be recognised or enforced in the forum; and

choice of law: even if the forum court has – and will – exercise the jurisdiction to decide the case, whether it will decide the case in accordance with the law of the forum *(lex fori)*, or in accordance with the law of the other state or country. Is the forum or foreign law to be 'the law of the cause' *(lex causae)* that disposes of the case, and how does the forum court choose one or the other? This question is, naturally, only important if application of the forum's law is likely to give a different result

51 Graeme Johnston, *The Conflict of Laws in Hong Kong* (2nd edn, Sweet & Maxwell 2012), para 2.086.

52 *Ibid.*, 2.060.

53 Sir Lawrence Collins and others (eds), *Dicey, Morris and Collins on the Conflict of Laws Volume 1* (14th edn, Sweet & Maxwell 2006), para 1–001.

54 James Fawcett and Janeen M. Carruthers, *Cheshire, North & Fawcett Private International Law* (14th edn, Oxford University Press 2008), 7.

> to the application of the foreign law: that is, where there is a 'conflict of laws'.[55]

Given the nature of private international law, it is not difficult to envisage that private international law, in fact, permeates all aspects of the OBOR arrangement – for example, a loan transaction between a Chinese commercial bank and a company in one of the OBOR countries, or a sale and purchase transaction between a company in China and a company in Eastern Europe.

Of course, there have been attempts to harmonise different aspects of private law so as to reduce conflict of laws problems. These attempts have been made by various international organisations such as the International Institute for the Unification of Private Law (UNIDROIT), the United Nations Commission on International Trade Law (UNCITRAL) and the Hague Conference on Private International Law. However, no complete harmonisation has ever been achieved. Perhaps the most successful attempt at harmonising was that of the UNCITRAL in the form of the Convention on the Recognition and Enforcement of Foreign Arbitral Awards (New York, 1958), or known as the 'New York Convention', which attracted ratification from 157 countries around the world.[56] With no complete harmonisation, it is difficult in the extreme to envisage how seamless commercial activities, which are the core of the OBOR project, can be materialised.

Addressing private international law concerns in the context of the OBOR

This book addresses some private international law issues that are of concern in the context of the OBOR project. To address these, the editors have engaged academics from different countries along the OBOR route so as to bring in different national perspectives. Chapters in the book are arranged following familiar judicial proceedings starting from party autonomy and ending with the recognition and enforcement of foreign judgments.

In this book, Sooksripaisarnkit examines diverse approaches to the issue of party autonomy in the context of choice of law among countries along the OBOR route. He reveals that problematic and ambiguous wording of the Principles on Choice of Law in International Commercial Contracts combined with their non-binding status make them not ideal for harmonising rules on party autonomy within these OBOR countries. He thus proposes that an international convention should be agreed among all states participating

55 Reid Mortensen and others, *Private International Law in Australia* (3rd edn, LexisNexis Butterworths 2015), 3.

56 United Nations Commission on International Trade Law, 'Status: Convention on the Recognition and Enforcement of Foreign Arbitral Awards (New York 1958)' <www.uncitral.org/uncitral/en/uncitral_texts/arbitration/NYConvention_status.html> accessed 30 August 2017.

in the OBOR, perhaps with the People's Republic of China taking a lead in convening the drafting of such a convention.

Guo and Fu explore trends in different jurisdictions where electronic services of process, for example, via social media, are feasible. They also explore recent developments in the People's Republic of China, where electronic service of process is increasingly recognised in civil and commercial cases. Finally, they propose the construction and promotion of a regional system for electronic services abroad among countries along the OBOR route even though they are aware of limitations such as different levels of advancement in technologies and opportunities for online access among these jurisdictions. Hence, they propose gradual promotion of such means of service.

On the issue of jurisdiction, Yip analyses a recent judicial development in Singapore with the creation of the Singapore International Commercial Court and what impacts this newly established judicial organ may have on commercial cases relating to OBOR projects or on disputes involving parties from OBOR countries. She explores jurisdictional rules of the Singapore International Commercial Court against the background of the recent ratification of Singapore to the Convention of 30 June 2005 on Choice of Court Agreements. She admits complexity caused by such jurisdictional rules which can pose challenges to the resolution of OBOR disputes. Yet she remains optimistic that more frequent use of the Singapore International Commercial Court will gradually bring familiarity with the frameworks. She also encourages a precise drafting of the jurisdictional clause.

Concerning conflict of law issues relating to OBOR transactions, Garimella takes a comparative approach to examine private international law rules of India with the judicial guidance of the Supreme People's Court of China. Noting the uncertainty around India's participation in the Belt and Road Initiative, she prefixes the comparative approach with a chronicling of the legal regime affecting transnational commercial and sales contracts. She concludes that despite the political uncertainty in India about participation in the OBOR, accession to harmonised legal platforms could help usher much-needed clarity within the governance of transnational contracts.

Kunda discusses the application of regional law beyond its intended geography, in the context of the European Union. She exemplifies the scenario through a few EU legal instruments whose scope is sometimes blurring the line of territorial limitation to the region. She attempts to identify the underlying policies explaining such normative structure. Illustrating through the normative regime in the domains of competition law and the General Data Protection Regulation, she suggests that non-EU-based companies, attempting to enter or remain in the global market, could benefit from realigning their business strategies to the prevailing regulatory requirements, else they could run the risk of administrative penalties and civil liability.

Huo examines problems of proof of foreign law from the perspective of Chinese courts. Through an empirical approach, the author flags the diversity in the normative regime on the reception of foreign law in the legal systems of nations along the OBOR and suggests, amongst others, the establishment of a judicial assistance regime exclusively for the Belt and Road Initiative and the enactment of clear rules to implement the B & R Opinion of the Supreme People's Court.

Zeller attempts to explore the possibility of realising the economic value of OBOR's promise by flagging the practical concerns that need to be addressed within the initiative. He begins with the premise that diverse legal systems within the supply chain interacting with each other would be at the same level of diversity. Illustrating the collateral concerns that arise from the legal transaction costs, he suggests that the OBOR cannot realise its promise as long as transnational laws are not ratified and, importantly, embraced by the business community. He further suggests that economic value could be realised only through accession to harmonised legal platforms like the UN Convention on Contracts for the International Sale of Goods (CISG).

Trade facilitation draws much strength from the conjugation between the conflict of laws regime and the policy initiatives. Chunchaemsai discusses this important aspect in the context of Thailand and the member-states of the ASEAN region, a vital part of the OBOR covering ten nations. Discussing the need to fuse the policy related to conflicts of laws within the region with a collectivistic approach to the public policy mechanism, the author holds the opinion that such effort could contribute significantly to the success of the Belt and Road Initiative.

Mega-trade and investment partnerships spread across diverse legal systems hold the possibility of governance-related concerns, especially with regard to transparency and accountability. The inevitable presence of public funds would require increased scrutiny and an effective legal system to engage with such purpose. John and Gulati emphasise the need for checks and balances to prevent the misuse of any funds and an effective regulatory regime to address cross-border corruption cases. The authors note that while many countries of the Asian region are signatory to the UN Convention against Corruption, a comprehensive framework that provides rules governing questions concerning jurisdiction, applicable law and the recognition and enforcement of foreign judgments in civil corruption cases has not yet been developed. They suggest that OBOR would benefit from addressing these questions and adopting a global viewpoint with regard to handling graft-related problems.

Tsang discusses the special place of Hong Kong within the dispute resolution processes related to the OBOR. The author maps the various instruments related to reciprocal judicial arrangements between China's mainland and the Hong Kong Special Administrative Region and suggests that Hong Kong can play an important role as facilitator in OBOR-related dispute resolutions because of the many advantages offered by its private international law rules.

Elbalti discusses the importance of Recognition and Enforcement of Foreign Judgments for the success of OBOR, characterised as 'an ambitious connectivity project'. The author turns the searchlight on potential participant regions – the Persian Gulf nations and the countries of the Middle Eastern region. Illustrating the problem of inconsistency in the recognition practice amongst the nations of these regions, the author suggests law reform in order to align it to internationally accepted standards for judgments recognition. Further enhanced regional cooperation through establishing and/or adhering to multilateral instruments that guarantee the free movement of judgments among the potential OBOR countries is also suggested.

Bozkurt discusses the roadblocks to OBOR as a result of the legal diversity amongst its participants, in particular with regard to key issues concerning the foundational element of international commerce – contracts of carriage and their enforcement. Exemplifying through the law in another potential participant, Turkey, the author suggests law reform in the space of substantial as well as procedural law affecting contractual, maritime and carriage-related commercial laws as well as dispute resolution laws.

The following pages hold forth the importance of addressing the potential conflicts in law-related issues that are inevitable in this mega-trading project. The chapters also attempt to address these issues and follow the path of suggesting ways in which these concerns can be addressed. Leafing through the pages of this volume of scholarly essays, the reader, it is hoped, would be able to walk through the wonderful world of private international law in the context of OBOR – the world of diversity and, increasingly, of harmonisation.

Part I

Party autonomy

2 Harmonisation of choice of law rules in commercial contracts in the One Belt One Road countries

Will the Hague principles on choice of law in international commercial contracts serve as a good model?

Poomintr Sooksripaisarnkit

Introduction

In October 2013, President Xi Jinping of the People's Republic of China proclaimed his nation's big *dream* of the One Belt One Road (hereinafter the 'OBOR') initiative. This project comprises the building of the 'Silk Road Economic Belt' and the '21st-Century Maritime Silk Road'.[1] Its primary aim is to bring closer cooperation among countries in Asia, Africa, and Europe to enhance cross-border trade supported by seamless infrastructure. This dream is ideal only if countries along the OBOR route have the same legal system and adopt the same laws. In reality, the world is far from ideal. Diverse legal systems and laws will impede a vision of the seamless economy. The Hague Conference on Private International Law on 19 March 2015 approved a text of the 'Principles on Choice of Law in International Commercial Contracts' (hereinafter the 'Principles').[2] Although these Principles are not a binding international convention, they may, as stated in the Preamble, 'be used as a model for national, regional, supranational, or international instruments'.[3] Moreover, courts or arbitral tribunals may refer to the Principles in reaching their decision.[4] It is doubtful to what extent courts can utilise the Principles, bearing in mind they are bound by national conflict of laws rules. Far from harmonising the choice of law rules in international commercial contracts as

1 Xinhua, 'Vision and Actions of Jointly Building Silk Road Economic Belt and 21st-Century Maritime Silk Road: Issued by the National Development and Reform Commission, Ministry of Foreign Affairs, and Ministry of Commerce of the People's Republic of China, with State Council authorization' (28 March 2015) <news.xinhua.net/english/china/2015–03/28/c_134105858.htm> accessed 30 June 2017.

2 The Hague Conference on Private International Law, 'Principles on Choice of Law in International Commercial Contracts' <https://assets.hcch.net/docs/5da3ed47-f54d-4c43-aaef-5eafc7clf2a1.pdf> accessed 30 June 2017.

3 *Ibid.*

4 *Ibid.*

the 'Rome I Regulation'[5] does on the European level, the focus of the Principles is limited to upholding and reinforcing a concept of 'party autonomy'.[6]

While the concept of party autonomy is enshrined in contemporaneous statutes and international conventions, the concept does not gain universal acceptance.[7] Exceptions or limitations to the party autonomy also vary among the laws of each country.[8] The hope is that the Principles will come into play purportedly to bridge such differences. Nevertheless, it is highly questionable to what extent the Principles are likely to achieve their aims. The author argues in this chapter that this new 'brainchild' of the Hague Conference on Private International Law is likely to meet with limited use and no success. As a long saga that led to the drafting of the Principles was well-elaborated in the Commentary attached to the Principles, it will not be repeated here. Nor is it possible to examine all 12 provisions – many of which are problematic. In this chapter, the author will focus his attention on certain aspects of the Principles to elaborate on his argument. These provisions are chosen for consideration in this chapter because they are contentious, they give rise to problems of interpretation, or else they do not reflect practices in certain OBOR jurisdictions. Of course, it is not possible and the author will not pretend that he has surveyed all conflict of law rules of all 67 countries along the OBOR route. To the extent possible, the author will refer to conflict of law rules of some of these countries for comparative purposes. This chapter is divided into two parts. In the first part, the concept of 'party autonomy' will be broadly explained and the author will then focus on the contentious Article 4, which purports to enhance the concept of party autonomy by allowing the parties to choose non-state laws. Also, in the same part, a short note will be made with regard to Article 5, addressing the tacit or the implied choice of law. In the second part, the author will discuss the exceptions to the party autonomy – namely overriding mandatory rules and public policy in Article 11.

Party autonomy in the Principles

Before proceeding with the analysis, some points should be noted at the outset. As the name suggests, the Principles only involve *commercial* contracts – 'where each party is acting in the exercise of its trade or profession'.[9] Therefore,

5 Regulation (EC) No. 593/2008 of the European Parliament and of the Council of the 17 June 2008 on the law applicable to contractual obligations.

6 The Hague Conference on Private International Law, 'Commentary on the Principles on Choice of Law in International Commercial Contracts' <https://assets.hcch.net/docs/5da3ed47-f5fd-4c43-aaef-5eafc7c1f2a1.pdf> accessed 30 June 20177 (hereinafter 'The Commentary'), see in particular paras 1.4–1.5.

7 See Jürgen Basedow, *The Law of Open Societies: Private Ordering and Public Regulation in the Conflict of Laws* (Brill Nijhoff 2015), paras 187–191.

8 Symeon C. Symeonides, *Codifying Choice of Law Around the World: An International Comparative Analysis* (Oxford University Press 2014), 115–116.

9 Article 1(1).

it is sensible that consumer and employment contracts are excluded from the scope of the Principles.[10] Certain other matters are also excluded from the scope of the Principles as per Article 1(3) on the basis of 'the lack of consensus on whether to characterise them as contractual issues or on whether to subject them to party autonomy'.[11] Such commercial contracts which fall within the ambit of the Principles must be *international* in nature. Instead of defining 'internationality', the Principles define a contract which is *not* international, that is, one in which 'each party has its establishment in the same State and the relationship of the parties and all other relevant elements, regardless of the chosen law, are connected only with that State'.[12]

The concept of party autonomy is then affirmed in Article 2(1) which states in general: 'A contract is governed by the law chosen by the parties'. This is also the position of the Anglo-common law countries. They have been following what Lord Wright said in *Vita Food Products, Inc. v Unus Shipping Co*[13] that 'where there is an express statement by the parties of their intention to select the law of the contract, it is difficult to see what qualifications are possible, provided the intention expressed is bona fide and legal'.[14] The passage of Lord Wright has been cited with approval, for example, in Singapore,[15] Hong Kong,[16] and India.[17] Indeed, in his judgment, Lord Wright gave very wide meaning to the party autonomy. Speaking in the context of the case concerning carriage of herrings from Newfoundland to New York with a bill of lading providing for the contract to be governed by English law,[18] Lord Wright explained:

> Connection with English law is not as a matter of principle essential. The provision in the contract (e.g. of sale) for English arbitration imports English law as the law governing the transaction, and those familiar with international businesses are aware how frequent such a provision is even where the parties are not English and the transactions are carried on completely outside England.[19]

10 *Ibid.*
11 The Commentary (n 6), para 1.24.
12 Article 1(2). Article 12 further provides: 'If a Party Has More than One Establishment, the Relevant Establishment for the Purpose of These Principles Is the One Which Has the Closest Relationship to the Contract at the Time of Its Conclusion'.
13 *Vita Food Products, Incorporated v Unus Shipping Company, Limited (in liquidation)* [1939] AC 277.
14 *Ibid.*, 290.
15 *Peh Teck Quee v Bayerische Lamdesbank Girozentrale* [2000] 1 SLR 148; [1999] SGCA 79, [12] (Singapore Court of Appeal).
16 *Credit Agricole Indosuez v Shanghai Erfangji Co Ltd and Another* [2002] HKCFI 94, [29] (Hong Kong Court of Appeal].
17 *National Thermal Power Corporation v Singer Company & Ors* 1992 (3) SCC 551 (Supreme Court of India).
18 *Vita Food Products* (n 13), 284–286.
19 *Ibid.*, 290.

It is not as clear within the context of India whether this latter part of Lord Wright's judgment is adopted there.[20] Yet the Principles make it clear that no connection between the chosen law and the transaction is required.[21] It is yet to be seen how the Principles may encourage Indian judges to settle the law on this matter. The concept of party autonomy is enshrined likewise in the private international law rules of other countries involved in the OBOR initiative, notably the People's Republic of China,[22] Japan,[23] and Thailand.[24]

However, certain countries in the Middle East which are included in the OBOR initiative do not uphold the party autonomy. Basedow quoted Article 968 of the Iranian Civil Code of 1935: 'Obligations arising out of contracts are subject to the laws of the place where the contract was concluded, except where the contracting parties are foreign nationals and have expressly or impliedly subjected the contract to another law'.[25] He further maintained that Saudi Arabia does not seem to 'honour choice of law agreements at all'.[26] In his research, he maintained that Yemen, Jordan, and Iraq have followed a similar scheme to that of the Egyptian Civil Code of 1948 where Article 19 states:

> the law applicable is (1) the law of the domicile where such domicile is common to the contracting parties or, otherwise (2) the law of the place where the contract was concluded; (3) contracts related to immovable property are governed by the law of the place in which the property is situated.[27]

20 Jan L. Neels, 'The Role of the Hague Principles on Choice of Law in International Commercial Contracts in Indian and South African Private International Law' (2017) 22(2) *Uniform Law Review* 443, 445.

21 Article 2(4).

22 Article 41 of the Law of the People's Republic of China on the Laws Applicable to Foreign-related Civil Relations (Adopted at the 17th session of the Standing Committee of the 11th National People's Congress, 28 October 2010) provides: 'The parties may by agreement choose the law applicable to their contract'. See World Intellectual Property Organization, 'Law of the People's Republic of China on the Laws Applicable to Foreign-Related Civil Relations' <www.wipo.int/edocs/lexdocs/laws/en/cn/cn173en.pdf> accessed 29 August 2017 (unofficial translation).

23 Article 7 of the Act on General Rules for Application of Laws (Act No.78 of June 21, 2006). See Japanese Law Translation, 'Act on General Rules for Application of Laws' <www.japaneselawtranslation.go.jp/law/detail/?id=1970&re=02> accessed 29 August 2017.

24 Section 13 of the Act on Conflict of Laws, B.E. 2481: 'The Question as to What Law Is Applicable in Regard to the Essential Elements or Effects of a Contract Is Determined by the Intention of the Parties to It . . .' Office of the Council of State, 'Act on the Conflict of Laws, B.E. 2481' <http://web.krisdika.go.th/data/outsidedata/outside21/file/Act_on_Conflict_of_Law_B.E._2481.pdf> accessed 29 August 2017.

25 Basedow (n 7), para 190.

26 *Ibid.*, para 191.

27 *Ibid.*

In these countries, choice of law may be allowed in limited circumstances in contracts relating to immovable property or in contracts where both parties have their domicile in other countries, but the legal position in these countries has been unclear.[28] It is to such countries that the drafters remain hopeful that the Principles will be the source of inspiration for lawmakers to adopt the concept of party autonomy following the guidance given in the Principles. However, any statutory changes in these countries, or indeed elsewhere, even if they are to occur, are unlikely to materialise in the near future. Even if they are to materialise, they may vary in details from choice of law rules in private international law of other jurisdictions along the OBOR route.

Setting out the concept of 'party autonomy', Article 3, subject to the *lex fori*, extends the party autonomy to the choice of 'non-state laws', that is, 'rules of law are generally accepted on an international, supranational, or regional level as a neutral and balanced set of rules'. From the perspective of the Anglo-common law jurisdictions, this extension is likely to be futile. Choosing non-state laws will not be possible. The oft-cited authority is that of the House of Lords in *Amin Rasheed Shipping Corporation v Kuwait Insurance Co.*[29] The facts of the case, which were about identifying an applicable law to a marine insurance contract, do not concern us here. However, attention should be drawn to what was said by Lord Diplock:

> The applicable English conflict rules are those for determining what is the "proper law" of a contract . . . To identify a *particular system of law* as being that in accordance with which the parties to it intended a contract to be interpreted, identifies *that system of law* as the "proper law" of the contract. The reason for this is plain; the purpose of entering into a contract being to create legal rights and obligations between the parties to it . . . This is not possible except *by reference to the system of law* by which the legal consequences that follow from the use of those words is to be ascertained.[30]

The only means by which non-state laws can have any role to play in the context of the Anglo-common law jurisdictions is by way of 'incorporation', which is different in nature from nominating them as governing laws for the contract. By way of incorporation, non-state laws will be deduced to merely terms of the contract, and the contract still has to be read within the context of a state law or an objectively determined applicable law.[31] Different from when state-laws are chosen as governing laws of the contract, any subsequent change or amendment to such laws will not affect the contract in case of the

28 *Ibid.*
29 [1984] 1 AC 50.
30 *Ibid.*, 60 (emphasis added).
31 Sir Lawrence Collins and others (eds), *Dicey, Morris & Collins: The Conflict of Laws Volume 2* (14th edn, Sweet & Maxwell 2006), para 32–088.

incorporation.[32] Indeed, the range of non-state laws that can be incorporated into the contract appear to be wider than such laws allowed to be chosen in the Principles. It must be remembered, under Article 3 of the Principles, non-state laws to be chosen must be: (1) 'accepted on an international, supra-national, or regional level' and (2) 'neutral and balanced'. These two qualifications are in themselves prone to problems of interpretation. The Commentary gave two examples. The first one is the 'United Nations Convention on Contracts for the International Sale of Goods (Vienna, 1980)' (CISG), when it is nominated by the parties to govern the contract, not by its having force of law as per the applicable law of any nation.[33] The second one is the 'UNIDROIT Principles of International Commercial Contracts 2010'.[34] As pointed out by Mankowski, taking the CISG as an example is rather dubious, and some countries have had reservations. In addition, parties to international sale transactions are not infrequently contracting out of the CISG.[35] A more fundamental problem, as convincingly raised by Mankowski, is that '[n]either Article 3 nor the comment indicate, and even less reveal, who is to judge whether the necessary degree of acceptance is reached or by which standards and based on which methodology such evaluation is to take place'.[36] Article 3 of the Principles is at best elusive, and it is unlikely to serve as a model for countries whose private international law rules are still unclear on whether the choice of non-state laws can be upheld. In the People's Republic of China, for example, the point is regarded as uncertain.[37] While some commentators appear to be of the view that, under Chinese private international law, the parties can choose an international convention not ratified by the People's Republic of China,[38] Tu argued that this suggestion is too far-fetched because 'it would have the effects that private parties could "force" China to accept a treaty that China might not want to ratify'.[39] Similar to China, the position within the Japanese private international law on this point is also uncertain even though the weight of academic commentators appears to be of the view that choosing non-state laws is not feasible.[40] Likewise, in Thailand, there is no clear view on this.[41] With the failure to bring clarity on this point, the Principles are likely to stir confusion.

32 *Ibid.*, 32–090.

33 The Commentary (n 6), para 3.5.

34 *Ibid.*, para 3.6.

35 Peter Mankowski, 'Article 3 of the Hague Principles: The Final Breakthrough for the Choice of Non-State Law?' (2017) 22(2) *Uniform Law Review* 369, 379.

36 *Ibid.*, 373.

37 Zheng Sophia Tang and others, *Conflict of Laws in the People's Republic of China* (Edward Elgar Publishing 2016), para 8.20.

38 *Ibid.*, para 8.22.

39 Guangjian Tu, *Private International Law in China* (Springer 2016), para 140.

40 Yuko Nishitani, 'Party Autonomy and Its Restrictions by Mandatory Rules in Japanese Private International Law: Contractual Conflict Rules' in Jürgen Basedow and others (eds), *Japanese Private International Law in Comparative Perspective* (Mohr Siebeck 2008), 87.

41 Soemsit Sirijaroensuk, 'A Comparative Study of Rome I and Thai Private International Law: Focus on the Applicable Law Rules in Contract' B.E. 2554 (2011) 3(3) วารสารกฎหมายกระทรวงยุติธรรม

The Principles provide further that the proper law can be identified by way of the tacit choice. In this sense, it means the choice that 'appear[s] clearly from the provisions of the contract or the circumstances'[42] and that the choice of court or the arbitration clause in itself does not determine the choice of law.[43] Speaking of the position under the Chinese private international law rules, the implied choice is not recognised.[44] However, it has been noted from the Chinese court practices that if the party to the litigation invoked the law of one country and the other party did not argue otherwise or that both parties submitted the law of the same country, in such situation the courts would be prepared to find the law of that particular country was chosen.[45] Other than in this context, the implied choice is unlikely to be accepted in the law of the People's Republic of China in the near future.[46] Likewise, under Japanese private international law, the readiness to find the implied choice to exist is uncertain. Reading Article 7 of the Japanese private international law statute which provides that '[t]he formation and effect of a juridical act shall be governed by the law of the place chosen by the parties at the time of the act' along with Article 8 which provides where there is no choice, the formation and effect of a juridical act shall be governed by the law of the place with which the act is closely connected and such place is taken to be the habitual residence of the party effecting the characteristic performance, Nishitani is inclined to be of the view that the implied choice has no place in Japanese private international law unless there are strong pointers to the parties' intention. Such pointers may be gleaned from 'choice-of-court agreement, arbitration agreement, choice of a single place of performance, or reference to certain specific legal institutions of the state concerned'.[47] As one may remember, these pointers run counter to the recommended approach in the Principles. Likewise, as noted by Sirijareonsuk, the Thai Supreme Court in its decision no. 1645/2538 found the implied choice of the English law from the arbitration clause appointing arbitrators in the United Kingdom.[48] Speaking from the Anglo-common law perspective, the courts are more ready to find the implied choice from a choice of jurisdiction clause or an arbitration clause. Academic commentators observed that '[i]n practice, where parties have agreed to litigation or arbitration in a particular country, the court is likely to conclude that

(Court of Justice Law Journal) 41, 64 <http://elib.coj.go.th/Article/cpt2011_3_2.pdf> accessed 8 September 2017.

42 Article 4.

43 *Ibid.*

44 Tu (n 39), para 142. Article 3 of the Law of the People's Republic of China on the Laws Applicable to Foreign-related Civil Relations: 'The parties may explicitly choose the law applicable to their foreign-related civil relation in accordance with the provisions of this law'.

45 *Ibid.*

46 *Ibid.*

47 Nishitani (n 40), 86.

48 Sirijareonsuk (n 41), 63.

the contract is governed by the law of that country'.[49] An obvious example is the judgment of the English Court of Appeal in *The Komninos S*.[50] The factual situation involved damages to the cargo of steel coils shipped from Thessaloniki in Greece to Ravenna in Italy.[51] In the Queen's Bench Division, Mr Justice Leggatt (as he then was) in determining the proper law to the contract of carriage considered the following connecting factors:[52]

For English Law	*For Greek Law*
Clause 24: 'All dispute [sic] to be referred to British courts'.	The contract of carriage was concluded in Greece.
Clause 8 refers to the term 'Act of God'.	Parties: Greek shipowners and Greek managers v Cypriot shipowners.
Clause 17: Adjustment of general average in London and in £ Sterling.	Cargo: Steel coils from Greece to Italy.
Clauses 20 and 21: Limitation of liability in certain circumstances was expressed in £ Sterling.	Freight: Greek currency – according to Greek exchange control regulations.

Mr Justice Leggatt found the reference to the 'British courts' in Clause 24 to be vague and that other references to the English terminologies 'may have been influenced by the use of English as the language of commerce'.[53] Therefore, he found the proper law to be the Greek law.[54]

In the Court of Appeal, Bingham LJ (as he then was) considered the argument that the reference to 'British courts' was ambiguous. The argument was that 'British courts' can connote the courts in Scotland or Northern Ireland or in Hong Kong (the then British colony) or even in Gibraltar or in the Falkland Islands.[55] He rejected this argument:

> It is widely known that the Commercial Court and the Admiralty Court, both parts of the High Court, deal on a daily basis with a wide range of international maritime business, much if not most of it referred by agreement to English law or jurisdiction. No doubt for historical and geographical reasons, no other court in the United Kingdom enjoys that reputation or dispatches that business.[56]

49 C.M.V Clarkson and Jonathan Hill, *The Conflict of Laws* (4th edn, Oxford University Press 2011), 211.

50 *Hellenic Steel Co and Others v Svolamar Shipping Co. Ltd and Others (The "Komninos S")* [1991] 1 Lloyd's Rep. 370.

51 *Hellenic Steel Co and others v Svalomar Shipping Co. Ltd and Others (The "Komninos S")* [1990] 1 Lloyd's Rep. 541.

52 *Ibid.*, 544.

53 *Ibid.*

54 *Ibid.*

55 *The Komninos S* (n 50), 373.

56 *Ibid.*, 374.

Different in outcome from that of the House of Lords in *Compagnie D'Armement Maritime S.A v Compagnie Tunisienne de Navigation S.A*,[57] while not departing from the overall *ratio decidendi* of the case, Bingham LJ explained that the method of finding an implied term and the method of determining the 'closest connection' in the absence of both the express and the implied choices are similar in that overall circumstances have to be taken into account. However, a fine distinction lies in the purpose. For finding the implied choice, the overall circumstances become relevant 'to ascertain the parties' contractual intention (meaning their actual, not their imputed intention: what they would have said if asked at the time)'.[58] On the other hand, the consideration of the overall circumstances for finding the closest connection in the absence of choice 'involves the application of a rule of law, not a process of contractual construction'.[59] He found in this instance that the parties' contractual intention can be inferred from Clause 24 which referred to the British courts. He added:

> If cl.24 did not exist, it would . . . be impossible to draw any inference as to the parties' intentions . . . I would accept the Greek system of law is that with which the transaction had its closest and most real connection.[60]

In the *Compagnie D'Armement Maritime* case, the House of Lords reached a different conclusion in a seemingly analogous factual circumstance. The case involved a Tunisian company, through the shipbrokers in Paris, approaching the French shipowners to supply ships to carry a cargo of oil between two ports in Tunisia.[61] It was agreed that the ships to be supplied did not necessarily have to be those under the ownership of the said French shipowners. Such ships could be 'controlled or chartered' by them.[62] The contract contained a clause: 'This contract shall be governed by the laws of the flag of the vessel carrying the goods', but the vessel particulars in the contract were left blank.[63] The contract also contained an arbitration clause: 'Any dispute arising during execution of this charterparty shall be settled in London, owners and charterers each appointing an arbitrator – merchant or broker'.[64] Approaching the matter via slightly different routes, all their Lordships unanimously held the contract to be governed by French law.[65] Yet, as Bingham LJ in *The Komninos S*

57 [1971] AC 572.
58 *The Komninos S* (n 50), 374.
59 *Ibid.*
60 *Ibid.*, 376.
61 *Compagnie D'Armement Maritime* (n 57), 582.
62 *Ibid.*
63 *Ibid.*, 591.
64 *Ibid.*
65 *Ibid.*, 584 (Lord Reid), 590–591 (Lord Morris of Borth-y-Gest); 593 (Viscount Dilhorne); 593 (Lord Wilberforce); 609 (Lord Diplock).

correctly pointed out,[66] one can take as *ratio decidendi* emphasis their Lordships placed on the weight of the jurisdiction clause and the arbitration clause in determining the implied choice. For example, in the speech of Lord Wilberforce, '[a]n arbitration clause must be treated as an indication, to be considered together with the rest of the contract and relevant surrounding facts. Always it will be a strong indication'.[67] Likewise, in the speech of Lord Diplock, 'an arbitration clause is generally intended by the parties to operate as a choice of the proper law of the contract as well as the curial law and should be construed unless there are compelling indications to the contrary'.[68] As such, although the wording of Article 4 of the Principles correctly reflects the legal positions adopted in different jurisdictions, it does somewhat downplay the weight one should attribute to the arbitration or the jurisdiction clause in the contract and such wording does not reflect practices in different countries. The author would put forward a suggestion that the wording of the last part of Article 4 should be altered to read:

> An agreement between the parties to confer jurisdiction on a court or an arbitral tribunal to determine disputes under the contract in itself provides a rebuttable presumption as to a choice law, unless there are overwhelming connecting factors to the contrary.

Exceptions to the party autonomy in the Principles

The Principles provide for two grounds of exceptions or limitations to the party autonomy in Article 11 – overriding mandatory provisions of the law of the forum and public policy *(order public)* of the law of the forum. One observation that can be made at the outset is that the Principles do not accommodate the 'bad faith' limitation – a condition so vividly pronounced in the passage of Lord Wright. There is no case in common law jurisdictions which explicitly explains this 'bad faith' limitation, indeed this condition had not been recognised prior to the judicial pronouncement by Lord Wright in the Privy Council.[69] Yet there are subsequent authorities both in Australia and in Singapore which discussed this condition.

In *Golden Acres Limited v Queensland Estates Pty Ltd*,[70] the fact of the case, in short, involved the purported claim to the entitlement for commission from the sale of land.[71] An agreement between parties contained a clause: 'For all purposes arising under this agreement, the same shall be deemed to be entered

66 *The Komninos S* (n 50), 375–376.
67 *Compagnie D'Armement Maritime* (n 57), 600.
68 *Ibid.*, 609.
69 Tan Yock Lin, 'Good Faith Choice of a Law to Govern a Contract' [2014] *Singapore Journal of Legal Studies* 307, 310.
70 (1969) Qd. R. 378.
71 *Ibid.*, 383.

into in the colony of Hong Kong'.[72] This type of agreement was said to be in breach of a local statute in Queensland in that the claimant in this case was not a registered real estate agent and the agreed commission exceeded the amount imposed by the said statute.[73] Despite the argument that the law of Hong Kong was chosen because there was intention 'to find purchasers of land in the Far East and a number of buyers were, in fact, residents of Hong Kong', Hoare J found the claimant had calculated legal problems had Queensland law governed the contract.[74] He, therefore, found the intention to choose Hong Kong law not to be in good faith. What is unclear was his subsequent explanation:

> The Queensland legislature has seen fit to enact legislation closely regulating the operation of real estate agents in Queensland . . . one can see that it certainly could be contrary to the public interest if the operation of the statute as a whole could be circumvented by the simple device of agreeing that some other law will apply to a contract which would otherwise be subject to the restrictions imposed by the Act . . . generally speaking it would be contrary to public policy for the legislative intention to be stultified by parties to a contract, of which the proper law would be Queensland, selecting some other law for the purpose of avoiding the application of Queensland law.[75]

It is unclear because the good faith condition, according to Hoare J, appears to be subsumed in the public policy condition. It must be remembered that Lord Wright referred to these two conditions as separate concepts.

The passage of Hoare J on the good faith condition was referred to with approval by the Court of Appeal in Singapore.[76] The case involved a loan facility agreement between a Singapore branch of a German bank and an individual residing in Malaysia. A number of documents containing the terms and conditions of the agreement were issued by the bank. Among them, Clause 20 of the standard terms and conditions provided: 'This agreement shall be construed and have effect in all respects in accordance with the laws of Singapore'.[77] It was argued by the concerned individual that at the time the facility agreement was signed, the standard terms and conditions had not been sent by the bank. Hence, at the relevant time he was not aware of the choice of law clause.[78] In addition, the facility agreement was indeed in breach of Malaysian statutes, and the bank was aware of this but took an indifferent

72 *Ibid.*
73 *Ibid.*
74 *Ibid.*, 384.
75 *Ibid.*, 384–385.
76 *Peh Teck Quee* (n 15), [17].
77 *Ibid* [2]–[4].
78 *Ibid* [15].

approach to ensuring compliance. So, the argument went on, in continuing ignorance the bank 'was tantamount to a reckless disregard . . . for the laws of Malaysia and thus showed both a lack of bona fides and of any intention to comply with Malaysian law'.[79] Importantly taking into account the comity of nations as a public policy, the courts in Singapore should not give effect to the law of Singapore chosen to evade the application of Malaysian compulsory statutes.[80] The Court of Appeal treated the signature to provide a conclusive evidence of the agreed choice of law:

> The only rider to this is the principle that if the only purpose for choosing Singapore law was to evade the operation of Malaysian law, the court would likely to hold that the choice of law was not bona fide on the basis of the evidence before it.[81]

However, it found upon the fact that there were reasons for the parties to agree on Singapore law, including that the bank was operating from Singapore, all relevant accounts were in Singapore, and the bank had paid taxes relevant to the facility agreement in Singapore.[82] So, in effect, the Court of Appeal in Singapore affirmed in principle the approach of Hoare J that the bad faith intention involves intention to evade mandatory laws of a particular country. The argument in the case before it failed on the basis that such intention to evade could not be established. But the difference between this case of the Court of Appeal in Singapore and that of the *Golden Acres* case is that what had to be considered by the court in this case was the intention to evade 'foreign' compulsory statutes, and in this respect, the author thinks that the Court of Appeal in its judgment focused its mind on establishing that the objective choice of law in this case was Singapore law and did not give sufficient weight or provide elaborated analysis as to the potential breaches of the compulsory Malaysian statutes. Again, the line was not drawn between the intention to evade the mandatory laws that constitutes bad faith and the public policy exception.

If Hoare J's approach represented correct interpretation of the good faith limitation propounded by Lord Wright, then this condition does not seem to be of much use and indeed it appears redundant. Most instances of evading a country's mandatory laws will be caught by the public policy condition. However, as shall be seen ahead, the analysis does not go as simply as this.

Article 11 of the Principles encapsulates both the overriding mandatory provisions and the public policy exceptions. From the Anglo-common law standpoint, some academic commentators were of the view that '[t]he issue of how mandatory rules ought to be treated in the private international law of

79 *Ibid.*
80 *Ibid* [16].
81 *Ibid* [17].
82 *Ibid.*

contracts is historically connected with, yet to be kept separate from, the role of public policy'.[83] These commentators, however, did not justify why these two deserve separate consideration. Other scholars prefer not to treat these two as conceptually distinct. As Davies and others explain:

> A contractual choice-of-law clause . . . may not be enforced on grounds of public policy where the public policy is considered sufficiently powerful to override parties' generally respected freedom of contract . . . Such public policy will typically be in the form of a statute of the forum state . . . A statute that operates to override what would otherwise be the governing law of the contract . . . is commonly referred to as a mandatory law of the forum.[84]

The drafters of the Commentary to the Principles attempted to provide, with respect, rather unhelpful explanations in order to distinguish these two concepts:

> In the case of overriding mandatory provisions, the applicability of the chosen law is supplemented or displaced by the application of the mandatory provision of another law. In the case of public policy, the applicability of the chosen law is limited only to the extent that its application is manifestly incompatible with fundamental notions of public policy.[85]

The explanation along the same tenor also appears in another paragraph of the Commentary.[86]

At first sight, this explanation appears problematic. In reality, however, this line of distinction is not different from the application of the doctrine of public policy as recognised in the Anglo-common law jurisdictions. The public policy 'can only be used as a shield (to deny the application of an otherwise applicable foreign law) and not as a sword (to invoke the application of an otherwise inapplicable law)'.[87] So, the public policy, as far as it is relevant, only renders the violated part of the chosen law ineffective. But it does not lead to the application of, for example, the law of the forum, in place of the ineffective chosen law. On the other hand, a mandatory provision, in addition to rendering the relevant parts of the chosen law ineffective, also replaces those parts. The problem still is on the actual distinction between the domain of the public policy and the domain of the mandatory provision, as there is no guideline or

83 Roy Goode and others, *Transnational Commercial Law: Texts, Cases and Materials* (2nd edn, Oxford University Press 2015), para 2.53.
84 Martin Davies and others, *Nygh's Conflict of Laws in Australia* (9th edn, LexisNexis Butterworths 2014), para 19.39.
85 The Commentary (n 6), para 11.6.
86 *Ibid.*, 11.11.
87 Clarkson and Hill (n 49), 51.

yardstick for the determination of public policy.[88] In the absence of definitions provided in the Principles, the reality is more complicated.

In fact, there are two levels of public policy – one applies at the domestic level and the other one applies 'even in an international context'.[89] Within the context of the Anglo-common law legal traditions, public policy of a country operates in two ways. First, it refuses application of the foreign law that is contrary to the country's public policy. Second, it aims to preserve comity between that country and other nations.[90] It has been observed that it is possible for the courts to apply the mandatory rules of the other countries by invoking the forum's public policy to maintain comity.[91] Article 11(4) of the Principles refers to the *lex fori* on whether the forum court has to consider whether the public policy of the objective proper law country should be taken into account. It is difficult for the forum court to try to justify and elaborate on the public policy of another country with entirely different social context and background to that of the forum, should it have to apply. As the court may need to consider the public policy of the objective proper law country for the sake of comity, will it be correct for one to presume that the court can take notice of such public policy without the parties to the litigation having to draw this to the forum court's attention?

In relation to mandatory rules, it must be observed that Article 11, in fact, employs the term 'overriding mandatory provisions', not *simply* mandatory provisions. To understand this term, as explained by Symeonides, reference must be made to the Rome I Regulation at the European level.[92] In Article 9 of the Rome I Regulation:

> Overriding mandatory provisions are provisions the respect for which is regarded as crucial by a country for safeguarding its public interests, such as its political, social or economic organisation, to such an extent that they are applicable to any situation falling within their scope, irrespective of the law otherwise applicable to the contract under this Regulation.

The concept is complicated because whether a provision is an *overriding* mandatory one is 'a question of interpretation'.[93] Plus, under the Rome I Regulation, the determination of the overriding mandatory provision is a matter of the Member States of the European Union and, thankfully, the Member States

88 Reid Mortensen, *Private International Law in Australia* (3rd edn, LexisNexis Butterworths 2015), para 8.56.

89 Adeline Chong, 'The Public Policy and Mandatory Rules of Third Countries in International Contracts' (2006) 2 *Journal of Private International Law* 27, 29.

90 *Ibid.*, 30.

91 See *Ibid.*, 33–35.

92 Symeon C. Symeonides, 'The Hague Principles on Choice of Law for International Contracts: Some Preliminary Comments' (2013) 61 *The American Journal of Comparative Law* 873, 886.

93 Clarkson and Hill (n 49), 233.

do not take a uniform approach on the interpretation of Article 9.[94] Under the English legal position, much influenced by the European legal thinking, one has to further distinguish two kinds of mandatory provisions – *internal* and *international*. For *internal* mandatory rules, they 'would be applicable when the governing law of a contract is also that of the law containing that particular mandatory rule'.[95] For *international* mandatory rules, they apply regardless of the law which governs the contract.[96] The overriding mandatory rules in the context of Article 9 are only relevant to these *international* mandatory rules.[97] Presumably, the same can be said for Article 1 of the Principles. It is to this distinction between the *internal* and the *international* mandatory rules that one is reminded of the approach of Hoare J to the good faith condition in the *Golden Acres* case discussed earlier. As one may remember, Hoare J was of the view that the Queensland statute he considered in the case, if anything, is only an *internal* mandatory provision as he said 'one can see that it certainly could be contrary to public interest if the operation of the statute as a whole could be circumvented by the simple device of agreeing that some other law will apply'.[98] So Hoare J seems to elevate the status of the *internal* mandatory provision to an *international* one by backdoor resorting to the good faith condition. Article 11 of the Principles is silent on this back door approach.

Now, how can one distinguish between an *international* public policy and an *international* mandatory provision? The distinction becomes crucial in the context of the Principles because in the case of the former it does not displace the chosen law of the contract, whereas in the latter it does. Also, while Article 11(4) provides that by the *lex fori* the forum court may apply the public policy of the objective proper law country, Article 11(2) provides, again referring to the *lex fori*, that the forum court may apply 'overriding mandatory provisions of another law'. The term 'another law' is explained as 'the law of a State other than that of the forum or of the law chosen by the parties'.[99] Such broad language being used without any potential limitation is problematic. The drafters of the Principles appear to contemplate only those States with rather well-developed and mature *lex fori* to delineate details on when or in what situations the international mandatory provisions of which country have to be taken into account by the court. However, this is apparently not the case in many countries along the OBOR route.

In the People's Republic of China, according to Article 4 of its private international law statute, '[w]here a mandatory provision of the law of the People's

94 Jan-Jaap Kuipers, *EU Law and Private International Law: The Interrelationship in Contractual Obligations* (Martinus Nijhoff Publishers 2011), 125.
95 Chong (n 90), 31.
96 Richard Fentiman, *International Commercial Litigation* (Oxford University Press 2010), para 3.42.
97 *Ibid.*, para 3.51.
98 *Golden Acres* (n 70), 384–385.
99 The Commentary (n 6), para 11.19.

Republic of China ("PRC") exists with respect to a foreign-related civil relation, that mandatory provision shall be applied directly'. Under Chinese private international law, there is no distinction between the internal and the international mandatory rules as such and any reference to 'mandatory rules' in domestic legislation only connotes the sense of international mandatory rules: 'In the Chinese concept, overriding mandatory rules are unilaterally applicable, which can be directly applied without the need to refer to conflict rules'.[100] Taking reference from the Rome I Regulation, it would be wrong, however, for one to assume that every international mandatory rule recognised in Chinese law is equivalent to those described in Article 11 of the Principles. In the Japanese private international law statute, the provision related to the international mandatory rules is simply absent even though the provisions of the Japanese law which are regarded as being international mandatory ones are applied 'taken for granted *de lege lata*'.[101] In Thai private international law, there is simply no notion of international mandatory rules as such. The only provision relevant for this purpose is Section 5 which provides: 'Whenever a law of a foreign country is to govern, it shall apply in so far as it is not contrary to the public order or good morals of Siam'.[102] The 'public order' constitutes 'matter[s] involved in the benefit of the country or the majority of the population which affect on the national security, economy and family institution'.[103] On the other hand, 'good morals' refers to 'the great tradition of society which can be changed in generation that one society assumes it is good morals while another might not'.[104] If anything, these can be analogous to the concept of 'public policy' but it is doubtful if these can be read as analogous to international mandatory rules. It is hard to see how judges in countries where the concept of overriding mandatory provisions does not exist trying to take the Principles into account and applying this notion, not to mention referring to the purported overriding mandatory rules of another country.

Conclusion

It is apparent that the Principles, being a non-binding instrument in nature, will have little or even no impact in harmonising the contractual choice of law rules as national courts are bound by their domestic private international law rules. Moreover, the scope of what the Principles address is narrowly limited to the concept of party autonomy. While the Principles may provide a source of inspiration for national courts or lawmakers to adopt certain aspects of them into domestic conflict of law rules, such process is likely to be evolved on a gradual basis and will take time. The OBOR project cannot wait that long.

100 Tang and others (n 37), para 8.86.
101 Nishitani (n 40), 79.
102 'Siam' is a former name of Thailand.
103 Sirijareounsuk (n 41), 65.
104 *Ibid.*

Bearing in mind the scale of countries involved in the Hague Conference on Private International Law's projects, making a binding international convention on contractual choice of law rules may be too difficult to attempt. However, within the OBOR project with its 67 participating countries, perhaps an international convention on choice of law rules among these countries, similar in style to the Rome I Regulation, is feasible to achieve and, from the point of view of the author, is sensible. As one would expect, it is perhaps a task for the People's Republic of China to convene the drafting of such an international convention.

As this chapter revealed, the wording of the Principles is not without flaws. Article 3 provides for the ability for the parties to choose non-state laws to govern their contract. While non-state laws are not unfamiliar in an arbitration context, the application of these within the judicial context is unlikely. Worse still, the drafts added qualifications to non-state laws to be recognised such that identifying these becomes quite an insurmountable task. Then, the Principles reflect the tacit choice in Article 4. Yet negative wording in relation to the use of the arbitration clause and the jurisdiction clause in identifying the implied choice of law does not really reflect practices among different jurisdictions. Article 11 is highly insensible in the sense that the public policy and the overriding mandatory provisions, which are largely overlapping, are set out in the same provision with different treatment. Neither in the Principles nor in the Commentary is a guideline provided on how to distinguish between these.

Therefore, even if in the future the Principles are implemented into the laws of certain countries, experiences from international conventions suggest that there will be a degree of disparity in how the wording of the Principles is construed, regardless of the Commentary. In certain jurisdictions, such as in the Anglo-common law jurisdictions with long-established fundamental principles on conflict of laws or in the People's Republic of China with a well delineated conflict of laws statute, it is hard to see in which context the Principles can be of use.

Part II

Service of process

3 On the construction of electronic service abroad system under the 'Belt and Road' Initiative

Yujun Guo and Pengyuan Fu

Introduction

Service abroad is of vital importance to international civil and commercial lawsuits. However, in real international civil and commercial cases, there exist problems of slow service and low success rate, which put the processing of judicial activities in a difficult position. Moreover, with the development of communication technology and the popularity of computers and the Internet, an increasing number of countries, including the United Kingdom, the United States, Australia, New Zealand and China, have begun to serve by the efficient electronic means. In China, the relevant rules on electronic service abroad first appeared in the Interpretation of the Supreme People's Court on the Application of the Special Maritime Procedure Law in 2003 and finally became legislation in the Civil Procedure Law of the People's Republic of China (2012 Amendment)[1] (hereinafter 'Civil Procedure Law'). But up until now, there is no international treaty to stipulate and adjust this new way of service, including the Convention on the Service Abroad of Judicial and Extrajudicial Documents in Civil or Commercial Matters (hereinafter 'Hague Service Convention').

As the political and economic cooperation among the countries along the 'Belt and Road' are more frequent than ever with the implementation of the 'Belt and Road' Initiative, those countries also need to pay attention to exchange and cooperation in the legal field. It is of great benefit to promote judicial cooperation in electronic service abroad among countries along the 'Belt and Road', which will not only make huge contributions to the effectiveness of the settlement of civil and commercial cross-border disputes, but also provide a fair and efficient legal environment for the 'Belt and Road' area.

The development of electronic service abroad

In international civil and commercial litigations, electronic service abroad refers to the act conducted by judicial authorities or plaintiffs to serve judicial

1 Effective date: 1 January 2013.

and extrajudicial documents to the defendants abroad or other parties by electronic means such as telex, fax, email and social networking site (SNS) based on laws of countries concerned or rules of international conventions.[2]

The germination of electronic service abroad

Electronic service abroad came on stage in the 1980s when a federal court of the United States first allowed electronic service abroad by modern communication technology. In 1980, in *New England Merchants National Bank v Iran Power Generation & Transmission Co.*[3] (hereinafter '*New England Merchants* case'), the plaintiff could not serve the Iranian defendant effectively by various means due to the tension between the United States and Iran as well as the defendant's intentional evasion. At last, the US District Court for the Southern District of New York made the decision to permit the plaintiff to serve the defendant via telex. The *New England Merchants* case marks the beginning of electronic service abroad, in which the courts realised the role of modern communication technology in pursuing values of justice and efficiency in litigation and became willing to make use of the convenience brought by technology in judicial practice with a positive and open mind.

The evolution of electronic service abroad

At the turn of the century, especially the beginning of the twenty-first century, human beings gradually stepped into the Internet Age in the wake of the rapid development of computer technology and communication technology. Accordingly, electronic service abroad entered a steady stage of development. The United Kingdom and the United States successively applied their existing rules of civil procedure flexibly, allowing the service of process via fax and email.

In 1996, the Queen's Bench Division of the Royal Courts of Justice authorised the attorneys in the London law firm of Schilling & Lom to serve court orders to the defendant outside the jurisdiction via email, which is the first case permitting service abroad via email in the world.[4] In this case, Schilling & Lom received a series of emails aiming at a media celebrity client of the firm, in which the sender threatened to spread defamatory materials against the client on the Internet. To ensure legal remedy for the client before the materials were

2 See Han Depei and Xiao Yongping, *Private International Law* (3rd edn, Higher Education Press and Peking University Press 2014), 512; Ju Haiting, 'Research on the Electronic Service of Process' (2006) 5 *People's Justice* 67, 67; Song Chaowu, 'The Confliction of Tele-justice Practice and Rules' (2011) 6 *Journal of China University of Political Science and Law* 62, 65.

3 [1980] SDNY, 495 F Supp 73 (SDNY).

4 Frank Conley, 'Service with a Smiley: The Effect of Email and Other Communications on Service of Process' (1997) 11 *Temple International and Comparative Law Journal* 407, 408.

leaked on the Internet, the attorney at Schilling & Lom sought an injunction from the court. Under Order 65 of the Rules of the Supreme Court of the United Kingdom, an order of injunction must be served in person.[5] However, as the defendant could be contacted only via email and provided no traditional contact information, the attorney of the plaintiff could not serve the injunction by traditional means. As a result, the court granted the attorney to serve via email according to Order 65 r.4(1) and r.5(1).[6]

Later in 2000, a federal court of the United States allowed service via fax and email for the first time in *In Re International Telemedia Associates, Inc.*[7] (hereinafter '*Broadfoot v Diaz* Case'), a bankruptcy case. In this case, the defendant Diaz was abroad of uncertain whereabouts and refused to provide the plaintiff with a fixed postal address but offered long-term valid fax number and email address for contact. Considering the previous situation, the Bankruptcy Court for Northern District Georgia made the decision to approve the plaintiff's motion and allow the service abroad via fax, email and mail to Diaz's last known postal address. The court held that Rule 4(f)(3) of *Federal Rules of Civil Procedure* offers a non-exhaustive list of alternative means of service abroad and gives the discretion to choose other means as long as the means is not prohibited by international agreement.[8]

In 2002, the United States Court of Appeals for the Ninth Circuit confirmed the legal validity of the plaintiff's service to the defendant abroad via email in *Rio Properties, Inc. v Rio International Interlink*[9] (hereinafter '*Rio*'), in which the Court of Appeals approved service abroad via email for the first

5 Under Order 65, r.1/2(1), an injunction, as an order to which obedience may be enforced by committal, must be served in person.

6 Order 65, r.4(1) provides in relevant part as follows: 'When it appears to the Court that it is impracticable for any reason to serve [the] document in the manner prescribed, the Court may make an order for substituted service of that document'.

Order 65, r.5(1) provides in relevant part as follows: 'Service of any document [with noted exceptions] . . . may be effected – . . . (d) in such other manner as the Court may direct'.

7 245 B.R. 713 (Bankr. N.D. Ga. 2000).

8 When the courts of the United States decide whether to allow the parties to carry out service of process abroad through electronic means, the main legal basis is Article 4(f)(3) and Article 4(h)(2) of the Federal Rules of Civil Procedure. Federal Rules of Civil Procedure 4(f)(3) provides in relevant part as follows: '(f) Serving an Individual in a Foreign Country. Unless otherwise provided by federal law, an individual – other than a minor, an incompetent person, or a person whose waiver has been filed – may be served at a place not within any judicial district of the United States: . . . (3) by other means not prohibited by international agreement, as the court orders. Federal Rules of Civil Procedure 4(h)(2) provides in relevant part as follows: (h) Serving a Corporation, Partnership, or Association. Unless federal law provides otherwise or the defendant's waiver has been filed, a domestic or foreign corporation, or a partnership or other unincorporated association that is subject to suit under a common name, must be served: . . . (2) at a place not within any judicial district of the United States, in any manner prescribed by Rule 4(f) for serving an individual, except personal delivery under (f)(2)(C)(i)'.

9 [2002] 9th Cir, 284 F3d 1007 (9th Cir).

time. While acknowledging the advantages of service via email, the Court pointed out certain limitations such as no effective method to acknowledge if the person to be served has actually received. Therefore, when judging whether electronic service abroad is to be allowed, the court shall balance the limitations of email service against its benefits in any particular case.

The diversification of electronic service abroad

With further development of the Internet, social networking sites (SNS) gradually became a daily contact tool for a majority of people[10] while the advancement of science and technology as well as the development of communication means also promote the evolution of means of judicial service. Since the late 2000s, electronic service abroad has entered a recent diversified stage of development, characterised by the adoption of more diverse means of communication and being applied in an increasing number of countries under relatively loose conditions.

Australia is the first country to allow service via Facebook. In 2008, the Capital Territory Court of Appeal permitted the plaintiff to serve the two defendants via Facebook in *MKM Capital Prop. Ltd. v Corbo and Poyser*[11] (hereinafter '*MKM Capital*'). However, the court also ordered the plaintiff to serve via email and by leaving documents at the last known address of the defendants.[12]

In 2009, the Supreme Court of New Zealand allowed the plaintiff to serve via Facebook in *Axe Market Gardens v Craig Axe.*[13] In this case, a father sued his son for his unauthorised transfer of 241,000 NZD from the account of their family business. The defendant lived in the United Kingdom at an unknown address, so the means of service in the Hague Service Convention were not applicable. Considering that the defendant transferred the sum of money via online banking, contacted the plaintiff via email and had a Facebook account, the court finally granted the plaintiff's request to serve the defendant via Facebook.[14]

10 Hans Van Horn, 'Evolutionary Pull, Practical Difficulties, and Ethical Boundaries: Using Facebook to Serve Process on International Defendants' (2013) 26 *Pacific McGeorge Global Business & Development Law Journal* 555, 565.

11 [2008] ACTCA 608 (SC).

12 See 'Facebook Used to Find Defendants in Australian Court Case' (Ottawa Citizen, 15 December 2008) <www.ottawacitizen.com/technology/technology/1081894/story.html> accessed 7 October 2016. See also Bonnie Malkin, 'Australian Couple Served with Legal Documents via Facebook' (*Telegraph.Co.UK*, 16 December 2008) <www.telegraph.co.uk/news/newstopics/howaboutthat/3793491/Australian-couple-served-with-legal-documents-viaFacebook.html> accessed 7 October 2016.

13 CIV: 2008–485–2676 (New Zealand 2009).

14 John. G. Browning, 'Served Without Ever Leaving the Computer' (2010) 73 *Texas Bar Journal* 180, 181. See also Ian Llewellyn, 'NZ Court Papers Can Be Served via Facebook' (Judge Rules, 16 March 2009) <www.nzherald.co.nz/nz/news/article.cfm?c_id=1&objectid=10561970> accessed 7 October 2016.

In 2009, in *Knott v Sutherland*,[15] a Canadian court issued a judge order to permit the plaintiff to serve by two means: (1) posting a copy of litigation document at the human resources department where the defendant formerly worked; (2) sending a message to the defendant's Facebook account as an alternative means.[16]

In 2011, under circumstance of the attorney's failure to serve the defendant (debtor) by various means in the Hague Service Convention, the court of Hastings County, England, invoked *MKM Capital*, the 2008 Australian case, and allowed the plaintiff's attorney to serve court summons to the defendant via Facebook as an alternative.[17]

The US court began to allow service via Facebook from 2011 in *Mpafe v Mpafe*,[18] in which Jessica in Minnesota filed for divorce with her husband whom she had not seen for years. She did not know the exact address of him, only having one clue that he might have returned to Côte d'Ivoire. Jessica asked for the court's permission to serve by general delivery (sending mail to the post office to be received by the defendant), but the judge considered it only as a waste of energy. Besides, the judge held the same opinion for service by notice in the newspaper, because nobody, especially not the poor, would read legal newspapers to acknowledge a divorce lawsuit he is facing. While the traditional means of notice has been outdated with a relatively large cost, technology has provided cheaper and more effective means of service. Therefore, the judge decided that the plaintiff could serve by notice on the Internet, including via social networking sites (SNS) such as Facebook and Myspace, email and other means which could be sought on online search engines like Google.

The legislation of electronic service abroad

After over 30 years' development, the legality of electronic service abroad has been acknowledged by an increasing number of countries, and the relevant rules are made mainly in the following two ways:

First, in some countries, that electronic means can be used in service abroad is expressly provided in legislation. For example, Article 162 of Spain's Civil

15 [2009] Edmonton 0803 002267 (Alta.Q.B.M.).

16 See Browning (n 14), 182. See also Shaunna Mireau, 'Substitutional Service via Facebook in Alberta' (SLAW.CA, 24 September 2009) <www.slaw.ca/2009/09/24/substitutional-service-via-facebook-inalberta/> accessed 8 October 2016.

17 See 'British Lawyer Uses Facebook to Serve Court Summons' (*The Telegraph*, 14 March 2011) <www.telegraph.co.uk/technology/facebook/8382570/British-lawyer-uses-Facebook-to-serve-court-summons.html> accessed 8 October 2016. See also Sarah, 'UK Solicitor Serves First Court Summons by Facebook' (Law & Legal, 16 March 2011) <www.lawandlegal.co.uk/careers/uk-solicitor-serves-court-summons-facebook/> accessed 8 October 2016.

18 No. 27-FA-11–3453 (D. Minn. 2011) <https://zh.scribd.com/document/70014426/Mpafe-v-Mpafe-order> accessed 8 October 2016. See also Van Horn (n 10), 566.

Procedure Law provides the possibility of service of legal documents by electronic means, but there are some requirements: the court and the person to be served shall have relevant technical devices; the authenticity and integrity of documents shall be guaranteed; the time of sending and receiving shall be indicated. Article 117 of Lithuania's new Civil Procedure Law provides that service via email is allowed under the litigants' agreement.[19] Besides, Rule 5(b)(2)[20] and Rule 5(b)(3)[21] of Federal Rules of Civil Procedure of the United States provide that with written consent of the person to be served, electronic means could be used to serve documents including court orders, answer briefs, motions and discovery documents. New Zealand's Construction Contracts Regulations 2003 allows service by email or other electronic means under certain conditions, such as the consent by the person to be served. Also, under some special circumstances, documents could be served via fax between New Zealand and Australia.[22]

Second, in other countries, no explicit legislation concerning the electronic service abroad exists; however, the court may approve electronic service abroad case by case at discretion authorised by law. For example, the major legal bases for the US court to judge whether electronic service abroad should be permitted are Rule 4(f)(3)[23] and Rule 4(h)(2)[24] of Federal Rules of Civil Procedure. According to the rules, the plaintiff could serve summons or copies of pleading abroad by means appointed by the court and not prohibited by international conventions. Moreover, electronic service abroad approved by the court must meet the requirements of principle of due process explained

19 See He Qisheng, *Studies on Service of Process* (1st edn, Peking University press 2006), 180.

20 Federal Rules of Civil Procedure 5(b)(2)(E) provides in relevant part as follows: '(2) Service in General. A paper is served under this rule by: . . . (E) sending it by electronic means if the person consented in writing – in which event service is complete upon transmission, but is not effective if the serving party learns that it did not reach the person to be served'.

21 Federal Rules of Civil Procedure 5(b)(3) provides: '(3) Using Court Facilities. If a local rule so authorizes, a party may use the court's transmission facilities to make service under Rule 5(b)(2)(E)'.

22 See He Qisheng, 'Electronic Service Abroad and Hague Service Convention' (2005) 10 *Litigation Law Review* 535, 537.

23 Federal Rules of Civil Procedure 4(f)(3) provides in relevant part as follows: '(f) Serving an Individual in a Foreign Country. Unless otherwise provided by federal law, an individual – other than a minor, an incompetent person, or a person whose waiver has been filed – may be served at a place not within any judicial district of the United States: . . . (3) by other means not prohibited by international agreement, as the court orders'.

24 Federal Rules of Civil Procedure 4(h)(2) provides in relevant part as follows: '(h) Serving a Corporation, Partnership, or Association. Unless federal law provides otherwise or the defendant's waiver has been filed, a domestic or foreign corporation, or a partnership or other unincorporated association that is subject to suit under a common name, must be served: . . . (2) at a place not within any judicial district of the United States, in any manner prescribed by Rule 4(f) for serving an individual, except personal delivery under (f)(2)(C)(i)'.

by the Supreme Court of the United States in the *Mullane* case, that is, the service shall be 'reasonably calculated, under all the circumstances, to apprise interested parties of the pendency of the action and afford them an opportunity to present their objections'.[25] Australia's Uniform Civil Procedure Rules provides that when personal service is not applicable, other means which will effectively notify the defendant of the proceedings in all possible circumstances can be used for the service under the court's approval.[26] The Rule 4(1) and Rule 5(1)[27] of Order 65 of the Rules of the Supreme Court of United Kingdom have similar regulations. Besides, Article 138 of Code of Civil Procedure of Quebec, Canada, provides that the judge or the clerk could authorise other means of service according the plaintiff's motion as the case may require.[28]

The conditions for application of electronic service abroad

In deciding whether the plaintiff is to be allowed to serve abroad by electronic means, as required by the principle of due process, the US courts usually conduct a case-by-case balancing test where the following four factors are mainly concerned:

First, whether the traditional means have been attempted. In *Rio*, the plaintiff Rio Properties tried to serve the defendant Rio International Interlink to its address in Miami, Florida, which was used in its registration of domain name of a betting site. However, the address actually belonged to an international express corporation of the defendant, which was not authorised to receive the service on behalf of the defendant. Besides, the defendant's attorney in Los Angeles, California, also refused to receive service on behalf of his client. As a result, the plaintiff could try to serve only by direct means, but failed to acquire the defendant's address in Costa Rica, only finding out that the defendant agreed to contact via email and the express corporation in

25 See *Mullane v Central Hanover Bank & Trust Co.*, 339 U.S. 306 (1950). See also Matthew R. Schreck, 'Preventing You've Got Mail from Meaning You've Been Served: How Service of Process by E-Mail Does Not Meet Constitutional Procedural Due Process Requirements' (2005) 38 *John Marshall Law Review* 1121, 1123–1125.

26 Rule 116(1) of the Australian Uniform Civil Procedure Rules permits substituted service 'where, in effect, there is a practical impossibility of personal service and that the method of service proposed is one which in all reasonable probability, if not certainty, will be effective in bringing knowledge or notice of the proceedings to the attention of the defendant'.

27 Order 65, r.4(1) provides in relevant part as follows: 'When it appears to the Court that it is impracticable for any reason to serve [the] document in the manner prescribed, the Court may make an order for substituted service of that document'.

Order 65, r.5(1) provides in relevant part as follows: 'Service of any document [with noted exceptions] . . . may be effected – . . . (d) in such other manner as the Court may direct'.

28 See David P. Stewart and Anna Conley, 'E-mail Service on Foreign Defendants: Time for an International Approach' (2007) 38 *Georgetown Journal of International Law* 755, 786–787.

Miami. Under such circumstance, the plaintiff filed an emergency motion to the court of first instance and was approved to serve the defendant by mail to the attorney and the express corporation as well as via email. Furthermore, in *Ryan v Brunswick Corp.*,[29]the US District Court for the Western District of New York allowed the plaintiff to serve the defendant via mail, fax and email and held that Rule 4(f)(3) of Federal Rules of Civil Procedure has a prerequisite that the plaintiff must reasonably prove the attempts of service.

Second, the feasibility of traditional means. Attention shall be paid to whether the address of the person to be served is known or not known, whether the person to be served is evading the service, whether traditional means would cause undue burden to the plaintiff, and so forth. For example, in *Broadfoot v Diaz*, the defendant Diaz was abroad of uncertain whereabouts and refused to provide a long-term address, which constituted serious evasion of service. In *Hollow v Hollow*,[30] the defendant was the plaintiff's husband who had emigrated to Saudi Arabia and contacted his wife in the United States only via Yahoo Email, which made it hard for the service to be received both by international service corporation and by the employer of the defendant while the service means under Saudi Arabian laws would take from one year to one and a half years. According to the laws of New York State, when the service means stipulated by the law is not applicable, the court may authorise the plaintiff to use other means.[31] Thus the court approved the plaintiff to serve via email to the defendant's last known email address and at the same time via international registered mail and standard mail.

Third, the possibility of notifying the defendant by electronic means. Considerations would be whether the email address and Facebook account actually belongs to the person to be served, whether the electronic contact information is provided by the person to be served, the degree and frequency of using the electronic communication means by the person to be served, whether the person to be served uses the electronic means in daily business, whether the two parties have contacted each other via the electronic means, and so forth.[32] In *Broadfoot v Diaz*, as the defendant chose to be contacted by fax and email and the use of the two means has been rather popular in the context of globalisation and informatisation, the court held after reasonable consideration that service via fax and email could effectively notify the defendant of the pending action. In the *Rio* case, the defendant Rio International Interlink was exactly a company which generated great profits from its online operation method

29 No. 02 – CV – 0133E(F), 2002 WL 1628933, (W.D.N.Y. 2002).

30 747 N.Y.S.2d 704 (N.Y. Sup. Ct. 2002).

31 See N.Y.Civ.Prac. L. & R. § 308[5] (McKinney 2002). It provides: 'Personal service upon a natural person shall be made by any one of the following methods: . . . [5] in such manner as the court, upon motion, without notice, directs, if service is impracticable under paragraphs one, two or four of this section'.

32 See Stewart and Conley (n 28), 764–772. See also Melodie M. Dan, Social, 'Networking Sites: A Reasonable Calculated Method to Effect Service of Process' (2010) *1 Case Western Reserve Journal of Law, Technology & the Internet* 183, 212–218.

and designated email as its preferred contact means on its website. In *FTC v PCCare247, Inc.*[33] (hereinafter '*FTC* case'), the defendants cheated through Internet and email, and one of their email addresses was used to contact with the plaintiff and the court. Moreover, plenty of facts could prove that the Facebook account to be served was truly owned by the defendants. Therefore, the court considered service via email and Facebook could satisfy the requirements for the due process.

Finally, the court would also consider whether electronic service is prohibited by international convention or the law of the country where the person to be served lives. In the *Rio* case, the United States Court of Appeals identified Rule 4(f)(3) and Rule 4(h)(2) of Federal Rules of Civil Procedure applicable to the case. Moreover, there is no sequence of application among the means stipulated in Rule 4(f)(3), Rule 4(f)(1) and Rule 4(f)(2), but the alternative means approved by the court could not violate international convention. In the *FTC* case, the court held that the United States and India were both state parties to Hague Service Convention which did not prohibit service via email and Facebook and that the plaintiff could thus serve via email and Facebook according to Rule 4(f)(3) of Federal Rules of Civil Procedure.

The methods of electronic service abroad

In the early stage of development, electronic service abroad adopted means of telex and fax. With the development of computer and Internet, the court has gradually allowed means of email, short message service (SMS) and social networking site (SNS) such as Facebook and Twitter for service abroad.

In terms of new technological means, the US court had a classical exposition in the *Broadfoot v Diaz* case: the permission of service by new technological means is just logical extension of the permissions of personal service, service by mail, service by publication and service via telex in previous cases, and people turning a blind eye to the fact and advantages of new technological development are no different from hiding their head in the sand.[34] In the *Rio* case, the court clarified that the due process stipulated by the Constitution of United States does not restrict service means within given ones but requests the service means to be reasonably considered and able to notify and give defense opportunity to the person to be served. This broad standard liberates the court from the restriction of outdated means of service and makes it possible to adopt new technology in service.

In 2008, the *MKM Capital* case heard by Capital Territory Court of Appeal of Australia was the first case to allow service via Facebook in the world. In this case, the plaintiff was a loan corporation, and the defendants Carmel Corbo and Gordon Poyser were a couple who defaulted on a residential loan

33 [2013] SDNY, WL 841037 (SDNY).

34 See *In Re International Telemedia Associates, Inc.*, 245 B.R. 713, 719, 722 (Bankr. N.D. Ga. 2000).

of 150,000 AUD and lost the lawsuit due to their absence on court. After failing to serve by private investigation firm, newspaper notice and personal service at the defendants' residential address, MKM Capital applied to the court for service via Facebook. As the plaintiff established that the personal information of the defendants accorded with that of the Facebook account to be served and proved that the account belonged to the defendants, at last, the court authorised the plaintiff to serve the defendants via Facebook message.[35] However, the court also ordered the plaintiff to serve via email and by leaving copies of documents at the last known address of the defendants.[36]

Afterwards, Australia's Federal Magistrates Court and Federal Court successively permitted the plaintiff to serve the defendant via text message in the 2008 *Child Support Registrar Applicant v Leigh* and the 2010 *Jemella Australia Pty Ltd. v Bouobeid*, respectively. In addition, in the latter case, the court presumed that the defendant would be served in five business days.[37]

In 2009, in *Donal Blaney v Persons Unknown*, the Supreme Court of the United Kingdom first permitted the plaintiff to serve an injunction via Twitter.[38] The plaintiff Donal Blaney was a famous lawyer as well as a Twitter celebrity, whereas the defendant was an anonymous man who registered a Twitter account with Donal's picture, linked the account to Donal's and imitated Donal's tone to tweet. Because the address of the defendant was unknown, the Supreme Court finally permitted the attorney of the plaintiff to serve the link of the injunction via Twitter message, in which the defendant was requested to tell his real identity and stop tort.[39]

In 2013, in *FTC*, the plaintiff Federal Trade Commission had already served the summons and copies of pleading, thus the US District Court for the Southern District of New York permitted other documents to be served via email and Facebook to the defendant in India. Nevertheless, the court considered

35 See Nick Abrahams, 'Australian Court Serves Documents via Facebook' (*Sydney Morning Herald*, 12 December 2008) <www.smh.com.au/articles/2008/12/12/1228585107578.html> accessed 7 October 2016. See also Noel Towell, 'Lawyers to Serve Notices on Facebook' (*Sydney Morning Herald*, 16 December 2008) <www.smh.com.au/articles/2008/12/16/1229189579001.html> accessed 7 October 2016.

36 See 'Facebook Used to Find Defendants in Australian Court Case' (n 12). See also Malkin (n 12).

37 Claire M. Specht, 'Text Message Service of Process – No LOL Matter: Does Text Message Service of Process Comport with Due Process' (2012) 53 *Boston College Law Review* 1929, 1953.

38 See Frances Gibb, 'High Court to Serve Injunction Through Twitter' (*TIMES*, 2 October 2009) <www.thetimes.co.uk/tto/technology/article1859704.ece> accessed 8 October 2016.

39 Jeremy Kirk, 'U.K. High Court Serves Injunction Over Twitter' (*IDG News Service*, 2 October 2009) <www.cio.com/article/2424271/legal/u-k—high-court-serves-injunction-over-twitter.html> accessed 8 October 2016. See Martha Neil, 'UK's High Court OKs Serving Injunction on Anonymous Blogger Via Twitter' (*ABA Journal*, 2 October 2009) <www.abajournal.com/news/article/uk_high_court_uses_twitter_to_serve_injunction_on_anonymous_blogger/> accessed 8 October 2016.

email itself enough for the service, and service via Facebook, as a relatively new means, just plays the role of complement and guarantee for the email means.

China's legislation and practice on electronic service abroad

China's provisions on electronic service abroad first appeared in Special Maritime Procedure Law[40] promulgated in 1999 and its Judicial Interpretation[41] in 2003. Article 80.1.3 of the Special Maritime Procedure Law provides that the service of legal documents in maritime actions can be conducted ' in other appropriate ways whereby such service can be acknowledged'. To be specific, according to Article 55 of the Judicial Interpretation in 2003, 'other appropriate ways may include fax, email (including personal website of the person to be served), etc'.

In 2006, Several Provisions of the Supreme People's Court on the Service of Judicial Documents of Foreign-related Civil or Commercial Cases[42] expanded the application of electronic service abroad to all foreign-related civil and commercial cases in addition to maritime cases.[43] The Civil Procedure Law marks the first time in China that electronic service abroad has been adopted in legislation. According to Article 267, service of judicial documents to defendants who have no residence in China may 'use means which can confirm receipt by the person to be served, such as fax and email'.[44]

In judicial practice, electronic service abroad was adopted in developed regions of Eastern China at early times. For instance, in the case of share transfer dispute between Zheng Bangchuan (plaintiff) and Lin Zhicheng (defendant of Singaporean citizenship), the Intermediate People's Court of Xiamen served judicial documents to the two email addresses of the defendant, which

40 The Law on the Special Procedures for Maritime Proceedings of the People's Republic of China, Effective date: 1 July 2000.

41 Interpretation of the Supreme People's Court on the Application of the Law on the Special Procedures for Maritime Proceedings of the People's Republic of China, Effective date: 1 February 2003.

42 The Several Provisions of the Supreme People's Court on the Service of Judicial Documents of Foreign-related Civil or Commercial Cases, Effective date: 22 August 2006.

43 Specifically, Article 10 of the Several Provisions of the Supreme People's Court on the Service of Judicial Documents of Foreign-related Civil or Commercial Cases. In addition, Article 3 of the Several Provisions of the Supreme People's Court on the Service of Litigation Documents in Taiwan Region-related Civil Matters (Effective date: 23 April 2008) and Article 8 of the Several Provisions of the Supreme People's Court on the Issues concerning the Service of Judicial Documents of Hong Kong SAR and Macao SAR-related Civil and Commercial Cases (Effective date: 16 March 2009) also include similar stipulations.

44 In addition, Article 135 of the Interpretation of the Supreme People's Court on the Application of the Civil Procedure Law of the People's Republic of China (Effective date: 2 February 2015) provides: 'Process may be served electronically via fax, email, mobile communications and other specific systems'.

were provided by staff of his company, and the defendant acknowledged receipt and responded by replying via email.[45] Besides, the court of Longhu District, Shantou, used email as a supplementary means for contacting the Canadian defendant in a foreign-related divorce case. The Court of Nanhu District, Jiaxing, also adopted service via email in a foreign-related divorce case.[46] From the aforementioned cases, it can be seen that electronic service abroad plays a positive role in resolving the difficulty in service in judicial practice of foreign-related civil and commercial cases.

Prospect of electronic service abroad system under the 'Belt and Road' Initiative

Currently with smooth promotion of the 'Belt and Road' Initiative, the economic and trade exchanges among countries alongside are more frequent than before, although the differences in legal system, history and culture unavoidably make cross-border civil and commercial disputes complicated. These disputes shall be settled timely and fairly in case of relevant trade and investment activities interrupted and even terminated. However, the service means provided in Hague Service Convention are of long period and low efficiency, resulting in the inability to start legal proceedings due to failure in service in many foreign-related civil and commercial cases.[47] Moreover, quite a few countries alongside are not state parties to the Hague Service Convention,[48] and therefore the service means provided in the Convention cannot be adopted. It is desirable to actively promote the construction of regional system of electronic service abroad in countries along the 'Belt and Road'. This will contribute to satisfying the need of judicial practice of foreign-related civil and commercial cases, shortening the period of service abroad, enhancing the efficiency of settlement of cross-border disputes and creating a fair and effective judicial environment for the region along the 'Belt and Road'.

As development level varies from country to country in the region along the 'Belt and Road', the construction of electronic service abroad system will

45 He Qisheng, (n 22), 543.

46 See Zheng Zhangxia, 'A Brief Analysis on the Electronic Service Means under Foreign Related Cases in Practice – The Thought on Guangdong Province's Implementation of Electronic Service' (2015) 15 *Journal of Changchun Institute of Education* 20, 20.

47 See Wan Exiang, 'Judicial Reform and Foreign-Related Civil and Commercial Trials After China's Entry into WTO' (2002) 6 *International Economic Law Review* 1, 18.

48 The countries along the 'Belt and Road' which have already entered the Hague Service Convention are 33 in total: China, Albania, Armenia, Belarus, Bosnia and Herzegovina, Bulgaria, Croatia, Cyprus, Czech Republic, Egypt, Estonia, Greece, Hungary, India, Israel, Lithuania, Latvia, Montenegro, Poland, Moldova, Romania, Russia, Serbia, Slovakia, Slovenia, Sri Lanka, Turkey, Macedonia, Ukraine, Vietnam, Kazakhstan, Kuwait, Pakistan. See HCCH's website <www.hcch.net/en/instruments/conventions/status-table/?cid=17> accessed 8 October 2017. For the list of countries along the 'Belt and Road', see Chapter 1 of this book.

face challenges as follows: first, the uneven distribution of Internet users in the relevant countries. Although the total number of Internet users in the world reached 3.5 billion by the end of 2016, accounting for 47% of global population (the number in 2000 was 6%), such increase was unevenly scattered around the world and was polarised between developed and developing countries.[49] Along the 'Belt and Road', there are developed European countries and a large number of developing Asian and African countries. The gaps in the development level of network communication determine that currently there seems to be no realistic foundation for a multilateral convention on electronic service abroad. Second, certain problems and limitations still exist in today's electronic service in terms of privacy, security, institution and regulation, social convention and infrastructure. On the one hand, a reasonable and perfect system has not yet been established, electronic service abroad might potentially put a brake on procedural justice, privacy and security, and bring about certain conflicts between high judicial efficiency and weak procedure guarantee. Moreover, different procedures have different levels of requirement for procedure guarantee.[50] On the other hand, the infrastructure of countries along the 'Belt and Road' varies to a great extent, which results in relatively significant differences in daily communication means. By studying the history of electronic service abroad, it could be found out that relevant institutions and regulations shall be gradually established and improved with the development of technical devices and communication habits.

In response to the challenges mentioned earlier, we suggest the gradual promotion of construction of electronic service abroad system in the region along the 'Belt and Road' in the following two aspects.

First, from the perspective of international cooperation, the relevant countries shall actively advance the judicial cooperation, promote consensus on electronic service abroad among courts of different countries, holding interchange activities such as China-ASEAN Justice Forum, and build consensus preliminarily in non-conventional form like *Nanning Declaration*.[51] On the basis of consensus, China may further make use of existing results of bilateral judicial cooperation,[52] negotiate with countries who has concluded civil and

49 See International Telecommunications Union, 'In 2016, There Were About 3.9 Billion People Who Had Not Access to the Internet Worldwide' *(199 IT Internet Data Center)* <www.199it.com/archives/518381.html> accessed 8 October 2017.

50 See Song Chaowu, 'Research on Civil Electronic Service' (2008) 6 *Jurist* 125, 128–129.

51 Nanning Declaration was approved at the 2nd China-ASEAN Justice Forum on 8 June 2017 in Nanning, Guangxi Province, China.

52 The countries along the 'Belt and Road' which have concluded treaties on judicial assistance in civil and commercial matters with China are as follows: Mongolia, Kazakhstan, Kyrgyzstan, Tajikistan, Uzbekistan, Singapore, Thailand, Vietnam, Laos, Kuwait, UAE, Egypt, Turkey, Russia, Ukraine, Belarus, Poland, Bulgaria, Romania, Bosnia and Herzegovina, Hungary, Greece, Cyprus, Lithuania. See The Ministry of the Foreign Affairs of the People's Republic of China, 'The Present Situation of China's Judicial Assistance and Extradition Treaties' <www.fmprc.gov.cn/web/ziliao_674904/tytj_674911/wgdwdjdsfhzty_674917/t1215630.shtml> accessed 8 October 2017.

commercial judicial assistance treaties with China, to extend the mutual application of electronic service in the Contracting States by way of interpreting the means of electronic service not in violation of the treaties, and lay emphasis on providing the conditions for application and the acknowledge of receipt proof of electronic service abroad.

Second, from the perspective of system design, the range and conditions for application of electronic service abroad, the newly emerging means of service, should be gradually expanded. China's legislation on its range of application has gone through different stages – it could be adopted only in special maritime procedures at first and has gradually been applied universally to foreign-related civil and commercial cases. Therefore, the construction of electronic service abroad system in countries along the 'Belt and Road' cannot be achieved overnight in terms of system design. Instead, it is necessary to make detailed rules on applicable case type, document type, service target and feasible means for different judicial procedures, respectively, so as to develop the system step by step beginning from limited applicability and ultimately realise the goal of universal applicability in the future.

Conclusion

Around 4000 years ago, the *Code of Eshnunna* provided the plaintiff must shout out the defendant's name and wait until the defendant's response before the lawsuit could continue. With thousands of years passed, the means of service has developed into personal service, and then to mail, publication and telex. In the future, social development will further drive the means to develop from tangible literary service to intangible electronic service.[53]Currently at the new age of deep implementation of the 'Belt and Road' Initiative, we shall conform to the trend of the global development, base ourselves upon the present social situation of countries alongside and gradually promote the construction of system of electronic service abroad in those countries from perspectives of international cooperation as well as system design.

53 See Conley (n 4), 417–423.

Part III

Jurisdiction

4 Navigating Singapore's private international rules in the age of innovative cross-border commercial litigation framework

*Man Yip**

Introduction

In the last decade, Singapore has been consistently working on consolidating its position as the leading dispute resolution hub in Asia. China's ambitious 'One Belt One Road' initiative ('OBOR') affords an invaluable opportunity to Singapore to foster its role in dispute resolution services. Conversely, the success of the OBOR is in part dependent upon the availability of reliable and efficient dispute resolution mechanisms to handle the commercial disputes that will inevitably arise.[1] Singapore looks poised to contribute to the success of the OBOR in that respect, in light of its mature and business-friendly legal system, sophisticated commercial jurisprudence and well-developed judicial experience.

Coincidentally, China announced its OBOR in the same year (2013) that the Chief Justice of Singapore, Sundaresh Menon, mooted his idea to create an innovative 'international' court to handle an expected increase in international commercial disputes in the region. In January 2015, following a series of consultations, the Singapore International Commercial Court ('SICC') was launched. In 2016, to increase the portability of its judgments abroad, Singapore signed on to the Hague Convention on Choice of Court Agreements 2005 (the 'HCCCA') and it has been implemented by way of local legislation in October the same year.[2]

However, these recent developments have also made the Singapore High Court's *in personam* civil jurisdictional framework as well as the rules on recognition and enforcement of foreign judgments far more complex than

* The author would like to thank her colleagues, Goh Yihan and Kenny Chng for their helpful comments on earlier drafts. All views and error are the author's own.

1 See generally Guiguo Wang, 'The Belt and Road Initiative in Quest for a Dispute Resolution Mechanism' (2017) 25 *Asia Pacific Law Review* 1.

2 Singapore has also participated in the bigger Hague Conference 'Judgments Project', focused on the recognition and enforcement of judgments. See The Hague Conference on Private International Law, 'The Judgements Project' <www.hcch.net/en/projects/legislative-projects/judgments> accessed 7 November 2017.

before. This chapter focuses on the jurisdictional rules of the Singapore High Court. It suggests that the challenge posed by Singapore private international rules is not that they are underdeveloped to deal with the likely increase in disputes in the region, which may be the more commonly encountered problem in other countries. To the contrary, the challenge is one of navigating the web of sophisticated and, in some respects, innovative rules.

The discussion in this chapter comprises two parts. The first part, immediately following this introduction, provides an overview of the complex *in personam* civil jurisdictional rules of the Singapore High Court[3] (of which the SICC is a division). The succinct description is written with the aim of helping readers appreciate the distinctions in and interplay between the different jurisdiction regimes under Singapore law. The second part examines the challenge posed by Singapore's private international rules. This part of the discussion highlights the main challenge is one of navigating the complex web of jurisdictional rules of the Singapore High Court. This in turn bears on the broader question of whether Singapore's jurisdictional rules would impact upon its ability to provide a viable court-based dispute resolution mechanism for disputes arising from the OBOR initiative. This chapter concludes that the challenge is not insurmountable, and it should instead be embraced.

Jurisdictional framework of the Singapore High Court

Traditional framework

The *in personam* civil jurisdiction of the Singapore High Court is founded on the Supreme Court of Judicature Act ('SCJA').[4] Before the establishment of the SICC and the implementation of the HCCCA, the High Court has jurisdiction if: in accordance with the Rules of Court,[5] the defendant has been served with originating process while he is present[6] in Singapore or served abroad with the leave of court;[7] if the defendant has submitted to the jurisdiction of the High Court;[8] and if the High Court is vested with jurisdiction by any other written law.[9]

Conceptually, it would be helpful to think of the High Court's jurisdictional framework by reference to two core distinctions at play. First, there is a distinction between *existence* of jurisdiction and *exercise* of jurisdiction. The High Court may decline to exercise jurisdiction even if it is established that

3 Hereinafter, references to 'Singapore High Court' and 'High Court', in the absence of provision to the contrary, shall refer to the Singapore High Court sans the SICC.

4 Cap 332, 2007 Rev Ed.

5 Cap 332, R5, the subsidiary legislation of the SCJA.

6 SCJA, s 16(1) (a) (i); transient presence shall suffice: *HRH Maharanee Seethadevi Gaekwar of Baroda v Wildenstein* [1972] 2 QB 283 (CA).

7 SCJA, s 16(1) (a) (ii).

8 SCJA, s 16(1) (b).

9 SCJA, s 16(2) and s 17.

it has jurisdiction. Second, there is a distinction to be drawn between *territorial* jurisdiction (service within jurisdiction) and *extraterritorial* jurisdiction (service out of jurisdiction). Territorial jurisdiction is established as of right.[10] Extraterritorial jurisdiction, on the other hand, is discretionary and subject to more stringent requirements, owing to the traditional judicial attitude that this involves an exercise of 'exorbitant' jurisdiction.[11] As such, leave of court is required for service of process on a foreign defendant.

Given that this collection examines the possible challenges to the success of the OBOR initiative caused by the conflict of law problems, the discussion in this part shall focus on the discussion of extraterritorial jurisdiction, as this most readily relates to cross-border disputes that are likely to proliferate as a result of increasing economic integration.

Turning now to consider extraterritorial jurisdiction in greater detail, as mentioned, leave of court is required for service abroad on a foreign defendant.[12] The burden of obtaining court's leave is on the plaintiff, who must establish the following:

1 the case falls within a head of jurisdiction under one of the heads prescribed in Order 11, rule 1 of the Rules of Court on the basis of 'a good arguable case';
2 a serious issue to be tried on the merits; and
3 Singapore is a proper forum to try the action.

It is noteworthy that even where parties' contract contains a choice of court agreement in favour of the Singapore High Court, service on a foreign defendant cannot be made without the leave of court, unless there is contractual provision for a means of service in Singapore.[13] In the absence of contractual provision for local service of process, to establish that the case is a proper one for service out of Singapore, a plaintiff in a dispute involving a forum jurisdiction agreement may specifically avail of the heads of jurisdiction under Rules of Court, Order 11, rules 1(d)(iv) and (r).[14]

As for demonstrating that Singapore is a 'proper forum to try the action',[15] the applicable test is that enunciated by the House of Lords in *Spiliada*

10 Based on service of process on the defendant in Singapore, the defendant's submission to the Singapore High Court, or where special provisions had been made in other written laws. See a detailed description in *Halsbury's Laws of Singapore* (LexisNexis Singapore 2013 Reissue) vol 6(2), paras 75.005–75.028.
11 *Zoom Communications Ltd v Broadcast Solutions Pte Ltd* [2014] SGCA 44, [2014] 4 SLR 500 [72] [*Zoom Communications*].
12 Rules of Court, Order 11, rules 1 and 2.
13 Rules of Court, Order 10, rule 3: in such a scenario, jurisdiction is established as of right.
14 Depending on the facts of the dispute, other heads of jurisdiction may be applicable.
15 This is part of showing that the Singapore High Court has (extraterritorial) jurisdiction. Procedurally, the plaintiff makes an *ex parte* for leave of court for service out of jurisdiction. After service abroad has been made, at the *inter parties* stage, if the defendant

Maritime Corp v Cansulex Ltd,[16] commonly referred to as the *Spiliada* test. In Singapore, whilst English cases on the application of the test remain persuasive, a sizeable pool of local authorities[17] is now available to provide direct guidance. Lying at the heart of the *Spiliada* test is a comparison between holding trial in the forum court and holding trial in the foreign court by reference to the interests of all the parties involved and the ends of justice. The characteristic features of the *Spiliada* test, as is well known, are that it comprises two stages of inquiry, and at each stage, the court is called upon to exercise discretion. The first stage is focused on examining forum appropriateness by primarily considering factors of expense and convenience. The second stage is concerned with the question of whether substantial justice can be obtained in the *prima facie* natural forum that is established in the first stage.

Where there is a choice of court agreement in place, the determination of forum appropriateness is more complex. Where the choice of court agreement is exclusive, the *Spiliada* test is displaced and the 'strong cause' test[18] is applied instead. For instance, in a case where the parties have by agreement submitted their disputes to the exclusive jurisdiction of the Singapore High Court, the court would uphold the parties' agreement to litigate in Singapore, unless the defendant can show 'strong cause' amounting to exceptional circumstances justifying the breach of contract to bring the suit elsewhere.

Where the choice of agreement is non-exclusive in nature, on the other hand, the Singapore Court of Appeal has recently clarified in *Orchard Capital I Ltd v Ravindra Kumar Jhunjhunwala*[19] that the *Spiliada* test would apply and the choice of court agreement is one of the factors in the evaluation exercise. In that case, the choice of court agreement was in favour of Hong Kong courts. It is not clear that the Singapore court would apply the same approach where the choice of court agreement is in favour of Singapore courts.[20] It has been observed that there are English and Hong Kong authorities in favour

chooses to challenge the High Court's *exercise* of jurisdiction and applies for a stay of the Singapore proceedings, the burden lies on him to show that Singapore is not the most appropriate forum in accordance with the *Spiliada* test. If the defendant instead challenges the High Court's *existence* of jurisdiction on the basis that Singapore is not the proper forum for the trial, the burden remains with the plaintiff to show that Singapore is indeed the proper forum on the basis of the *Spiliada* principles. Strategically, the defendant should opt for a setting aside application if the argument is one based on forum appropriateness: see further *Zoom Communications* [2014] SGCA 44, [2014] 4 SLR 500 [77]–[80].

16 [1987] AC 460 (HL).

17 See, for example, *JIO Minerals FZC v Mineral Enterprises Ltd* [2010] SGCA 41, [2011] 1 SLR 391; *Zoom Communications* [2014] SGCA 44, [2014] 4 SLR 500; *Rotary Engineering Ltd v Kioumji & Eslim Law Firm* [2017] SGCA 24, [2017] 1 SLR 907.

18 *The 'Jian He'* [1999] SGCA 71, [1999] 3 SLR(R) 432.

19 [2010] SGCA 16, [2012] 2 SLR 519.

20 The overall tenor of the judgment does not distinguish between a foreign jurisdiction agreement and a forum jurisdiction agreement.

of a forum-biased approach where the case concerns a forum choice of court agreement.[21]

SICC framework

Innovative court system

After the announcement to establish a specialist court in January 2013, the SICC was launched into operation two years later on 5 January 2015.[22] According to the *Report of the Singapore International Commercial Court Committee* released on 3 December 2013, owing to the continued growth of cross-border investment and trade in Asia, there is a need for 'a neutral and well-regarded dispute resolution hub in the region' to resolve transnational disputes that are expected to increase in the coming years.[23] As a matter of national strategy, the SICC forms part of Singapore's multi-pronged approach to foster the jurisdiction as a hub for dispute resolution. The other two prongs are the Singapore International Arbitration Centre ('SIAC'),[24] as well as the recently launched Singapore International Mediation Centre, working in tandem with the Singapore International Mediation Institute.[25]

Notably, the SICC's docket comprises international commercial disputes. Its design and capabilities, for this reason, reflect strong influence from international arbitral model, a dispute mechanism that is favoured by the international business community for the resolution of commercial disputes. The

21 Yeo Tiong Min, 'The Contractual Basis of the Enforcement of Exclusive and Non-Exclusive Choice of Court Agreements' (2005) 17 *Singapore Academy of Law Journal* 306.

22 See, generally, Denise H. Wong, 'The Rise of the International Commercial Court: What Is It and Will It Work?' (2014) 33 *CJQ* 205; Sundaresh Menon (Chief Justice of the Supreme Court of Singapore), 'International Courts: Towards a Transnational System of Dispute Resolution' (Opening Lecture for the DIFC Courts Lecture Series 2015, 19 January 2015) <www.supremecourt.gov.sg/data/doc/ManagePage/5741/Opening%20Lecture%20-%20DIFC%20Lecture%20Series%202015.pdf > accessed 7 November 2017.

23 Singapore International Commercial Court Committee, *Report of the Singapore International Commercial Court Committee* (2013) <www.mlaw.gov.sg/content/dam/minlaw/corp/News/Annex%20A%20-%20SICC%20Committee%20Report.pdf> accessed 7 November 2017.

24 See Singapore International Arbitration Centre, 'Statistics' <www.siac.org.sg/2014-11-03-13-33-43/facts-figures/statistics> accessed 7 November 2017.

25 The Singapore International Mediation Centre entered into a Memorandum of Understanding with the Mediation Centre of the China Council for the Promotion of International Trade/China Chamber of Commerce 19 September 2017 to promote the use of international commercial mediation to resolve business disputes arising from the OBOR initiative and to encourage the use of each other's mediators and mediation services. See 'Singapore, China sign MOU for Belt and Road Initiative dispute mediation' (*Channel News Asia*, 19 September 2017) <www.channelnewsasia.com/news/singapore/singapore-china-sign-mou-for-belt-and-road-initiative-dispute-9226612> accessed 7 November 2017.

motivation is to create a court-based dispute resolution mechanism that the business community is familiar with but which engenders greater accountability and transparency in processes.[26] As Justice Steven Chong has described, the SICC framework is 'a careful marriage between litigation and arbitration'.[27]

In sum, a hallmark feature of the SICC's procedural framework is the greater latitude for party autonomy and flexibility, a feature that is evident in the international commercial arbitration model. Space constraint does not permit a comprehensive exposition of the procedural rules and other innovative capabilities.[28] It suffices to highlight three key capabilities for illustration. First, whilst the SICC litigation model envisages open court hearings and publication of its judgments, parties may apply for a confidentiality order for (a) the proceedings to be heard in camera, (b) the non-disclosure of information or document, or (c) sealing of court file.[29] Second, in SICC proceedings, it is possible for questions of foreign law to be determined on the basis of submissions instead of proof.[30] Finally, parties may apply for foreign rules of evidence or rules of evidence not forming part of foreign law to be applied to their case heard by the SICC.[31] Notwithstanding some similarities with the arbitral model, it must not be missed that party autonomy does not conclusively decide whether the arbitration-inspired features would apply in the SICC proceedings. The decision ultimately lies with the SICC.

Further, a significant selling point of the SICC is its panel of International Judges – in addition to its panel of distinguished local judges – from which the Chief Justice of the Singapore may appoint to hear disputes brought before the SICC. There are currently fifteen International Judges, drawn from both

26 See common criticisms of the international commercial arbitration regime: Denise H. Wong, 'The Rise of the International Commercial Court: What Is It and Will It Work?' 33 *CJQ* 205, 217–219; Sundaresh Menon C.J., 'Adjudicator, Advocate or Something in Between? Coming to Terms with the Role of the Party-Appointed Arbitrator' (*Herbert Smith Freehills-SMU Asian Arbitration Lecture* 24 November 2016) <www.supremecourt.gov.sg/Data/Editor/Documents/CJ%20speech%20at%20CIArb%20Presidential%20Lecture%202016.pdf > accessed 7 November 2017.

27 Justice Steven Chong, 'The Singapore International Commercial Court: A New Opening in a Forked Path', speech delivered at the British Maritime Law Association Lecture and Dinner (21 October 2015) <www.supremecourt.gov.sg/Data/Editor/Documents/J%20Steven%20Chong%20Speeches/The%20SICC%20-%20A%20New%20Opening%20in%20a%20Forked%20Parth%20-%20London%20(21.10.15).pdf> accessed 7 November 2017.

28 See Man Yip, 'Special Reports – Singapore International Commercial Court: A New Model for Transnational Commercial Litigation' (2015) 32 *Chinese (Taiwan) Yearbook of International Law and Affairs* 155.

29 Rules of Court, Order 110, rule 30, read with *Singapore International Commercial Court Practice Directions* [97] <www.supremecourt.gov.sg/docs/default-source/default-document-library/sicc-practice-directions – effective-from-1-jan-2017.pdf> accessed 7 November 2017. See also Rules of Court, Order 110, rule 31 (reports of judgments of major legal interest).

30 SJCA, s 18L; Rules of Court, Order 110, rule 25.

31 SCJA, s 18K; Rules of Court, Order 110, rule 23.

civilian and common law backgrounds as well as from both Western and Asian jurisdictions.[32] Although the appointment of international jurists to hear a case in a domestic court is mildly reminiscent of the arbitral system, unlike the arbitral system, parties do not have a say at all in the appointment process. They can neither nominate candidates nor indicate any form of preference. Party autonomy is irrelevant here.

We now move on to examine the jurisdictional rules of the SICC, which is the focus of this chapter. Structurally, the SICC is established as a division of the High Court. Its jurisdiction is derived from section 18D of the SCJA. Notably, the *in personam* jurisdiction of the SICC is bound up with its subject-matter jurisdiction.[33] The SICC hears cases that are 'international' and 'commercial' in nature, although these terms are broadly defined.[34] A case may be considered international[35] or commercial[36] if the parties are agreed that it is of such nature. There are two principal ways in which disputes could be brought before the SICC. First, where parties have by a written jurisdiction agreement submitted their disputes to the SICC.[37] Second, where proceedings have been transferred from the High Court to the SICC.[38] Thus far, the disputes decided by the SICC have been transfer cases.[39]

Written jurisdiction agreement

Where there is a written jurisdiction agreement in favour of the SICC, service of originating process on a foreign defendant does not require leave of court.[40] Other requirements for establishing existence of jurisdiction, pursuant to Order 110, rule 7 of the Rules of Court, are that the claim is international and commercial in nature and parties are not seeking any form of prerogative relief.

Further, under the SICC rules, there are limited grounds for the SICC to decline exercising jurisdiction where existence of jurisdiction is established on the basis of a written jurisdiction agreement. Order 110, rule 8(1) of the Rules of Court provides that the SICC may refuse to exercise jurisdiction in a dispute only if 'it is not appropriate for [it] to be heard in the [SICC]'. However, differing from the traditional regime, the *Spiliada* test is not applicable in this context. Indeed, Order 110, rule 8 of the Rules of Court makes clear

32 See Singapore International Commercial Court, 'Judges' <www.sicc.gov.sg/Judges.aspx?id=30> accessed 1 November 2017.

33 SCJA, section 18D(a), read with Rules of Court, Order 110, rule 7(1)(a).

34 Rules of Court, Order 110, rules 1(2) (a) and (2) (b).

35 Rules of Court, Order 110, rule 1(2) (a) (iv).

36 Rules of Court, Order 110, rule 1(2) (b) (iii).

37 Rules of Court, Order 110, rule 7.

38 Rules of Court, Order 110, rules 12(3B) and (4).

39 See Singapore International Commercial Court, 'Recent Judgments' <www.sicc.gov.sg/HearingsJudgments.aspx?id=72> accessed 7 November 2017.

40 Rules of Court, Order 110, rule 6(2).

that the SICC 'must not decline to assume jurisdiction in a claim solely on the ground that the dispute between the parties is connected to a jurisdiction other than Singapore'.[41] The only other statutory guidance on 'inappropriateness' is found in sub-rule (3) which provides that the court 'shall have regard to [the action's] international and commercial character'. It has thus been commented elsewhere that the concept of 'inappropriateness' under the SICC requires clarification in order to provide certainty for users of this specialist court.[42]

Another observation that may be made of Order 110, rule 8 is that its wording does not distinguish between an exclusive jurisdiction agreement and a non-exclusive jurisdiction agreement.[43] But there is scope to argue that the concept of 'inappropriateness' may take into account the precise content of the jurisdiction agreement.[44]

Transfer

We now turn to consider the SICC's jurisdiction founded on transfer of proceedings. As this chapter examines conflict of law issues, the discussion will not consider transfer of proceedings as a matter of exercise of internal allocation of jurisdiction between the High Court and the SICC. Only one point relating to conflict of law rules that warrants highlighting. Where proceedings are first commenced in the High Court, there may be instances where the question for transfer of proceedings to the SICC arises before the High Court has ruled on its own jurisdiction.[45] If the defendant contests the High Court's jurisdiction, the question of transfer is bound up with the question on the High Court's jurisdiction over the claim.

In *Rappo v Accent Delight International Ltd*, the Singapore Court of Appeal said that the 'presence of the SICC and its capabilities are potentially relevant to the [*Spiliada*] analysis'.[46] The court gave the example of the possibility of determining issues of foreign law based on submission instead of proof, a salient procedural feature of the SICC framework.[47] It explained that

41 Emphasis added.

42 Man Yip, 'The Resolution of Disputes Before the Singapore International Commercial Court' (2016) 65 *ICLQ* 439, 456–460.

43 Relevantly, SCJA, section 18F provides that, save where there is express provision to the contrary, a written jurisdiction agreement in favour of the SICC shall be *presumed* to be exclusive. There is debate as to whether this presumption is rebutted where the jurisdiction agreement is governed by foreign law. See TM Yeo, 'Staying Relevant: Exercise of Jurisdiction in the Age of the SICC' *(Eighth Yong Pung How Professorship of Law Lecture 2015)* <https://law.smu.edu.sg/sites/default/files/law/CEBCLA/YPH-Paper-2015.pdf> accessed 7 November 2017.

44 *Ibid.*, see also Man Yip (n 42), 457.

45 For example, where the plaintiff applies for transfer of proceedings to the SICC or if the High Court raises the question on its own motion.

46 [2017] SGCA 27, [2017] 2 SLR 265 [116] *[Accent Delight]*.

47 *Accent Delight* [2017] SGCA 27, [2017] 2 SLR 265 [122].

this capability of the SICC would reduce the weight of governing law being foreign law in the *Spiliada* analysis 'if the Singapore courts, through their International Judges in the SICC, are familiar with and adept at applying that foreign law'.[48] Given that comparison of competing fora lies at the heart of the *Spiliada* exercise, in principle, it is hard to object to the Court of Appeal's enlightened approach. However, it does mean that the presence of the SICC, where the question of transfer is raised at the jurisdictional stage, introduces further complications to the *forum non conveniens* analysis.

We now move onto the consider the jurisdictional rules under the HCCCA.

HCCCA framework

Background

The objective of the HCCCA is to promote international trade and investment through fostering judicial cooperation by way of a uniform set of rules on jurisdiction and recognition and enforcement of foreign judgments in civil and commercial matters.[49] The chief appeal of the HCCCA lies in the recognition and enforcement of a judgment from a Contracting State in another Contracting State, subject to a limited list of defences. This is the reason why Singapore has signed up to the HCCCA: to increase the number of jurisdictions in which Singapore judgments (including the SICC judgments) could be recognised and enforced. The enhanced portability of Singapore judgments abroad would in turn increase the attractiveness of the Singapore courts to users. At the time of writing, the HCCCA has entered into force in Singapore, Mexico and Member States of the European Union (excluding Denmark). Signatories which have yet to ratify the HCCCA are China, Montenegro, the United States and Ukraine.[50]

Jurisdiction

The HCCCA applies in 'international cases to exclusive choice of court agreements concluded in civil or commercial matters'.[51] The implementing legislation of the HCCCA in Singapore is the Choice of Court Agreements Act 2016 ('CCAA'), which came into force on 1 October 2016. For jurisdictional

48 *Ibid.*
49 The Hague Conference on Private International Law, 'Full Text: 37: Convention of 30 June 2005 on Choice of Court Agreements' <www.hcch.net/en/instruments/conventions/full-text/?cid=98> accessed 1 November 2017.
50 See The Hague Conference on Private International Law, 'Status Table: 37: Convention of 30 June 2005 on Choice of Court Agreements' <www.hcch.net/en/instruments/specialised-sections/choice-of-court> accessed 7 November 2017.
51 HCCCA, art 1(1).

purposes,[52] section 4(1) of the HCCCA defines an 'international case' widely: a case is international unless the parties to the case reside in the same Contracting State and their relationship as well as all other elements relating to the dispute are connected only with that Contracting State. The CCAA, reflecting the HCCCA, does not directly define what are considered 'civil' or 'commercial' matters. It, however, expressly excludes certain matters from its scope under section 9, a number of which would be regarded as 'civil' or 'commercial' by the ordinary meaning of these words.[53]

Section 3(2) of the CCAA provides that a choice of court agreement is 'deemed to be exclusive . . . unless the parties to the agreement expressly provide otherwise'. Notably, unlike the common law, the choice of court agreement that falls within the scope of the HCCCA must be exclusive in respect of all parties.[54] Further, a choice of court agreement that designates the courts of more than one jurisdiction (e.g. either X or Y) to resolve the disputes would fall outside of the HCCCA regime.

The HCCCA framework is a mandatory one with no opt-out provision. It is characterised by three basic rules. First, the chosen court must hear the case, unless the jurisdiction agreement is null and void under the law of the chosen court. This is reflected in section 11 of the CCAA. Section 11(3) provides that the Minister of Singapore may provide for further circumstances in which the Singapore court may decline to exercise jurisdiction. To date, no such provision has been made. The *Spiliada*/'strong cause' test is not relevant.

Second, the non-chosen court must refuse to hear the case. This is reflected in section 12 of the CCAA. It provides that 'a Singapore court must stay or dismiss any case or proceeding' if Singapore courts are not the designated courts, unless a limited list of exceptions apply. Again, the *Spiliada*/'strong cause' test is not relevant.

Third, a judgment from a chosen court must be recognised and enforced in other Contracting States, subject to a limited list of defences. This is reflected in Part 3 of the CCAA. This chapter does not consider the rules on recognition and enforcement of judgments.[55]

52 A separate definition of 'international' is provided under HCCCA, art 1(3) in the context of recognition or enforcement of judgments. In that context, a case is considered 'international' where it concerns the recognition or enforcement of a foreign judgment.

53 For example, employment matters as well as matters relating to the carriage of passengers and goods are excluded.

54 R.A. Brand and P.M. Herrup, *The 2005 Hague Convention on Choice of Court Agreements: Commentary and Documents* (Cambridge University Press 2008), 175–176.

55 For the impact of the HCCCA on Singapore's rules on recognition and enforcement of foreign judgments, see generally TM Yeo, 'Hague Convention on Choice of Court Agreements 2005: A Singapore Perspective' (2015) 114 *Journal of International Law and Diplomacy* 50; T.M. Yeo, 'Common Law Developments Relating to Foreign Judgments' (*Ninth Yong Pung How Professorship of Law Lecture* 18 May 2016) <https://law.smu.edu.sg/sites/law.smu.edu.sg/files/law/Paper2016_YPH.pdf> accessed 7 November 2017.

Transfer

For completeness, a few words must be said of transfer of proceedings from the High Court to the SICC. The HCCCA allows the courts of the Contracting States to apply their own rules on internal allocation of jurisdiction amongst its domestic courts. Article 5(3) (b) of the HCCCA, however, directs that where the chosen court has discretion in respect of transfer of proceedings, 'due consideration should be given to the choice of the parties'. If such consideration is not accorded to parties' choice, the resultant judgment may be refused recognition and enforcement in other Contracting States. Article 8(5) of the HCCCA provides that 'recognition or enforcement of the judgment may be refused against a party who objected to the transfer in a timely manner in the State of origin'.

What is noteworthy is that in cases where the CCAA is engaged, transfer of proceedings from the High Court to the SICC can be made only if the parties consent to the transfer.[56] Simply put, the Singapore implementation of the HCCCA imposes a higher threshold than is required under the HCCCA.

Challenge

Navigating the maze – interplay between the different regimes

Although the SICC and HCCCA bring great practical benefits for Singapore, it is undeniable that they also introduced new layers of complexity for the jurisdictional rules of the Singapore High Court (including the SICC). Navigation between the different regimes is no easy task. This chapter offers the following key points by way of guidance.[57]

First, where there is no choice of court agreement, the traditional jurisdictional framework of the High Court would apply. However, this does not mean that the case will remain in the High Court. As discussed earlier, the case may be transferred to the SICC. In fact, a plaintiff may apply for a transfer of proceedings for strategic reasons, either as a dilatory tactic to frustrate the defendant or to increase the prospects of the case being heard in Singapore.

Second, where there is a written choice of court agreement in favour of the Singapore High Court, one cannot assume that (a) the SICC rules apply, (b) the CCAA rules apply, or (c) both the SICC rules and the CCAA rules apply. The SICC regime is not coterminous in scope with the CCAA regime. The SICC, for purpose of jurisdiction, accords similar treatment to exclusive and non-exclusive choice of court agreements. The CCAA deals only with cases

56 Rules of Court, Order 110, rule 12(3B). In this connection, see also Rules of Court, Order 110, rule 13A(2).

57 For a detailed discussion on the complexities, see also Kenny Chng, 'The Impact of the Singapore International Commercial Court and Hague Convention on Choice of Court Agreements on Singapore's Private International Law' (2018) *CJQ* (forthcoming).

to which an exclusive choice of court agreement applies, though a choice of court agreement, in the absence of provision to the contrary, shall be deemed to be exclusive. The CCAA also does not adopt the common law concept of exclusive choice of court agreement. Further, the two regimes do not adopt identical meanings of 'international'. Moreover, as discussed earlier, some clearly 'commercial' matters are excluded from the CCAA regime. Finally, and most importantly, one must take great care to read the choice of court agreement to determine its precise content and effect.

Third, the date on which the choice of court agreement was concluded is crucial. Where the agreement was concluded before 1 October 2016, the CCAA is irrelevant as the legislation was not yet in force. Further, an agreement designating the 'High Court' and concluded before 1 October 2016 does not of itself constitute an agreement to designate the SICC.[58] Where an agreement designating the 'High Court' was concluded on or after 1 October 2016, it shall be construed as 'including an agreement to submit to the jurisdiction of the [SICC], unless a contrary intention appears in the agreement'.[59]

Fourth, in a case where there is a written exclusive choice of court agreement designating the SICC specifically and the case falls within the ambit of the CCAA, sections 11 and 12 of the CCAA are applicable to determine existence and exercise of jurisdiction.[60] However, where the case involves service of originating process out of Singapore on a foreign defendant, Order 110, rule 6(2) of the Rules of Court is applicable. In other words, leave of court is not required for service of process on the foreign defendant.

Fifth, in a case where the parties' exclusive choice of court agreement designates the High Court but explicitly excludes the SICC and the case falls within the ambit of the CCAA, the SICC rules are not engaged. If the defendant is abroad, service out of jurisdiction requires leave of court. However, leave of court can be readily obtained by reason of section 11 of the CCAA.

Sixth, where parties' written non-exclusive choice of court agreement specifically designates the SICC, the CCAA is not engaged. The SICC jurisdictional rules would apply. What is not clear is whether Order 110, rule 8 of the Rules of Court – which governs the SICC's assumption of jurisdiction – should be interpreted as calibrating the threshold of 'inappropriateness' by reference to the precise content of the jurisdiction agreement.

Drafting considerations

In the age of the SICC and the CCAA, precise and considered drafting of choice of court agreements is crucial. In deciding to submit future commercial disputes to the courts of Singapore, parties must make clear in the wording

58 Rules of Court, Order 110, rule 1(2)(c).
59 Rules of Court, Order 110, rule 1(2)(ca).
60 Rules of Court, Order 110, rules 7 and 8 are displaced.

whether they wish to submit these disputes to the SICC[61] or the High Court and whether the clause is intended to be exclusive or non-exclusive.[62]

The aim is to work out beforehand which regime would be most beneficial and to be engaged and conversely, which regime is to be avoided. The forward planning in this sense must include consideration of what kind of disputes would be appropriate for which court and the implications in respect of recognition and enforcement of the judgment abroad.

Singapore courts as a viable dispute resolution mechanism?

The discussion in the preceding sections should give a real sense of how complex the web of jurisdictional rules of the Singapore High Court (including the SICC) have become, as a consequence of the establishment of the SICC and the implementation of the HCCCA locally. These initiatives are meant to strengthen Singapore's position as a leading dispute resolution hub. However, coupled with some uncertainties in the SICC rules, there may be concern as to whether the potential users of the SICC may be deterred by the legal intricacies that they (and their legal advisors) would have to navigate. The concern is not an unreal one. The SICC was set up to attract more judicial business from the region. Yet if one were to cast a glance at the other ASEAN member states, it can be fairly said that the member states differ in legal traditions, stage of legal development as well as socio-cultural philosophies.[63] Not every potential user would be familiar or comfortable with utilising the legal services of foreign courts. The broader question is this: can Singapore courts, especially the SICC, become a viable court-based dispute resolution mechanism for transnational commercial disputes arising from the OBOR initiative? Simply put, are the Singapore courts (particularly the SICC) sufficiently user friendly from the private international law perspective?

I am not denying that there is a degree of complexity in nimbly navigating Singapore's jurisdictional rules. But I would suggest that the challenge is not insurmountable. We need to first appreciate that the SICC and HCCCA regimes embody sophisticated approaches to private international law issues. The challenge is in one sense unavoidable and a familiar facet of legal development. In the initial stage that these approaches are introduced, working out their interplay with the traditional framework will no doubt take some

61 One consideration would be whether these disputes would fall within the subject-matter jurisdiction of the SICC.

62 Explicit provision on the nature and effect of the choice of court clause is essential given the presumption of exclusivity under section 18F of the SCJA and the deeming provision under section 3(2) of the CCAA.

63 For example, the underpinning cultural philosophy of the Indonesian society is to seek to resolve disputes amicably and avoid litigation where possible. See Karen Mills, 'National Report for Indonesia (2016)' in Jan Paulsson and Lise Bosman (eds), *ICCA International Handbook on Commercial Arbitration* (Kluwer Law International, Supplement No 88, March 2016), 1.

effort. But it should not be missed that there is potential for the more sophisticated frameworks to influence reform within the traditional framework, so that greater alignment could be achieved and thereby minimising the degree of complexity.

Moreover, increasing use of the new frameworks will promote familiarity and confidence. Education, research and reflection are crucial corroborative efforts. Further, a number of the conceptual complexities may not cause real or enduring difficulties in practice. For instance, the date on which the choice of court agreement is concluded, as discussed earlier, has implications in respect of the construction of the effect of the agreement. This is a matter which careful drafting could avoid. The number of cases where parties can legitimately claim that they do not appreciate the legal implications are likely to be few. In this connection, the promotion of use of model clauses may help to allay some of the concerns.

I further suggest that challenge is to be embraced. The changes brought about by the SICC and HCCCA would encourage business parties to be more proactive in considering whether to enter into a choice of court agreement and if they do, to be more considered and precise in the drafting. On a broader level, the SICC and the HCCCA may inspire greater innovation in developing new dispute resolution mechanisms that are suited to the resolution of disputes arising from the creation of OBOR 'economic corridors'. Traditional thinking tends to sharply distinguish between litigation in domestic courts and international commercial arbitration, with clear preference for the latter for the resolution of cross-border commercial disputes.[64] Litigation in domestic courts of a foreign jurisdiction is generally considered to be undesirable owing to fears of bias and unfamiliar procedures. The SICC, being a hybrid of the two frameworks, provides a platform to reconsider the spread of options that can be offered to disputants. Indeed, its internationalist and arbitral-like design may make litigation outside of one's home jurisdiction less unfamiliar. Of course, the main advantage of arbitration lies in the enforceability of awards in more than 150 jurisdictions by reason of the New York Convention on the Recognition and Enforcement of Foreign Arbitral Awards 1958 (the 'New York Convention').[65] Presently, there is no equivalent regime for court-based dispute resolution. But the HCCCA, to which China is a signatory, has the potential to become the litigation counterpart of the New York Convention.

At the very minimum, the SICC and the HCCCA (and their development in the next few years) can form the base templates for the conceptualisation

64 Queen Mary University of London, '2015 International Arbitration Surveys: Improvements and Innovations in International Arbitration' <www.arbitration.qmul.ac.uk/research/2015/index.html> accessed 7 November 2017.

65 Azmi & Associates (Philip Teoh), 'China's One Belt One Road: Managing Risks and Disputes' <www.lexology.com/library/detail.aspx?g=8c4e6abb-9df5-4f5e-ad4b-961fa42eb850> accessed 7 November 2017.

of supranational dispute resolution mechanisms designed specifically for the OBOR initiative. The capabilities of the SICC, in particular, help us not only reimagine how litigation can operate, but also conceive workable reforms for arbitration.[66]

Conclusion

This chapter has examined the intricate web of jurisdictional rules of the Singapore High Court (including the SICC) that are brought about by the launch of the SICC and the implementation of the HCCCA. The challenge posed by the Singapore private international rules is thus one of navigating the web of rules and ensuring that the users of Singapore court-based dispute resolution services could achieve their desired litigation objectives through appropriate drafting of jurisdiction clauses. The broader question is whether the sophisticated and overlapping jurisdictional frameworks would make Singapore courts, especially the SICC, less user friendly such that they do not constitute viable dispute resolution mechanism for disputes arising from the economic integration engendered by the OBOR. I have argued that the challenge is not insurmountable. The challenge can be dealt with by thoughtful drafting of choice of court agreements, and the challenge will also abate over time with increasing familiarity in engaging the frameworks. Indeed, the challenge is one to be embraced if we are to look forward to innovation and progress, a theme that will undoubtedly run deep in the implementation of the OBOR initiative.

66 For example, to introduce an appeal mechanism to the arbitral process. Under the SICC regime, parties may limit their right to appeal: see *Singapore International Commercial Court Practice Directions* [139] <www.supremecourt.gov.sg/docs/default-source/default-document-library/sicc-practice-directions – effective-from-1-jan-2017.pdf> accessed 7 November 2017.

Part IV

Conflict of laws

5 OBOR and the syncretic private international law rules in India

Time for accession to harmonised legal regimes

*Sai Ramani Garimella**

Introduction

Although the OBOR initiative is an economic value creator for the nations involved, the interaction of diverse legal, political, economic, cultural, and religious systems in the districts along the Road means that conflict of law scenarios seem inevitable. The problem is compounded by the fact that few major sub-regions falling within the geography of this initiative have, as yet, not acceded to international harmonisation efforts. The correct choice and application of the relevant law and the provision of judicial services, therefore, becomes a roadblock in building One Belt One Road.

This chapter attempts to critique the guidance of China's Supreme People's Court and its similarity with the law in India. The chapter is sensitive to the uncertainty around India's participation within the OBOR. Hence it attempts to chronicle the private international law rules applicable under Indian law to transnational sales contracts. The chapter is arranged in two parts – the first part traces the Indian private international law rules as applicable to transnational contracts existing in India. The second part of the chapter makes a comparative analysis of the Chinese judicial guidance on the OBOR with the Indian law. The chapter concludes with a plea for accession to harmonised laws, such as the UN Convention on Contracts for the International Sale of Goods (CISG).

International private law addresses issues with a foreign element that could include a conflict in the application, to the same facts, of different laws prescribed in different jurisdictions. The domain also addresses the gaps in the regulatory regime concerning transnational commerce and helps states address the law reform activity through harmonised law. The OBOR initiative, a mega-economic partnership, exemplifies as well as heightens the importance for states and legal systems to be prepared with regard to conflict of laws rules between the participant states, as well as others, given that it is inevitable that non-members would also be affected by the initiative.

* The author thanks Ravneet Sandhu, Graduate Student at South Asian University, for her research assistance.

Part I – Private international law rules in India

The law applicable to a foreign element in interpersonal conflicts[1] is largely derived from the jurisprudence developed by the higher judiciary, as contrasted with countries of the other geographies which have either used the legislation method to regulate conflict issues or subscribed to unified laws.

Interpersonal conflicts, especially those related to contractual obligations and tortious liability, are subjected to a *de minimis* regime that includes legislative provisions on the recognition and enforcement of foreign judgments[2] and the law related to limitation.[3] Further to the treaty obligations as a founder-signatory to the New York Convention on Enforcement of Foreign Arbitral Awards, 1958 (hereinafter the 'New York Convention'), the Indian Parliament enacted the Arbitration and Conciliation Act, 1996[4] to usher in a comprehensive regime for domestic and international commercial arbitration as well as conciliation mechanisms for dispute resolution.

Much of the jurisprudence related to the law on obligations involving a foreign element is a derivation from the judicial decisions. It has been a stated part of the early literature on the subject[5] that the common law principles have had a significant impact on the handling of a foreign element within a dispute.

Success with the New York Convention notwithstanding, membership with international organisations working in the private law space, such as the Hague Conference on Private International Law (HCCH) and the International Institute for the Unification of Private Law (UNIDROIT), could not as yet encourage an address to substantive legal issues in disputes with a foreign element.

Jurisdiction of the Indian courts

It is a general rule of private international law that courts do not assume jurisdiction over foreign immovables. The Supreme Court, in *CtA.Ct. Nachiappa Chettiar v CtA.Ct. Subramama Chettiar*,[6] concerning the division of certain immovable properties situated in Burma (Myanmar), reiterated its engagement with this general rule and held against the Indian courts' jurisdiction

1 Interpersonal conflicts are conflicts involving two or more individuals or organisations where the legal systems that the parties are connected to view the same facts of the dispute differently. See T.S. Rama Rao, 'Private International Law in India' (1955) 4 *The Indian Yearbook of International Affairs* 219.

2 Code of Civil Procedure, 1908, Sections 13, 44A.

3 The Limitation Act, 1963.

4 Inspired by the UNCITRAL Model Law the legislation has since been amended in 2015.

5 See, for instance, P.V. Raja Mannar, 'The Future of Private International Law in India' (1952) 1 *The Indian Yearbook of International Affairs* 20; V.K. Thiruvenkatachari, 'Developments in the field of Private International Law' (1953) 2 *The Indian Yearbook on International Affairs* 195.

6 AIR 1960 SC 307.

for determination of questions of title in respect of immovable properties in foreign countries or to direct division thereof. It observed:

> Where a court has no jurisdiction to determine any matter in controversy such as the question of tide in respect of the foreign immovable property it has no jurisdiction to refer it for the determination of the arbitrators.[7]

Inbound jurisdiction

The inbound jurisdiction of the civil courts in India, which are lower than the high courts, is specified within the Code of Civil Procedure, 1908 (hereinafter the CPC). Section 9 reads:

> *9. Courts to try all civil suits unless barred.*
>
> The Courts shall (subject to the provisions herein contained) have jurisdiction to try all suits of a civil nature excepting suits of which their cognizance is either expressly or impliedly barred.
>
> [1][Explanation I].- A suit in which the right to property or to an office is contested is a suit of a civil nature, notwithstanding that such right may depend entirely on the decision of questions as to religious rites or ceremonies.
>
> [2][Explanation II].- For the purposes of this section, it is immaterial whether or not any fees are attached to the office referred to in Explanation I or whether or not such office is attached to a particular place.].

This jurisdiction is normally subject to territorial and pecuniary limitations further set out in the Code and the concerned state law creating the civil court.

In *Hakam Singh v Gammon (India) Ltd*,[8] the Supreme Court of India held that parties, by agreement, cannot confer jurisdiction on a court which it does not possess under the Code. However, it clarified that in a scenario where two courts or more have jurisdiction under the Code to try a suit or proceeding, an agreement between the parties that the dispute between them shall be tried in one of such courts is not contrary to public policy under Section 28 of the Indian Contract Act, 1872.[9]

7 *Ibid.*, 312.

8 AIR 1971 SC 740; see also, *Globe Transport Corporation v Triveni Engineering Works*, 1983 (4) SCC 707.

9 28 Agreements in restraint of legal proceedings, void. – [17] [Every agreement, –
(a) by which any party thereto is restricted absolutely from enforcing his rights under or in respect of any contract, by the usual legal proceedings in the ordinary tribunals, or which limits the time within which he may thus enforce his rights; or
(b) Which extinguishes the rights of any party thereto, or discharges any party thereto, from any liability, under or in respect of any contract on the expiry of a specified period so as to restrict any party from enforcing his rights, is void to that extent].

Anti-suit injunctions – Indian courts

Judicial opinion has indicated that anti-suit injunctions/restraining orders against foreign proceedings (flowing from the idea that such foreign forum could be a *forum non conveniens*) may be issued only if those proceedings seem vexatious and oppressive. In appropriate cases, proceedings in India may stay if the court could perceive that proceedings in the foreign court could better serve the ends of justice.[10] Opining in a dispute not involving a foreign element, the court cautioned against anti-suit injunctions unless absolutely essential for the ends of justice.[11] The author suggests heightened caution in disputes before foreign proceedings involving a foreign element, as it would relate to the principle of comity.

The Supreme Court in *Modi Entertainment Network v WSG Cricket Pte Ltd*[12] clarified the position on anti-suit injunctions in disputes before foreign proceedings:

- the defendant against whom an injunction is sought must be amenable to the personal jurisdiction of the court;
- the said injunction may be granted, only if the absence of it would lead to frustrating the ends of justice and perpetration of injustice;
- respect for the principle of comity of courts; and
- where there is more than one forum, the court in the exercise of its discretion to grant anti-suit injunction has to examine and determine the appropriate forum *(forum conveniens)* – that is, the convenience of the parties and may grant an anti-suit injunction in regard to proceedings which are oppressive or vexatious or in a *forum non-conveniens.*

Forum selection clauses

The Indian law lends validity to the forum selection clauses. In *ABC Laminart Pvt. Ltd. v A.P. Agencies, Salem*,[13] the Court outlined the rules explaining the validity of contracts ousting or conferring jurisdiction on courts:

- Ousting jurisdiction of a court, which otherwise would have jurisdiction, by a contract, is void.
- Conferring jurisdiction on a court, which otherwise does not have any jurisdiction, by a contract, is void.
- Where two or more courts have jurisdiction to try a matter, then limiting the jurisdiction to a particular court is valid. However, such contract should be

10 See, for example, *Vanichand Rajput v Lakshmichand Manekchand* (1919) 21 Bom LR 955; *Jethabhai Versey & Co v Amarchand Madhavji & Co.* AIR 1920 Bom 20.

11 *Manohar Lal Chopra v Seth Hiralal* AIR 1962 SC 527.

12 AIR 2003 SC 1177.

13 AIR 1989 SC 1239.

> clear, unambiguous and specific. Ouster clauses may use the words 'alone', 'exclusively' and 'only' and the same pose no difficulty in interpretation.[14]

In the *British India Steam Navigation Co., Ltd. v Shanmughavilas Cashew Industries and Ors*,[15] the Court held that clauses conferring jurisdiction outside India, either to the courts in the nationality/domicile of one of the parties or to a third (neutral) forum are not violative of the Indian Contract Act, 1872, the Code of Civil Procedure. In *Modi Entertainment Network*,[16] the Court held that preventing a party from approaching a contractually designated forum would amount to aiding a breach of contract. Further, if parties contracted, in a non-exclusive forum selection clause, to approach a neutral foreign forum and to be governed by the law applicable to it for the dispute resolution, ordinarily no anti-suit injunction will be granted in regard to proceedings in such a *forum conveniens* on the presumption that the parties have thought over their convenience and all other relevant factors before submitting to non-exclusive jurisdiction of the court of their choice which cannot be treated just as an alternative forum.[17]

In *Kumarina Investment Ltd. v Digital Media Convergence Ltd. and Another*,[18] the Court held that the question of jurisdiction is to be determined as per the jurisdictional clauses of the contract especially when the petitioner is a foreigner and the parties have preferred a specific law as the applicable law to govern their contract and disputes. It, however, identified a few situations when a non-chosen court could exercise jurisdiction:

- the contracting parties being subject to the municipal law of the country with which the case has the connection or where the cause of action may have arisen;
- the governing law clause of the contract is violative of the public policy of the country and such clause does not confer exclusive jurisdiction on the forum chosen; or
- it is possible according to the chosen applicable law to override the chosen forum.[19]

Admiralty jurisdiction

The Indian courts have emphasised the submission to the jurisdiction by the defendant. To illustrate this, especially in the context of admiralty jurisdiction, the author refers to the decision in *M.V Elisabeth v Harwan Investment*

14 *Ibid* at [03].
15 [1990] 3 SCC 481.
16 *Supra* (n 12)
17 *Ibid* at 15.
18 (2010) SCC Online TDSAT 641.
19 *Ibid.*, 69.

and Trading Pvt. Ltd, Goa.[20] The Court explained that an action *in rem* lies against an outward foreign ship as a defendant in an admiralty court, where the defendant against whom the maritime claim existed was within the jurisdiction of the Court. Indian courts could exercise jurisdiction *in rem* against the foreign ships on the cause of action concerning the carriage of goods from an Indian port to a foreign port. The apex court's observations, in this case, were not confined to the assertion of admiralty jurisdiction of the High Courts in India. Emphasising the relevance of the admiralty jurisdiction to the growing demands of international trade, the Court also referred to the general principles of private international law applicable to these disputes. Interestingly, in its obiter, the Court lamented the non-ratification/adoption/accession to various international conventions that help facilitate international commerce,[21] thus leaving the Court to follow a circuitous route for using the principles incorporated in the conventions as part of the common law of India for the enforcement of maritime claims against foreign ships. It recommended:

> Such a specialized body of legal and technical experts can facilitate the adoption of internationally unified rules by national legislation. It is appropriate that sufficient attention is paid to this aspect of the matter by the concerned authorities. Perhaps the Law Commission of India, endowed as it ought to be with sufficient authority, status and independence, as is the position in England, can render valuable help in this regard. Delay in the adoption of international conventions which are intended to facilitate trade hinders the economic growth of the nation.[22]

This recommendation, albeit in the context of admiralty jurisdiction, could be seen as applicable in other areas affecting transnational commerce, especially in the area of sales contracts.

In *World Tanker Carrier Corporation v SNP Shipping Services,*[23] the court's jurisdiction over liability limitation actions was the issue. While the High Court's admiralty jurisdiction allowed a determination of claims related to liability limitation actions, a limitation action cannot be filed in a court when all the claimants who are defendants to the action are foreigners residing outside India, who do not carry on business in India. It held that with no part of the cause of action having arisen within the jurisdiction of the Bombay High Court, it had no jurisdiction to entertain the admiralty suits. The Court also ruled that the presence of a foreign defendant who appears under protest to contest jurisdiction cannot be considered as conferring jurisdiction on the court to take action.[24]

20 AIR 1993 SC 1004.
21 *Ibid* at 1012.
22 *Ibid* at 1060.
23 (1998) 5 SCC 310.
24 *Ibid.*, 326.

Choice of law

A logical extension of the principle of party autonomy is the freedom of the parties to choose the governing law applicable to their contract. Indian courts have on a few occasions delineated the law on express, implied and objective choice of law applicable to a commercial contract.

In *Dhanrajamal Gobindram v Shamji Kalidas and Co*,[25] the Court held that choice between the *lex loci contractus* or *lex loci solutionis* for the decision on a proper law of the contract is a matter of presumption.[26] The determination is, however, to be founded upon accepted rules. An expressed intention of the parties regarding the choice of law overrides any presumption. In the absence of an express intention regarding the choice of law, the applicable law is to be inferred from the terms and nature of the contract and from the general circumstances of the case.

The determination of the proper law of the contract has moved away from any presumptions and founded itself upon the consideration of all relevant factors. In *Delhi Cloth and General Mills v Harnam Singh*,[27] the grouping of elements test was applied in order to ascertain the proper law of contract, thus endorsing the objective approach.

In *Rabindra N. Maitra v Life Insurance Corporation of India*,[28] the Supreme Court listed the factors to be considered while imputing the objective choice of law by the court – the place where the contract was made, place of performance, place of domicile, residence or business of the parties, national character of corporation, subject matter of contract, and all other facts that help localise the contract. Amongst these, the Court underscored the importance of the law of the place of performance of the contract as a determinant factor because of the contract's closer connection with *that* law than any other.

In *British India Steam Navigation Co., Ltd. v Shanmughavilas Cashew Industries and Ors*,[29] the Court ruled on the 'fixed' nature of the proper law of the contract and explained that there cannot be a 'floating' proper law.[30] Choice of law, founded upon the freedom of the parties, ought to be *bona fide* legal and not impinge upon public policy.[31] Courts in India possess the residual power to strike down the wholly unconnected choice of law clauses.

The Supreme Court in *National Thermal Power Corporation v Singer Company and Ors*[32] explained that an express choice of law, to be considered valid, ought to be explicit, emphatic, unambiguous, *bona fide* legal, and not opposed to public policy. The term 'proper law of a contract' refers to the system of

25 [1961] 3 SCR 1029.
26 *Ibid* [37].
27 AIR 1955 SC 590.
28 AIR 1964 Cal 141.
29 (1990) 3 SCC 481.
30 *Ibid* at [29].
31 *Ibid* [31].
32 [1992] 3 SCR 106.

law by which the parties intended the contract to be governed. This intention is either expressed or to be inferred from the circumstances of the case. In the absence of such choice of the proper law, the courts could impute an intention by applying the objective test to determine what the parties would have intended as regards the applicable law had they applied their minds to the question. Relevant factors for the objective test could be the place, form and object of the contract, place of performance, the place of residence or business of the parties, and reference to courts having jurisdiction play an important role for the courts to determine the system of law with which the transaction has its closest and most real connection:

> Rule 180 – The term 'proper law of a contract' means the system of law by which the parties intended the contract to be governed, or, where their intention is neither expressed nor to be inferred from the circumstances, the system of law with which the transaction has its closest and most real connection.
>
> (Dicey & Morris, *The Conflict of Laws* (Vol. 11) pp. 1161–1162)

> The expression 'proper law of a contract' refers to the legal system by which the parties to the contract intended their contract to be governed. If their intention is expressly stated or if it can be clearly inferred from the contract itself or its surrounding circumstances, such intention determines the proper law of the contract.
>
> . . . .
>
> Where, however, the intention of the parties is not expressly stated and no inference about it can be drawn, their intention as such has no relevance. In that event, the courts endeavour to impute an intention by identifying the legal system with which the transaction has its closest and most real connection.[33]

In the absence of an express choice of law as the proper law of the contract, the same could be inferred by applying sound ideas of business, convenience, and sense to the language of the contract itself:

> Where the parties have not expressly or impliedly selected the proper law, the courts impute an intention by applying the objective test to determine what the parties would have as just and reasonable persons intended as regards the applicable law had they applied their minds to the question. The judge has to determine the intention of the parties by asking himself "how a just and reasonable person would have regarded the problem"
>
> *The Assunzione (1954) P. 150; Mount Albert Borough Council v. Australasian Temperance and General Mutual Life Assurance Society Ltd.* (1938) A.C. 224.[34]

33 *Ibid* [13].
34 *Ibid* [16].

The *NTPC v Singer* ratio related to an arbitration issue with a designated proper law of the contract – the Indian law. Hence much of the import of the decision on the proper law is an obiter. Nevertheless, the decision addressed an important issue in private international law – the choice of the forum and its impact on the tacit choice of law. In the absence of an expressed choice of law, such choice may be clearly inferred on the basis of the contract and the surrounding circumstances.[35] The Court observed that if the contract did not have a choice of law, the law of the 'closest and real connection' must be applied to the proper law.[36] Neels commented that a choice of forum provision may nevertheless be seen as one of the *indiciae* of a tacit choice of law, corroborated by other factors indicating to such an intention.[37] While the decision accepted only a rebuttable presumption with regard to a choice of forum indicating a tacit choice of law, the Court clearly indicated that such choice of forum would not, on its own, be sufficient to deduce a choice of law. It shall only serve as a rebuttable presumption.[38]

In *Shreejee Traco (I) Pvt Ltd. v Paperline International Inc.*,[39] the Supreme Court, in a matter related to arbitrator appointment, referred to the *NTPC v Singer* decision and ruled in favour of a presumption of linkages between the choice of forum and a tacit choice of law. It is commented that the instant decision made a mistaken reading of a presumptive linkage, where the precedent only recommended a casual linkage and a possible factor for consideration. It is hoped that in an appropriate dispute before it, the apex court will make an authoritative precedent, drawing upon the international practice, and especially the import of Article 4 of Hague Principles on Choice of Law in Commercial Contracts, 2015.[40]

Recognition and enforcement of foreign judgments

Section 2, The Code of Civil Procedure, 1908 defined 'foreign Court' and 'foreign judgments' as:

(5) "foreign Court" means a Court situate outside India and not established or continued by the authority of the Central Government;
(6) "foreign judgment" means the judgment of a foreign Court;

35 Jan L. Neels, 'Choice of Forum and Tacit Choice of Law: The Supreme Court of India and the Hague Principles on Choice of Law in International Commercial Contracts (An Appeal for an Inclusive Comparative Approach to Private International Law)' in *Eppur si Muove: The Age of Uniform Law Essays in Honour of Michael Joachim Bonell to Celebrate His 70th Birthday* (UNIDROIT 2016), 358, 366.
36 *Supra* (n 36) [13] & [17].
37 *Supra* (n 39), 367.
38 *Supra* (n 36), headnote [5].
39 (2003) 9 SCC 79.
40 India was represented at the HCCH on the Choice of Law Principles, and at the adoption on 19 March 2015.

The judgment of a foreign court imposes upon the defendant a legal obligation to fulfil, and Indian courts, as courts elsewhere, are under a legal obligation to enforce such judgments. The common law 'doctrine of obligation'[41] has been turned into a legal obligation within Section 13, which specifies the instances where such judgment is considered inconclusive, and hence not creating an obligation:

> **13. When foreign judgment, not conclusive.** A foreign judgment shall be conclusive as to any matter thereby directly adjudicated upon between the same parties or between parties under whom they or any of them claim to litigate under the same title except, –
>
> (a) where it has not been pronounced by a Court of competent jurisdiction;
> (b) where it has not been given on the merits of the case;
> (c) where it appears on the face of the proceedings to be founded on an incorrect view of international law or a refusal to recognize the law of India in cases in which such law is applicable;
> (d) where the proceedings in which the judgment was obtained are opposed to natural justice;
> (e) where it has been obtained by fraud;
> (f) where it sustains a claim founded on a breach of any law in force in India.

The scope of Section 13 has been explained in *extenso* by the apex court in *R. Viswanathan v Rukn – Ul- Mulk Syed Abdul Wajid*:[42]

> A judgment which is the result of bias or want of impartiality on the part of a judge will be regarded as a nullity and the trial *corum non judice*.[43]
>
> A foreign judgment of a competent court is conclusive even if it proceeds on an erroneous view of the evidence or the law if the minimum requirements of the judicial process are assured; correctness of the judgment in law or on evidence is not predicated as a condition for recognition of its conclusiveness by the Municipal Court.[44]

The *Viswanathan* ratio prescribed the standard for conclusiveness of foreign judgments:

- 'conclusiveness' refers to the final adjudication and not the reasons;
- it is to be interpreted only in the context of the section; and

41 According to this doctrine, when a foreign court of competent jurisdiction by its judgment creates a right in favour of a person, it becomes obligatory on the other party to comply with it.

42 AIR 1963 SC 1.

43 *Ibid.*, 25.

44 *Ibid.*, 71.

- the question whether the principle of effectiveness[45] formed the basis of conclusiveness of the foreign judgment is debatable.

In an '*action in personam*', the plaintiff before a foreign court cannot, in the wake of a judgment against him, deny the jurisdiction of such court. The foreign court's competence in delivering the judgment in question under Section 13 is to be understood in the international sense and not merely by the law of the foreign state under which the court functions.

Application of the law of limitation

The Limitation Act 1963 applies to the foreign judgments enforceable under the Code of Civil Procedure, the period of limitation being:

- for the execution of a decree granting a mandatory injunction, three years from the date of the decree or the date fixed for performance; and
- for the execution of any other decree, 12 years from the date of its enforceability; in decrees for payment of money or delivery of goods, limitation period begins upon default of such performance (provided that an application for the enforcement or execution of a decree granting perpetual injunction will not be subject to any period of limitation).

Judgment-holders from a non-reciprocating territory are required to file a civil suit before the competent court in India within three years of the date of the foreign judgment or decree.

Rule of reciprocity

Under Section 44A of the CPC, a decree of a superior court of any reciprocating territory[46] is executable as a decree passed by the domestic court. Decrees from a non-reciprocating territory could be enforced through a civil suit[47]where the foreign court's order could be a cause of action. The foreign court's order could, however, be of evidentiary value against the defendant. Interim relief orders of a foreign court are not enforceable under Section 13.

45 Principle of effectiveness: a court should pronounce judgment only in a case where it can execute a decree within its own territory. Such a decree cannot, therefore, be passed if at the time of the service of the writ the defendant does not reside within such jurisdiction and is a foreigner, being the subject or citizen of another independent country. See *I&G Investment Trust v Raja of Khalikote* [1952] AIR (CHC) 508, 524.

46 The List of Reciprocating Territories under the Civil Laws in India are United Kingdom, Singapore, Bangladesh, UAE, Malaysia, Trinidad & Tobago, New Zealand, the Cook Islands (including Niue), and the Trust Territories of Western Samoa, Hong Kong, Papua and New Guinea, Fiji, and Aden.

47 *Moloji Nar Singh Rao v Shankar Saran* AIR 1962 SC 1737.

Procedure of enforcement of foreign judgments

A foreign judgment, recognised as conclusive according to Section 13, could be enforced by either:

- instituting a suit on such judgment; or
- by instituting execution proceedings.

A suit on a foreign judgment must be filed within a period of three years from the date of the judgment.

The foregoing narrative explains that the grounds for refusing enforcement of foreign judgments are wider than those for non-enforcement of arbitral awards,[48] and Indian courts have often been reluctant to enforce foreign judgments without subjecting them to some measure of scrutiny on their merits. Importantly for international arbitration, Indian courts have emphasised the implicit difference between off-shore litigation and off-shore arbitration, thereby calling for exclusive application of the law as per the method of dispute resolution. In *Max India Limited v General Binding Corporation*,[49] the Court distinguished litigation action from the arbitration proceedings, thereby reiterating the position that foreign judgments and foreign arbitral awards shall be subject to mutually exclusive legal regimes.

Part II – OBOR: the guidance from the Supreme People's Court

The varied legal systems that dot the OBOR also bring forth the scenario of the inevitability of disputes flowing from the contracts.[50] The economic causeway's functionality could be significantly affected by issues related to conflict of laws and the provision of judicial services for the resolution of these conflicts. The existing legal architecture on civil and commercial disputes resolution includes the Convention on the Service Abroad of Judicial and Extra-judicial Documents in Civil or Commercial Matters, 1965; the Convention on the Taking Evidence Abroad in Civil or Commercial Matters, 1970; and, in the space of arbitration, the New York Convention. Additionally, 34 out

48 The Code of Civil Procedure, through Section 13, allows the courts in the enforcement jurisdiction to make a subjective analysis of the judgment for reasons including natural justice. Further, the jurisprudence of Section 13 also renders a foreign judgment unenforceable if such order was in disregard of the law governing the contractual relationship or the *lex loci contractus*. International arbitration is subjected to the settled law under the New York Convention on Enforcement of Foreign Arbitral Awards, 1958 and the Arbitration and Conciliation Act, 1996.

49 (2009) 112 DRJ 611 (DB).

50 See, for example, Zhu Weidong, 'Some Considerations on the Civil, Commercial and Investment Dispute Settlement Mechanisms Between China and the Other Belt and Road Countries' (2017) 14(3) *TDM* 1, 3.

of the 64 countries associated with the OBOR have modelled their arbitration legislations on the UNCITRAL Model Law on International Commercial Arbitration. A significant concern with regard to dispute resolution is the enforcement of foreign judgments. The China-driven OBOR is not insulated from this concern either. In China, the enforcement of foreign judgments has also been reportedly challenging in recent years.[51] Developments over the past two years indicate a potential shift by Chinese courts, which appear increasingly proactive in establishing reciprocity.[52] The People's Republic of China has also signed the Hague Convention on Choice of Court Agreements, 2005[53] to facilitate judicial cooperation in the field of jurisdiction and the recognition and enforcement of judgments. China now joins 12 other OBOR countries within the Convention's membership.

Supreme People's Court's guidance

On 16 June 2015, the Supreme People's Court issued guidance on the provision of judicial services and guarantee for the construction of 'one way'.[54] The guidance envisages that the People's Courts would consider their trial function in an enhanced manner and provide effective services for the smooth building and functioning of the Belt and Road Initiative. Pending reciprocal arrangements for judicial assistance between China and certain Belt and Road countries, Chinese courts may provide judicial assistance to parties from relevant countries to facilitate the formation of reciprocity.

The *Several Opinions* stressed the need for accurate application of international treaties and foreign laws and for respect of the parties' right to choice

51 See Yuliya Zeynalova, 'The Law on Recognition and Enforcement of Foreign Judgments: Is It Broken and How Do We Fix It?' (2013) 31 *Berkeley Journal of International Law* 150, 174; Arthur Anyuan Yuan, 'Enforcing and Collecting Money Judgments in China from a U.S. Judgment Creditor's Perspective' (2004) 36 *George Washington International Law Review* 757, 758; Ramon E. Reyes, Jr., 'The Enforcement of Foreign Court Judgments in the People's Republic of China: What the American Lawyer Needs to Know' (1997) 23 *Brooklyn Journal of International Law* 241, 260 (stating 'when there is no treaty between [China and another nation], the principle of mutual reciprocity must be used').

52 The Wuhan Intermediate Court's decision in the *Application to Recognize and Enforce a Foreign Civil Judgment by Liu Li v. Tao Li and Tong Wu* (2015 E Wuhan Zhong Min Shang Wai Chu Zi No. 00026, 30 June 2017) acknowledged juridical reciprocity between China and the United States and ruled that a US civil court order be recognised as legally binding in China; The Nanjing Intermediate Court's decision in *Case of Application by Kolmar Group AG and Jiangsu Textile Industry (Group) Import & Export Co., Ltd for Recognition and Enforcement of Civil Judgment and Ruling Special Procedure by Foreign Court* (2016 Su 01 Xie Wai Ren No. 3, 9 December 2016).

53 China deposited the signature to the Convention on 12 September 2017 <www.hcch.net/en/news-archive/details/?varevent=569> accessed 10 October 2017.

54 *Several Opinions on Providing Judicial Services and Guarantee for the Building of One Belt One Road by People's Courts* (No.9 [2015] of the Supreme People's Court) (hereinafter *Several Opinions*).

of law and the content of such law. People's Courts have the responsibility of ascertaining foreign laws, the focus being on the development of regulations on the identification and application of foreign laws in the relevant countries under the 'Belt and Road Initiative'.[55]

Responsibility to provide extensive judicial services and security for the 'One Way'

The guidance calls for recognition of the responsibility to respond to the judicial concerns that may arise out of the interactions of Chinese and foreign markets. It calls for a commitment to create an environment of rule of law and implement the principle of equality of law and equal protection of the legitimate interests of the Chinese and foreign parties, thereby effectively maintaining fair competition, and a harmonious and win-win regional cooperation environment.

Enhanced role of the trial function for effective judicial services

People's Courts will utilise their trial function to provide, on a reciprocal promise, judicial assistance. They will, in accordance with international treaties, actively advocate and explain the scope of international judicial assistance in the area of judicial documents, investigate and collect evidence, recognise and enforce foreign judicial decisions, and provide efficient and quick judicial relief for the legitimate rights and interests of Chinese and foreign parties.

Establish and strengthen mechanisms along the 'One Way' to enhance rule of law

People's Courts will strive to develop a wide range of dispute resolution mechanisms of utility for the 'One Way', including respect for the voluntary choices made by the parties. They will increasingly participate in the international rule-making activity on international trade and investment law and international maritime rules.

Strengthen the work of guidance and strive to improve the judicial services along the 'One Way'

People's Courts will continuously engage in training for effective judicial services. They will work towards preparation and implementation of the guidance through the template of cases for future reference.

55 Supreme People's Court Issues Service to Ensure Belt and Road Initiatives (with Typical Cases) <http://szlhqfy.chinacourt.org/article/detail/2015/07/id/1663903.shtml> accessed 15 October 2017.

The guidance II – typical cases likely under the OBOR

The Supreme People's Court has also released eight typical cases, the ratio of which could be a guidance on dispute resolution related to OBOR. In *ThyssenKrupp Metallurgical Products Gmbh v Sinochem International Overseas Pte Ltd.*[56] (hereinafter *Sinochem*) the Court was called upon to decide the applicable law and whether ThyssenKrupp's supply of substandard goods constituted a fundamental breach of contract. The governing law of the contract was the law of New York, and the UN Convention on Contracts for the International Sale of Goods (CISG) applies to the concerns of contractual rights and obligations. The Court embarked upon a vivisection of the contract to identify the issues covered under the CISG and those for which the governing law would be applicable, carefully ensuring that these issues did not overlap. Goods delivered by ThyssenKrupp were not in conformity with the contract and constituted a breach, but because Sinochem was able to sell them for a reasonable value, the breach did not constitute a fundamental breach under the CISG. Setting aside the order of the High People's Court of Jiangsu Province, the Court held against fundamental breach of contract and ordered ThyssenKrupp to refund part of the payment for the goods and to pay for demurrage charges. The case offers an interesting insight into the Chinese private international law rules – employing private international law rules for harmonious interpretation of parties' chosen applicable law with the content of international instruments. The *Sinochem* decision prioritised international treaties, recoursing to the chosen national law on issues that were not the subject of treaty law. The trial function of the courts in cases where foreign law is an issue includes the ascertainment and confirming the content of the law. The Court accepted ThyssenKrupp's submission on the Uniform Commercial Code (UCC) of New York, which was not contested by Sinochem. Further, the Court, upon an examination of the domicile of the parties, Germany and Singapore respectively, found that parties are within their contractual right to nominate the CISG to govern their contractual rights and obligations. The trial function requires the verification of the validity of the contract, irrespective of the issue being contested by either of the parties. The governing law, the UCC, was held applicable, to decide contractual validity, because the CISG was silent on this issue. Thus, the decision exemplified the principle of harmonious interpretation of treaty law and general principles in a given case.

In *Zhejiang Yisheng Petrochemical Co. Ltd v Luxembourg INVISTA Technology Co. Ltd*,[57] the Court was called upon to affirm the validity of an arbitration clause that was worded in a seemingly incompatible language with the prevailing arbitration law:[58]

56 No.35 (2013) Final Civil Division IV, Supreme People's Court.

57 (2012) Zhejiang Ningbo Zhong Zi No. fourth.

58 See《中华人民共和国仲裁法》(Arbitration Law of the People's Republic of China), Article 16, passed and issued on 31 August 1994, effective as of 1 September 1995, amended on and effective as of 27 August 2009 <www.npc.gov.cn/wxzl/wxzl/2000-12/05/content_4624.htm

> The arbitration shall take place at China International Economic Trade Arbitration Centre (CIETAC), Beijing, P. R. China and shall be settled according to the UNCITRAL Arbitration Rules as at present in force.[59]

The Supreme People's Court, hearing a review from the decision of the Ningbo Intermediate Court, opined:

> The parties used the expression 'take place at' in the arbitration clause; the phrase following [this expression] was generally understood to be [a reference to] the place [of arbitration]. However, according to the teleological method of interpretation [that supports the adoption of a meaning] conducive to realizing the parties' wishes to arbitrate, [the phrase] could be understood to also include agreement on the arbitration institution.[60]

The *Zhejiang* ratio is significant, as it recognised the validity of arbitration clauses that specified China-seated arbitrations under UNCITRAL Arbitration Rules. Adopting a teleological interpretation of the arbitration clause to ensure its validity, thereby ensuring realisation of the parties' intention to arbitrate in:

> a situation where the arbitration clause did not clearly limit the authority arbitration institution, [the court] determined that the parties' agreement concerning the application by a permanent arbitration institution of another [organisation's set of] arbitration rules should be understood as [an agreement] that the institution would manage the entire arbitration process in accordance with that [set of] arbitration rules.[61]

The decision is significant, as it helps promote diversified dispute resolution mechanisms, supports the institutionalisation of arbitration, and enhances the credibility of arbitration.

Comparing the Indian and the Chinese law

The Supreme Court of India's ratio in the *Enercon (India) Ltd. & Ors. v Enercon GmBH & Anr*[62] is an interesting decision within the arbitration space,

---

and www.gov.cn/flfg/2009–08/27/content_1403326.htm> (providing for the requirement of designating, in an arbitration agreement, an arbitration commission for handling the case); Stanford Law School, 'China Cases Guiding Project, case 6' <https://cgc.law.stanford.edu/wp-content/uploads/sites/2/2016/11/B-and-R-TC6-English.pdf> accessed 14 September 2017.

59 *Ibid.*, case 6, at 3.

60 *Ibid.*

61 *Ibid* at 4.

62 (2014) 5 SCC 1.

in the wake of the *BALCO*,[63] a ratio that authoritatively stated the law on seat-centric arbitration in India.[64] The *Enercon* ratio exemplifies the principle of teleological interpretation of the arbitration clause, an interpretation that rings similarity with the *Zheijiang* ratio of the Chinese Supreme People's Court. In *Enercon*, the appellants contended that the Intellectual Property License Agreement that contained an arbitration clause was not strictly a contract and therefore, an arbitration agreement. They further pleaded against an application for reference to arbitration under Section 45 of the Arbitration and Conciliation Act.[65] Applying the tested principle of separability of the arbitration clause, the Supreme Court held that Section 16[66] recognised that the substantive agreement and the arbitration agreement formed two separate contracts and the legitimacy and validity of the latter could not be affected even if one claims that the former is void or voidable or unconcluded.[67] The Supreme Court clarified that legislative mandate under Section 45 of the Act not to refer a dispute to arbitration in cases where the agreement is 'null and void, inoperative or incapable of being performed'[68] is applicable only to the arbitration agreement and a party must contend and prove one of these infirmities to exist in the arbitration agreement itself, as against the substantive agreement, which would be the domain of the arbitral tribunal. The appellants contended that the Arbitration Agreement was unworkable as it prescribed for a three-member arbitral tribunal but provided for the procedure of appointment for only two of these arbitrators. The Supreme Court, ruling in favour of the respondents, held that courts ought to adopt a pragmatic, reasonable business person's approach (and not a technical approach) while interpreting or construing an arbitration agreement and must strive to make a seemingly

63 *Bharat Aluminum Company Limited v Kaiser Aluminum Technical Service, Inc*, (2012) 9 SCC 552.

64 Seat-centric arbitration is a term used to explain the importance of restoring the arbitration to its jurisdictional venue. The phrases 'seat of arbitration' is understood to mean the legal jurisdiction to which an arbitration is attached. See, Simon Greenberg, Christopher Kee and J. Romesh Weeramantry, *International Commercial Arbitration an Asia-Pacific Perspective* (Cambridge 2011), 55; see also, Sai Ramani Garimella, 'Seat-Centric Arbitration – Decoding the Indian Law on the Choice of a Foreign Seat' (2017) 6 *Young Arbitration Review* 28.

65 Power of judicial authority to refer parties to arbitration. – Notwithstanding anything contained in Part I or in the Code of Civil Procedure, 1908 (5 of 1908), a judicial authority, when seized of an action in a matter in respect of which the parties have made an agreement referred to in section 44, shall, at the request of one of the parties or any person claiming through or under him, refer the parties to arbitration, unless it finds that the said agreement is null and void, inoperative or incapable of being performed.

66 Reliance has been placed upon the interpretation of Section 16 of the Act in the decision of *Reva Electric Car Company Private Limited v Green Mobil* (2012) 2 SCC 93.

67 *Supra* (n 63), 80.

68 *Ibid.*, 75.

unworkable arbitration agreement workable,[69] to fulfil the legislative mandate of the 1996 Act.

The *BALCO*[70] ratio is a significant statement on the method of construction to be adopted between the two parts of the legislation and any interrelationship that might exist between them.[71] The Court held that the jurisdiction of Indian courts is non-existent in arbitration held outside India. The opposite conclusion, reached in *Bhatia International*,[72] stood overruled:

> The exclusion of 'only' in Section 2(2) is not a case of *casus omissus* and the omission is not a mistake. A plain reading of Section 2(2) makes it clear that part I do not apply to arbitrations held outside India.[73]

Restoring[74] to seat-centric arbitration, the Court ruled that the omission of the word 'only' in Section 2(2) of the Act, which was subjected to much discussion in *Bhatia International* and the decisions that followed its ratio, was not an indication of deviation from the territorial principle. The restoration of the fulcrum of arbitration to the seat in the *BALCO* ratio heralded a pro-arbitration scenario and further a commitment to uphold the parties' choice of dispute resolution mechanism, an approach that has a similar tone to the guidance in the *Zheijiang* ratio and the import of *Several Opinions* of the Supreme People's Court – respecting parties' intention to arbitrate and promoting the internationalisation of arbitration as a dispute resolution mechanism for the 'One Way'.

69 *Ibid.*, 53, 68, 69, 83.

70 *Supra* (n 63).

71 Sai Ramani Garimella, 'The BALCO Rationale – A Shift to the Territoriality Principle in International Commercial Arbitration' (2014) 4 *CNLU LJ* 26, 27.

72 *Bhatia International v Bulk Trading SA & Anr.* (2002) 4 SCC 105; see also, *Venture Global v Satyam Computer Services* (2008) 4 SCC 190, *M/S. Indtel Technical Services v W.S. Atkins Plc.* AIR 2009 SC 1132.

73 *Supra* (n 63), 60–63 The Court's authoritative observation in the *BALCO* meant that the applicability of either of the Parts (I and II) is dependent upon the jurisdictional location of the arbitration. The Court observed that the nationality of the parties is not the determinant factor for the applicability of either of Parts of the legislation.

74 Seat-centric arbitration is not unknown to India. In *Yograj Infrastructure Limited v Ssang Yong Engineering and Construction Company Limited* (2011) 9 SCC 735, the Court opined that even if the agreement is subject to the laws of India, where the parties expressed a choice of the seat at Singapore and the application of the SIAC Rules, Part I is deemed to have been excluded. The judgment in this case also averred to the non-applicability of Part I of the Arbitration Act, 1996 in situations where the substantive law of the contract was the Indian Law, owing to the fact that parties have agreed to the foreign curial law, as in the law of the seat of arbitration. Thus, *Yograj* judgment effectively meant the absence of jurisdiction to the Indian Courts in an international arbitration during the arbitral proceedings for any interim relief. For similar judicial opinion, see *Paramita Constructions v UE Development India* (2008) 3 An L T 440; *Jyoti Turbo Power Services v Shenzhen Shandong Nuclear Power Corporation* AIR 2011 AP 111: See, further, F.S. Nariman, 'Ten Steps to Salvage Arbitration in India: The First LCIA-India Arbitration Lecture' (2011) 27 *Arbitration International* 115.

Part III – Accession to harmonised legal platforms: the way forward

The syncretic private international law rules in India present two concerns:

- they attempt to address complex and intersectional concerns through few underdeveloped principles; and
- the syncretic arrangement of these rules, scattered in the judicial opinion and a few legislative provisions borrowed from domestic law instruments, are handicapped by the absence of cross-referencing, an important feature of international law instruments, especially in private law.

As could be seen from India's experience with international arbitration, acceding to international treaties could help improve the domestic law and its implementation by borrowing shared experiences from other jurisdictions. As a potential OBOR participant, to gain value from this economic partnership, India should address the above two concerns as a priority. The primitive state of the law, outlined in the narrative in the first part, calls out for modernisation through accession to uniform laws. Ernst Rabel, noting the inadequacy of domestic law to regulate international trade, observed:

> Common legal science is a greater benefit than is generally imagined. Within each country, the international sales law would rival the domestic law by intrinsic strength, as did in Rome the *ius gentium with the ius civile.*[75]

CISG attempts to reduce trade barriers by providing advance and uniform international sale of goods rules to govern the contractual relations between the parties.[76] The globalisation of sale of goods contracts demonstrates the need for a uniform international sale of goods law and the CISG is the best functional example available that has an appeal beyond the regional geographies.[77] The Sale of Goods Act, 1930, a legislation wrought with uncertainty, has limited application to the sale of goods contracts with Indian law as the designated proper law of the contract. The CISG removes the uncertainties

75 Ernst Rabel, 'A Draft of an International Law of Sales' (1938) 5 *University of Chicago Law Review* 543 <http://chicagounbound.uchicago.edu/cgi/viewcontent.cgi?article=1572&context=uclrev> accessed 23 July 2017.

76 Berman observed 'in no other branch of law is there more uniformity among the principal legal systems of the world than in the law of international sales'. Harold J. Berman, 'The Uniform Law on International Sale of Goods: A Constructive Critique' (1965) 30 *Law and Contemporary Problems* 354 <https://scholarship.law.duke.edu/lcp/vol30/iss2/7> accessed 20 February 2017.

77 Bruno Zeller, 'Four-Corners – The Methodology for Interpretation and Application of the UN Convention on Contracts for the International Sale of Goods' (2003) <www.cisg.law.pace.edu/cisg/biblio/4corners.html> accessed 15 July 2017.

associated with the characterisation of issues within a transnational sales contract, as it allows for freedom of contract and the freedom of form – two features that address the diversity in private international law.

Cross-border trade involves high transaction costs, incomparable with those in the domestic contracts. There are also accrued transaction costs in case of disputes. It was, therefore, advisable to preserve the effects of the contract insofar as possible and to favour curing any deficiency in performance rather than offering immediate contract termination. This approach explains why under the CISG the contract may be declared avoided only if a fundamental breach has occurred, and often after offering an additional opportunity to perform on the part in default. Fundamental breach of the contract is a breach that deprives one of the parties, in full or essentially, of its reasonable expectations.[78]

The adoption of the CISG increases the predictability of the law applicable to the contract for the international sale of goods, thus simplifying the resolution of disputes arising from those contracts. Therefore, the CISG may contribute to decreasing the duration of litigation and to reducing associated costs, including judiciary workload.[79]

Given that the CISG may not address all aspects related to transnational contracts, the law reform effort in India should engage in cross-referencing of its laws to ensure clarity and predictability within the regulatory framework. Furthermore, an address for harmonised legal platforms should be coupled with ensuring improved judicial services, especially recognition and enforcement of foreign judgments. India should also consider accession to the Hague Convention on Choice of Court Agreements, 2005. The Convention's intention to enhance judicial cooperation between states is explained in its provisions on the presumptive exclusivity of a choice of court clause.[80] Exclusive/non-exclusive clause notwithstanding, the forum selected by the parties shall exercise jurisdiction to the exclusion of any other court. The Convention, with rules also on recognition and enforcement of judgments, is an important step towards international harmonisation of national conflict rules on forum selection clauses. Accession to the Convention could help India facilitate global transactions and provide certainty for Indian parties/litigants. It would help erase the concerns of interference in foreign proceedings through injunctive relief. Additionally, accession would ensure replacement of the procedure of

78 CISG art. 25: 'A breach of contract committed by one of the parties is fundamental if it results in such detriment to the other party as substantially to deprive him of what he is entitled to expect under the contract, unless the party in breach did not foresee and a reasonable person of the same kind in the same circumstances would not have foreseen such a result'.

79 L.G. Castellani, 'CISG and Harmonization of Asian Contract Law' <www.nysba.org/Sections/International/Seasonal_Meetings/Vietnam/Program_4/CISG_Paper.html> accessed 15 July 2017.

80 See, for example, Ved P. Nanda, 'The Landmark 2005 Hague Convention on Choice of Court Agreements' (2007) 42 *Texas International Law Journal* 773.

recognition through notification of countries under the Code of Civil Procedure. The Convention attempts to provide a viable alternative to arbitration.[81] As a potential participant within the Belt and Road Initiative, India could do well to seize the opportunity to update its legal platforms through harmonisation.

81 *Ibid.*, 787–788.

6 European Union legislation

How far does it reach beyond the EU border?

Ivana Kunda

Introduction

Increasing economic interdependence on a global scale has brought about the need to engage intensely in regulatory activities, which extend beyond state borders. Irrespective of the form it takes, such regulatory globalisation[1] is always intended to moderate and manage the undesirable effects appearing in a state that are attributable to the particular normative system or practices established abroad.[2] Intensifying economic relations within the framework of the One Belt One Road initiative (OBOR), entails operation of some businesses from the Eurasian countries outside the European Union (EU) on the territory of EU and thus also subject to EU legislations. Nonetheless, these businesses might unexpectedly find themselves subject to EU law also in situations in which their activities were only marginally connected to the EU territory.

The purpose of this chapter is to examine the "unilateral regulatory globalisation"[3] efforts originating from the EU. The tendency to employ the method of broadening the territorial scope of the EU law[4] seems to be correlated to the economic strength of the EU,[5] increasing risks to the EU's market

1 See, for example, Jonathan R. Macey, 'Regulatory Globalization as a Response to Regulatory Competition' (2003) *Faculty Scholarship Series Paper* 1418, <http://digitalcommons.law.yale.edu/fss_papers/1418>; John Braithwaite and Peter Drahos, *Global Business Regulation* (Cambridge University Press 2000).

2 Joanne. Scott, 'The New EU "Extraterritoriality"' (2014) 51(5) *Common Market Law Review* 1343.

3 Anu Bradford, 'The Brussels Effect: The Rise of a Regulatory Superstate in Europe' (2015) 107(1) *Northwestern University Law Review* 1.

4 Traditional concept to describe these methods is extraterritoriality. However, there are different positions as to whether a certain method is extraterritorial. There is also a concept of territorial extension recognised in the scholarship which tends to explain the situations where there is a territorial connection but the conduct or circumstances abroad are taken into account (see Joanne Scott, 'Extraterritoriality and Territorial Extension in EU Law' (2014) 62 *American Journal of Comparative Law* 87, 90). Given its different focus, this chapter will not discuss inconsistencies between these concepts and their definitions or attempt to characterize any of the norms as one or the other.

5 Yusuf Akbar, 'The Extraterritorial Dimension of US and EU Competition Law: A Threat to the Multilateral System?' (1999) 53(1) *Australian Journal of International Affairs* 113, 119.

stability[6] and strengthening of particular values, such as human rights.[7] It is present particularly in areas which demonstrate deep-seated national policies. Obvious cases in EU law include competition law, intellectual property law, labour law, transport law, consumer protection law and, more recently, areas such as environmental law,[8] human rights law[9] including data protection and privacy[10] and financial markets.[11]

When it comes to a state's prescriptive jurisdiction, generally accepted principles of public international law are the nationality principle according to which its citizens, including when they are acting outside of the national boundaries, are subject to its jurisdiction, and the territoriality principle, according to which a state has power to make laws affecting the conduct of people within its territory. The latter principle is codified in Article 349 of the Treaty on the Functioning of the European Union, pursuant to which the EU law applies to all EU Member States. It does not apply outside of this defined territory, which is in correspondence with the territoriality principle of public international law. Strictly applied, this principle would result in lack of protection of certain vital rights and interests (sometimes regarded as part of *ordre public*) against acts originating from outside the EU. Therefore, the principle of territoriality has been extended in classic international law theory to cover situations in which the act sanctioned under the law of a state has its origin abroad but is completed or implemented within its territory. This concerns a situation equivalent to those of "multilocal crimes" or "cross-border crimes" in criminal law, or "multilocal tort" in private

6 Scott (n 2), 1365.

7 Mistale Taylor, The EU's Human Rights Obligations in Relation to Its Data Protection Laws with Extraterritorial Effect (2015) 5(4) *International Data Privacy Law* 246.

8 Natalie Dobson and Cedric Ryngaertm, 'EU "Extraterritorial" Regulation of Maritime Emissions' (2017) 66 *International and Comparative Law Quarterly* 295; Tomasz Koziel, 'Extraterritorial Application of EU Environmental Law – Implications of the ECJ's Judgment in Air Transport Association of America' (2012) 19 *Columbia Journal of European Law* <www.law.columbia.edu/sites/default/files/microsites/journal-european-law/files/koziel.pdf> accessed 6 January 2018.

9 Lorand Bartels, 'The EU's Human Rights Obligations in Relation to Policies with Extraterritorial Effects' (2015) 25(4) *European Journal of International Law* 1071; Samantha Besson, 'The Extraterritoriality of the European Convention on Human Rights: Why Human Rights Depend on Jurisdiction and What Jurisdiction Amounts to' (2012) 25(4) *Leiden Journal of International Law* 857.

10 Francesca Bignami, Giorgio Resta, 'Human Rights Extraterritoriality: The Right to Privacy and National Security Surveillance' in Eyal Benvenisti and Georg Nolte (eds), *Community Interests Across International Law* (Oxford University Press forthcoming) available as GWU Law School. Public Law Research Paper No. 2017–67 <https://scholarship.law.gwu.edu/cgi/viewcontent.cgi?referer=www.google.hr/&httpsredir=1&article=2562&context=faculty_publications> accessed 6 January 2018.

11 Charles Dallara, Containing Extraterritoriality to Promote Financial Stability (2013) *Financial Stability Review* 47; Jan D. Lüttringhaus, 'Regulating Over-the-Counter Derivatives in the European Union – Transatlantic (Dis) Harmony After Emir and Dodd-Frank: The Impact on (Re) Insurance Companies and Occupational Pension Funds' (2011) 18(3) *Columbia Journal of European Law* 19.

international law,[12] where the act and consequence thereof are connected to two or more territorially distant places, which when located in different states cause the conflict of prescriptive and adjudicative jurisdiction. According to ubiquity theory, a crime/tort is considered to have occurred both in the place of the action of the perpetrator *(locus actus)* and in the place where the harm occurred *(locus damni)*. States in which both places are situated might have an interest in imposing regulation over the actors.[13] Compliance with two or more regulatory schemes and involvement in the proceedings in two or more jurisdictions on the same issue with potentially differing outcomes presents a burden for the transnational and global business players by increasing the transaction cost and overall legal uncertainty. Typically, it is the state which provides for the strictest rules that is perceived the most problematic and often its rules are criticised for having too long a reach beyond its borders. While this has regularly caused tensions between public international law subjects such as states or regional economic organisations, nowadays it is the business owners who feel strong enough to raise objections themselves.[14] Whilst major players are burdened by these compliance costs, they also benefit as potential new entrants may perceive these costs as strong barriers and be deterred from entering the market.[15]

Discussion on broadening the territorial scope of application of law is often concerned with analysing the phenomenon from a technical point of view, such as by distinguishing methodologies and approaches to regulatory actions. Alternatively, it is concerned with substantive effects so that the discussion revolves around the specific topics and underlying policies. In this chapter, the analysis is focused around two areas of EU law in which recent and exciting new developments are taking place. One area under scrutiny is competition law, where legal doctrines adopted in the course of five-decades-long case law have eventually been complemented by the application of the "qualified effects" doctrine further weakening the traditional territoriality principle, yet stepping aside from the long-term US position on the issue. Although many

12 Confirmed in EU case law by many cases commencing with the ECJ, Judgment of 30 November 1976, *Handelskwekerij G. J. Bier BV v Mines de potasse d'Alsace SA*, Case 21–76, EU:C:1976:166.

13 While in public law proceedings traditionally the law of the forum applies, in the civil proceedings this is not necessarily the case, but private international law accommodates the need for respect of fundamental national provisions by a method other than conflict of laws – the method of internationally mandatory rules or overriding mandatory provisions. See Ivana Kunda, Defining Internationally Mandatory Rules in European Private International Law of Contracts, (2007) 4(5) *Zeitschrift für Gemeinschaftsprivatrecht* 210.

14 Cedric Ryngaert, 'Editorial: Symposium Issue on Extraterritoriality and EU Data Protection', (2015) 5(4) *International Data Privacy Law* 221.

15 David J. Stute, 'Privacy Almighty? The CJEU's Judgment in Google Spain SL v. AEPD' (2015) 36(4) *Michigan Journal of International Law* 649, 677; Anna Zeiter, 'The New General Data Protection Regulation of the EU and Its Impact on IT Companies in the U.S.' (2014) *Stanford-Vienna TTLF Working Paper* 20 <http://law.stanford.edu/wp-content/uploads/2015/07/zeiter_wp20.pdf> accessed 6 January 2018.

of the past EU cases have involved US-based companies, it is not a far-fetched scenario that in the future, for instance, a company from China and another from Russia form a cartel whereby they implement uniformly fixed prices in the EU market, or that a former company is abusing its dominant position to delay or cancel the sale of the latter's competitive product on a global scale. Questions arise as to whether these situations are captured by the EU law and thus within jurisdiction of the European Commission[16] and, if so, under which conditions. The other examined area is personal data protection which is just emerging and where the EU legislator has embraced broadening the scope of application of its laws *inter alia* due to the importance that cross-border data flow has in the globalised and informaticised world. An illustrative example may be one of a Japanese company acting as an information society service provider which is collecting, processing and transferring the personal data of its customers, some of whom are domiciled in EU. Is such a company within the scope of the EU data protection legislation, and may enforcement agencies in the EU Member States act upon this? With these questions in mind, the following sections attempt to provide a picture of the current state of affairs, which naturally includes the understanding of the developments that led to it.

Competition law

The basic provisions concerning competition in the EU are set out in Articles 101 and 102 of the Treaty on the Functioning of the European Union (hereinafter TFEU),[17] formerly Articles 81 and 82 of the Treaty Establishing the European Community (hereinafter EC Treaty),[18] and initially Articles 85 and 86 of the Treaty Establishing the European Economic Community (hereinafter EEC Treaty).[19] The requirement that the conduct sanctioned under Articles 101 and 102 of the TFEU "may affect trade between Member States", existing in all earlier versions as well, is completely unaffected by whether an undertaking in question has its establishment in or outside the EU. In an early 1970s case, *Commercial Solvents*, the European Court of Justice (hereinafter ECJ), stated:

> This expression is intended to define the sphere of application of Community rules in relation to national laws. It cannot therefore be interpreted

16 The connectedness between the prescriptive jurisdiction and adjudicative jurisdiction warrants being noted here. As opposed to private law where the court having jurisdiction may apply its own or the law of another State, public law is characterised by the congruence of the two due to the principle of sovereignty.

17 Consolidated version of the Treaty on the Functioning of the European Union, OJ C 202, 7.6.2016, 50–199.

18 Consolidated version of the Treaty establishing the European Community, OJ C 325, 24.12.2002, 33–184, C 340, 10.11.1997, 173.

19 Treaty establishing the European Economic Community, 1957.

as limiting the field of application of the prohibition which it contains to industrial and commercial activities supplying the Member States.[20]

Thus, very early on, the principle was laid down that competition law of the EEC or EC then, and EU now, may be applicable to an undertaking established in a non-EU Member State. Over a half of a century, the three grounds for such application of EU competition law emerged: the doctrine of "single economic unit", the "implementation" doctrine and the "qualified effects" doctrine.

The doctrine of the "single economic unit"

The doctrine of the "single economic unit", according to some opinions, emanates from the principle of nationality,[21] which recognises the right of a state to assert jurisdiction over the acts of its nationals, even when these acts take place abroad. Some authors describe it as notionally on the basis of the principle of territoriality.[22] In its essence, the doctrine entails that an "undertaking" referred to in Article 101 of the TFEU may comprise several legal or natural persons forming a "single economic unit", the consequence of which is the prescriptive and enforcement jurisdiction against persons belonging to that unit regardless of the fact that they are based outside the EU Member States.[23]

In the leading case known by the name *Dyestuffs*[24] and decided in 1972, the then ECJ asserted jurisdiction over a parent company, whose registered office was outside the then EEC, in the United Kingdom which at the time was not an EU Member State. The prohibited conduct consisted in restricting competition by illegal price fixing of dyestuffs by subsidiary companies located in the EEC over which the parent undertaking exercised control. The ECJ held that the fact that a subsidiary has separate legal personality is not sufficient to exclude the possibility of imputing its conduct to the parent company. It further explained that such may be the case in particular where the subsidiary, although having separate legal personality, does not decide independently

20 ECJ judgment of 6 March 1974, *Istituto Chemioterapico Italiano S.p.A. and Commercial Solvents Corporation v Commission of the European Communities*. Joined cases 6 and 7–73., EU:C:1974:18, para 31. Confirmed recently in GC judgment of 12 June 2014, *Intel Corp. v European Commission*, case T-286/09, EU:T:2014:547, para. 248.

21 Julie Clarke, *International Merger Policy: Applying Domestic Law to International Markets* (Edward Elgar 2014), 141.

22 Some authors describe it as notionally on the basis of the principle of territoriality. See, for example, Florian Wagner-von Papp, 'Competition Law in EU Free Trade Cooperation Agreements (and What the UK Can Expect After Brexit)' in Marc Bungenberg et al. (eds), *European Yearbook of International Economic Law* (Springer 2017) 301, 312; August J. Braakman, 'Brexit and Its Consequences for Containerised Liner Shipping Services' (2017) 23(4) *The Journal of International Maritime Law* 254, 256. 22.

23 Okeoghene Odudu and David Bailey, 'The Single Economic Entity Doctrine in EU Competition Law' (2014) 51(6) *Common Market Law Review* 1721, 1722–23.

24 ECJ judgment of 14 July 1972, *Imperial Chemical Industries Ltd. v Commission of the European Communities*, Case 48–69, EU:C:1972:70.

upon its own conduct on the market, but carries out, in all material respects, the instructions given to it by the parent company. Where a subsidiary did not enjoy real autonomy in determining its course of action in the market, the prohibitions set out in Article 85 of the EC Treaty (now Article 101 of the TFEU) may be considered inapplicable in the relationship between it and the parent company with which it forms a single economic unit. In view of the unity of the group thus formed, the actions of the subsidiaries may in certain circumstances be attributed to the parent company,[25] and such parent company's conduct could be considered as conduct inside that territory of such a nature as to justify the exercise of legal jurisdiction. The ECJ stated that by asserting jurisdiction and applying Article 85 of the EC Treaty to conduct restricting competition adopted outside the territory of the then EEC on the grounds of economic repercussions which that conduct produced within the EEC, the European Commission did not violate international law.

Similar reasoning is to be found in the 1973 ECJ judgment in *Continental Can*.[26] There the ECJ confirmed the criteria for application of the EEC competition law, in this case regarding the application of the former Article 86 of the EEC Treaty on abuse of dominant position. Dismissing the objection of lack of competence by the European Commission to decide on this case against a company established outside the EEC, the ECJ stated that separate legal personality of a subsidiary company Europemballage, established both in Wilmington, Delaware, United States, and Brussels, Belgium, does not suffice to exclude the possibility that its conduct may be attributed to the parent company Continental, based in New York. This is so particularly in cases where the subsidiary company does not determine its market behaviour autonomously but basically follows directives of the parent company. The ECJ concluded the acquisition, on the basis of which the European Commission made the contested decision, was to be attributed not only to Europemballage, but also and first and foremost to Continental. Drawing on these facts, the ECJ held that EEC law is applicable to such an acquisition, as it influenced market conditions within the EEC. The circumstance that Continental did not have its registered office within the territory of one of the Member States was not sufficient to exclude it from the application of the EEC law.

According to the *Dyestuffs* line of case law, in order to qualify for the single economic unity, a parent company has to exercise "decisive influence" over the conduct of its subsidiary. In assessing this influence, the size of the shareholding, the representation on the board of the directors of the subsidiary company or the actual ability to influence the latter's dealings are some of the

25 ECJ judgment of 14 July 1972, *Imperial Chemical Industries Ltd. v Commission of the European Communities*, Case 48–69, EU:C:1972:70, para 132–135. See also CJEU judgment of 21 February 1973, *Europemballage Corporation and Continental Can Company Inc. v Commission of the European Communities*, Case 6–72, EU:C:1973:22.

26 ECJ judgment of 21 February 1973, *Europemballage Corporation and Continental Can Company Inc. v Commission of the European Communities*, Case 6–72, EU:C:1973:22.

identified pertinent considerations.[27] Regardless of the controversies it raised, the "single economic unit" doctrine remained and also today forms part of the EU competition law.[28]

The "implementation" doctrine

The "implementation" doctrine emerged out of the *Wood Pulp* case[29] decided in respect of the concerted practices between wood pulp producers established outside the then EEC affecting selling prices to purchasers established within the EEC. Unlike in the previously cited cases,[30] none of the foreign wood pulp producers had subsidiary companies within the EEC. The sole link to the EEC territory was in that they sold their products into the EEC market. For the reasons indicated ahead,[31] the ECJ was probably not keen on the "effects doctrine" but sought an alternative approach to justify the jurisdiction of EEC authorities, one which was more in line with the traditional concept of territoriality. The ECJ reasoned that an infringement of Article 85 of the EEC Treaty, such as the conduct of a horizontal agreement with the aim of exchanging price information which has the effect of restricting competition within the EEC market, consists of conduct made up of two elements, the "formation" of the agreement, decisions or concerted practice and the "implementation" thereof. The ECJ went on to say that if the applicability of prohibitions laid down under competition law are to depend on the place where the agreement, decision or concerted practice is formed, the result would obviously be to give undertakings an easy means of evading those prohibitions. The ECJ held that it is immaterial whether the producers use subsidiaries, agents, sub-agents, or branches inside the EEC or act directly on the EEC market. The decisive factor is, therefore, the place where the prohibited concerted practice is implemented, and the jurisdiction of the EEC to apply competition rules to such conduct is covered by the territoriality principle as universally recognised in public international law.[32]

Soon after the ECJ judgment in *Wood Pulp*, the European Commission invoked this judgment when issuing decisions having against foreign companies.[33] The "implementation" doctrine was applied a decade later in a Court of

27 Richard Whish, David Bailey, *Competition Law* (Oxford University Press 2012), 469.

28 *Ibid.*

29 ECJ judgment of 27 September 1988, *Ahlström Osakeyhtiö and others v Commission of the European Communities* and other, joined cases C-89/85, C-104/85, C-114/85, C-116/85, C-117/85 and C-125/85 to C-129/85, EU:C:1988:447.

30 See section 2.1.

31 See section 2.3.

32 ECJ judgment of 27 September 1988, *Ahlström Osakeyhtiö and others v Commission of the European Communities* and other, joined cases C-89/85, C-104/85, C-114/85, C-116/85, C-117/85 and C-125/85 to C-129/85, EU:C:1988:447, para 16–18.

33 89/190/EEC: Commission Decision of 21 December 1988 relating to a proceeding pursuant to Article 85 of the EEC Treaty (IV/31.865, PVC), OJ L 74, 17.3.1989, 1–20:

First Instance (hereinafter CFI) judgment in *Gencor*.[34] The case was brought before the CFI by an action for annulment of the European Commission decision declaring a concentration incompatible with the common market. The concentration concerned Gencor, a company incorporated under South African law and the parent company of a group operating mainly in the mineral resources and metals industries. Gencor and Lonrho, incorporated under English law, proposed concentration between the South-African interests of the two companies.

The European Commission applied the Regulation on the control of concentrations between undertakings,[35] and the CFI confirmed the application of the Regulation. Provoked by the applicant in this case, the CFI declared itself about the "implementation" doctrine. It stated that Gencor could not have had, by reference to the judgment in *Wood Pulp*, relied on the criterion as to the implementation of an agreement to support its interpretation of the restricted territorial scope of the Regulation. Far from supporting *Gencor*'s view, the ECJ held that the criterion for assessing the link between an agreement and EC territory, in fact, precludes it. The ECJ confirmed that, according to the judgment in *Wood Pulp*, the criterion as to the implementation of an agreement is satisfied by mere sale within the EC, irrespective of the location of the sources of supply and the production plant. The CFI held that Gencor was captured by the EC competition law on the non-disputed fact that Gencor and Lonrho carried out sales in the EC before the concentration and

the Commission stated: 'The fact that Norsk Hydro had its main business centres and production facilities outside the Community does not affect its liability in respect of any agreement implemented within the Community. The Community is a primary market for Norsk Hydro and accounts for some 60 % of its turnover in PVC. [. . .] In so far as the agreements were implemented inside the Community, the applicability of Article 85 (1) of the EEC Treaty to a Norwegian producer is not precluded by the free trade agreement between the European Economic Community and Norway'; 89/191/EEC: Commission Decision of 21 December 1988 relating to a proceeding pursuant to Article 85 of the EEC Treaty (IV/31.866, LdPE), OJ L 74, 17.3.1989, 21–44: The Commission stated: 'Dow is a United-States-owned company but is one of the largest LdPE undertakings operating in the Community and its European LdPE production facilities are located in the Netherlands and in Spain. The fact that Chemie Holding, Neste Oy and Statoil have their LdPE production as well as their main business centres outside the Community does not affect their liability in respect of any agreement implemented within the Community. [. . .] In so far as the agreements were implemented inside the Community, the applicability of Article 85 (1) of the EEC Treaty to the Austrian, Finnish and Norwegian producers is not precluded by the free trade agreements between the European Economic Community on the one hand and Austria, Finland and Norway on the other'.

34 CFI judgment of the of 25 March 1999, *Gencor Ltd v Commission of the European Communities*, case T-102/96, EU:T:1999:65.

35 Council Regulation (EEC) No 4064/89 of 21 December 1989 on the control of concentrations between undertakings, OJ L 395, 30.12.1989, 1–12. This Regulation is no longer in force, as it was repealed and replaced by the Council Regulation (EC) No 139/2004 of 20 January 2004 on the control of concentrations between undertakings (the EC Merger Regulation), OJ L 24, 29.1.2004, 1–22.

would have continued to do so thereafter.[36] Thus, EC competition authorities have jurisdiction in a situation where a foreign undertaking sells its products directly to purchasers in EC.

Thus, in order to apply EU competition law on the basis of the "implementation" doctrine, two elements to the prohibited act have to be distinguished: the "formation" of the restraint of competition, which in *Wood Pulp* was price fixing, and the "implementation" of the restraint of competition, which in that case was selling of products on the market at cartelised prices. While the location where an agreement, decision or a concerted practice is formed does not play a role, what matters is that it was implemented within the EU.[37] Analysing this judgment, the commentators also recognised that plausibility of the reasoning depends on whether both the former and the latter make part of the conduct prohibited by EU competition rules. As such, it amounts to objective territoriality principle which covers conduct originating abroad but completed within the territory of the state applying its law.[38] It was also argued that, in addition to being implemented in the EU, an agreement, decision or a concerted practice must have appreciable effect on intra-EU trade,[39] which as mentioned is the requirement for the application on EU law against the national laws of the EU Member States.[40]

Under this doctrine, the prohibited agreements entered into by companies established outside the EU may also be captured by EU competition law or agreements using previously fixed prices.[41] On the other hand, limitations arising out of the "implementation" doctrine mean that EU competition law would not apply where EU-based companies enter into a prohibited agreement on the territory of the EU but the agreement is implemented and restricts competition in a non-EU Member State. Such an agreement remains outside the scope of the EU competition law unless there are certain effects felt in the EU.[42] Interestingly, some authors have contrasted the EU "implementation" doctrine and the US "effects" doctrine. One of the conclusions

36 CFI judgment of the of 25 March 1999, *Gencor Ltd v Commission of the European Communities*, Case T-102/96, EU:T:1999:65, para. 87.

37 Walter Frenz, *Handbook of EU Competition Law* (Springer 2016), 135; Alina Katzorowska, *European Union Law* (Routledge 2013), 780.

38 Peter Behrens, 'The Extraterritorial Reach of EU Competition Law Revisited – The "Effects Doctrine" Before the ECJ' (2016) *Europa-Kolleg Hamburg Institute for European Integration Discussion Paper 3*, 11, <www.econstor.eu/bitstream/10419/148068/1/87238506X.pdf> accessed 6 January 2018.

39 Alina Katzorowska (n 37) citing CFI judgment of 27 September 2006, *Archer Daniels Midland Co. v Commission of the European Communities*, case T-329/01, EU:T:2006:268.

40 See section 2.

41 Walter Frenz (n 37), 135.

42 Alina Katzorowska (n 37), citing ECJ judgment of 10 July 1980, *Distillers Company Limited v Commission of the European Communities*, case 30/78, EU:C:1980:186 and ECJ judgment of 28 April 1998, *Javico International and Javico AG v Yves Saint Laurent Parfums SA (YSLP)*, case C-306/96, EU:C:1998:173.

points out that under the former the EU law would not apply to a situation where a proscribed agreement is entered into outside the EU, prohibiting sales within the EU or purchases from EU producers, whereas under the latter the US competition law would be applicable provided that such an agreement is directed at the US market.[43] There is a filler to this gap as evident from the subsequent EU case law explained in the following section.

The "qualified effects" doctrine

Generally speaking, the effects doctrine is recognising the state's power to exercise jurisdiction solely on the basis of the effects felt in its territory, whereas the nationality or the place of conduct are rendered irrelevant.[44] When the previously cited cases were brought before the ECJ, there were voices calling for the employment of the effects doctrine. Regardless of the statements by the European Commission[45] and Advocate Generals[46] confirming the effects doctrine, the Courts of Justice of the European Union (CJEU) has for a long time declined to explicitly accept it. This was explained by the fact that at the time the political élite in the EU, especially in the United Kingdom, expressed strong criticism of the effects doctrine when it started to be practised by the US authorities.[47] Legal scholarship was also loud in characterising it contrary to the principle of the sovereignty of states.[48] Owing to the developments and

43 Joseph Griffin, 'Foreign Governmental Reactions to US Assertions of Extraterritorial Jurisdiction' (1998) 6(3) *George Mason Law Review* 505. See also Richard Whish, David Bailey (n 27), 467.

44 Julie Clarke (n 22), 142.

45 64/233/CEE: Décision de la Commission, du 11 mars 1964, relative à une demande d'attestation négative présentée conformément à l'article 2 du règlement n° 17 du Conseil (IV/A-00061 – Grosfillex-Fillistorf), OJ 58, 9.4.1964, 915–916; 2006/897/EC: Commission Decision of 19 January 2005 relating to a proceeding under Article 81 of the EC Treaty and Article 53 of the EEA Agreement against Akzo Nobel NV and others, OJ L 353, 13.12.2006, 12–15. See further references in Florian Wagner-von Papp (n 21), 311, (n 35). See also Working Party No. 3 on Co-operation and Enforcement, *Roundtable on Cartel Jurisdiction Issues, Including the Effects Doctrine*, 21.10.2008, 4 <http://ec.europa.eu/competition/international/multilateral/oecd_submissions.html>, accessed 6 January 2018.

46 Opinion of Advocate Ge'neral Mr Mayras of 2 May 1972, *Imperial Chemical Industries Ltd. v Commission of the European Communities*, joined cases 48–69–57–69, EU:C:1972:32, section II.A et seq.; Opinion of AG Damon, joined cases C-89/85 (Ahlström Osakeyhtiö et al. V. Commission), EU:C:1988:258, paragraph 4 et seq.

47 Damien Gradine, March Reyesen and David Henry, 'Extraterritoriality, Comity and Cooperation in EU Competition Law', in Andrew T. Guzmán (ed), *Cooperation, Comity, and Competition Policy* (Oxford University Press 2011), 21, 26; August J. Braakman (n 21), 257; Rober Cannon, 'Laker Airways and the Courts: A New Method of Blocking the Extraterritorial Application of U. S. Antitrust Laws' (1985) 7 *Journal of Comparative Business and Capital Market Law* 63.

48 See, for example, Aidan Robertson and Marie Demetriou, '"But That Was Another Country . . .": The Extra-Territorial Application of the US Antitrust Laws in the US Supreme Court' (1994) 43 *International and Comparative Law Quarterly* 417.

practice on both sides of the Atlantic which led to a certain degree of convergence in broadened scopes of application of some laws over the past decades, the international public law seems to have taken the "new orientation" to be more permissive of what some term as "extraterritoriality" in competition law.[49] Against this background, the Courts of Justice of the European Union's recent stance of explicitly recognising the effects doctrine should not come as a surprise. However, getting there was a thorny path, as evident from the formerly explained EU case law.

It was actually in *Gencor* that the CFI's reasoning was overtly rested on the term "effect" to justify application of the Council Regulation (EC) No 139/2004 of 20 January 2004 on the control of concentrations between undertakings (hereinafter EC Merger Regulation).[50] This Regulation provides EU turnover thresholds which result in the undertakings' obligation to notify the European Commission of the concentration whenever they operate within the EU market at a certain level called the "EU dimension". In addition to a certain volume of sales in the EC, the CFI considered that application of the Merger Regulation in *Gencor* to have been justified as a matter of public international law because "the three criteria of immediate, substantial and foreseeable effect [in the EC] are satisfied in this case".[51] This sentence lists three qualifiers which need to be verified against the facts of each particular case in order for the application of the doctrine to result in the jurisdiction of the EU competition authorities and hence EU competition law.

Subsequent practice of the General Court (hereinafter GC) and the Courts of Justice of the European Union reaffirms the "qualified effects" doctrine. Deciding on the challenge against the European Commission decision in *Intel I*,[52] the CG had to decide on the jurisdiction in a case concerned with abuse of dominant position by Intel, a US-based company producing *inter alia* processors used in computers. The abuse manifested through rebates and naked restrictions applied to some of the large computer manufacturers (Dell, Lenovo, HP, NEC and Acer), and one of the large retailers (Media Saturn), thus virtually excluding the processors made by a smaller rival manufacturer (AMD) from the market. As much as this judgment stirred the debate about the substantive holding that there is no need to demonstrate effects by means of an as-efficient-competitor (AEC) test once a loyalty scheme is established, it also represents an important step towards the unreserved acceptance of the "qualified effects" doctrine as one of the alternative bases for the application

49 Jürgen Basedow, 'Competition Policy in a Globalized Economy: From Extraterritorial Application to Harmonization' in Manfred Neumann and Jürgen Weigand (eds), *The International Handbook of Competition* (Edward Elgar 2004), 321, 323.

50 OJ L 24, 29.1.2004, 1–22.

51 CFI judgment of the of 25 March 1999, *Gencor Ltd v Commission of the European Communities*, case T-102/96, EU:T:1999:65, para. 92–111.

52 GC judgment of 12 June 2014, *Intel Corp. v European Commission*, case T-286/09, EU:T:2014:547.

of EU competition law for foreign companies.[53] To satisfy the requirements of substantial, direct and foreseeable effects in the EU, it is not necessary to prove that the actual effects have taken place, it suffices that a threat to the effective competition structure in the common market is demonstrated, which did not materialise or has not yet materialised, otherwise the Commission's task to ensure that competition within the internal market is functioning would not be fully attainable.[54] This was followed by testing each of the types of prohibited conduct against the three qualifiers.

This judgment was appealed before the last instance – the CJEU. The part of the CJEU judgment[55] regarding the jurisdiction confirms that the "qualified effects test", likewise the "implementation test", pursues the objective of preventing conduct which, while not adopted within the EU, has anti-competitive effects liable to have an impact on the EU market. As such, these tests derive from Articles 101 and 102 of the TFEU.[56] Intel argued that the GC erred in establishing that the 2006 and 2007 agreements with Lenovo concerning processors for delivery in China would have qualified effects in the EU. In response, the CJEU for the first time affirmed the positions of the Commission and the GC that, under the "qualified effects test", the application of EU competition law is consistent with public international law provided it is foreseeable that the conducts in question have an immediate and substantial effect on the EU internal market. In carrying on this analysis, it is necessary to consider the conduct in question as a whole. The CJEU agreed with the GC which ruled that Intel's conduct *vis-à-vis* Lenovo formed part of an overall strategy aimed at foreclosing AMD's access to the most important sales channels, leading to the conclusion that the "qualified effect test" is satisfied. It also agreed with the Commission that to conclude otherwise would result in an artificial fragmentation of comprehensive anti-competitive conduct, capable of affecting also the EU internal market structure.[57] In the end, the CJEU simply stated that for the jurisdiction in this case it is sufficient to rely on the "qualified effect test", whereas the CG's application of the "implementation test" was examined for the sake of completeness.[58]

Thus, for the very first time, the CJEU in its judgment in *Intel* expressly adopted the "qualified effects" doctrine, justifying the application of EU competition law to foreign companies concluding agreements abroad to be implemented abroad, but with effects on the EU market. Practically speaking, this should not bring about the extensive structural changes in the system of

53 *Ibid.*, para. 231 and 236.
54 *Ibid.*, para. 250–252.
55 CJEU judgment of 6 September 2017, *Intel Corp. v European Commission*, case C-413/14 P, EU:C:2017:632.
56 *Ibid.*, para. 42 and 45.
57 *Ibid.*, para. 48–58.
58 *Ibid.*, EU:C:2017:632, para. 62.

extraterritorial application of EU competition law. There is a huge area of cases which will actually be captured both by the formerly instituted "implementation" doctrine and the recently endorsed "qualified effects" doctrine. Due to this overlap, only a few cases, such as the prohibiting sales within the EU or purchases from EU producers as explained earlier,[59] will call for the use of the "qualified effects" doctrine.

Data protection

In the EU, the applicable legal instrument to protection of personal data until 25 May 2018 is the Data Protection Directive (hereinafter DPD).[60] Together with the E-Privacy Directive, the DPD is to be replaced by the General Data Protection Regulation (hereinafter GDPR)[61] bringing along important changes in the territorial scope of EU data protection law. It seems important to note as well that the right to protection of personal data is codified in Article 8 of the Charter of Fundamental Rights of the European Union (hereinafter EU Charter).[62]

DPD's reach

Article 4(1) of the DPD states that its provisions apply where (a) the processing is carried out in the context of the activities of an establishment of the controller on the territory of the EU Member State, (b) the controller is not established on the EU Member State's territory, but in a place where its national law applies by virtue of international public law,[63] and (c) the controller is not established on EU territory and, for purposes of processing personal

59 See section 2.2.

60 Directive 95/46/EC of the European Parliament and of the Council of 24 October 1995 on the protection of individuals with regard to the processing of personal data and on the free movement of such data, OJ L 281, 23.11.1995, 31–50. The Directive 2002/58/EC of the European Parliament and of the Council of 12 July 2002 concerning the processing of personal data and the protection of privacy in the electronic communications sector, OJ L 201, 31.7.2002, 37–47, complements the DPD for the purposes of the telecommunication sector, and in its Article 3(1) states that it applies to the processing of personal data in connection with the provision of publicly available electronic communications services in public communications networks in the EU.

61 Regulation (EU) 2016/679 of the European Parliament and of the Council of 27 April 2016 on the protection of natural persons with regard to the processing of personal data and on the free movement of such data, and repealing Directive 95/46/EC, OJ L 119, 4.5.2016, 1–88.

62 Proclaimed in 2000, the EU Charter has become legally binding on the EU with the entry into force of the Treaty of Lisbon, in December 2009. OJ C 306, 17.12.2007, 135. The EU Charter is consistent with the European Convention on Human Rights adopted in the framework of the Council of Europe.

63 Because this ground has not changed at all in the GDPPR, it is jointly addressed in the respective section. See section 3.2.3.

data, makes use of equipment, automated or otherwise, situated on the territory of the said Member State, unless such equipment is used only for purposes of transit through the territory of the EU.

Location in the EU of the controller's "establishment" in sub-paragraph (a) and "equipment" in sub-paragraph (c) function as territorial triggers for application of the DPD[64] under Article 4(1) against non-EU-based controllers and regardless of the fact that personal data are entirely processed outside the EU. The Article 29 Data Protection Working Party advises that "neither the nationality or place of habitual residence of data subjects, nor the physical location of the personal data, are decisive" for the purpose of establishing applicable law.[65]

"Establishment" criterion

The notion of "establishment" was interpreted by the CJEU in the notorious *Google Spain* case[66] and several intra-EU cases. In *Google Spain*, Mr Mario Costeja Gonzalez, a Spanish national residing in Spain, was granted by the Spanish Data Protection Agency (hereinafter AEPD) the request against Google Spain, established in Spain, and Google, established in the United States, ordering them to withdraw his personal data from their index and prevent future access to those data. Both companies challenged the AEDP decision before the Spanish court which asked the CJEU for a preliminary ruling on the several important questions, one of which is whether a global internet search engine operator such as Google is subject to EU data protection law.[67] Upon stating that the very display of personal data on a search results page constitutes processing of such data and hence characterising internet search

64 It is actually the national law of a particular EU Member State which applies in a given case on the basis of the territorial connection and not the DPD itself, as it does not have an effect on private parties unless implemented by virtue of the national law. But for the purpose of simplicity and in a view of its topic, this chapter will generally address the applicability of the DPD.

65 Article 29 Data Protection Working Party, Opinion 8/2010 on applicable law, 16 December 2010, 0836–02/10/EN WP 179, <http://ec.europa.eu/justice/policies/privacy/docs/wpdocs/2010/wp179_en.pdf>, 8 accessed 6 January 2018.

66 CJEU judgment of 13 May 2014, *Google Spain SL and Google Inc. v Agencia Española de Protección de Datos (AEPD) and Mario Costeja González*, case C-131/12, ECLI:EU:C:2014:317.

67 This judgment is perhaps better known by the establishing the right of data subjects to request the internet search engines not to use their personal name to trigger certain internet pages, which is given many different names including "right to deletion", "right to be delisted", right to erasure", "right to oblivion" and "right to be forgotten". Among many contribution on the topic see, for example, F. Gilbert, 'The Right of Erasure or Right to Be Forgotten: What the Recent Laws, Cases, and Guidelines Mean for Global Companies' (2015) 18(8) *Journal of Internet Law* 14; D. Lindsay, 'The "Right to Be Forgotten" by Search Engines Under Data Privacy Law: A Legal Analysis of the Costeja Ruling' (2014) 6(2) *Journal of Media Law* 159.

engine operators as data controllers,[68] the CJEU went on to examine the territorial reach of the EU data protection law under Article 4(1)(a) of the DPD.

The CJEU dismissed Google's arguments that processing of the personal data at issue is carried out exclusively by Google Inc., which operates Google Search without any intervention on the part of Google Spain and that the latter's activity is limited to providing support to the Google group's advertising activity which is separate from its search engine service. The CJEU first held that Google Spain, a subsidiary of Google on Spanish territory, is an "establishment" within the meaning of the cited provision in conjunction with the recital 19 in the preamble to the DPD according to which an "establishment on the territory of a Member State implies the effective and real exercise of activity through stable arrangements".[69] Furthermore, by applying the methods of extensive and teleological interpretation, the CJEU held that the other requirement of Article 4(1)(a) was met because processing of personal data by Google is "carried out in the context of the activities" of Google Spain on Spanish territory.[70] It reasoned that the activities of Google, as the operator of the search engine, and those of Google Spain, are "inextricably linked" because the activities relating to the advertising space constitute the means of rendering the search engine at issue economically profitable and that engine is, at the same time, the means enabling those activities to be performed.[71] This is in line with what the Article 29 Working Party declared in 2008 when stating that the processing operation is carried out "in the context of the activities" of the establishment if a search engine provider establishes an office in a Member State that is involved in the selling of targeted advertisements to the inhabitants of that State.[72] Another example is where the news portal operated by a US company provides a subscription-only service to individuals in the EU

68 See critical appraisal Giovanni Sartor, 'Search Engines as Controllers: Inconvenient Implications of a Questionable Classification' (2014) 21(3) *Maastricht Journal of European and Comparative Law* 564.

69 CJEU judgment of 13 May 2014, *Google Spain SL and Google Inc. v Agencia Española de Protección de Datos (AEPD) and Mario Costeja González*, case C-131/12, ECLI:EU:C:2014:317, para. 48 and 49. See critical appraisal in Brendan Van Alsenoy, Marieke Koekkoek, 'Internet and Jurisdiction After Google Spain: The Extraterritorial Reach of the "Right to Be Delisted"' (2015) 5(2) *International Data Privacy Law* 105, 109.

70 It was suggested that in assessing this requirement, the degree of involvement in the activities and their nature have to be taken into account. Article 29 Data Protection Working Party (n 65) 14. However, the CJEU did not make reference to these criteria in its *Google Spain* judgment.

71 CJEU judgment of 13 May 2014, *Google Spain SL and Google Inc. v Agencia Española de Protección de Datos (AEPD) and Mario Costeja González*, case C-131/12, ECLI:EU:C:2014:317, para. 56.

72 Article 29 Data Protection Working Party, Opinion 1/2008 on Data Protection Issues Related to Search Engines, 00737/EN/WP 148, 4 April 2008 <>http://ec.europa.eu/justice/data-protection/article-29/documentation/opinion-recommendation/files/2008/wp148_en.pdf>, 10, accessed 6 January 2018.

who have to provide their personal data to the service's EU establishments. In such an instance, the processing of personal data by the US newspaper to provide the online service in the EU is carried out in the context of the activities of the EU establishments, because that processing is "inextricably linked" to the subscription management activities of the EU establishments – the US online newspaper cannot be accessed in the EU except through the activities of the EU establishments.[73] The CJEU added that, if a contrary interpretation is to be preferred in order to narrow the territorial scope of the DPD, individuals would be deprived of the effective and complete protection of their fundamental rights and freedoms, and in particular their right to privacy, with respect to the processing of personal data protected under the DPD and guaranteed under the EU Charter.[74]

The CJEU was confronted with different reactions to its holding regarding the scope of application of the DPD in *Google Spain*, ranging from harsh disapproval for imposing the EU regulatory regime over non-EU controllers which has "potentially broad practical implications on web-based business activity"[75] and reluctance to accept the CJEU's intervention "in order to save individual data protection on the basis of an outdated instrument",[76] to cautious acceptance as a consequence of intensifying "EU's obligations under human rights law to protect its citizens' personal data when such data are processed outside EU territory"[77] and praise for ensuring "effective protection of fundamental rights".[78] Whichever opinion one decides to side with, there is no doubt that the ruling has brought about new elements to the internet business environment, however, not as severe as to cause restructuring of Google operations in the EU, although that seems as a potential effect.[79] It also echoed in

73 Update of Opinion 8/2010 on applicable law in light of the CJEU judgment in Google Spain – WP 179 update, 16 December 2015, 176/16/EN, WP 179 update <>http://ec.europa.eu/justice/data-protection/article-29/documentation/opinion-recommendation/files/2015/wp179_en_update.pdf>, 12, accessed 6 January 2018.

74 CJEU judgment of 13 May 2014, *Google Spain SL and Google Inc. v Agencia Española de Protección de Datos (AEPD) and Mario Costeja González*, case C-131/12, ECLI:EU:C:2014:317, para. 53 and 54.

75 Christopher Wolf, 'Impact of the CJEU's Right to Be Forgotten: Decision on Search Engines and Other Service Providers in Europe' (2014) 21(3) *Maastricht Journal of European and Comparative Law* 547.

76 Paul de Hert and Vagelis Papakonstantinou, '*Google Spain*: Addressing Critiques and Misunderstandings One Year Later' (2015) 22(4) *Maastricht Journal of European and Comparative Law* 524, 630.

77 Mistale Taylor, 'The EU's Human Rights Obligations in Relation to Its Data Protection Laws with Extraterritorial Effect' (2015) 5(4) *International Data Privacy Law* 246, 256.

78 Hielke Hijmans, 'Right to Have Links Removed: Evidence of Effective Data Protection' (2014) 21(3) *Maastricht Journal of European and Comparative Law* 555.

79 This was suggested by Dan Jerker B Svantesson, 'Extraterritoriality and Targeting in EU Data Privacy Law: The Weak Spot Undermining the Regulation' (2015) 5(4) *International Data Privacy Law* 226, 230.

other jurisdictions.[80] The subsequent CJEU case law offers some fine tuning in interpreting Article 4(1) (a), with the most relevant one still to be decided.

In *Weltimo*, the CJEU established that formal registration in Slovakia does not prevent the Hungarian data protection authority from applying Hungarian law pursuant to Article 4(1) (a). This is based on the conclusion that Weltimo's establishment is in Hungary as it pursues a real and effective activity in Hungary (its websites concern properties situated in Hungary where it charges fees and are written in Hungarian), and the processing (the publication on its websites of data relating to the owners of those properties and of the use of those data for the purpose of invoicing for advertisements) is carried out "in the context of the activities" of that establishment.[81] Following the *Weltimo* judgment, the CJEU in *VKI* ruled that Amazon EU, a company registered in Luxembourg and addressing consumers residing in Austria via a website with a top-level domain name, .de, may have its establishment in an EU Member State other than Luxembourg. This is to be determined on the basis of "any real and effective activity, even a minimal one, exercised through stable arrangements", which need not include a subsidiary or a branch, but at the same time cannot exist merely because of the accessibility of the website there.[82] In assessing whether there is an "establishment" in an EU Member State, both the degree of stability of the arrangements and the effective exercise of activities in the EU Member State in question must be assessed.[83] In this judgment, the CJEU simply repeated the criteria to be employed by the national authorities in characterising the respective activities, leaving the characterisation entirely open. Interestingly enough, this judgment might be seen as coming against the background of the well-known practice by multinational companies of establishing formally in Luxembourg for various, mostly tax, benefits and incentives, while conducting their business operations in one or more other EU Member States.[84]

80 See, for example, *Equustek Solutions Inc. v Jack*, 2014 BCSC 1063 (CanLII), para. 59 (citing the judgment in *Google Spain* on the "inextricable link" to conclude in favour of the Canadian court territorial competence over Google Inc. on the application for an interim injunction restraining Google Inc. and Google Canada Corp. from including by indexing or referencing the defendants' websites in search results generated by Google's search engines).

81 CJEU judgment of 1 October 2015, *Weltimmo s. r. o. v Nemzeti Adatvédelmi és Információszabadság Hatóság*, case C-230/14, EU:C:2015:639, para. 30–38.

82 CJEU judgment of 28 July 2016, *Verein für Konsumenteninformation v Amazon EU Sàrl*, case C-191/15, EU:C:2016:61, para. 75–77.

83 CJEU judgment of 1 October 2015, *Weltimmo s. r. o. v Nemzeti Adatvédelmi és Információszabadság Hatóság*, case C-230/14, EU:C:2015:639, para. 29; CJEU judgment of 28 July 2016, *Verein für Konsumenteninformation v Amazon EU Sàrl*, case C-191/15, EU:C:2016:61, para. 77.

84 See case European Commission, SA.38944 $ – Aid to Amazon – Luxembourg, <http://ec.europa.eu/competition/elojade/isef/case_details.cfm?proc_code=3_SA_38944> accessed 6 January 2018. In the absence of the text of the decision as yet, see press release of 4 October 2017 in which the European Commission states that Luxembourg granted

The most recent case still pending before the CJEU, *Wirtschaftsakademie*, also referred to by the name *Facebook Fan Pages*, poses interesting questions along the *Google Spain* lines. It concerns "web tracking" employed by Facebook, which consists in the observation and analysis of the behaviour of Facebook users on the internet for commercial and marketing purposes. The issue of applicable law revolves around the particular corporate structure within Facebook which differentiates this case from *Google Spain*. Facebook Inc., being a US-based company providing a social networking service, has several subsidiaries in the EU, such as Facebook Ireland which is designated for data protection and subsidiaries in several other responsible for the sale of advertising space. This having been said, Facebook's services, in the same vein as those of Google, are offered to their users for no actual payment but usually in exchange for the right to use their personal data, which optimises their other service – advertising, and wherefrom the social networking service is financed, closing the business circle. Besides qualifying as controllers, all three entities: Facebook Inc., Facebook Germany and users of the Facebook fun pages, which might be controversial in itself, the Advocate General Bot in his opinion[85] states that application of the factors in Article 4(1) (a) leads to the conclusion that German law is to be applied by the data protection authority in Germany in this case. Reasons rely on the fact that Facebook Germany has a registered office in Hamburg through which it carries out its business, which qualifies for an "establishment". Given that Facebook Germany is responsible for marketing to Facebook users in Germany, the data are processed "in the context of the activities" of Facebook Germany.[86] Thus, the Advocate General has discarded the opinion which stresses the fact that an Irish office should qualify only under Article 4(1) (a) if exclusively designated to act as controller within the EU. Opined that data processing also takes place "in the context of" the operations of the German subsidiary, the Advocate General re emphasised the economic link between the data processing and the advertising revenue established in the CJEU judgment in *Google Spain*.

That the scope of Google Spain is not limited to search engines only[87] was also confirmed by the Article 29 Data Protection Working Party in its

undue tax benefits to Amazon of around €250 million and found this to be illegal under EU State aid rules because it allowed Amazon to pay substantially less tax than other businesses.

85 Opinion of Advocate General Bot of 24 October 2017, *Unabhängiges Landeszentrum für Datenschutz Schleswig-Holstein v Wirtschaftsakademie Schleswig-Holstein GmbH, in the Presence of Facebook Ireland Ltd, Vertreter des Bundesinteresses beim Bundesverwaltungsgericht*, case C-210/16, EU:C:2017:796.

86 Opinion of Advocate General Bot of 24 October 2017, *Unabhängiges Landeszentrum für Datenschutz Schleswig-Holstein v Wirtschaftsakademie Schleswig-Holstein GmbH, in the presence of Facebook Ireland Ltd, Vertreter des Bundesinteresses beim Bundesverwaltungsgericht*, case C-210/16, EU:C:2017:796, para. 89–107.

87 The limited in scope seems to be preferred reading of *Google Spain* judgment by Dan Jerker B. Svantesson, Article 4(1)(a) 'establishment of the controller' in 'EU data privacy

updated Opinion on applicable law. Not only that the judgment may apply to non-EU companies whose business model relies on offering "free services" within the EU, which are then financed by making use of the personal data collected from the users (such as for advertising purposes), but also to non-EU companies offering their services in the EU in exchange for membership fees or subscriptions, such as those seeking donations, provided this is done "in the context of" one or more establishments in the EU.[88] An earlier illustration offered by the Article 29 Data Protection Working Party involved a social network platform with headquarters in a non-EU Member State and an establishment in a Member State, the latter defining and implementing policies relating to data processing and targeting residents of all EU Member States, which constitute a significant portion of its customers and revenues. In this case, the Opinion states, the applicable law pursuant to Article 4(1) (a) is the law of the EU where the company is established. It is important to note that this illustration is related to situations in which the processing takes place in the context of the single establishment in the EU.[89] In the same Opinion, the Article 29 Data Protection Working Party also described a case of an internet service provider from outside the EU which also has establishments in various EU Member States: the data centre in Hungary involved in technical maintenance only, the commercial offices in different EU Member States organising general advertising campaigns and the office in Ireland as the only establishment within the EU with activities involved with effective processing of personal data. The conclusion was that the activities of the Irish office trigger the application of EU data protection law and the law applicable to processing carried out in the context of the Irish office's activities is Irish data protection legislation, regardless of whether the processing takes place in Portugal, Italy or any other Member State. Also, the data centre in Hungary would have to comply with Irish data protection law when processing users' data. The interesting part is where the Working Party explains the applicable law in the case of commercial offices based in other Member States. If their activity is limited to general non-user-targeted advertising campaigns which do not involve the processing of users' personal data, they are not subject to EU data protection laws. However, if they decide to conduct processing in the context of their activities involving the personal data of individuals in the country where they are established (such as sending targeted advertisements to users and possible future users for their own business purposes), they will have to comply with

law – time to rein in this expanding concept?' (2016) 6(1) *International Data Privacy Law* 210, 215.

88 Update of Opinion 8/2010 (n 73), 5.

89 Article 29 Data Protection Working Party, (n 65) 14; Update of Opinion 8/2010 (n 73), 2 (explaining that if there is more than one establishment in the EU, the social network could be subject to the national law of the respective Member State under Article 4(1)(a) depending on the 'inextricable link').

the local data protection legislation.[90] This is, however, inconsistent with the judgment in *Google Spain*, where the CJEU stated that Article 4(1) (a) of the DPD does not require the processing of personal data in question to be carried out "by" the establishment concerned itself, but only that it be carried out "in the context of the activities" of the establishment.[91] Against this background, it would come as a surprise if CJEU's analysis would lead to a different outcome than that proposed by the Advocate General Bot in *Wirtschaftsakademie*. Yet an interesting policy consideration is put forward that the presence of Facebook Ireland already ensures the application of EU law to Facebook operations in EU and the broad interpretation of the DPD's territorial scope is not needed to protect EU-based companies from the competitive advantage of Facebook or to guarantee effective and complete protection of fundamental rights.[92] Indeed, the dilemma in *Wirtschaftsakademie* is about the application of German or Irish law, not German or non-EU Member State law at all.

On a technical level, the reasoning in *Google Spain* reveals certain parallelisms to the doctrines employed in defining the scope of application of EU competition law. Putting an emphasis on the economic link between the search and advertising activities of the two companies and thus "following the money",[93] the CJEU danced near the notion of the "single economic unit".[94] Likewise, it was noted in the commentaries that the CJEU interpretation is quite compatible with the "effects" doctrine[95] and falls under the objective territoriality.[96]

"Equipment" criterion

Article 4(1) (c) provides for the application of the Member State law implementing the DPD if the controller "makes use of equipment, automated or otherwise, situated on the territory of the said Member State", regardless of the fact that it is established elsewhere. To ensure consistency within Article 4 and to avoid gaps in the application of data protection law, the application of Article 4(1) (c) should not be prevented by the existence of an establishment

90 Article 29 Data Protection Working Party (n 65), 16–17.

91 CJEU judgment of 13 May 2014, *Google Spain SL and Google Inc. v Agencia Española de Protección de Datos (AEPD) and Mario Costeja González*, case C-131/12, ECLI:EU:C:2014:317, para. 52.

92 Dan Jerker B. Svantesson (n 87), 216 – Article 4(1) (a) 'establishment of the controller'.

93 Stute (n 15), 662.

94 See more explicit reference in the opinion of Advocate General Jääskinen of 25 June 2013, *Google Spain SL and Google Inc. v Agencia Española de Protección de Datos (AEPD) and Mario Costeja González*, Case C-131/12, EU:C2013:424, para. 66. See section 2.1.

95 Van Alsenoy and Koekkoek (n 69), 109. See section 2.3.

96 Mistale Taylor, 'Permissions and Prohibitions in Data Protection Jurisdiction' (2016) 2(6) Brussels Privacy Hub Working Paper, 14 <http://brusselsprivacyhub.eu/BPH-Working-Paper-VOL2-N6.pdf> accessed 6 January 2018.

of the controller in the EU if that establishment is not a relevant establishment for the purposes of Article 4(1) (a) or where the processing is not carried out "in the context of" such an establishment.[97]

The criterion of "makes use of equipment, automated or otherwise, situated on the territory of the said Member State" in Article 4(1) (c) of the DPD seems somewhat close to the "implementation" doctrine,[98] the difference being that in the context of competition law implementation occurs by using the economic "equipment", whereas in data protection cases it is the technical equipment that is at stake.

In providing guidelines about Article 4(1)(c) of the DPD, the Article 29 Data Protection Working Party states that a high level of protection of individuals can only be ensured if websites established outside the EU but using equipment in the EU respect the guarantees for personal data processing, in particular the collection. Taking a relatively cautious approach to interpretation of the term "establishment" and "equipment", the Article 29 Data Protection Working Party explains that excluded from the definition of "equipment" are devices intended only for transition purposes such as networks (back bones, cables, etc.), which form part of the internet.[99] The concept of "making use" presupposes two elements: some kind of activity of the controller and the clear intention of the controller to process personal data.[100] Furthermore, the Article 29 Data Protection Working Party clarifies that for the determination of whether "the controller makes use of equipment for the purpose of processing personal data" it is not decisive if the controller has actual ownership or even control over the "equipment". They illustrate this by examples of (a) a company established outside the EU which collects personal data through cookies which are created using the user's personal computer located in the EU and stored on the same computer, or (b) a company established outside the EU, which is an advertiser, contracts with a search engine company, and uses java scripts to connect to the user's personal computer through which it collects personal data to personalise advertisements displayed for that particular user. In both situations, the Working Party sees the user's personal computer as the "equipment made use [of] by the controller".[101] There seems to be no reason to exclude from the notion of "equipment" some other similar devices which are not utilised purely for transition purposes, such as other nodes, including

97 Article 29 Data Protection Working Party (n 65) Opinion 8/2010 on applicable law, 16 December 2010, 0836–02/10/EN WP 179 <http://ec.europa.eu/justice/policies/privacy/docs/wpdocs/2010/wp179_en.pdf>, 29 accessed 6 January 2018.

98 See section 2.2.

99 Article 29 Data Protection Working Party, Working document on determining the international application of EU data protection law to personal data processing on the Internet by non-EU based web sites, 30 May 2002, 5035/01/EN/Final, WP 56, <>http://ec.europa.eu/justice/data-protection/article-29/documentation/opinion-recommendation/files/2002/wp56_en.pdf>, 9 accessed 6 January 2018.

100 Article 29 Data Protection Working Party (n 65), 29.

101 *Ibid.*, 10–12.

packet switches and modems. Provided that the user's personal computer or other equivalent piece of equipment is located in the EU, application of the EU personal data protection law is instantly triggered. This has been criticised on a technological basis[102] and as being "dysfunctional in its unnecessary complexity",[103] whereas some have considered this trigger to be sufficiently justified by the insistence on the "physical link" with the EU territory.[104]

It is worth noting that what matters in the previous illustrations is only the location of the personal computer: it is not necessary for the individual whose personal computer is being used to be an EU citizen or to be physically present or resident in the EU. Thus, the individuals affected may be US or Chinese nationals, and they would enjoy an equal level of personal data protection as any EU citizen. Although this might be seen as a long arm of EU data protection law, it is declared justified by a non-discrimination principle according to which all human beings, irrespective of their nationality, should enjoy data protection rights.[105]

Some additional examples show the scope of the DPD. One concerns a company based in New Zealand which uses cars globally, including in EU Member States, to collect information on Wi-Fi access points in order to provide a geo-location service to its clients, which regularly involves processing of personal data. The application of the DPD would be triggered in two ways under Article 4(1) (c): first, the cars collecting Wi-Fi information while circulating on the streets in the EU can be considered as equipment, and second, while providing the geo-location service to individuals, the controller will also use the mobile device of the individual (through dedicated software installed in the device) as equipment to provide actual information on the location of the device. The other example is related to cloud computing, where personal data are processed and stored on servers in several places around the world. The exact place where data are located is not always known and it can change in time, but this is not decisive in identifying the law applicable. It is sufficient under Article 4(1) (c) that that relevant "equipment" is located on the EU territory. Such is the situation in which the cloud service provider is a data controller, for instance, when it provides for an online agenda where private parties can upload all their personal appointments and it offers added value

102 Lokke Moerel, 'The Long Arm of EU Data Protection Law: Does the Data Protection Directive Apply to the Processing of Personal Data of EU Citizens by Websites Worldwide?' (2011) 1(1) *International Data Privacy Law* 28, 38.

103 Dan Jerker B. Svantesson, 'The Extraterritoriality of EU Data Privacy Law – Its Theoretical Justification and Its Practical Effect on U.S. Businesses' (2014) 50 *Stanford Journal of International Law* 53, 73.

104 Bernhard Maier, 'How Has the Law Attempted to Tackle the Borderless Nature of the Internet?' (2010) 18(2) *International Journal of Law and Information Technology* 142, 163.

105 Article 29 Data Protection Working Party (n 99), 7. For criticism of this, see Moerel (n 102), 29.

services such as synchronisation of appointments and contacts, and it uses "equipment" in the EU.[106]

Worried that the interpretation of the "use of equipment" provision, favouring a wide scope of the DPD's application, would result in application of EU data protection law to cases where there is a limited connection with the EU (e.g. a controller established outside the EU, processing data of non-EU residents, only using equipment in the EU), the Article 29 Data Protection Working Party puts forward a further condition to the application of this criterion in the form of the specific connecting factor of "targeting" of individuals on the given territory, with the aim of bringing more certainty in the future data protection framework.[107] The following section will reveal how those concerns are addressed in the GDPR.

GDPR's reach

The GDPR brings about important changes to the regulatory scheme of personal data protection in the EU. Besides one law for the entire EU market, increased fines, strengthened conditions for consent and some other substantive and procedural changes, the entry into force of the GDPR means extended scope of application of EU data protection law.

Estimating that the territorial scope of the DPD was ambiguous, that use of the "equipment criterion" was not satisfactory and probably due to criticism related to interpretation of the data processing "in context of an establishment" as in *Google Spain*, the legislator was inclined to provide more consistency and legal certainty by introducing improved or new rules. Article 3, titled "Territorial scope" provides for three grounds: establishment, subject's location and international law. The protection afforded by the GDPR is reserved for natural persons only, whatever their nationality or place of residence.[108]

"Establishment" criterion

According to Article 3(1), the GDPR applies to the processing of personal data in the context of the activities of an establishment of a controller or a processor in the EU, regardless of whether the processing takes place in the EU. The accompanying recital further details that establishment implies the effective and real exercise of activity through stable arrangements. The legal form of such arrangements, whether through a branch or a subsidiary with a legal personality, is not the determining factor in that respect.[109] This is basically the extension of the principle in Article 4(1) (a) of the DPD, while the

106 Article 29 Data Protection Working Party (n 65), 21–22.
107 *Ibid.*, 24.
108 Recital 14 of the GDPR.
109 Recital 22 of the GDPR.

explicit statement that the processing need not take place in the EU seems no more than a simple reiteration of the former rule.

Whereas the DPD pursuant to Article 4 applies only to controllers, the GDPR by virtue of Article 3(1) and 3(2) applies to data processing not only by controllers but also by processors. These notions are essentially the same in both legal instruments: the controller determines the purposes and means of the processing of personal data and the processor processes personal data on behalf of the controller.[110] By adding the place of establishment of the processor as a criterion, the EU legislator chose to expand the scope of application of the GDPR. However, the longest reach is said to be ensured by the following criterion.

"Subject's location" criterion

Pursuant to Article 3(2), the GDPR applies to the processing of personal data of data subjects who are in the EU by a controller or processor not established in the EU, where the processing activities are related to: (a) the offering of goods or services, irrespective of whether a payment of the data subject is required, to such data subjects in the EU or (b) the monitoring of their behaviour as far as their behaviour takes place within the EU.

In both paragraphs (a) and (b) there is a common requirement that processing concerns data of an individual "who is in the EU". This is the ultimate legislative choice, abandoning the earlier proposal on individual "residing in the EU",[111] which was meant to solve the problematic reach of the "equipment" criterion in the DPD, especially its potential to capture non-EU residents.[112] While it is likely that to ascertain whether an individual is residing in the EU would have been problematic, ascertaining the location of the person might prove even more difficult. While there are applications which may facilitate this task (such as geo-locators), they are not always used or available. Furthermore, a natural person may change the location much more easily than the residence. This creates a conflict-in-time issue: what if location changes during the course of data processing? It may be the case that at the time the processing commenced (e.g. by collecting and recording data) the person was not located in the EU, but soon after he or she relocated to the EU and was there for the most of processing (e.g. by structuring, consulting and/or disseminating data). And vice versa, a person located in the EU at the time the processing commences may change his or her location to stay outside the EU for the

110 Compare Articles 2(d) and 2(e) of the DPD to Articles 4(7) and 4(6) of the GDPR. Further on these notions see Article 29 Data Protection Working Party, Opinion 1/2010 on the concepts of "controller" and "processor", 00264/10/EN WP 169, 16 February 2010.

111 It seems that at least the Spanish language version has mistakenly retained the earlier phrase '*que residan en la Unión*'.

112 Taylor (n 96), 21–22.

most of the processing time and not come back to the EU until the data were no longer being processed. Assuming that there is an interest in applying EU law to the highest extent possible under the existing rules, there are at least two possible approaches. One approach is to resort to partial application of the law so that the processing operations performed during the subject's location in the EU are subject to EU law, while those performed during the subject's location outside the EU are not. In contrast, under the holistic approach, to render the EU law applicable, it would be sufficient that the subject has at any time during the processing been located in the EU. Although on the face of it the partial approach seems to be more foreseeable and less burdensome for the controllers and processors, in practice it probably would have the same result as the holistic approach. Thus, not even the lesser-evil principle could assist in choosing between the two.

There might be some indication in the additional condition under paragraph (b) that the legislator favours the partial approach. By the wording "the monitoring of their behaviour as far as their behaviour takes place within the EU" might be understood to limit the application to instances in which "behaviour takes place within the EU". However, while the use of the phrase with territorial connotation "as far as" rather than one with time connotation "as long as" might be purely accidental, pinpointing the relevant time does not seem to be intended by the legislator in either of the conditions. When read in its entirety, the condition in paragraph (b) is clearly aimed at defining the territorial connection of specific business operations with the EU. The condition in paragraph (a) refers to "offering of goods or services [. . .] to such data subjects in the EU", where "such data subjects" are "data subjects in the EU" so that the entire section would read "offering of goods or services [. . .] to [. . .] data subjects [in the EU] in the EU". Thus, the last phrase "in the EU" describes the "offering of goods or services" and not the "data subjects" who are already described by the term "such". Therefore, tying the relevant moment to that when the goods or services are offered to the data subject in question does not derive from the wording of the provision. In both paragraphs (a) and (b), the evident intention of the legislator was to slightly narrow the otherwise broad territorial scope of application. The intention behind such a broad scope is to ensure that natural persons are not deprived of the protection to which they are entitled under the GDPR, even when the controller or processor is not established in the EU.

Under 3(2)(a), the processing is subject to the GDPR, where it is related to offering goods or services in the EU to data subjects in the EU, irrespective of whether it is connected to a payment. In order to determine whether such a controller or processor is offering goods or services to data subjects who are in the EU, the GDPR preamble suggests that it should be ascertained whether it is apparent that the controller or processor envisages offering services to data subjects in one or more EU Member States.[113] Probably inspired by the

113 Recital 23 of the GDPR.

Article 29 Data Protection Working Party,[114] this introduces the "targeting" principle intended to further nuance the narrowing of the GDPR's territorial scope. Until now, "targeting"[115] has appeared in the CJEU practice in the context of ascertaining international jurisdiction for obligations arising out of internet activities, most notably in *Pammer*[116] and *Football Dataco.*[117] There, it was established that mere accessibility of the website on the territory does not create sufficiently strong connection to amount to jurisdiction. In the same vein, it is stated that mere accessibility of the controller's, processor's or an intermediary's website in the EU, of an email address or of other contact details, or the use of a language generally used in the third country where the controller is established, is insufficient to ascertain the controller's or processor's intention to offer services in the EU territory. Conversely, factors such as the use of a language or a currency generally used in one or more EU Member States with the possibility of ordering goods and services in that other language, or the mentioning of customers or users who are in the EU, may make it apparent that the controller envisages offering goods or services to data subjects in the EU.[118] As appealing as it might be to employ ready-made internet-tailored solutions tested in the consumer and intellectual property cases, it is not certain that they will ensure the desired legal certainty. The flaws are noted in the subjectiveness of the test and practical uselessness in the data protection context of the listed criteria.[119] Others, however, believe that a carefully blended cocktail of "targeting" criteria "could provide for a strong, or at least a less tenuous, connection to trigger jurisdiction".[120]

The processing of personal data of data subjects who are in the EU by a controller or processor not established in the EU is also subject to the GDPR when such processing is related to "the monitoring of the behaviour of such data subjects in so far as their behaviour takes place within the EU". In order to determine whether a processing activity can be considered to "monitor the

114 Article 29 Data Protection Working Party, (n 65) 21. Rather than targeting, it was suggested that 'enforceability' would be more appropriate criterion to narrow territorial scope of the EU data protection law. See Christopher Kuner, 'Extraterritoriality and Regulation of International Data Transfers in EU Data Protection Law' (2015) 5(4) *International Data Privacy Law* 235.

115 For analysis of the intention to target in another context, but still relevant to this discussion, see Ivana Kunda, 'Competencia Judicial Internacional Sobre Violaciones de Derechos de Autor y derechos Conexos en Internet' (2014) 13 *Anuario Español de Derecho Internacional Privado* 457.

116 CJEU judgment of 7 December 2010, *Peter Pammer v Reederei Karl Schlüter GmbH & Co. KG and Hotel Alpenhof GesmbH v Oliver Heller*, joined cases C-585/08 and C-144/09, EU:C:2010:740, para. 47 et seq.

117 CJEU judgment of 18 October 2012, *Football Dataco Ltd, Scottish Premier League Ltd, Scottish Football League and PA Sport UK Ltd v. Sportradar GmbH and Sportradar*, case C-173/11, EU:C:2012:642, para. 33 et seq.

118 Recital 23 of the GDPR.

119 Svantesson (n 79), 231–232.

120 Taylor (n 96), 18.

behaviour of data subjects", the legislator suggests in the GDPR preamble to ascertain whether natural persons are tracked on the internet, including potential subsequent use of personal data processing techniques which consist of profiling a natural person, particularly in order to take decisions concerning her or him or for analysing or predicting her or his personal preferences, behaviours and attitudes.[121] However, there seems to be circularity in the provision. The part of it which states "as far as their behaviour takes place within the EU" seems redundant, as it is already captured by the general condition of the "data subject in the EU". It is hard to imagine a behaviour of a person taking place in the EU while that person is not in the EU. It would be quite different if the condition would refer to the behaviour which takes "effect" within the EU, but this provision cannot be further from that.[122] In the attempt to classify the provisions of Article 3(2) of the GDPR, the scholars have concluded that it sways from the territoriality side of the spectrum towards passive personality.[123]

International law grounds

Article 3(3) provides that the GDPR applies to the processing of personal data by a controller not established in the EU, but in a place where EU Member State law applies by virtue of public international law. This corresponds entirely to the provision of Article 4(1) (b) of the DPD rendering the GDPR applicable to controllers established outside the EU, such as in diplomatic missions, embassies or consulates of the EU Member States, or on vessels and aircrafts under EU Member State flags.

Conclusion

Observing the development of the rules related to the territorial scope of the EU competition law and data protection law, it is evident that over the years, important changes have occurred in an attempt to respond to profound transformations of the business models, structures, scales and strategies brought about or facilitated by technological advancement and consequential social phenomena. While the tendency towards expanding the reach of EU law is owed to the fact that the EU Member States together make an important economic force and that pursued values are constitutionally or internationally recognised,[124] it is the equivalent developments in comparative law and

121 Recital 24 of the GDPR.

122 There is convincing argument made to the effect that the GDPR does not fall under the effects doctrine. See Taylor (n 96), 19.

123 *Ibid.*, 23; Dan Jerker B. Svantesson, *Extraterritoriality in Data Privacy Law* (Ex Tuto Publishing 2013), 141–142.

124 While the right to personal data protection is recognised as a human right (sometimes under different notions or legal labels), the free competition is considered a

gradual relaxation of public international law principles that make this road less bumpy.

While in the competition law landscape the "single economic unit" doctrine is well established and provides for relatively wide territorial reach of the EU competition law, it suffers from limitation in that a foreign company must have a subsidiary in the EU territory. The "implementation" doctrine went further in allowing jurisdiction to be stretched even to foreign companies and concluding prohibited agreements abroad, provided that these agreements are "implemented" on the territory of the EU. This "effects principle in disguise"[125] was the introduction into the "qualified effects" doctrine. The latter now resolves in the affirmative the question of whether an agreement between foreign entities not to supply customers in the EU which is implemented abroad and producing effects in the EU falls under the EU competition law. This is so provided that the effects in question are qualified by immediateness, substantiality and foreseeability.

In the data protection context, the applicable law scheme under the DPD underwent changes materialised in the territorial scope of the GDPR. While criteria under the international law are intact and the "establishment" trigger has only been refined, the "equipment" trigger has been replaced by a completely different concept cumulating two requirements – "data subjects are in the EU" and "the processing relates to controller's activities in EU". They come in junction with the "targeting" principle, which is requiring controller's intent to direct its activities to persons in the EU and steps towards its realisation, and which is rendering mere accessibility insufficient. The overall objective of this three-piece puzzle is to embrace more non-EU-based companies under the GDPR umbrella to ensure protection of such fundamental rights indiscriminately to all individuals in the EU.

There are issues related to compliance arising out of widening the territorial reach of the EU law. The GDPR is perhaps bringing the one-stop-shop, but shopping there comes at a price. Likewise, the EU expectations in creating and preserving the competitive market structure seems to favour big, skilful and abiding market players, yet sometimes it may hit them with ten-digit fees. And while up to now often the US-based companies were the most affected, it is predictable that in the future they are going to originate from other large economies, such as China and India, and their companies might be the focus. Therefore, it would appear very sensible for the non-EU-based companies, which strive to enter or remain in the global market, to stay on top of the relevant developments in EU law, including in the area of competition and data

constitutional value in the EU. See Alexandre de Streel, 'The Antitrust Activism of the European Commission in the Telecommunication Sector' in Philip Lowe and Mel Marquis (eds), *European Competition Law Annual 2012: Competition, Regulation and Public Policies* (Hart 2014), 197.

125 Jürgen Basedow, 'International Antitrust: From Extraterritorial Application to Harmonization' (2000) 60(4) *Louisiana Law Review* 1037, 1040.

protection, and to adjust their business strategies, plans and policies to the respective requirements, otherwise, they should calculate the risk of administrative penalties and civil liability. Then again, some may succeed in finding an innovative business approach facilitating the evasion of the EU law, although at this point this seems as unlikely as getting a camel through the eye of a needle.

Part V

Interpretation of foreign law and substantive harmonisation efforts

7 Proof of foreign law under the background of the Belt and Road Initiative

Zhengxin Huo

Introduction

Establishing the contents of foreign law may be an essential part of any litigation that involves transnational parties or transactions; however, it is by no means an easy task for a judge to fulfil. In fact, the failure to prove foreign law is one of the most important reasons why the percentage of foreign-related cases governed by foreign law in all such cases that Chinese courts have heard remains to be around 6% even after 1 April 2011, when China's new Private International Law Act (Act on the Application of Laws on Foreign-related Civil Relationships (Adopted at the 17th session of the Standing Committee of the 11th National People's Congress) was implemented.[1] Proof of foreign law, therefore, is believed to be a serious obstacle for China to improve the quality of international civil justice.

Now China is pushing its ambitious Belt and Road Initiative (hereinafter B&R Initiative) whose success, to a certain degree, depends on an efficient judicial assistance relationship between China on the one hand and the countries along the B&R routes on the other. Within such a setting, Chinese courts should be more friendly to foreign law especially when its private international law rules refer to a foreign legal system. If the countries along the B&R routes find that Chinese courts tend to close the door to their laws even though private international law demands their application, they will, needless to say, have doubts over China's sincerity to carry out the B&R Initiative on a win-win basis. Hence, if the issue of proving foreign law cannot be properly addressed, not only the quality of China's international civil justice will be distrusted, but also the B&R Initiative will be at stake.

As such, the purpose of this chapter is twofold. First, it provides a systematic review of Chinese legislation and judicial practice concerning proof of foreign law and an in-depth study on the challenges that Chinese courts are facing in proving law of the countries along the B&R routes. Second, after summarising

1 Wang Hui and Shen Wei, 'Lun Waiguofa Chaming Zhidu Shiling de Zhenjie ji Gaijin Lujin [The Problems of Failure to Prove Foreign Law and Solutions' (2016) 5 *Duiwaijinmaodaxue Xuebao* [*Journal of University of Foreign Economics and Trade*] 135, 136.

problems concerning proof of foreign law against the background of the B&R Initiative, it puts forward suggestions.

This chapter is composed of six parts including Introduction and Conclusion. Part II examines the existing Chinese legislation and judicial interpretation issued by the Supreme People's Court of China (hereinafter SPC) regarding proof of foreign law. Part III provides a review of Chinese judicial practice with regard to proving the content of foreign law since 2011 and critically analyses the problems thereof. Part IV outlines the challenges to prove foreign law before Chinese courts against the background of the B&R Initiative. Part V provides observations and comments on the latest efforts by Chinese courts to overcome the problems that have surfaced in the process of proving foreign law. Part VI concludes the discussion with corresponding suggestions.

Proof of foreign law under Chinese legislation and judicial interpretation

In China, the earliest rules concerning proof of foreign law can be dated back as far as the year 1988, when the SPC, in its capacity as interpreter of the application of law as prescribed by the Organic Law of the People's Courts,[2] issued the 'Opinions of the Supreme People's Court on Implementing the General Principles of Civil Law of the People's Republic of China' (hereinafter Opinions on the GPCL).

Pursuant to Article 193 of Opinions on the GPCL, the applicable foreign laws may be found out in the following ways: (1) provided by the litigants, (2) provided by the central authority of the foreign country having entered into the judicial assistance treaty with China, (3) provided by the Chinese embassy or consulate in this foreign country, (4) provided by the embassy of this foreign country in China, (5) provided by the legal experts at home and abroad. If the applicable foreign laws are unable to be found out with the aforementioned ways, the case shall be governed by the law of the People's Republic of China (hereinafter PRC).

Article 193 enumerates five methods to ascertain the content of foreign law which provides much needed help to Chinese judges when foreign law is referred to as the applicable law. However, there are several points which are worthy of discussion.

First, it fails to spell out who bears the burden of proof in general and in each specific situation. Second, the wording of 'may', instead of 'shall',

2 The Supreme People's Court may interpret points of law arising from the concrete application of law in the adjudicative work of the courts. This type of interpretation is known as 'judicial interpretation'. Documents of judicial interpretation issued by the Supreme People's Court have general binding force although they are not legislation archives in nature. *See* Feng Lin, *Constitution Law in China* (Sweet & Maxwell 2000), 221; Albert Hung-yee Chen, *An Introduction to the Legal System of the People's Republic of China* (3d edn, LexisNexis 2004), 118–128.

implies that it is unnecessary to exhaust the aforementioned ways before the conclusion that the applicable foreign law cannot be ascertained. Moreover, it indicates that these five ways are illustrative rather than exhaustive. For example, judicial practice shows that Intermediate People's Court of Wuxin City of Juangsu Province ascertained the content of German civil law according to the published Chinese translation of the German Civil Code in 2005,[3] and the First Intermediate People's Court of Shanghai identified the law of State of Delaware via LexisNexis, an online legal database, in 2006.[4] Third, it makes it clear that in the event that foreign law cannot be ascertained, rather than applying the most closely ascertainable law, Chinese courts will apply Chinese law instead.

On 28 October 2010, the PRC adopted its first statute on Private International Law titled 'Act on the Application of Laws on Foreign-related Civil Relationships' (hereinafter Private International Law Act) which came into force on 1 April 2011.[5] The enactment of the Private International Law Act is a historic event in Chinese legislative history, as it indicates China has modernised its conflict-of-law rules after many years of unremitting efforts made by legislators and scholars. Hence, after its implementation, the Private International Law Act becomes the major source of Chinese private international law.

The Private International Law Act contains 52 articles arranged under eight chapters, with headings that are indicative of their respective scope.[6] Among those 52 articles, the article that deals with proof of foreign law is located in Chapter One 'General Provision', as Article 10 provided that:

> The foreign law applicable to a foreign-related relationship shall be ascertained by the relevant People's Court, arbitration institution, or administrative agency; Where the parties choose to apply a foreign law, the parties concerned shall ascertain such foreign law; In case the foreign law cannot be ascertained or there is no pertinent rule of law after ascertainment, the law of the PRC shall apply.

A careful reading of the aforementioned Article indicates that some interesting changes have been made compared with Article 193 of Opinions on the GPCL.

3 *Sven Vorlop v FTE Ahrend Freizeit-Technologie GMBH* (2005) Xi Minsan Chuzi No. 0059.

4 Huan Jin el., *Zhongguo Guojisifa Sifashijian Yanjiu* [*A Study on Judicial Practice of Private International Law in China (2001–2010)*] Falv Chubanshe (China Law Press 2014), 210.

5 See Zhonghua Renmin Gongheheguo Shewai Minshi Falvguanxi Shiyongfa 2010 [Act on the Application of Laws on Foreign-related Civil Relationships/Private International Law Act] (P.R.C.).

6 For detailed discussion of the Private International Law Act, see Zhengxin Huo, 'An Imperfect Improvement: The New Conflict of Laws Act of the People's Republic of China' (2011) 60 *International and Comparative Law Quarterly* 1065–1093.

First, reflecting the civil law tradition, Article 10 of the Private International Law Act states expressly that, as a general principle, courts or other quasi-judicial institutions, shall ascertain the content of foreign law *ex officio*.

Second, it distinguishes a specific situation (i.e. the parties choose a foreign law as the governing law) where the parties concerned shall bear the burden of proof to ascertain the content of the chosen law. The rationale behind this provision is that because the parties have reached agreement on the applicable law, it is reasonable to presume that they are familiar with the law in question and possess sufficient materials to ascertain its content; therefore, it is logical to ask the parties to bear the burden of proof in this case.

Third, given the development of modern science and technology and the close exchange between countries across the globe, it does not enumerate the specific methods to ascertain foreign law. The lack of listing of the specific methods increases the flexibility of the Article, which will, in turn, facilitate the task of ascertaining foreign law.

Compared with Article 193 of Opinions on the GPCL, needless to say, Article 10 of the Private International Law Act represents a significant progress; nonetheless, the article ignores the suggestions put forward by Chinese scholars who argued that Chinese law should not apply automatically when foreign law cannot be ascertained or there is no pertinent rule of law after ascertainment. They hold such position because they worry that the application of the *lex fori* without exception would encourage the 'homeward trend', which has prevailed in Chinese judicial practice over the years.[7]

On 6 January 2013, the SPC promulgated 'Interpretation (I) on the Implementation of the Act on the Application of Laws over Foreign-related Civil Relationships of the People's Republic of China' (hereinafter Interpretation (I)).[8] The Interpretation (I) attempts to provide concrete explanations on the abstract articles mainly in Chapter One of the Private International Law Act and to create new provisions to close the legal loopholes.

Having acknowledged that proof of foreign law is a major obstacle for Chinese courts to improve judicial efficiency in foreign-related cases, the SPC considers it necessary to provide concrete provisions regulating proof of foreign law. Therefore, the Interpretation (I) provides more detailed rules, as Article 17 of this judicial interpretation states that:

> If a foreign law cannot be established pursuant to the methods provided by the international conventions to which China is a party, by the parties' submission, by expert witness, or other appropriate methods, the People's Court may hold that the foreign law cannot be proved.

7 *Ibid.*, 76.

8 Zuigao Renmin Fayuan Guanyu Shiyong Zhonghua Renmin Gongheguo Shewai Minshi Falv Guanxi Shiyongfa Ruogan Wenti de Jieshi Yi (Supreme People's Court, Interpretation (I) on the Implementation of Act on the Application of Laws on Foreign-related Civil Relationships of the People's Republic of China), Zuigao Renmin Fayuan Gongbao 24 [Bulletin of Supreme People's Court] (2012).

> Where the parties bear the burden of proving a foreign law chosen by them, the People's Court may hold that the foreign law cannot be proved if they fail to fulfill this duty within the reasonable period designated by the Court without due cause.

It merits particularly strong emphasis that Chinese judges are left with much more discretion under the Article 17 compared with Article 193 of Opinions on the GPCL, which is reflected in the following two aspects.

First, when a People's Court ascertains the content of foreign law *ex officio*, it shall fulfil its duty pursuant to Article 10 of the Private International Law Act and Article 17 of the Interpretation (I) which do not enumerate the specific methods. Second, when the parties bear the burden to prove foreign law, they shall fulfil the duty within a reasonable period specified by the People's Court; otherwise, they have to face the consequence that the law they chose is unable to be ascertained. Obviously, the SPC attempts to improve judicial efficiency by vesting judges with such wide discretion.

Nevertheless, given the failure to prove foreign law would lead to the application of the *lex fori* automatically, the author submits that Article 17 of the Interpretation (I) would encourage the 'homeward trend'. Indeed, as many Chinese judges are still reluctant to recognise the effect of foreign law in civil cases involving foreign elements, it is highly possible that this article would be manipulated by Chinese judges to expand the application of *lex fori*, and if this were the case, the underlying purpose of Private International Law Act would be defeated.

Furthermore, as Chinese judges are generally unfamiliar with foreign law, Article 18 of the Interpretation (I) states that the People's Court should listen to the parties' statement on the content of foreign law, should they reach agreement, the Court may confirm it; should they have different opinions, the Court shall examine and determine it. That is to say, if the parties reach an agreement on the content of a foreign law, the court may confirm it directly, even in the circumstance that the court shall ascertain the content of foreign law *ex officio*. The purpose of such an arrangement, apparently, is to alleviate the burden of Chinese judges, thus enhancing the judicial efficiency.[9]

Cases in which foreign law should be approved before Chinese courts

Since the implementation of the Private International Law Act, Article 10 of the Act has been invoked occasionally by Chinese courts to prove the content of foreign law. After systematically searching major online legal databases,

9 Zhengxin Huo, 'Two Steps Forward, One Step Back: A Commentary on the Private International Law Act of China' (2013) 42 *Hong Kong Law Journal* 685–713.

including China Judgments Online,[10] Beida Fabao,[11] and LexisNexis China,[12] the author has found 29 cases in which foreign law was needed to be proved before Chinese courts up to 30 June 2017.

Because of the huge amount of private international law cases that Chinese courts have heard during the past six years, the cases cannot cover all those in which proof of foreign law is relevant; however, those typical cases are illustrative of the attitude of Chinese courts towards foreign law and of the practical effect of Article 10 of the Private International Law Act in judicial practice, which, therefore, can provide the solid basis for further research. The information of those cases can be found in the following table.

Among the 29 cases in the previous table, 28 should be governed by foreign law, and one by an international convention to which China is a contracting party. Hence, for those 28 cases, it is necessary to prove the content of foreign law before Chinese courts. In this respect, how foreign laws was proved and whether it was able to be proved in those cases provide a good opportunity to observe the actual attitude of Chinese courts towards foreign law as well as the consequence of Article 10 of the Private International Law Act in judicial practice.

However, the previous table indicates that only nine out of 28 were eventually governed by the foreign law. The reason for the application of Chinese law in place of foreign law in the rest 19 cases is the same: the otherwise applicable foreign law could not be proved. Furthermore, among those 19 cases, there are 16 cases in which the conclusion that foreign law was unable to be approved was based on the fact that the parties failed to submit the relevant foreign law. In comparison, among the nine cases in which foreign law was applied, there are seven cases in which the parties proved the relevant foreign law. Expressed differently, among those 28 cases in which foreign law should be proved, there were but two cases in which the court ascertained the content of foreign law *ex officio*.

In light of the analysis of the previous cases, the following conclusions can be drawn: first, proof of foreign law, in general, is a difficult issue before Chinese courts. The failure to prove foreign law is a major reason why Chinese law is applied even though private international law rules refer to a foreign legal system.

Second, Chinese courts are reluctant to ascertain the content of foreign law *ex officio* even after the implementation of the Private International Law Act which states in Article 10 that, as a general principle, courts shall ascertain the content of foreign law *ex officio*. Therefore, in most occasions, it is the parties that bear the burden to prove foreign law.

Third, in cases where foreign law is chosen by the parties, the parties, in principle, should prove its content; otherwise, they have to accept the

10 http://wenshu.court.gov.cn/ accessed 25 August 2017.
11 http://en.pkulaw.cn/ accessed 25 August 2017.
12 www.lexisnexis.com.cn/zh-cn/products/lexis-china.page accessed 25 August 2017.

Case name and number	Date of judgment	Court decided the case	Applicable law	Law applied	Reasons for the application of law
The Hong Kong and Shanghai Banking Co. Ltd. v Hongfa International Packing Production Co. Ltd., (2016) Yue 0391, Min Chu No.611	28 June 2017	People's Court of Qianhai Cooperation Zone, Shenzhen	Hong Kong law (party autonomy)	Hong Kong law	The parties submitted Hong Kong law.
Guan Shijun v Li Zhengjian, (2016) Yun Min Zhong No. 795	23 May 2017	Higher People's Court of Yunnan	Burmese law (party autonomy)	Chinese law	The parties failed to submit Burmese law.
Hungarian Export Credit Insurance Pte. Ltd. v Xia Jingjun el., (2015) Zhe Yong Shang Waichuzi No.181	24 March 2017	Ningbo Intermediate People's Court, Zhejiang	Hungarian law	Hungarian law	The court entrusted ECUPL to ascertain the content of Hungarian law[13]
Gaomin International Trade Co. Ltd. v Huaheng International Industrial Co. Ltd., (2016) Zhe Min Zhong No.246	29 December 2016	Higher People's Court of Zhejiang 号	Australian law (party autonomy)	Australian law	The parties submitted Australian law.
Delixy Energy Pte. Ltd. v Dongming Zhongyou Petrochemical Fuel Co. Ltd., (2016) Lu Min Zhong No.1891	28 December 2016	Higher People's Court of Shandong	English law (party autonomy)	Chinese law	Though the plaintiff provided the English law submitted by Holman Fenwick Willan LLP, the court did not accept it.
Hang Seng Bank (China) Ltd., Shunde Sub-branch v Yaode Metal Decoration Co. Ltd., (2015) Fo Zhongfa Min Er Chuzi No. 32	15 December 2016	Intermediate People's Court of Foshan, Guangdong	Hong Kong Law (party autonomy)	Chinese law	The parties failed to submit Hong Kong law.

(*Continued*)

(Continued)

Case name and number	*Date of judgment*	*Court decided the case*	*Applicable law*	*Law applied*	*Reasons for the application of law*
Li Hanliu v Chen Shuangwei, (2016) Zhe 1121 Min Chu No.803	28 December 2016	People's Court of Qintian County, Zhejiang	Serbian law (party autonomy)	Chinese law	The parties failed to submit Serbian law.
Zhang Zuqiao v Zhang Minsheng & Dai Kairong, (2016) Xiang 1202 Min Chu No.1744	26 November 2016	People's Court of Hebi District, Huaihua City, Hunan	Ghanaian law (party autonomy)	Chinese law	The parties failed to submit Ghanaian law.
Bank of East Asia Co. Ltd. v Langdian Co. Ltd. el. Guarantors, (2016) Yue 0391 Minchu No. 713	15 November 2016	People's Court of Qianhai Cooperation Zone, Shenzhen	Hong Kong law (party autonomy)	Hong Kong law	The parties submitted Hong Kong law.
Hong Kong Yongfeng International Co. Ltd. v Xinjiang Mining Industry Co. Ltd., (2015) Wu Zhong Minsan Chuzi No. 64	19 August 2016	Intermediate People's Court of Urumqi, Xinjiang Uygur Autonomous Region	Hong Kong law (party autonomy)	Hong Kong law	The parties submitted Hong Kong law.
PICC P&C Sichuan Sub-branch v Yunnan Hongxin Logistics Co. Ltd., (2015) Yun Gao Min San Zhongzi No. 86	12 December 2015	Higher People's Court of Yunnan	Laotian law (party autonomy)	Chinese law	The parties failed to submit the content of Laotian law.
Tenghong Foreign Trade Co. Ltd. (Fu Gong Cuunty) v Chen Xiaoding el., (2015) Nu Zhong Minsan Zhongzi No.3	28 October 2015	Intermediate People's Court of Nujiang Lili Autonomous Prefecture, Yunnan	Burmese law (party autonomy)	Chinese law	The parties failed to submit Burmese law.

Daewoo Shipbuilding & Marine Engineering Co. Ltd. v Glory Advance Corporation, (2014) Xia Haifa Quezi No.1	25 January 2015	Maritime Court of Xiamen	Panamanian law (party autonomy)	Panamanian law	The plaintiff submitted the content of Panamanian law which had been notarised.
Jiangho Group Co. Ltd. v Xinhongda Group Co. Ltd. and Construction Bank of China, Xuzhou Chengzhong Sub-branch, (2014) Su Min Zhongzi No.0205	04 July 2014	Higher People's Court of Jiangsu	Saudi Arabian law	Chinese law	Saudi Arabian law cannot be proved.
Duizheng Import & Export Col. Ltd. v Hyundai Merchant Marine Co., Ltd., (2014) Yong Haifa Shang Chuzi No. 639	13 June 2014	Ningbo Maritime Court	Mexican law (party autonomy)	Chinese law	The parties failed to submit Mexican law.
Lei Jian v Zeng Xinmei and Zhouwei, (2014) Shen Zhongfa Min Zhongzi No. 274	10 June 2014	Intermediate People's Court of Shenzhen, Guangdong	Hong Kong law	Chinese law	The parties failed to submit Hong Kong law.
Mindongcongmao Shipping Industrial Co. Ltd. v Swiss Wärtsilä Co. Ltd., (2014) Xia Haifa Shang Chuzi No.212	27 May 2014	Maritime Court of Xiamen	Swedish law (party autonomy)	Swedish law	The parties submitted Swedish law.
Deng Jinahua v Chen Binsong, (2014) Zhong Zhongminfa Sizhongzi No.6	03 April 2014	Intermediate People's Court of Zhongshan, Guangdong	Hong Kong law	Hong Kong law	The court ascertained Hong Kong law *ex officio*.

(*Continued*)

(Continued)

Case name and number	*Date of judgment*	*Court decided the case*	*Applicable law*	*Law applied*	*Reasons for the application of law*
Zhang Zhen v Alibaba Group Holding Ltd., (2012) Hang Bin Shang Wai Chuzi No.53	28 November 2013	People's Court of Binjiang District, Hangzhou City, Zhejiang	Law of the Cayman Islands (party autonomy)	Chinese law	The parties failed to submit law of the Cayman Islands.
Xu Lin v Alibaba Group Holding Ltd., (2012) Hang Bin Shang Wai Chuzi No.52	28 November 2013	People's Court of Binjiang District, Hangzhou City, Zhejiang	Law of the Cayman Islands (party autonomy)	Chinese law	The parties failed to submit law of the Cayman Islands.
Lu Susheng v Wanning Shimeiwan Hotel Co. Ltd., (2013) Qiong Min San Zhongzi No. 75	18 November 2013	Higher People's Court of Hainan	English law (party autonomy)	Chinese law	The parties failed to submit English law.
Guangdong Kugao Investment Management Co. Ltd. v Hong Kon g & Macau International Hainan Investment Co. Ltd., (2013) Qiong Min San Zhongzi No. 79	10 September 2013	Higher People's Court of Hainan	Hong Kong law (party autonomy)	Chinese law	The parties failed to submit Hong Kong law.
Zhang Shuyi v Air France, (2013) Hu Yizhong Yimin Zhongzi No. 1689	04 September 2013	First Intermediate People's Court of Shanghai	Montreal Convention (party autonomy)	Montreal Convention	China is contracting party to Montreal Convention.

Long Zhongyong and Yongya (Private) Co. Ltd. v Bangzhe Shipping Co. Ltd., (2013) Wu Haifa Shangzi No.00845	19 August 2013	Wuhan Maritime Court	Singapore law (party autonomy)	Chinese law	The plaintiff requested to apply Chinese law, while the defendant did not appear before the court.
Haicheng Bangda International Logistics v Yantai Zhonglian Industrial Co. Ltd., (2013) Lu Minsi Zhongzi No.7	17 July 2013	Higher People's Court of Shandong	US law (party autonomy)	Chinese law	The parties failed to submit US law.
SEoIL Shipping Co. Ltd. v Tangshan Ganglu Iron & Steel Co. Ltd., (2012) Jin Gao Minsi Zhongzi No. 4	12 December 2012	Higher People's Court of Tianjin	English law (party autonomy)	English law	The parties provided the content of English and the court ascertained it *ex officio.*
Star Overseas v Zhang Yuqi, (2012) *Hu Yizhong Minyi* (Min) Zhongzi No. 2158	12 October 2012	First Intermediate People's Court of Shanghai	Hong Kong law (party autonomy)	Chinese law	The parties failed to submit Hong Kong law.
International Finance Co. v Zhejiang Glass Co. Ltd. & Feng Guangcheng, (2010) Zhe Shao Shangwai Chuzi No.76	02 November 2011	Intermediate People's Court of Shaoxing, Zhejiang	New York law (party autonomy)	Chinese law	The parties failed to submit New York law.
X Co. Ltd. v Chen Y, (2010) Pu Minyi (Min) Chuzi No.26514	08 October 2011	People's Court of Pudong New Area, Shanghai	Minnesota law (party autonomy)	Chinese law	The parties failed to submit Minnesota law.

consequence that the law they chose cannot be proved. It is worth noting that if both parties reached the agreement on the content of the relevant foreign law, Chinese courts would simply confirm it and then apply it; nonetheless, if one party submitted the content of foreign law while the other party challenged its authenticity, or if the two parties disagree on the content of foreign law that they chose, it is highly possible that Chinese courts conclude that foreign law cannot be proved.

Last, but not least, in cases where foreign law should be applied by the choice-of-law rules other than party autonomy, Chinese courts are more likely to ascertain the content of foreign law *ex officio*, as *Hungarian Export Credit Insurance Pte. Ltd. v Xia Jingjun el.* suggests.[13] However, it should be emphasised that though the parties are not requested to prove foreign law under such a circumstance, it is still possible for Chinese courts to jump to the conclusion that foreign law cannot be proved with no detailed explication provided, which is vividly reflected by *Jiangho Group Co. Ltd. v Xinhongda Group Co. Ltd. and Construction Bank of China, Xuzhou Chengzhong Sub-branch.*[14] In this case, the Saudi Arabian law should have governed the capacity of the plaintiff pursuant to Article 14 of the Private International Law Act; however, the court concluded that Chinese law should be applied on the ground that Saudi Arabian law could not be proved. Unfortunately, the conclusion was drawn without any detailed reasoning or analysis. It follows that the parties may run the risk that a foreign law that is otherwise applicable is disregarded if they fail to prove that law even when they do not bear the burden of proof under Article 10 of the Private International Law Act.

Overall, if the cases in the previous table are any indication, the combined effect of Article 10 of the Private International Law Act and Articles 17 and 18 of the Interpretation (I) apparently encourages the 'homeward trend' in judicial practice. In this light, the author's worry expressed in Part II is not irrational. As the new generation of Chinese leadership pledges to open the door wider to the outside world since 2012,[15] and the PRC is now promoting the ambitious B&R Initiative, the 'homeward trend', obviously, is an anachronism.

Challenges of proving foreign law against the background of the B&R Initiative

In September 2013, Chinese President Xi Jinping proposed a Silk Road Economic Belt, and in October, a 21st-Century Maritime Silk Road, together now referred to as the Belt and Road Initiative. It integrates the historical

13 (2015) Zhe Yong Shang Waichuzi No.181.

14 (2014) Su Min Zhongzi No.0205.

15 Xinhua, 'China Headlines: China Initiates New Round of Reform and Opening Up' (23 September 2015) <http://news.xinhuanet.com/english/2015-09/23/c_134651397.htm> accessed 12 August 2017.

symbolism of the ancient Silk Road with the new requirements of today. The Initiative is a Chinese program whose goal is to maintain an open world economic system, and achieve diversified, independent, balanced, and sustainable development, and also a Chinese proposal intended to advance regional cooperation, strengthen communications between civilizations, and safeguard world peace and stability.[16]

Spanning more than 65 countries and encompassing 4.4 billion people and up to 40% of the global GDP, the B&R Initiative aims to create a trade and infrastructure network to connect Asia with Europe and Africa along ancient trade routes. Since its announcement by President Xi Jinping, over 600 contracts have been signed by Chinese enterprises for projects in the countries along the B&R routes.[17] This number of cross-border contracts is set to continue to increase, especially as it has been projected that Asia alone needs about USD 8 trillion worth of basic infrastructure projects for the 2010–2020 period.[18] Other than infrastructure and related projects, logistics and maritime sectors are also likely to see heightened activity in the B&R regions. The significant opportunities of the B&R also come with significant risks of legal disputes arising. This is particularly the case given that the B&R sees commercial contracts being concluded between parties from the countries with very different legal systems and traditions.

Under such a circumstance, the number of the Initiative-related disputes has been increasing by leaps and bounds, and the challenges posed by the B&R for Chinese courts are unprecedented, as He Rong, Vice-President of the SPC, said in an exclusive interview with China Daily, '[T]he Initiative has brought a boom of foreign-related disputes, as well as challenges for us in case hearings.'[19] Indeed, given the context of the B&R Initiative, the author believes that proof of foreign law in the Initiative-related disputes would be a more challenging task before Chinese courts.

First, as the nature and category of the Initiative-related disputes are in wider variety, proving the content of foreign law becomes an even more burdensome task consequently. According to the latest statistics, the Initiative-related cases coming before Chinese courts during the past three years cover not only contracts, torts, family and succession issues, but also cases involving demand guarantees, international factoring, private equity funds, stock options in companies listed overseas, environment pollution, cross-border

16 Office of the Leading Group for the Belt and Road Initiative, ***Building the Belt and Road: Concept, Practice and China's Contribution*** (Foreign Languages Press 2017), 4.

17 Ministry of Commerce of China, 'Investment and Cooperation Statistics Along "One Belt and One Road" Countries from January–February in 2017' 24 March 2017.

18 The State Council of the People's Republic of China, 'How Malaysia Scholar Sees the Belt and Road Initiative', as cited by Hon Mr. Rimsky Yuen SC, Secretary for Justice of the Hong Kong SAR, 12 October 2016.

19 CAO Yin, 'Courts Handling "A Boom" of Belt and Road Cases' <www.chinadaily.com.cn/china/2017twosession/2017-03/15/content_28559326.htm> accessed 12 August 2017.

mergers and acquisitions, employment disputes, e-commerce, cross-border contract projects, international logistics, foreign currency and financial regulation, bonded trade disputes, and so forth.[20] As the types of the disputes proliferate, the difficulty of proving foreign law increases as a consequence.

Second, because of the huge political, economic, cultural, and historical differences among the countries along the B&R routes, their legal systems vary widely, some of which are either completely unfamiliar to Chinese judges or not easily accessible to Chinese courts, proving law of those countries is thus far more difficult.

Generally speaking, Chinese judges are more familiar with law of the European Continental countries, because modern Chinese law is largely based on European civil law system. Although Anglo-American law is essentially distinct from Chinese legal system, it is easily accessible before Chinese courts for the following reasons. First, English is the most popular foreign language in China, which means that there is little, if any, language barrier for the Chinese to understand law of these English-speaking countries. Second, major online legal services, such as LexisNexis, Westlaw, Heinonline, and so forth, have provided easy accesses to case law, statutes, administrative codes, newspaper and magazine articles, public records, law journals, law reviews, treatises, legal forms, and other information resources in Anglo-American jurisdictions.

In contrast, proving law of the countries along the B&R routes is usually more arduous before Chinese courts. First, a certain number of the countries along the B&R routes, those in the Middle East, and Central Asia, in particular, belong to Islamic law family, which is completely unfamiliar to Chinese judges and lawyers. Second, law of many countries along the B&R routes remains mysterious to the outside world out of language obstacles, non-transparent system or lack of online legal databases. Last, but not least, unlike the Western developed countries whose law schools receive a large number of Chinese students, most countries along the B&R routes are not attractive to Chinese law school students. Hence, it is not surprising that the number of the experts on law of those countries available in China is rather limited.

Third, China, so far, has not established an effective mechanism to ascertain law of the countries along the B&R routes via international treaty either bilaterally or multilaterally. By the end of 2016, among the 67 countries along the B&R routes, China has signed bilateral treaties on civil or criminal judicial assistance with 24, which means there is no such treaty between China and the remaining countries. Moreover, the existing bilateral judicial assistance treaties focus on service, taking of evidence, and recognition of judgments or awards; proof of foreign law, however, is, more or less, a neglected issue.[21]

20 Shi Jianpin, 'Waiguofachaming: Yidaiyilubeijingxia deXinsikao [Proof of Foreign Law: New Reflection Under the Background of the Belt and Road Initiative]' (2016) 6 *Lilun yuXiandaihua* [*Theory and Modernization*] 100.

21 Ministry of Justice of China, 'Introduction to Civil Assistance' <www.moj.gov.cn/sfxzws/node_219.htm> accessed 12 August 2017.

In this light, if law of a country along the B&R routes is designated as the applicable law by private international law rules, it is by no means easy to prove its content before a Chinese court. Given Chinese judges are left with much discretion in deciding how foreign law is proved and whether it can be proved under the current Chinese law and judicial interpretation, the author argues that the purpose of private international law as well as the B&R Initiative would be at stake if the 'homeward trend' cannot be effectively checked.

Latest efforts made by Chinese courts with regard to proof of foreign law

Fortunately, the SPC of the PRC has realised the challenges that the B&R Initiative has posed for Chinese courts. On 16 June 2015, the SPC issued a policy document entitled 'Several Opinions of the Supreme People's Court on Providing Judicial Services and Safeguards for the Construction of the Belt and Road by Peoples' Courts' (hereinafter B&R Opinion).[22] The B&R Opinion covers cross-border criminal, civil and commercial, and maritime as well as free trade zone-related judicial issues which also deals with the judicial review of arbitration. What merits particularly strong emphasis is Paragraph 7 of this document,[23] in which the SPC unambiguously requests the Peoples' Courts to 'fully respect the right of the parties to choose a governing law, actively

22 Zuigao Renminfayuan Guanyu Renminfayuan wei Yidaiyilu Tigong Sifa Fuwu he Baozhang de Ruogan Yijian [Several Opinions of the Supreme People's Court on Providing Judicial Services and Safeguards for the Construction of the Belt and Road by Peoples' Courts] No. 9 [2015].

23 This paragraph provides as follows:

The people's courts shall accurately apply international treaties and practices according to the law, accurately identify and apply foreign laws, and enhance the international credibility of judgments. They shall constantly improve the judicial capacities of applying international treaties and practices and accurately apply international treaties and practices in cases to which such international treaties and practices should apply according to the law. They shall thoroughly research international treaties of trade, investment, finance, and maritime transport concluded by countries along the Belt and Road and China or jointly participated in by them and in strict accordance with the Vienna Convention on the Law of Treaty and general definitions of terms of treaties, make bona fide interpretation on the basis of their contexts and by reference to the purposes and objectives of such treaties, and enhance the uniformity, stability, and predictability of the application of international treaties and practices in the trial of cases. They shall, in accordance with the provisions of the Act on the Application of Laws on Foreign-related Civil Relationships, take such foreign elements as the subject, object, and content of legal relationship, and legal facts into full consideration, fully respect the right of the parties to choose a governing law, actively identify and accurately apply foreign laws, and eliminate legal doubts of the parties of China and countries along the Belt and Road in international commercial affairs. They shall pay attention to differences in cultural and legal backgrounds of the parties in countries along the Belt and Road, apply such internationally recognized legal value concepts and legal principles as justice, freedom, equality, integrity, rationality, order as well as strict observance of contracts and estoppel, make argumentation in a common, concise, overall, and precise manner, and enhance the persuasive power of judgments.

identify and accurately apply foreign laws, and eliminate legal doubts of the parties of China and countries along the Belt and Road routes in international commercial affairs'.

Apparently, Paragraph7 indicates that the SPC clearly understands the importance of conflict of laws issues, proof of foreign law, in particular, for the smooth implementation of the B&R Initiative. As a matter of fact, in the author's opinion, the expression employed herein reveals the anxiety of SPC over the 'homeward trend'.

Since the promulgation of the B&R Opinion, Chinese courts at various levels have taken measures to 'actively identify and accurately apply foreign law'. So far, noticeable progress can be summarised as follows:

First, Chinese courts have established specialised academic platforms providing foreign law ascertainment service in collaboration with leading Chinese universities or social institutions, which, *inter alia*, include the following: the Foreign Law Ascertainment Center at China University of Political Science and Law (CUPL) in Beijing co-established by the SPC and the CUPL 2015,[24] the Foreign and Hong Kong Macao Law Ascertainment Center in Shenzhen co-established by the SPC and Benchmark Chambers International in 2016,[25] and the Foreign Law Ascertainment Center at East China University of Political Science and Law (ECUPL) in Shanghai co-established by the Higher People's Court of Shanghai and the ECUPL in 2014.[26] Judicial practice during the past years suggests that these academic platforms have played a positive role in helping judges and parties to ascertain or prove foreign law, especially law of the countries along the B&R routes. For example, in *Hungarian Export Credit Insurance Pte. Ltd. v Xia Jingjun el.*,[27] as listed in the table in Part III, it is the Foreign Law Ascertainment Base at ECUPL that proved the content of the relevant Hungarian law.

Second, the SPC plans to establish an Initiative-related case guidance and reference system for the lower courts, including model cases, guiding cases, and selected cases (i.e. as selected by the SPC), to guide and limit judges' discretion. For example, in order to provide more detailed guidance to Chinese judges when they hear the Initiative-related cases, the SPC has released 'Model Cases heard by People's Courts to Providing Judicial Services and Safeguards

24 Xinhua, 'Foreign Law Ascertainment Center at China University of Political Science and Law Is Established' (19 January 2015) <http://news.xinhuanet.com/legal/2015-01/19/c_1114051426.htm> accessed 12 August 2017.

25 China News Agency, 'Foreign and Hong Kong Macao Law Ascertainment Center is Established in Shenzhen' (20 September2015) <www.chinanews.com/gn/2015/09-20/7533945.shtml> accessed 12 August 2017.

26 'Higher People's Court of Shanghai and Each China University of Political Science and Law Signed Agreement on Proof of Foreign Law' (25 December 2014) <http://shfy.chinacourt.org/article/detail/2014/12/id/1523989.shtml> accessed 12 August 2017.

27 (2015) Zhe Yong Shang Waichuzi No.181.

for the Belt and Road Initiative' regularly since 2015.[28] Ascertaining foreign law accurately is a major issue that these model cases aim to illustrate.

Needless to say, these efforts are a step in the right direction; however, they are not enough. As long as proving the content of foreign law remains difficult before Chinese courts and the conclusion that foreign law is unable to be proved can be drawn by Chinese courts arbitrarily, the risk of expanding the application of *lex fori* by misusing Article 10 of the Private International Law Act would not be substantially reduced.

Hence, the author believes that more effective measures should be taken to facilitate proving foreign law on the one hand and to limit the discretionary powers of Chinese judges in applying Article 10 of the Private International Law on the other.

Conclusion

The very effectiveness of private international law depends upon whether the applicable law can be accurately identified and applied, especially when foreign law is at issue, and the purpose of private international law is to safeguard the security and prosperity of international exchange and business. It follows that the importance of proving foreign law for the B&R Initiative cannot be overemphasised.

Though Chinese authorities are taking steps to solve the problems that have surfaced in the process of proving foreign law before Chinese courts, further efforts need to be made to rise to the challenges under the background of the B&R Initiative. In view of this, the chapter concludes the discussion with the following suggestions. It is the author's hope that these suggestions will be helpful to Chinese authorities in improving the legislation and judicial policy and to discourage the dangerous 'homeward trend', which both China and foreign countries, those along the B&R routes in particular, would stand to benefit from.

First, the Chinese government should take steps to accelerating the shaping of judicial assistance regime under the framework of the B&R Initiative. At current stage, Chinese authorities should persuade more countries along the B&R routes to sign judicial assistance treaties with China. Among other things, exchange of law information and assisting the ascertainment of the law of the other country should be the important issues that such treaties cover. In the long run, the Chinese government should take into account the establishment of a multilateral judicial assistance regime under the framework of the B&R Initiative. Though establishing such a regime is destined to be a

28 'Supreme People's Court Released the Second Set of Model Cases heard by Peoples' Courts to Providing Judicial Services and Safeguards for the Belt and Road Initiative' (15 May 2017) <www.chinacourt.org/article/detail/2017/05/id/2863082.shtml> accessed 12 August 2017.

difficult and lengthy task, its significance to the success of the Initiative cannot be overstated.

Second, given the importance of online legal databases in proving foreign law and the lack of such database covering the legal information of most Initiative-related countries, the author suggests that the Chinese government consider building a B&R online legal database in cooperation with the partner countries which should contain legislation, case law, and other important legal information of the countries along the B&R routes. Once such a database is established, proving law of the countries along the B&R routes would be much easier.

Third, the SPC should enact concrete rules to implement the B&R Opinion and to see to it that Chinese courts:

> fully respect the right of the parties to choose a governing law, actively identify and accurately apply foreign laws, and eliminate legal doubts of the parties of China and countries along the Belt and Road routes in international commercial affairs.

As has been illustrated by the cases analysis in Section III, the 'homeward trend', to a considerable degree, is the consequence that Chinese judges misunderstand and even misuse Article 10 of the Private International Law together with Articles 17 and 18 of the Interpretation (I). Hence, it is of great necessity for the SPC to enact judicial interpretation to limit the discretionary powers of Chinese judges. Highlights of the rules are as follows:

1. When the private international rules other than the parties' choice refer to a foreign law, courts shall ascertain the content of that foreign law *ex officio*. In this case, it is the judges who bear burden of ascertaining foreign law; therefore, they cannot conclude that foreign law is unable to be proved merely on the ground that the parties failed to submit the content of the relevant foreign law.
2. In case where the parties choose a foreign law, they bear the burden of proving that law; however, certain requirements have to be satisfied before the conclusion can be drawn that foreign law is unable to be proved. In the first place, courts should grant the parties a reasonable period to submit the foreign law that they chose. Though 'reasonable period' is a flexible expression, necessary explanation should be provided to support its reasonability. Moreover, if the parties ask the court to extend the period with due causes, their request should be permitted. As a matter of fact, such requirements are implicit in Article 17 of the Interpretation (I); nonetheless, they have not been strictly followed by Chinese judges.
3. In case the parties have disagreement over the content of foreign law that they submitted, courts should ascertain it on its own instead of jumping to the conclusion that foreign law cannot be proved.

4 In all situations, the conclusion that foreign law cannot be proved must be supported by detailed reasoning and explication. The decision that foreign law cannot be proved without sufficient explanation is appealable.

Last, but not least, in order to help the academic platforms providing foreign law ascertainment service exert a more constructive role, the SPC should establish and improve the rules regulating the function and operation of these institutions. Important issues that have to be clarified include the following: (1) the qualifications of a foreign law expert at such institutions, (2) the nature and the weight of an opinion on the content of foreign law submitted by such institutions, (3) the allocation of cost in proving foreign law, (4) the duty as well as the remedy for a mistake in the content of foreign law submitted by such institutions. As long as these important issues cannot be properly addressed, it is unrealistic for those institutions to play an important role in proving foreign law before Chinese courts.

8 One Belt One Road – One law?

Bruno Zeller

Introduction

In late 2013, the President of the People's Republic of China, Mr Xi Jinping, announced the concept of the 'Silk Road Economic Belt', also referred to as the One Belt One Road (OBOR) project. This project has since witnessed momentum. As an example, at the end of April 2017, another train arrived in China, which had its origin in the United Kingdom. This is one of more than 1,700 trains that have made the transcontinental voyage between China and Europe.[1] The fact that China is looking at Europe is not accidental, as the European Union is China's largest trading partner. Indeed, one would witness a sharp increase of projects in Europe that have been funded by China. As Wilson observed:

> China is financing the upgrade of the Greek port of Piraeus and a €3 billion bullet train from Belgrade to Budapest. Another network of rails, roads and pipelines, starting in the Chinese central city of Xian, will stretch westward as far as Belgium. Beijing has already started building an eight-thousand-mile cargo rail route between the Chinese city of Yiwu and Madrid.[2]

Wilson further observed that the redirection of the capital abroad made good economic sense, as the Chinese domestic industries have been overbuilt.[3] Aside from financing projects in Europe, China has also invested in infrastructure in the Central Asian countries along the proposed Silk Road, and such investments have resulted in increased trade surpassing the trade volumes with another major trading partner, namely Russia.[4]

1 Wade Shepard, 'What the Newly Branded China-Europe "Silk Road" Trains Really Mean' *Forbes* (28 June 2016) <www.forbes.com/sites/wadeshepard/2016/06/28/what-the-newly-branded-china-europe-silk-road-trains-really-mean/#32cc86613487> accessed 10 July 2017.

2 William T. Wilson, 'China's Huge "One Belt, One Road" Initiative Is Sweeping Central Asia' *The National Interest* (27 July 2016) <http://nationalinterest.org/feature/chinas-huge-one-belt-one-road-initiative-sweeping-central-17150> accessed 10 July 2017.

3 *Ibid.*

4 *Ibid.*

The moot question is: how do the legal systems tie into the new logistics possibilities? A transhipment is not too difficult to understand as the World Trade Organization (WTO) legal regime does not affect transhipment. However, the issues will become more complicated once goods are offloaded and new goods are loaded onto the train. In essence, the shipping experience would need to be duplicated. The point is: how do customs work with this model?

To this end, the author, in this chapter, investigates practical problems that could arise from the interaction of diverse legal systems affecting the commerce between nations along the proposed Silk Road. In essence, he argues that diverse legal systems within the supply chain interacting with each other would be at the same level of diversity. As long as transnational laws are not ratified and, importantly, embraced by the business community and globally included into legal systems, a truly seamless trade system will not eventuate. As an example, the United Nations Convention on Contracts for the International Sale of Goods (Vienna, 1980) (CISG), with 84 member states, is hailed as the most important harmonised sales law. However, at the same time legal advisors are routinely excluding the CISG as a law governing international sale transactions. Another example is a consistent failure on the part of the European Union to enact a common contract law despite numerous attempts that ultimately sit on the shelf gathering dust.

The author argues further that it would be of advantage if the International Institute for the Unification of Private Law (UNIDROIT) and the United Nations Commission on International Trade Law (UNCITRAL) could be given mandate to devise necessary uniform trading laws. In addition, Free Trade Agreements (FTAs) and Bilateral Investment Treaties (BITs) within the Asian Region are still too diverse to be useful in overcoming roadblocks hindering trade. The roadblocks at borders are commonly customs procedures that can be costly and time-consuming. Roadblocks after borders are rules and regulations that are foreign to traders such as navigating through the Chinese court system.

In this chapter, the author will attempt to demonstrate that realising the economic value in the Silk Road would require law reform efforts towards harmonised domestic trade laws. The author will also attempt to document the emerging signs of harmonisation in aspects such as laws relating to letters of credit and exemption clauses in bills of lading. Of importance in this discussion is also the influence of more than 75 overseas economic and trade cooperation zones in 35 countries.[5] It will be argued here that the cooperation zones – through shaping taxes and creating jobs in the regions – will not overcome the necessity to streamline cross-border laws in order to reduce

5 Zhong Nan, 'Belt and Road Driving Growth' *China Daily* (24 February 2016) <www.chinadaily.com.cn/business/chinadata/2016-02/24/content_23614444.htm> accessed 10 July 2017.

costs. The author will also highlight issues that need a complete address within domestic laws, through harmonisation.

The Silk Road – effect on trade and investment

There is no doubt that the One Belt One Road (OBOR) is benefiting Asia and requires massive investments if it is to function efficiently. Six major cooperation corridors are proposed:

> On land, the plan is to build a new Eurasian land bridge and develop the economic corridors of: China-Mongolia-Russia; China-Central Asia-West Asia; the China-Indochina peninsula; China-Pakistan; and Bangladesh-China-India-Myanmar . . . On the seas, the initiative will focus on jointly building smooth, secure and efficient transport routes connecting major sea ports along the belt and road.[6]

With the fact that China is financing projects and investments and Chinese banks are expanding their influence into the OBOR markets, the OBOR has moved beyond a mere aspirational goal.[7] Developments in Pakistan illustrate well the scale and the rapid movement of the OBOR. The deep-sea port in Gwadar is being developed at an estimated cost of $46 billion over six years. As a result:

> It could open up an energy and trade corridor from the Gulf across Pakistan to western China, that could also be used by the Chinese Navy. The CPEC [China-Pakistan Economic Corridor] will give China land access to the Indian Ocean, cutting the nearly 13,000 km sea voyage from Tianjin to the Persian Gulf through the Strait of Malacca and around India, to a mere 2,000 km road journey from Kashgar to Gwadar.[8]

The decision of the United States to withdraw from the Trans-Pacific Partnership (TPP) could help give momentum to the China-backed OBOR projects.[9] Bottlier from the Johns Hopkins School of Advanced International Studies has been quoted as saying:

> I am concerned that its [the OBOR's] significance is underrated in the U.S. and the West in general. It is a very positive initiative and a major

6 Geoff Wade, 'China's "One Belt, One /Road" Initiative' (Parliament of Australia) <www.aph.gov.au/About_Parliament/Parliamentary_Departments/Parliamentary_Library/pubs/BriefingBook45p/ChinasRoad> accessed 19 August 2017.

7 *Ibid.*

8 'China-Pakistan Economic Corridor: Pakistan's Road of High Hopes' *The Indian Express* (18 April 2016) <http://indianexpress.com/article/explained/cpec-pakistan-china-nawaz-sharif-xi-jinping-2758111/> accessed 10 July 2017.

9 The Wharton School of the University of Pennsylvania, 'Where Will China's "One Belt, One Road" Initiative Lead?' <http://knowledge.wharton.upenn.edu/article/can-chinas-one-belt-one-road-initiative-match-the-hype/> accessed 19 August 2017.

> vision of how China can collaborate with countries in its neighbourhood, Europe, Latin America and Africa in a way that is in the long-term interest of China and [the global economy].[10]

However, a change in attitude of the United States could be witnessed from the fact that they did send a delegation to Beijing to attend China's recent Belt and Road summit.[11]

One Belt One Road – Australia's attempts at engagement

Despite Australia's not being identified as one of the countries along the One Belt One Road route, a sharp increase in Chinese investments in Australia can be seen in recent years. An example is the Port of Darwin, which gives access to Australia via the Northern Territory, having been leased to private investors from China.[12] This was viewed negatively by some as not a sound decision from a strategic point of consideration.[13]

Arguably, the OBOR initiative could be an accelerator also for increased investments in Australia by Chinese firms and vice versa investments in China by Australian firms. The OBOR will likely open opportunities for Australian industries in third countries.[14] It has been noted that key advantages of OBOR for Australia are:[15]

- For Australian industry to understand the intent of the Belt and Road Initiative as well as practical examples of projects that relate to specific industry sectors and regions; and

10 *Ibid.*

11 Wendy Wu, Zhuang Pinghui, and Stuart Lau, 'US to Send Top Adviser to China's Belt and Road Summit as Part of Sino-US Trade Deal' *South China Morning Post* (6 July 2017) <www.scmp.com/news/china/diplomacy-defence/article/2094085/us-send-top-adviser-chinas-belt-and-road-summit-part> accessed 19 August 2017.

12 The operations at the Port of Darwin were leased for 99 years to Landbridge, a Chinese company, for USD 506 million. The Chinese group would pay the full price of the lease but take only 80% ownership stake, and the Northern Territory's government announced that Landbridge will have to identify an Australian investor for the 20% retained stake. The enterprise agreement terminates in 2018. 'Chinese Company Landbridge to Operate Darwin Port Under $506m 99-Year Lease Deal' *ABC* (14 October 2015) <www.abc.net.au/news/2015-10-13/chinese-company-landbridge-wins-99-year-darwin-port-lease/6850870> accessed 27 October 2017.

13 Ben Smee and Christopher A. Walsh, 'How the Sale of Darwin Port to the Chinese Sparked a Geopolitical Brawl' *The Guardian* (18 December 2016) <www.theguardian.com/australia-news/2016/dec/18/how-the-sale-of-darwin-port-to-the-chinese-sparked-a-geopolitical-brawl> accessed 19 October 2017.

14 Jean Dong, Xu Wang and Gemma Cooper, 'One Belt One Road: Opportunities for Asia' (Australian Institute of International Affairs) (4 October 2016) <www.internationalaffairs.org.au/australianoutlook/one-belt-one-road-opportunities-for-australia/> accessed 19 August 2017.

15 *Ibid.*

- For Chinese enterprises to understand the areas in which Australian industries have strong competitive capabilities that can have direct application to Belt and Road priority areas (both in China and participating Belt and Road countries).

To engage on issues related to the OBOR and Australia, a not-for-profit organisation, the Australia-China Belt Road Initiative (ACBRI) has been established to provide information for Australian industry.[16] ACBRI has received much patronage from industry groups.[17] The Vice-Minister and Deputy China International Trade Representative, Mr Zhang Xiangchen (Ministry of Commerce), visited Melbourne and noted that the China-Australia Free Trade Agreement (ChAFTA) is a great start and called for further work in order to fully appreciate the OBOR.[18]

In addition, the Prime Minister of Australia and the President of China discussed OBOR-related bilateral engagement in 2016 when President Xi called for the 'alignment of China's Belt and Road initiative with Australia's northern development plan'.[19] This is in contrast to the exclusion of Australia from the map of the OBOR and is arguably in response to China's understanding of the importance of the resources trade from Western Australia and Queensland. Controversially, Chinese conglomerate Shanghai CRED, in conjunction with an Australian consortium, bought the iconic pastoral Kidman estate last year for A$386.5 million.[20] The size is 77,300 sq/km composing 1% of Australia and is said to produce 15,000 tons of beef per year.[21]

It remains to be seen whether Canberra can rise to the challenge and 'develop attractive projects to capitalise on this opportunity from the Prime Minister's visit'.[22]

One Belt One Road – identifying the legal challenges

It is obvious – given the location of the rail link – that challenges will need to be overcome. The issues, therefore, are twofold: first, will the physical

16 The initiative is supported by the Australian Government and the Australia-China Council. <www.australiachinaobor.org.au/> accessed 10 July 2017.

17 There are 12 companies and industrial bodies on the ACBRI from Australia. See Australia-China Belt & Road Initiative <www.australiachinaobor.org.au/#team> accessed 28 October 2017.

18 Australia-China Belt & Road Initiative, 'ACOBORI and CCCA Host Chinese Ministry of Commerce Vice-Minister and Deputy China International Trade Representative Mr Zhang Xiangchen in Melbourne, Victoria' (Media Release, 21 February 2017) <www.australiachinaobor.org.au/mediareleases/ViceMinisterMediaReleasev.pdf> accessed 10 July 2017.

19 Geoff Raby, 'Northern Australia Takes Its Place on Xi Jinping's New Silk Road Map' *Financial Review* (11 May 2016) <www.afr.com/opinion/columnists/northern-australia-takes-its-place-on-xi-jinpings-new-silk-road-map-20160511-gos84v> accessed 27 October 2017.

20 'Australia Kidman Bid: Gina Rinehart and Shanghai CRED Make New Offer' *BBC* (10 October 2016) <www.bbc.com/news/business-37604087> accessed 10 July 2017.

21 *Ibid.*

22 Raby (n 19).

infrastructure, that is train, road and shipping, be sufficiently secured and in place in order to create a seamless transport network? The second issue – the purpose of this chapter – is will the physical development be matched with legal reforms along the various transport routes?

Political uncertainty and investment risks would be the major problems, especially as more than half of the countries involved in the plan are considered 'sub-investment grade'.[23] It follows that economies and infrastructure have not yet developed in these countries. There is no doubt that sovereign debt factors will play an important role specifically in politically unstable nations as can currently be seen around the Middle East. An example is China's heavy investment in Libya. As Michael Kan and Belinda Yan noted:

> China has always been an avid supporter of infrastructure projects in developing countries, including Libya. Backed by immense economic resources, technical know-how and a relatively low cost labour force, Chinese state-owned enterprises and private contractors have penetrated and invested heavily in important industry sectors including real estate and construction, railroad, oil and telecommunications. Bilateral treaties and agreements were entered into between the Chinese and the Libyan governments to facilitate this. The aggregate value of those investments exceeded US$20 billion.
>
> Thus, when political unrest and eventually civil war broke out in Libya in 2011, Chinese investors stood to suffer massive economic loss.[24]

However, the bilateral trade in commodities and capital and consumer goods will be accelerated. It is, therefore, not surprising that China has invested heavily in industrial production capacity and will do so in the foreseeable future. By the middle of 2016, 'various bilateral and multilateral industrial capacity cooperation fund built by the Chinese side have amounted to more than 100 billion U.S. Dollars'.[25] To sum up:

> The "One Belt, One Road" plan is not a free trade agreement. It's more of a blueprint for integrating China's trading partners by developing their infrastructure – ports, roads, airports and railways – in a way that complements Beijing's own interests. Infrastructure-led development

23 Moody's Investor Service, 'Moody's: China's Belt and Road Strategy – Credit Positive for Emerging Market Sovereigns' <www.moodys.com/research/Moodys-Chinas-Belt-and-Road-Strategy-Credit-Positive-for-Emerging—PR_331106> accessed 10 July 2017.

24 Michael Kan and Belinda Yan, 'China's Investment in Libya' *The African Business Journal* <www.tabj.co.za/northern_africa/michael_kan_and_belinda_yan_assess_what_chinese_investors_will_n.html> accessed 27 October 2017.

25 'Wang Yi: "One Belt One Road" Initiative Achieves Series of Important Early-Stage Harvest' *Xinhua* (22 May 2016) <http://news.xinhuanet.com/english/2016-05/22/c_135377975.htm> accessed 10 July 2017.

worked well for China, in Beijing's view, and now it wants to expand that approach internationally.[26]

Arguably, therefore, the future of trade – or, more precisely, the development of trade – depends heavily on the success of the OBOR specifically in the creation of certainty in returns for all investors concerned, whether they are privately owned or supported by government resources.

The legal landscape

The challenge to industry is confined not only to infrastructure, finance and trade generally but also to the legal aspects that underpin the security of projects. The legal landscape could help with streamlining international trade laws and easing trade further.

As with all international trade, the foundation is the underlying contract. Any issues associated with transport, financial questions, dispute resolution and conflict of laws are supported by the contract. In addition, on a public international law level, the influence of the World Trade Organization (WTO) cannot be underestimated. However, in China, the Central Government has not yet overcome provincial patriotism. The WTO did note that local protectionism in China has resulted in distortions to the economy.[27] In the China – Rare Earths case,[28] China's provincial governments were found to be in breach of the WTO rules, which in turn forced the Central Government to defend the case at WTO arbitration. However, the outcomes of the WTO disputes led to an enhancement of transparency of trade policies, as exemplified in the efforts of China in accommodating WTO requirements.[29] Of significance in relation to the OBOR is the fact that many countries along the Silk Road were third parties to the WTO complaint – India, Oman, Saudi Arabia, Vietnam, Argentina, Australia, Indonesia, Turkey and the Russian Federation.[30]

Issues relating to public law and private law need to be outlined here. As noted within the foregoing discussion, the public law issues identified in the context of the OBOR relate to WTO compliance and the proliferation and construction of the FTAs and BITs. The private law space concerns itself with

26 The Wharton School of the University of Pennsylvania (n 9).

27 World Trade Organization, 'Trade Policy Review: Report by the Secretariat – People's Republic of China' (WT/TPR/S/161) <https://docs.wto.org/dol2fe/Pages/FE_Search/FE_S_S009-DP.aspx?language=E&CatalogueIdList=54155,68101,65948,67571,33013&CurrentCatalogueIdIndex=1&FullTextHash=&HasEnglishRecord=True&HasFrenchRecord=True&HasSpanishRecord=True> accessed 19 August 2017.

28 World Trade Organization, 'DS431: China – Measures Related to the Exportation of Rare Earths, Tungsten and Molybdenum' <www.wto.org/english/tratop_e/dispu_e/cases_e/ds431_e.htm> accessed 27 October 2017.

29 World Trade Organization, 'China – Rare Earths (DS431, 432, 433)' <www.wto.org/english/tratop_e/dispu_e/cases_e/1pagesum_e/ds431sum_e.pdf> accessed 27 October 2017.

30 World Trade Organization (n 28).

contractual issues such as the determination on jurisdictional issues and governing law.

In this chapter, the question of the utility to introduce a common contract model as the preferred option will be addressed.

Investment risk

Considering high-value inter-country investments, investment protection is a pertinent question. The International Centre for Settlement of Investment Disputes (ICSID) provides this protection and most countries along the proposed OBOR corridors have ratified the 'Convention on the Settlement of Investment Disputes between States and Nationals of Other States, Washington, 18 March 1965'. Concerns about non-accession and non-ratification of the ICSID Convention apart from the eventuality of a country terminating the BITs remain. Ecuador has just done so:

> On May 3, 2017, the Ecuadorian National Assembly approved a proposal to terminate Ecuador's BIT's with Argentina, Bolivia, Canada, Chile, China, Italy, the Netherlands, Peru, Spain, Switzerland, the United States and Venezuela. Ecuador announced its intention to renegotiate these and other investment treaties on terms that it considers more favourable.[31]

Arguably, ICSID will play an important role, as most of the Central Asian countries, including Russia, pose a substantial operational and credit risk.[32] This is pursuant to a report of the Economic Intelligence Unit, whose overall country credit-risk rating is derived by evaluating risk across sovereign, currency, banking sector, politics and economic structure.[33] The issue of sovereign risk also plays an important role. Venezuela 'has received a sizeable share of Chinese credit, struggles to repay its US$56 billion in loans as the oil price tumbles and its economy falters'.[34] Kazakhstan and other Central Asian countries are increasingly driven by nationalist agendas. The share of oil and gas owned by Chinese companies is of concern and any investor should consider hiring Kazak nationals where possible.[35]

However, in this context, consideration must also be given to the development in India in relation to BITs. India has suspended the Foreign Investment

31 Debevoise & Plimpton, 'Ecuador to Terminate Investment Treaties' (11 May 2017) <www.debevoise.com/~/media/files/insights/publications/2017/05/20170511a_ecuador_bit.pdf> accessed 10 July 2017.

32 The Economic Intelligence Unit, 'Prospects and Challenges on China's "One Belt, One Road" a Risk Assessment Report' (2015) <https://static1.squarespace.com/static/529fcf02e4b0aa09f5b7ff67/t/554c49cee4b06fc215162cb4/1431062990726/One+Belt%2C+One+Road.pdf> accessed 10 July 2017.

33 *Ibid.*

34 *Ibid.*, 10.

35 *Ibid.*, 11.

Promotion Board (FIPB), and it has also terminated BITs with key trading partners.[36] The relevant sectoral department would, henceforth, handle approvals for investments: '[G]iven that sectoral regulators would likely have a narrow sector-specific outlook when reviewing proposals, it is hoped that the government will draw on the expertise of former FIPB officials to ease the transition'.[37]

It would not be to India's advantage not to participate in the OBOR and also lose its status of a preferred investment state. It should be noted that India has signed BITs with more than 80 countries since 1994, although negotiations with the United States for a BIT have hit a roadblock on concerns related to the Investor-state Dispute Settlement (ISDS).[38] Of concern to investors is that '[i]n 2016, the Indian government also requested that counterparties to 25 existing BITs (including China, Mexico and Turkey) revise their BITs in line with India's joint interpretative statement'.[39]

Free Trade Agreements (FTAs)

China has concluded a few FTAs with ASEAN and Australasian countries; however, India and the European region, except for Switzerland, are yet to engage with China through FTAs. The existing FTAs are:[40]

- ASEAN — ASEAN-China Free Trade Area (2015)
- Australia — China-Australia Free Trade Agreement (2015)
- Hong Kong — Mainland and Hong Kong Closer Economic Partnership Arrangement (CEPA) (2003)
- Macau — Mainland and Macau Closer Economic Partnership Agreement (CEPA) (2003)
- New Zealand — New Zealand-China Free Trade Agreement (2008)
- Pakistan — China-Pakistan Free Trade Agreement (2007)
- Taiwan — Economic Cooperation Framework Agreement (2010)
- Singapore — China-Singapore Free Trade Agreement (2008)
- South Korea — China-South Korea Free Trade Agreement (2015)
- Switzerland — China-Switzerland Free Trade Agreement (2014)
- Georgia — China-Georgia Free Trade Agreement (2017)

36 Debevoise & Plimpton, 'India Disbands the FIPB and Endangers BITs: One Step Forward, Two Steps Back?' (30 June 2017) <www.debevoise.com/~/media/files/insights/publications/2017/06/20170630_india_disbands_the_fipb_and_endangers_bits_one_step_forward_two_steps_back.pdf> accessed 10 July 2017.

37 *Ibid.*

38 Nayanima Basu, 'US Junks Bilateral Investment Treaty Talks' *The Hindu Business Line* (28 June 2017) <www.thehindubusinessline.com/economy/policy/us-junks-bilateral-investment-treaty-talks/article9740501.ece> accessed 28 October 2017.

39 Debevoise & Plimpton (n 36).

40 See The Ministry of Commerce, People's Republic of China, 'China FTA Network' <http://fta.mofcom.gov.cn/english/fta_qianshu.shtml> accessed 27 October 2017.

While FTAs could be trade facilitators, more FTAs with the same country, but with different rules, is not conducive for Small and Medium-sized Enterprises (SMEs), as they struggle with the regulatory requirements. In addition, the lag time for commencement is sometimes ten years. Hence, no immediate benefits will accrue. Most importantly, the accrual of FTA-related benefits is only at the border but does not reach beyond the border, namely the creation of a common contract law.

Contract issues

Many international conventions and model laws notwithstanding, the main issue where there is no real cohesion is in the area of contract law. The question always is which governing law and relevant jurisdiction is applicable. Of course, it is possible – if both parties agree – to nominate a commonly used law and a jurisdiction – which is used within the trade. As an example, English laws are chosen for many commodity sales and London is nominated as the seat for arbitration to resolve disputes in these transactions. London courts have developed expertise in managing maritime disputes. However, as far as the underlying sale of goods contract is concerned, this is not the case.

Two issues need to be addressed: a review of contract designs and the introduction of harmonised contract laws. Both approaches need to be in tandem with each other in order to gain maximum benefits. Frydlinger and others have argued:

> Indeed, 2016 Nobel prize winner Oliver Hart has showed that most contracts are incomplete. As we have written, today's business environment is complex, fast moving and unpredictable. Supply and demand change quickly. Market threats come from all angles, ranging from new competitors, customer hypes, disrupting technology, regulation and unpredictable events such as dramatic fluctuation of oil prices. Essentially, we are dealing with a growing volume of the unknown or the unknowable. Relationships must be designed, not to eliminate these realities, but to cope with them. The transactional contract has no mechanisms for achieving the much needed flexibly and collaboration that is demanded by today's environment.[41]

With the complexity of commerce along the China-EU corridor, relational contracts could come of importance as the OBOR opens new opportunities in international trade and, therefore, the rise of a new economy.

41 David Frydlinger and others, 'Unpacking Relational Contracts' (Haslam College of Business, University of Tennessee, Knoxville) <www.vestedway.com/wp-content/uploads/2016/10/Unpacking-Relational-Contracting_v19.pdf> accessed 27 October 2017 (available upon registration), see page 16.

Relational contracts

A relational contract has been described as:

> *A legally enforceable written contract establishing a commercial relationship within a flexible contractual framework based on social norms and jointly defined objectives, prioritizing a relationship with continuous alignment of interests before the commercial transactions.*[42]

In essence, it incorporates a social norm that is a cultural element into a formal contract. This is always valued in Asia, as exemplified in China, where there is the desire to renegotiate contracts through amicable discussion of mutually acceptable solutions, rather than through litigation.

Relational contracts are formal contracts; hence they include the more formalistic view expressed in Europe. Contracts are often based on price and power, but they also involve problem solving and joint working as well as personal relationships. Economists and psychologists have also been concerned with the notable factors in designing a successful relational contract.[43] In brief, the objective of a relational contract should be outcome based or output based, such as increasing customer satisfaction or gaining market share.[44] However, the end goal that is outcome-based must take into consideration factors such as risk allocation and – importantly – changes in the market place. The occurrence of market-related as well as strategic changes is often an inevitability and hence a capacity to shift priorities must be inbuilt into a relational contract.[45] The best example of focusing on an end-goal is supplied by the OBOR itself, where China is investing billions of dollars to create a network of trade which – costly in the development stage – will benefit the country in the long term.

Importantly, the relational contract is not a benevolent model. Profit is still important, otherwise, businesses would come to a standstill. However, the purpose of the relational contract is to create continuous alignment of interests:

> The very process of creating the relational contract enables the parties to solve the often toughest part of any commercial negotiation – the price/value negotiation. As a result of adopting the guiding principles, the parties will be both obliged and incentivized to find a model that,

42 *Ibid.*, 5 (Italics contained in the original text).

43 See, for example: Daniel Kahneman, *Thinking, Fast and Slow* (Farrar, Straus and Giroux 2011); Susan Helper and Rebecca Hendersen, 'Management Practices, RelationalContracts, and the Decline of General Motors' (2014) 28(1) *The Journal of Economic Perspectives* 49; Kate Vitasek and others, 'Unpacking Collaborative Bidding: Harnessing the Potential of Supplier Collaboration While Still Using a Competitive Bid Process' (The Haslam College of Business, The University of Tennessee, Knoxville) <www.vestedway.com/wp-content/uploads/2017/08/Unpacking-Collaborative-Bidding_2017.pdf> (accessed 27 October 2017 – available upon registration).

44 Frydlinger (n 41), 31.

45 *Ibid.*

> without usage of power, respects loyalty and equity, i.e. that treats both parties' interests with equal value and apply proportion between risk and rewards.[46]

The OBOR by definition will create a complex network of opportunities and hence strategic agreements are necessary in sourcing the relevant economic assets that are required to grow a business. As Frydlinger and others put it:

> The relational contract will and should not replace the transactional contract. Instead, it is necessary to incorporate transactional and relational contracts into a more comprehensive system that explains the characteristics of both, including explaining when each contract model is needed.[47]

Transnational contracting could be further improved and rationalised through harmonised sale laws. Legal cost-reduction apart, importantly both parties would be relying on the same contract structure. To that end, the CISG as a Convention and the UNIDROIT Principles as model law should be used in tandem.

Harmonised contract law

Considering the multitude of countries participating in the OBOR, a harmonised contract law is, in the short term, out of reach. Considering that the EU has not yet managed to agree on a model – despite three versions of a harmonised contract law having been devised – speaks for itself. The three attempts were the Principles of European Contract Law, the Draft Common Frame of Reference and the Common European Sales Law. Despite these attempts, a common contract law has not been established. A further complication is that specifically in the Asian region the uptake of the CISG has been less than desirable, and in particular it should be noted that the South Asian region countries have not taken to the Convention. Because China, the driver of the OBOR, is a Convention country, as are many of the European countries along the OBOR route, non-Convention countries along the OBOR might be persuaded to adopt the CISG, leading to the Convention becoming the governing law for contracts. Simply put, this Convention could become the choice of law within the OBOR. Of significance is the fact that infrastructure investment and construction, supported by the export of equipment and machinery, is a contractual issue involving goods.

The facts speak for themselves, considering that 88 countries so far have introduced the CISG into their domestic legal systems.[48] It is estimated that

46 *Ibid.*, 32.
47 *Ibid.*, 42.
48 The United Nations Commission on International Trade Law, 'Status: United Nations Convention on Contracts for the International Sale of Goods (Vienna 1980)' <www.uncitral.org/uncitral/en/uncitral_texts/sale_goods/1980CISG_status.html> accessed 27 October 2017.

80% of the world's trade in goods is potentially governed by the CISG.[49] In addition, a gradual removal of reservations by Contracting States has contributed to an international harmonisation of the CISG. It should be remembered that the drafters' intent when the uniform rules were being designed was to:[50]

> take into account the different social, economic and legal systems [which] would contribute to the removal of legal barriers in international trade and promote the development of international trade.

Even if most OBOR countries will ratify the CISG, the legal system in every country will take some time to adjust to the new regime. In Vietnam – a country that has recently ratified the CISG – contracts are rooted in statutes, a reminder of the French colonial influence. The Economic Intelligence Unit has set it out as follows:

> Judges think little of contradicting themselves or the rulings of other courts. Moreover, there is little in the way of historical case law to provide foreign investors with fair warning of potential pitfalls. Contract negotiations can be lengthy and obtaining project approval from the government is often delayed. Businesses are advised to consider whether it is worth including clauses in contracts that allow disputes to be dealt with by the Singapore Court of Arbitration. Before attempting to resolve a contractual matter in the courts or through arbitration, it is advisable first to exhaust all avenues of negotiation.[51]

Unfortunately, the CISG is not a code and gaps still need to be filled by domestic law, which reduces the efficiency of a common contract law. Another issue is that many companies routinely exclude the application of the CISG despite its usefulness. One of the misconceptions is that the legal profession in many instances has not recognised that the correct interpretation of conventions and model laws can create an economic benefit as it alleviates the need to learn the rules of a different legal system or hire lawyers familiar with the applicable foreign law. The advantage of uniform rules has been noted as early as 1980 by the House of Lords in *Fothergill v Monarch Airlines Ltd*[52] interpreting the 'Convention for the Unification of certain rules relating to international carriage by air, 12 October 1929' ('Warsaw Convention'). Lord Scarman summed it all up when he stated:

> Rules contained in an international convention are the outcome of an international conference; if, as in the present case, they operate within

49 Ingeborg Schwenzer and Christopher Kee, 'International Sales Law – The Actual Practice' (2011) 29 *Penn State International Law Review* 425, 428.

50 The United Nation Commission on International Trade Law, 'United Nations Convention on Contracts for the International Sale of Goods' www.uncitral.org/pdf/english/texts/sales/cisg/V1056997-CISG-e-book.pdf> accessed 27 October 2017, see Preamble at paragraph 3.

51 The Economic Intelligence Unit (n 32), 11.

52 [1981] A.C. 251.

> the field of private law, they will come under the consideration of foreign courts; and uniformity is the purpose to be served by most international conventions, and we know that unification of the rules relating to international air carriage is the object of the Warsaw Convention. It follows that our judges should be able to have recourse to the same aids to interpretation as their brother judges in the other contracting states. The mischief of any other view is illustrated by the instant case. To deny them this assistance would be a damaging blow to the unification of the rules which was the object of signing and then enacting the Convention. Moreover, the ability of our judges to fulfil the purpose of the enactment would be restricted, and the persuasive authority of their judgments in the jurisdictions of the other contracting states would be diminished.[53]

These words have a parallel in the desire of the Chinese government in the implementation of the OBOR. Obviously, a successful OBOR would require simplification of the logistics in tandem with simplifying the legal issues emanating from transport and contracts. The two issues that need consideration here are whether regional harmonisation of contract law contributes effectively in reducing barriers to trade, and whether the CISG should be expanded.

As far as the first issue is concerned, the failed attempts in Europe and the negative reception of the Principles of Asian Contract Law have shown that this is not a successful path to take in the unification process of contract law.[54]

As to the second issue, the Villanova Conference in 2013 emphatically rejected the notion of an expansion of the CISG through the proposed Swiss initiative at the 45th meeting at the UNCITRAL.[55] Also suggestions that a protocol should be adopted to overcome some of the gaps in the CISG is equally doomed to fail.[56] Either proposal would require ratifications by States and the problem which could arise is that two 'versions' of the CISG are in existence which would certainly not contribute to a global harmonising of at least sale laws. The best example is found in shipping law where the 'International Convention for the Unification of Certain Rules of Law relating to Bills of Lading signed at Brussels, 25th August 1924' (The 'Hague Rules'), as amended by the Protocols signed at Brussels on 23rd February 1968 and by the Protocol signed at Brussels on 21st December 1979 (the 'Hague-Visby Rules'), still dominate the field but the 'United Nations Convention on

53 *Ibid*., 294.

54 See Shiyuan Han, 'Principles of Asian Contract Law: An Endeavour of Regional Harmonisation of Contract Law in East Asia' (2013) 58 *Villanova Law Review* 589; see also Bruno Zeller, 'Regional Harmonisation of Contract law – Is It Feasible?' (2016) 3(1) *Journal of Law, Society and Development* 85.

55 See, in general, Keith Loken, 'A New Global Initiative on Contract Law in UNCITRAL: Right Project, Right Forum?' (2013) 58 *Villanova Law Review* 509.

56 See, in general, Jadranka Petrovic and others, 'The Exclusion of the Validity of the Contract from the CISG: Does It Still Matter?' (2017) 2 *Journal of Business Law* 101.

the Carriage of Goods by Sea, Hamburg, 31stMarch 1978' (the 'Hamburg Rules') have also been ratified albeit by a small and relatively unimportant group of nations. In the case of the 'United Convention on Contracts for the International Carriage of Goods Wholly or Partly by Sea, signed at Rotterdam on 23rd September 2009' (the 'Rotterdam Rules'), there is no sign of this coming into force for at least the foreseeable future.

The question of regional harmonisation has not found traction and can arguably be dismissed as not being superior to a simple acceptance of the CISG.[57] In addition, any regional contract principles are only model laws and require inclusion into the contract in order to have the force of law.

A far superior proposition is to include the 'UNIDROIT Principles on International Commercial Contracts 2010' into a contract in addition to the CISG. Kronke, supporting the conjunctive reading of the UNIDROIT Principles and the CISG, observed:

> What we see looking at the two instruments – the CISG as the mother of all modern conventions on the law of specific contracts and the [UNIDROIT Principles] as the (inevitably) soft-law source of modern general contract law – are neither competitors nor apples nor pears. What we see is actually, and even more, potentially a fruitful coexistence. . . [T]he UNIDROIT Contract Principles are, obviously, complementary in that they address a wide range of topics of general contract law which neither the CISG nor any other existing or future convention devoted to a specific type of transaction would ever venture to touch upon.[58]

The UNIDROIT-recommended model clause reads:

> **The contract shall be governed by the United Nations Convention on Contracts for the International Sale of Goods (CISG) interpreted and supplemented by the UNIDROIT Principles of International Commercial Contracts.**
>
> **(2010)**[59]

The author is of the opinion that this clause is best used in scenarios involving the Convention as the governing law of the contract. In other cases, it

57 See, in general, Bruno Zeller, 'The Development of a Global Contract Law: Still a Dream?' in UNIDROIT (ed), *Eppur si muove: The Age of Uniform Law: Essays in Honour of Michael Joachim Bonell to Celebrate His 70th Birthday Volume 2* (The International Institute for the Unification of Private Law 2016) 1179. See also Bruno Zeller (n 54).

58 Herbert Kronke, 'The UN Sales Convention, The UNIDROIT Contract Principles and The Way Forward' (2005) 25 *Journal of Law and Commerce* 451, 458–459.

59 International Institute for the Unification of Private Law, 'Model Clauses for the Use of the UNIDROIT Principles of International Commercial Contracts' <www.unidroit.org/instruments/commercial-contracts/upicc-model-clauses> accessed 28 October 2017 (bold font followed the original text).

would be appropriate to also include into the clause the governing law to fill gaps left by the Convention and the UNIDROIT Principles, as they require the assistance of a governing domestic law in order to cover gaps. It must be noted that neither of the two instruments are codes and hence gaps are inevitable. Specifically in the Convention, gaps exist because States in the ratifying process could not agree on the inclusion of certain principles such as validity of contract as noted in Article 4.[60]

The UNIDROIT Principles do include matters which are outside the Convention but are relevant in contracting such as authority of agents, defects of consent, set-off – just to mention a few. Of importance is the treatment of third party rights under the UNIDROIT Principles.[61] It is modelled on the civil law maxim of *alteri stipulari nemo potest*, that is, to quote the Swiss Code of Obligations, Article 112(1):

> A person who, acting in his own name, has entered into a contract whereby performance is due to a third party is entitled to compel performance for the benefit of said third party.[62]

This aspect is most important if exemption clauses are envisaged which attempt to protect all participants within the supply chain such as independent contractors. They still adhere to the privity rule, which states that a person who is not a party to a contract can neither enforce a contract (i.e. to take benefits from it) nor incur any liability. This rule was firmly established in English law in *Dunlop Pneumatic Tyre Company, Limited v Selfridge and Company, Limited*.[63]

Interpretation of harmonised contract

It needs to be noted that no contract – relational or otherwise – is ever complete. Hence interpretation of contracts, although a malediction and a benediction at the same time,[64] is inevitable.

The tools of interpretation differ and are dependent upon the chosen jurisdiction. One fact is clear – in a changing environment, to include the 'entire agreement' clause into the contract is not as wise as the written contract alone is decisive.

60 Article 4 of the CISG provides: 'This Convention governs only the formation of the contract of sale and the rights and obligations of the seller and the buyer arising from such a contract. In particular, except as otherwise expressly provided in this Convention, it is not concerned with: (a) the validity of the contract or of any of its provisions or of any usage; (b) the effect which the contract may have on the property in the goods sold'.

61 See Articles 5.2.1 – Article 5.2.6 of the UNIDROIT Principles.

62 'Federal Act on the Amendment of the Swiss Civil Code (Part Five: The Code of Obligations)' <www.admin.ch/opc/en/classified-compilation/19110009/201704010000/220.pdf> accessed 28 October 2018.

63 [1915] A.C. 847.

64 Guyla Eorsi, 'General Provisions' in Nina M. Galston and Hans Smith (eds), *International Sales: the United Nations Convention on Contracts for the International Sale of Goods* (M. Bender 1984), paras 2–1–2–36.

Hence the Convention and the UNIDROIT Principles, specifically the principles on the interpretation of contracts and the behaviour of parties, based on good faith and the subjective intent, are of immense assistance in interpreting contracts in the light of the aspiration of the parties. Article 8 of the Convention and Articles 4.1 to 4.8 of the UNIDROIT Principles – in contrast to the common law – allow for consideration of the subjective intent of the parties expressed either in pre-contractual, contractual or post-contractual negotiations. Article 8 – in effect duplicated into the UNIDROIT Principles – states:

1 For the purposes of this Convention statements made by and other conduct of a party are to be interpreted according to his intent where the other party knew or could not have been unaware what that intent was.
2 If the preceding paragraph is not applicable, statements made by and other conduct of a party are to be interpreted according to the understanding that a reasonable person of the same kind as the other party would have had in the same circumstances.
3 In determining the intent of a party or the understanding of a reasonable person would have had, due consideration is to be given to all relevant circumstances of the case including the negotiations, any practices which the parties have established between themselves, usages and any subsequent conduct of the parties.

The first issue arises with the division of subjective and objective intent of the parties. Article 8(1) directs the courts to investigate the subjective intent first and only if subsection (1) is not applicable can subsection 8(2), namely the objective intent, be applied.

The only difference, therefore, is that Article 8(1) relies on the parties to show that there was a 'meeting of the mind', whereas Article 8(2) relies on the reasonable person (*vernünftige* person) test if the first approach does not supply an answer. It can be argued that as both approaches look at the same matter – that is, not only the conduct of the parties but also the statement made by the parties – logically the subjective issue is to be resolved first before an objective approach is to be attempted.

Obviously, statements made by each party need to be objectively tested before they can be treated as facts. In a transnational setting, this approach is arguably superior to the common law approach where only the objective approach is applied, namely the parol evidence rule.[65] McLauchlan asked the penetrating question:[66]

65 'If there be a contract which has been reduced into writing, verbal evidence is not allowed to be given of what passed between the parties, either before the written instrument was made or during the time that it was in a state of preparation, so as to add to or subtract from or in any matter to vary or quality the written contract. This is the classical exposition of the so-called parol evidence rule, a rule which, in truth, extends to all extrinsic evidence, whether oral or otherwise, and which, moreover, is in some respects a rule of substantive law rather than a mere rule of evidence'. Ewan McKendirck, *Goode on Commercial Law* (4th edn, Penguin Books 2010), 101.

66 David McLauchlan, 'Common Assumptions and Contract Interpretation' (1997) 113 *Law Quarterly Review* 237, 242.

> Why allow evidence of the fact that the parties have "united in rejecting" a particular meaning, but disallow evidence of the fact that the parties have united in accepting a particular meaning?

The CISG as well as the UNIDROIT Principles have answered this question by first looking at the subjective intent of the parties in order to ascertain what the particular meaning is which the parties have established amongst themselves. How to determine the intent of the parties has been explained in subsection 8(3). By using the terms such as 'including' and 'determining the intent' which are replacing interpretation indicates that the court is at liberty to define the intent of the parties to their satisfaction. To illustrate the point, *TeeVee Toons, Inc v Gerhard Schubert GMBH*[67] is of interest. One of the clauses was a merger clause which reads:

> This quotation comprises our entire quotation. On any order placed pursuant hereto, the above provisions entirely supersede any prior correspondence, quotation or agreement. There are no agreements between us in respect of the product quoted herein except as set forth in writing and expressly made a part of this quotation.[68]

There is no doubt that under common law such a clause would be valid and enforced, as the parol evidence rule recognises the merger clause as the complete writing. However, under the Convention, to interpret the whole contract including the merger clause Article 8 is applied. Hence the question is: what did the parties subjectively know or should not have been unaware what the terms of the contract were? Casey J noted that 'only if both Schubert and TVT shared the intent to be bound by the Merger Clause contained in the "Terms and Conditions" is the Merger Clause operative'.[69] The Court further noted that prior extrinsic evidence can have the effect to disregard boilerplate language that includes a merger clause, and therefore it trumps the written merger clause itself.[70]

The United States District Court of Colorado in *Alpha Prime Development Corporation v Holland Loader Company, LLC; and Steven Michael Svatek*[71] noted two important facts. First, '[t]he text and commentary to the CISG show that a writing between the parties is not conclusive of the terms of their agreement'[72] and that second '[a] writing is one, but only one, of many

67 No 00 Civ. 5189 (RCC) (United States District Court, Southern District of New York. The full text is available at <http://cisgw3.law.pace.edu/cases/060823u1.html> accessed 10 July 2017.

68 *Ibid.*

69 *Ibid.*

70 *Ibid.*

71 Civil Action NO.09-cv-01763-WYD-KMT (United States District Court of the District of Colorado). The full text is available at <http://cisgw3.law.pace.edu/cases/100706u1.html> accessed 10 July 2017.

72 *Ibid.*

circumstances to be considered when establishing and interpreting the terms of a contract'.[73]

On the surface, it might show that the Convention does not foster certainty as a writing is not conclusive proof of the terms of the contract, as the subjective view can even change merger clauses. However, the fact is – as indicated earlier – contracts are never complete, as not all intentions of the parties are locked into a contract. By analogy, a person writing a letter to a friend will not include facts both know. As correctly stated by the United States District Court of the Eastern District of Pennsylvania in *ECEM European Chemical Marketing B.V v The Purolite Company*:

> The standard UCC inquiry regarding whether a writing is fully or partially integrated has little meaning under the CISG and courts are therefore less constrained by the "four corners" of the instrument in construing the terms of the contract.[74]

It is not the clarity of the terms which is the primary consideration but whether the parties intended otherwise clear terms to be included into their contractual obligations. With this ability of Article 8, merger clauses and other terms or conditions cannot be given a literal interpretation if they run contrary to the intentions of the parties. In *MCC-Marble Ceramic Center Inc v Ceramica Nuova D' Agostino, S.p.A*,[75] the court ruled clearly under this mandate and noted:

> [The buyer] did not intend to agree to the terms on the reverse of the form contract. The acknowledgement that [seller's] representatives were aware of [the buyer's] subjective intent puts this case squarely with article 8(1) of the CISG, and therefore requires the court to consider [buyer's] evidence as it interprets the parties' conduct.[76]

The previous narrative, drawing from case law from common law jurisdictions to explain Article 8, clearly indicates that contrary to the parol evidence rule, the true intent of the parties can be elicited and the four corners of the contract are not a constraint. Subsection 8(3) indeed explains the circumstance which can be taken into account when interpreting the contract. The four

73 *Ibid.*

74 Civil Action No. 05–3078 (United States District Court for the Eastern District of Pennsylvania). The full text is available at <http://cisgw3.law.pace.edu/cases/100129u1.html> accessed 10 July 2017 quoted from *Calzaturifio Claudia S. n c v Olivieri Footwear Ltd* (United States District Court, Southern District of New York) 1998 U.S. Dist. Lexis 4586.

75 No. 97–4250 (United States Court of Appeals for the Eleventh Circuit). The full text is available at <http://cisgw3.law.pace.edu/cases/980629u1.html> accessed 10 July 2017.

76 *Ibid.*

corner rule[77] came to be included as being part of Article 8(3) by the Court of Appeal *(Obergericht)* of the Canton of Thurgau:[78]

> According to Art.8(3) CISG, the enquiry into a party's actual intent as well as into the recipient's perspective must take into account all relevant circumstances, such as the mentioned established practices, usages and subsequent conduct of the parties . . . The Convention requires that the interpretation take account of the contract as a whole. Individual clauses must be considered as an integral part of the contract and are to be interpreted in their context rather than in isolation.

Conclusion

This chapter has indicated that a project of such magnitude as China's OBOR will pose challenges for businesses not only to adjust their dealings but also to develop a legal framework which will take account of the new opportunities. In addition, governments also need to adjust FTAs and BITs in view of the challenges, which in size herald a new economic plan.

The OBOR could be the opportunity to usher a new transnational legal landscape where harmonised laws are applicable not just at the border but also beyond the border regulations. The CISG as well as the UNIDROIT Principles in tandem are perfect tools with which to establish a harmonised contact law, which in turn would help augment the supply lines along the road. In addition, relational contracts are best suited to take advantage of a harmonised contract law, as one constant factor has become part of the negotiations. The importance in the combination of a Convention and a Model Law is that it covers the multitude of jurisdictions along the Silk Road and will enhance the benefits of the proposed new economic orders.

77 See Bruno Zeller, '*Four-Corners* – The Methodology for Interpretation and Application of the UN Convention on Contracts for the International Sale of Goods' <http://cisgw3.law.pace.edu/cisg/biblio/4corners.html> accessed 10 July 2017.

78 ZBR.2006.26 (Court of Appeal *(Obergericht)* of the Canton of Thurgau, Switzerland *(Building Materials Case)*. The English translation is available at <http://cisgw3.law.pace.edu/cases/061212s1.html> accessed 10 July 2017.

9 Thai conflict of law rules, China's One Belt One Road initiative and ASEAN trade facilitation

One common path with many exit routes

Kittiwat Chunchaemsai

Introduction

Once the Chinese government has implemented the One Belt One Road initiative, reinventing new trade routes to the world, opportunities for prosperity will be generated across the globe. Thailand as well as most, if not all, ASEAN countries are invited to take part. To implement such a great enterprise, plans are in progress to build infrastructure such as roads and rail across the connecting countries in order to respond to the New Silk Road initiative. Completion of such physical infrastructure will create necessary links along the route, and undoubtedly these can be constructed within a calculable period of time.

However, what about the regulatory infrastructure? What about the law and legal systems along this gigantic transnational network? Does a unified law or perhaps a harmonious legal system need to be developed throughout the road and rail networks so as to facilitate trade flows along the Belt and the Road countries within the ASEAN region? To be more specific, should a collective public policy be established among ASEAN members? Where the function of private international law or conflict of laws is to reveal the law of only one (i.e. the most connected) country that shall govern a legal issue arising out of a transnational transaction, application of such law is not an easy task when the *lex fori* offers underlying escape devices. Should the my-country-first approach be adopted, it could result in a perhaps undesired scenario wherein the law of not one but many countries applies, depending on where or in which country the truck or the train is forced to make a stop.

This chapter, despite limited availability of academic resources, attempts to articulate the conjugation between policy and conflict of laws surrounding China's initiative and the ASEAN trade facilitation. The introduction is followed by an elaboration of the clash of policy and law in the next part. This section also expounds the policy among the member-countries and China, building the foundation for a common path. Subsequently, in the following section, in contrast, is an attempt to point out some legal issues on conflict of laws that are unlikely to support the hard infrastructure. Its focus is on a simple question of public policy, prescription, and conflict of laws. In the last part, this chapter author attempts a diagnostic approach, suggesting possible methods for resolving the concerns and closing as many exit routes as possible. The conclusion is then drawn with a plea for further engagement on the subject.

Policy and law as soft infrastructure in one common path

Weaving a common legal system, either as a hard-law or soft-law infrastructure, threading together the linkages between nations presents a significant challenge for countries along the OBOR. As 'markets require a legal infrastructure',[1] and a legal infrastructure requires a political will,[2] a collective political resolve among relevant countries then drives the legal infrastructure reform and, hence, the market development.

It is well acknowledged that Southeast Asia is diverse. Legal traditions are individualised according to the municipal domains and units of each country so that, perhaps greatly, some may differ from others. To avoid conflict-of-laws problems, unification and harmonisation either of substantive law or private international law are occasionally called upon, although not much progress seems to have been made.[3] The ASEAN way of consultation and consensus alongside policy-based approach and soft-law mechanisms is strongly embedded within the region's operation. A rule-based approach and hard-law mechanisms seem to be less available. It is, therefore, suggested here that establishing firm common policy goals is the very first step towards regional legal infrastructure and market.

ASEAN's collective policy goals and commitment

Based on the soft mechanism, collective policy goals responding indirectly, if not directly, to the Chinese initiative seem to be well progressed in the

1 Tamar Frankel, 'The Legal Infrastructure of Markets: The Role of Contract and Property' (1993) 73 *Boston University Law Review* 389, 404; Edward S. Knight, 'Legal Infrastructure for the New Global Marketplace' (2000) 34 *The International Lawyer* 211.

2 Richard A. Posner, 'Creating a Legal Framework for Economic Development' (1998) 13(1) *The World Bank Research Observer* 1.

3 Bajuseto Hardjowahono, *The Unification of Private International Law on International Commercial Contracts Within the Regional Legal System of ASEAN* (Hephaestus Publishers 2005); Gary Bell, 'Harmonisation of Contract Law in ASIA – Harmonising Regionally or Adopting Global Harmonisations – The Example of the CISG' (2005) *Singapore Journal of Legal Studies* 362; Erman Rajagukguk, 'Harmonization of Law in ASEAN Countries Towards Economic Integration' (2012) 9 *Jurnal Hukum Internasional* 529; Joanne Wong, 'On Legal Harmonisation Within ASEAN' (2013/2014) 5 *Juris* <www.singaporelawreview.com/juris-illuminae-entries/2015/on-legal-harmonisation-within-asean> accessed 15 December 2017.

ASEAN community. From the course of cooperation, trade facilitation has been advanced continuously. Declared in its Blueprint 2015, the ASEAN Economic Community (AEC) has envisioned 'trade facilitation' in the following:

> Simple, harmonised and standardised trade and customs, processes, procedures and related information flows are expected to reduce transaction costs in ASEAN which will enhance export competitiveness and facilitate the integration of ASEAN into a single market for goods, services and investments and a single production base.[4]

With the vision translated into action,[5] the AEC Blueprint 2025 has recognised the progress of its predecessor and has carried on this task.[6] 'Accelerate and deepen the implementation of trade facilitation' is the current target. Strategic measures have been emphasised for the economic purpose of enhancing participation in Global Value Chains (GVC).[7] More importantly, in terms of transport facilitation cooperation, a vision towards 'greater connectivity, efficiency, integration, safety and sustainability of ASEAN transport to strengthen ASEAN's competitiveness and foster regional inclusive growth and development' has also been targeted.[8] These policy measures could ensure ASEAN's enhanced contribution to the OBOR.

Towards the development of legal infrastructure in ASEAN, several international and regional instruments have played an important role. Under the sharing-of-policy goal in establishing an ASEAN single market proclaimed by the ASEAN Charter,[9] the ASEAN Trade Facilitation Framework (ATFF) has been adopted. This regional framework is similar to the Trade Facilitation Agreement (TFA) under the World Trade Organization (WTO) and the Revised International Convention on the Simplification and Harmonization of Customs Procedures (the revised Kyoto Convention) under the World Customs Organization (WCO). The scope of ATFF covers general areas of (a) customs and transport facilitation, (b) transparency of trade regulation and procedures, (c) standards and conformance, and (d) private sector engagement and business facilitation, as well as specific areas of, for example, ASEAN Single Window (ASW), ASEAN Customs and Transit System (ACTS), ASEAN Trade Repository (ATR), ASEAN-wide system of Self-Certification, and ASEAN Solutions for Investments, Services and Trade (ASSIST).[10] To drive such a framework and to enhance coordination among the ASEAN members, the ASEAN Trade Facilitation Joint Consultative Committee (ATF-JCC) has been

4 AEC Blueprint 2015, para 16.
5 *Ibid.*
6 AEC Blueprint 2025, paras 9 and 10.
7 *Ibid.*, para 24.
8 *Ibid.*, para 46.
9 ASEAN Charter, art 1 (5).
10 ASEAN Trade Facilitation Framework, para 5.

established. In addition, in the context of transportation, two more frameworks have been proclaimed by ASEAN. One is the Framework Agreement on the Facilitation of Goods in Transit and the other is the Framework Agreement on the Facilitation of Inter-State Transport.[11] They reinforce the willingness to create integrated and efficient logistics and transportation systems within and beyond the region. The ASEAN Transport Strategic Plan 2016–2025 announced the transportation network plan within and outside the AEC. On implementation, these frameworks would help build facilities within the region that would together further the cross-border trade flowing from the Chinese trucks and trains to the ASEAN region's road and rail network and vice versa.

Thailand – current developments in conflict of laws

Thailand's response to the global and regional movements has been on similar lines to that of ASEAN. Trade facilitation has been declared as one of the country's strategic plans responding to both regional and international developments. According to Thailand's Twelfth National Economic and Social Development Plan (2017–2021), developing trade facilitation infrastructure and logistic and transport systems to meet international standards has been placed as one of the schemes under Part 4 Development Strategies, Strategy 3: Strategy for Strengthening the Economy, and Underpinning Sustainable Competitiveness.[12] This is to communicate to government agencies that a more proactive operation to reinforce and facilitate trade while focusing on supporting measures rather than controlling measures should be adopted and executed. Furthermore, in Strategy 7 in the same part, Strategy for Advancing Infrastructure and Logistics, transportation infrastructure, is also a means for improving competitiveness and efficiency of trade facilitation mechanisms in Thailand.

Thailand has been actively pursuing development strategies, similar to the recommendations related to ease of doing business measures publicised by the World Bank Group within its upstream administrative structure. Law Reform Commissions have been formulated in order to extensively review and reform laws and regulations in areas that may, for example, hinder business activities, place too much burden on people's lives, or be obsolete.[13] The World Bank Group Doing Business Report 2018 ranked Thailand at the 26th place out of 190 economies of small and medium enterprises around the world, as compared with the 48th place in 2017. Additionally, the country is admired as 'one of top 10 economies that have improved most in the ease of doing

11 See, respectively, ASEAN Framework Agreement on the Facilitation of Goods in Transit 1998 and ASEAN Framework Agreement on the Facilitation of Inter-State Transport 2009.

12 'The National Economic and Social Development Plan' *(Nesdb.go.th)* <www.nesdb.go.th/nesdb_en/ewt_w3c/main.php?filename=develop_issue> accessed 29 December 2017.

13 *(Thailawreform.go.th)* <www.thailawreform.go.th> accessed 15 December 2017.

business in the last year worldwide'.[14] Thailand so far seems to be sufficiently prepared for participating in the OBOR.

It could possibly be derived that policy and law as soft infrastructure among ASEAN countries, and especially in Thailand, share one common path. ASEAN's One Vision, One Community appears to correspond with the OBOR, and therefore conflicts of policy as well as regulatory competition could be diminished. Nonetheless, a recent field research study[15] has shown that, although under the collective policy targets and affiliated legal instruments, occurrence of conflict of laws is a reality. While policy could be loosely united through cooperation, legal regime unification may not be easy. For instance, in terms of trade facilitation issues between Thailand and CLMV countries (Cambodia, Laos PDR, Myanmar, and Vietnam), although they are all committed to the WTO's TFA and the ATFF, the laws and regulations in these countries vary. With implementation being individualised, regional integration could be possible only through extensive collaboration.

Conflict of laws as a legal junction to many exit routes

To sustain a common path among countries of the region, collective policy goals may be deployed while legal conflicts still remain. On the basis of the findings of the research jointly conducted by economists and lawyers, trade flows in the ASEAN are highly likely hampered by laws.[16] Outdated, incompatible, and inefficient laws and regulations of the ASEAN countries furthered by underdeveloped unification or harmonisation cause inconvenience in transnational business operations. Legal conflicts related to cross-border trade are prominent.[17] Of the laws affecting international trade in Thailand and CLMV legal systems, arbitration law seems to be the only area that is, to a certain extent, systematised, because all ASEAN members are Contracting States of the Convention on the Recognition and Enforcement of Foreign Arbitral Awards, 1958.[18] Other areas affecting international trade such as customs, transportation, intellectual property, dispute resolutions outside arbitration,

14 'Thailand Moves Up in Global Doing Business Ranks' (*World Bank* 2017) <www.worldbank.org/en/news/press-release/2017/11/01/thailand-moves-up-in-global-doing-business-ranks> accessed 15 December 2017; generally also World Bank, *Doing Business 2017: Equal Opportunity for All*, A World Bank Group Flagship Report (14th edn, World Bank 2017).

15 Kaewkwan Tangtipongkul (Project leader), Anin Aroonruengsawat, Kittiwat Chunchaemsai, Sittikorn Nippaya, Supachai Srisuchart, Aimpaga Techa-apikun, and Kriengkrai Techakanont, 'Analysis of the Effects and Utilization of Agreements and Cooperative Frameworks Related to Economics and International Trade in ASEAN Community', Thailand Research Paper, International Institute on Trade and Development, Thailand (forthcoming).

16 *Ibid.*

17 *Ibid.*

18 'Status' *(Uncitral.org)* <www.uncitral.org/uncitral/en/uncitral_texts/arbitration/NYConvention_status.html> accessed 17 December 2017.

and sales laws are underdeveloped, leading to the inevitability of conflict of laws situations. Given the notion that economic growth and legal systems are interrelated and interact with one another,[19] such conflict could certainly affect the advancement of the OBOR in the ASEAN.

Conflict of laws in context

A contemporary scenario on conflict of laws is characterised by individualisation rather than harmonisation. Harmonisation could be an important method by which to resolve the divergence of laws among countries through the application of appropriate connecting factors and subsequent governing law. Conflict of laws has taken some flak for the shortcomings[20] of its diverse approaches and complex methodologies, and the prevalence of forum laws are *inter alia* potential drawbacks in the determination of the appropriate applicable law in the ASEAN judicial systems. Availability of resources regarding the rules and their detailed application in the ten ASEAN member-states is also an area of difficulty.

There has been significant research on the harmonisation of the law related to international commercial contracts within the regional legal traditions of ASEAN.[21] Without overstating the achievements of harmonisation, this chapter advances an argument that harmonisation is not effective and efficient if the my-country-first approach is still embedded. To avoid such individualistic operation and be more harmonious, a regional approach should be mutually established, especially desisting from the diverse and complex methodologies of conflict of laws. This includes but is not limited to typical escape devices that may easily lead to the law of the country in which a legal action is heard, instead of the law of the connected foreign country.

Difficult, debatable, but unavoidable questions concerning traditional conflict of laws' approaches and methodologies applied as escape devices are to be raised as follows.

1 *renvoi*
2 proof of foreign law

19 Anthony Ogus, 'The Importance of Legal Infrastructure for Regulation (and Deregulation) in Developing Countries' (2003) 47 *Philippine Journal of Public Administration* 251; Daniel M. Klerman, 'Legal Infrastructure, Judicial Independence, and Economic Development' (2007) 19 *Global Business & Development Law Journal* 427.

20 Hardjowahono (n 3).

21 *Ibid*; see, Lim Yew Nghee, 'Towards a Uniform Conflict of Laws Regime in ASEAN Governing International Commercial Transactions: Uniformization of Choice of Law Rules in Contract and Tort' (LLM thesis, McGill University 2000); Bruno Zeller, 'Facilitating Regional Economic Integration: ASEAN, ATIGA and the CISG' in Ingeborg H. Schwenzer and Lisa Spagnolo (eds), *Towards Uniformity: The 2nd Annual MAA Schlechtriem CISG Conference* (Eleven International Publishing 2011); Shiyuan Han, 'Principles of Asian Contract Law: An Endeavor of Regional Harmonization of Contract Law in East Asia' (2013) 58 *Villanova Law Review* 589.

Should ASEAN member-states not take notice of the laws of fellow members, instead of calling for proof of such law(s)?

3 public policy

The following narrative attempts to present the possibility of collectivising public policy within the region. In other words, should public policy of the forum still be a powerful tool used for avoiding the application of other ASEAN members' laws?

The question needs to be addressed from the perspective of ASEAN trade facilitation, especially in the context of participation in the OBOR. The issue is whether a country's *lex fori* approach should be superseded by the region's *lex fori* approach, and if seen as complementary, the *lex causae* of other ASEAN countries or of ASEAN itself be supplemented to the law of the forum.

For conflict of laws to work effectively, an application of foreign law, where appropriate, is a must. Avoiding foreign applicable law, where possible, is not of its main purpose. However, the situation in Thailand is quite different. Under the Act on Conflict of Laws, Buddhist Era 2481, of Thailand,[22] several conflict-of-law rules have been, from time to time, applied as escape devices. Not proving foreign law has been the most popular channel. Public policy has been ranked second to not proving foreign law, whereas no reported case has ever been decided on the basis of the *renvoi* doctrine or the other conflict of laws approaches and methodologies.

Conflict in conflict of law devices

Consider three escape devices – that is, *renvoi*, proof of foreign law, and public policy – incompatibility is not hard to find. Conflict in conflict of laws is a regular occurrence in the pluralistic legal systems of the ASEAN community. This chapter attempts to articulate the application of these devices in Thailand and other ASEAN countries.

Renvoi

According to the Act on Conflict of Laws, Buddhist Era 2481, Section 4: 'Whenever the law of a foreign country is to govern and under that law it is

22 There has not yet been an English version of textbook explaining the Act in its entirety. At the time of writing, the author is working on it. For a summative explanation, see Chinnawat Thongpackdee and Vanina Sucharitkul in Alejandro Carballo Leyda, *Asian Conflict of Laws: East and South East Asia* (Kluwer 2015), 233; for a comparative discussion on Thai conflict of laws on contract, see Prasit Pivavatnapanich, 'Choice of Law in Contract and Thai Private International Law: A Comparative Study' <www.thailawforum.com/articles/choiceoflaw3.html> accessed 19 December 2017.

the law of [Thailand] which shall be applied, the internal law of [Thailand] governs, and not the [Thai] rules on conflict of laws'. The implication of this rule is remission. If a foreign law is the governing law, such reference shall include the conflict of law rules of that foreign legal system. However, where, by the foreign conflict of laws, it is the law of Thailand that shall govern, the relevant substantive law of Thailand shall apply to the case. There is no judicial delineation on this statutory provision relating to *renvoi*. Recent research published in Thai language argues for the exclusion of *renvoi* in part, if not *in toto*.[23]

The *renvoi* doctrine in other ASEAN countries, such as Vietnam, a civil law tradition, is akin to that of Thailand. While *renvoi* by remission is clearly accepted by legislation, in the Vietnamese Civil Code (2005), *renvoi* in the form of transmission is omitted.[24] In the common law system in Myanmar, the conflict of law rules are silent on *renvoi*,[25] whereas Malaysia's conflict of law rules, citing English common law, seem to accept in principle *renvoi* in the form of remission.[26] In the Philippines, operating in a mixed legal system, *renvoi* is very likely to be accepted through judicial decisions.[27] Despite all that, when a reference is made to what is claimed to be the Asian Principles of Private International Law (APPIL), an advanced proposal is that *renvoi* shall be excluded and that the foreign law shall be limited only to substantive rules of that foreign country.[28]

Proof of foreign law

Possibly, the most popular conflict of law provisions entertained in Thailand is Section 8. It prescribes:

> Whenever the law of a foreign country which is to govern is not proved to the satisfaction of the Court, the internal law of [Thailand] shall apply.

Much of case law from the Thai courts establishes the fact that foreign law has not been applied in many cases where it could have possibly been, for reasons

23 Kittiwat Chunchaemsai, 'The Abolition of *Renvoi* Doctrine in Conflict of Laws' (2017) 46 *Thammasat Law Journal* 69.

24 Thi Hong Trinh Nguyen, *Private International Law in Vietnam: On General Issues, Contracts and Tort* (Mohr Siebeck 2016), 56.

25 Adrian Briggs, *Private International Law in Myanmar* (University of Oxford, Faculty of Law 2015), 77.

26 R.H. Hickling and Wu Min Aun, *Conflict of Laws in Malaysia* (Butterworths Asia 1995), 32.

27 Jorge R. Coquia, 'A Restate of Conflict of Laws (Private International Law) for the Philippines' (1992) 67 *Philippine Law Journal* 121, 127; Fr Ranhilio Callangan Aquino, *Elements of Philippine Private International* Law (3rd edn, Centralbooks 2016), 151.

28 Weizuo Chen and Gerald Goldstein, 'The Asian Principles of Private International Law: Objectives, Contents, Structure and Selected Topics on Choice of Law' (2017) 13 *Journal of Private International Law* 411, 423.

of not being proved in the Thai courts.[29] This may result from the fact that such burden placed on the claimant is too much to bear or too unworthy to carry out. It may also be the legislative provision itself that is vague, or it may be the court's standard of proof that is unclear.

Considering the APPIL as an example, the principle of *ex officio* is put forward. This is, of course, against the usual practice of lawyers in Thailand. Similar to Malaysia and the Philippines, foreign law is considered as a matter of fact and the onus of proof is on litigants, although method of proof is likely to be more specified and exercised in the latter two countries than in the former.[30] Myanmar's legal system has similar provision – the judge has neither the power nor the duty to apply foreign law *ex officio*.[31] However, no firm stand is taken in the Vietnamese legislation on conflict of laws. A mixed approach between facultative and mandatory systems seems to be activated.[32]

Public policy[33]

Now, the last resort for a forum to exclude or evade an application of foreign law is public policy, or *order public* or, in Thai terminology, 'public order and good morals'. Section 5 of the Act on Conflict of Laws, Buddhist Era 2481 states: 'Whenever a law of a foreign country is to govern, it shall apply in so far as it is not contrary to the public order or good morals of [Thailand].' The internal law of Thailand would supplant foreign law when contrary to Thai public order or good morals.

APPIL offers a special rule on mandatory rules in a similar, but less restrictive, manner as the European law.[34] Vietnamese as well as Myanmar conflict of laws' publications also acknowledge and distinguish the application of mandatory rules out of the public policy principles.[35] However, it should be noted that under Thai conflict of laws rules, no specific rule dealing with mandatory rules has been legislated. Where the mandatory rules prevail over foreign laws, they are applicable as being within the scope of public policy descriptions. Provided that any Thai law or mandatory regulation relevant to the case at bench stems from public order or good morals of Thailand, such Thai law or

29 See, for instance, Thai Supreme Court Judgments No. 530/2568, No. 1950/2529, No. 3223/2525, and No. 3537/2546.

30 Respectively, Hickling and Aun (n 26), 44; Aquino (n 27), 100.

31 Briggs (n 25), 72.

32 Nguyen (n 24), 48.

33 This point will be elaborated in detail in the following part.

34 Chen and Goldstein (n 28), 430; also, for example, of European private international law rules, art 9 of the Regulation (EC) No 593/2008 on the law applicable to contractual obligations ('Rome I Regulation') and art 16 of the Regulation (EC) No 864/2007 on the law applicable to non-contractual obligations ('Rome II Regulation').

35 Respectively, Nguyen (n 24) 61; Briggs (n 25) 79 and 100.

regulation shall apply. No judicial notice towards foreign laws could be given for law and regulation of such mandatory nature.

Public policy exception has diverse application within the conflict of laws rules among national legal systems. Its application is 'not just an exception to the usual choice-of-law process because it chooses local law in circumstances which are an exception to the usual choice-of-law process'.[36] If no limitation is in place and the public policy's applicable scope is widened, the forum's public policy itself will overrule the forum's private international law.[37] Just as a matter of expression, while 'public policy' is deployed in Malaysia, Myanmar, and probably also in the Philippines,[38] the Vietnamese private international law's terminology uses the term 'basic principles of the law'.[39] The generic term of 'public policy' depends on a lot of factors differing from one society to another.

Public policy mechanism in conflict of laws: a common path or an exit route

With various escape devices underlying conflict of laws in a country, public policy is of major concern. From the beginning, collective policy goals towards trade facilitation and participation in OBOR have been cooperatively established in ASEAN public domains. Legal diversity in ASEAN generates conflicts rather than supports common policy. Conflict in conflict of laws accelerates the issues rather than resolves the diversity. This part attempts to enumerate inconsistent scenarios of law and policy resulting from the collision between regionalisation and individualisation.

Individualistic approach to public policy

Occasionally, the law of the forum, to preserve or to protect the forum's public interest, may supersede the law of a foreign country that ought to be applicable. It is acknowledged that public policy may cover many types of rules, standards, and regulations under various sources of law, and its definition and coverage could not be firmly framed. Even under European private international law, the term 'public policy' of the forum has not been clarified. The word 'manifestly' has been inserted in order to limit, more or less, public policy's damaging application.[40] As a regional integration, it had been once

36 Alex Mills, 'The Dimensions of Public Policy in Private International law' (2008) 4 *Journal of Private Internal Law* 201, 209.

37 Charles B. Nutting, 'Suggested Limitations on the Public Policy Doctrine' (1935) 19 *Minnesota Law Review* 196.

38 Respectively, Hickling and Aun (n 26), 3, 50; Briggs (n 25), 82; Aquino (n 27), 136.

39 Nguyen (n 24), 60.

40 See, for instance, art 21 of the Rome I Regulation and art 26 of the Rome II Regulation; Geert van Calster, *European Private International Law* (2nd edn, Hart Publishing 2016) 235 and 273.

argued that 'as a matter of common law, there is no such thing as "European public policy" ':[41]

> The danger of a doctrine so vague as this is that it may be interpreted to embrace such a multitude of domestic rules as to provide a fatally easy excuse for the application of the law of the forum and thus to defeat the underlying purpose of private international law.[42]

If it does so, it would be as what has been said that '[the] theory of public policy has never been anything but an escape device'.[43]

Unless it were to be collectively regionalised, application of the public policy mechanism would have been, as it is, based on a country's individual approach to each legal action existing at a particular moment.

The Thai Supreme Court Judgment No. 1583/2511 concerning a legal issue on prescription is an important statement on the subject. The facts are as follows: a contract was agreed to be governed by the law of Denmark. Such choice of foreign law could simply be applicable according to Section 13 of the Act on Conflict of Laws, Buddhist Era 2481. However, with regard to prescription, it was decided that where prescription or statutory period of limitation is the law relating to Thai public order or good morals, the choice of Danish law agreed by the contracting parties could not be applied. Consequently, it is the internal law of Thailand that governed the matter. Applying Section 5, the Court was able to evade the application of foreign law. The foreign law is inapplicable to a dispute or a claim so far as an underlying issue concerns public order or good morals of Thailand. To put it differently, applying such foreign law to the dispute would be against Thai public policy. Nevertheless, limitation of action under the Civil and Commercial Code,[44] reading together with the Civil Procedure Code of Thailand, is regarded as substantive, and not procedural, in nature.[45] The reason for this is that '[when] prescription has not been set up as a defence, the court cannot dismiss the claim in the ground of prescription',[46] as this ground is not categorised as a legal issue on public order and good morals in the context of the Civil Procedure Code. The claim can thus still be brought before the court, it is merely that '[after] the lapse of the period of prescription for [the claim], the debtor is entitled to refuse

41 Adrian Briggs, *The Conflict of Laws* (3rd edn, Oxford University Press 2013), 211.

42 James Fawcett, Janeen M. Carruthers and Peter North, *Cheshire, North & Fawcett: Private International Law* (14th edn, Oxford University Press 2008), 121.

43 Travor C. Hartley, *International Commercial Litigation: Text, Cases and Materials on Private International Law* (2nd edn, Cambridge University Press 2015), 567.

44 The English translation is derived from Khemchai Chutiwong and others, *The Civil and Commercial Code: English Version* (rev edn, Winyuchon 2016).

45 For the division of prescription into procedural and substantive natures which is claimed to be the common law jurisdictions' demarcation, see, Fawcett, Carruthers and North (n 42), 80.

46 s 193/29.

performance in accordance with [the claim]',[47] but if the debtor acts otherwise, '[any] act of performance in satisfaction of [the claim] barred by prescription, regardless of the value, may not be demanded back'.[48] Despite all that, '[the] parties cannot agree to exempt, extend, or reduce the periods of prescription specified by law'.[49] This immediate substantive nature is debatably a basis for rendering prescription as being within the sphere of public order in Thailand.

The reader might be curious about the inclusion of limitation period as public policy of Thailand. For example, in a case decided by the Slovak Republic's Court in Bratislava, the question of expiration of the limitation period was considered to be simply subject to the law of a foreign country – that was the Austrian law. No attention to public policy exceptions had been reported.[50] The European private international law states that the law applicable to a contract by virtue of a European regulation shall govern in particular 'prescription and limitation of actions'.[51] The question of prescription and limitation of actions is, therefore, regarded as a substantive matter, hence not being subject to the *lex fori*,[52] 'irrelevant whether such provisions are deemed substantive or procedural under the *lex causae*'.[53] This matter is, in other words, outside the realm of the forum's public policy or mandatory rules. Considering the rules of another continent, the 1994 Inter-American Convention on the Law Applicable to International Contracts endorsed by the Organization of American States (OAS) has also opened for a foreign law to govern principally 'prescription and lapsing of actions'.[54] The question herein is what will happen in ASEAN if a question of prescription and limitation of action is raised in a legal action involving the OBOR operations.

47 s 193/10.
48 s 193/28.
49 s 193/11.
50 CLOUT Case 946 *Krajský súd v Bratislave*, 26CB/114/1995 (11 October 2005) <www.uncitral.org/clout/clout/data/svk/clout_case_946_leg-2599.html> accessed 19 December 2017.
51 Art 12(1)(d) of the Rome I Regulation; also art 15(h) of the Rome II Regulation whereby the law applicable to non-contractual obligations under this Regulation shall govern in particular 'the manner in which an obligation may be extinguished and rules of prescription and limitation, including rules relating to the commencement, interruption and suspension of a period of prescription or limitation.'
52 Pippa Rogerson, *Collier's Conflict of Laws* (14th edn, Cambridge University Press 2013), 299 and 345; generally also Andrew Dickinson, *The Rome II Regulation: The Law Applicable to Non-Contractual Obligations* (Oxford University Press 2008).
53 Janeen Carruthers, 'Has the Forum Lost Its Grip?' in John Ahern and William Binchy (eds), *The Rome II Regulation on Law Applicable to Non-Contractual Obligations: A New International Litigation Regime* (Martinus Nijhoff 2009), 44.
54 Art 14(d); generally also Harold S Burman, 'International Conflict of Laws, The 1994 Inter-American Convention on the Law Applicable to International Contracts, and Trends for the 1990s' (1995) 28 *Vanderbilt Journal of Transnational Law* 367, 380.

Scholarly writings on Malaysian conflict of laws[55] state that limitation of actions is a subject of classification between substance and procedure. However, drawing content from the old English common law, this issue is regarded as procedural matter, hence being governed by *lex fori*. The approach of Myanmar, another common law tradition, is different. Forms of limitation period are divided into two kinds: time bar rules which are procedural in nature and those which are substantive in nature. While the former restrains judicial enforcement of a party's claim and may be dealt with only by Myanmar law, the latter is merely a substantive defence to the claim and can, only under certain circumstances, be governed by the law of foreign country.[56] In the Philippines, prescription is characterised as a matter of procedural law. It is, therefore, the Philippines' prescriptive period of time that will be applied to a case containing foreign elements.[57]

Additionally, in Singapore, a legislation has operated in that

> [where] a claim is governed by foreign law, it is the limitation period of that foreign law and not of Singapore law that will apply, unless such an application would conflict with public policy or cause undue hardship to a party or potential party.[58]

Another country that seems to give a room for an application of foreign prescriptive law is Vietnam, as its conflict of laws has opened that '[statutes] of limitation [for lawsuits regarding] a civil relation involving a foreign element will be governed by the law applicable to the dispute'.[59]

How should Thais and other ASEAN peoples engage with a legal problem or action concerning limitation period of action? Should they have a trial in a country where the *lex causae* or the foreign limitation law is applicable? Or should they go to a country where the *lex fori* always triumphs? No decisive answer could easily be ascertained, as this matter concerns the facts of a case and the time period laid down in the law of the relevant countries. The ASEAN situation on this subject is akin to what has been revealed by an African scholar. Among African countries, where a settled principle is that 'issues of procedure are governed by the *lex fori* and matters of substance by the *lex causae*', '[whether] limitation periods should be characterised as procedural

55 See, for example, Hickling and Aun (n 26), 35.

56 Briggs (n 25), 69.

57 Elizabeth H. Aguiling-Pangalangan, 'Philippines' in Alejandro Carballo Leyda (ed), *Asian Conflict of Laws: East and South East Asia* (Kluwer 2015), 288 (citing *Cadalian v Philippine Overseas Employment Association*, GR No L-104776 (1994)); Aquino (n 27) 146.

58 Harish Kumar and Jonathan Toh, 'Singapore' in Leyda (n 57), 209 (citing Foreign Limitation Periods Act 2012, s 3(1) and 4(1)).

59 Nguyen Thi Xuan Trinh and Konrad Hull, 'Vietnam' in Leyda (n 57), 288 (referring to art 777 of the Vietnamese Civil Code).

or substantive has been subject to debate' and 'remains to be seen'.[60] For lawyers conducting their legal operations in transnational perspectives across these regions, forum shopping is materialised.[61] Practically speaking, requiring litigants to sacrifice their own interest by suing their opponent in a country that is most closely connected to the action, even if they have to lose the case on the grounds of time bar, may be too harsh.

To resolve this conflicting situation, three options could be advanced. Should individual, regional, or global approaches be adopted? The first option is that a country could amend its own internal law avoiding regulatory competition[62] and embrace the same period of prescription. This could be difficult as countries also see a benefit in regulatory competition. Regional understanding could be a possibility if the enormous legal diversity could be lessened to a level of reconciliation. Should a regional agreement be difficult to achieve, joining an international legal framework, such as ratifying the Convention on the Limitation Period in the International Sale of Goods (New York, 1974), is another available alternative.[63] Still, implementation of an international instrument may raise a basic question as to what has been said in another context, '[should] Asian [or ASEAN] countries adopt these compromises drafted mainly by Westerners or international organisations, or are there issues peculiar to Asia [or ASEAN] which should be considered in commercial matters [or else]?'[64]

For ASEAN to issue a regional legal framework or to regionally become part of an international instrument, a consensus of all ASEAN members is required. To grow such a consensus, regional opinion supporting one of the three approaches is an indispensable condition. To obtain such a whole regional consent, forming collective public policy is of great importance, and this is an issue that is peculiar to the ASEAN way of regional integration.

Collectivistic approach to public policy

Guided by shared aims, purposes, and fundamental principles, the three pillars of the ASEAN Community are Political-Security Community, Economic

60 Richard Frimpong Oppong, *Private International Law in Commonwealth Africa* (Cambridge University Press 2013), 10–11.

61 See, for a general explanation of this topic, Andrew S. Bell, *Forum Shopping and Venue in Transnational Litigation* (Oxford University Press 2003).

62 See, for a general discussion on the topic, Dale D. Murphy, *The Structure of Regulatory Competition: Corporations and Public Policies in a Global Economy* (Oxford University Press 2006); specifically also, Stefan Vogenauer, 'Regulatory Competition Through Choice of Contract Law and Choice of Forum in Europe: Theory and Evidence' (2013) 21 *European Review of Private Law* 13.

63 Until the present time, no ASEAN country has become a member of this Convention. Text and detail of the Convention is available at <www.uncitral.org/uncitral/en/uncitral_texts/sale_goods/1974Convention_limitation_period.html> accessed 24 December 2017.

64 Bell (n 3); Angelo Chianale, 'The CISG as a Model Law: A Comparative Law Approach' (2016) *Singapore Journal of Legal Studies* 29.

Community, and Socio-Cultural Community.[65] Should this imply that the ASEAN countries do have collective policy? Could, among other things, 'preserving regional peace and stability',[66] reinforcing 'regional economic integration',[67] and 'lifting the quality of life of its people through cooperative activities'[68] be achieved without harmonious law, regulation, and public policy among ASEAN members? For one desiring and believing in the ASEAN integration, the ASEAN public policy has been formulated through the ASEAN Charter, the Blueprints, and other declarations. It needs to be translated into the public policy mechanism in conflict of laws. Should collective definition, coverage, application, limitation, interpretation, and so on, of 'public policy' in conflict of laws be regionally established? Should 'the forum's perception of justice and fairness'[69] be supplemented by the region's one? Should 'an escape device to protect a particular socio-national community', 'the superiority of some fundamental principles of a domestic community', and the national 'proximity', 'relativity' and 'seriousness of the breach' of public policy[70] be influenced by principles and values of the cofounded regional community?

To demand that ASEAN countries abolish the public policy device entirely would be, as well as in the European Union, 'a step in the wrong direction' as ASEAN countries are, compared with the European context, 'far from having a substantial synchronization of private law'.[71] The necessity of the public policy mechanism is still significant in ASEAN's legal plurality. In economic spheres, by contrast, provided that ASEAN's public policy is affirmative and operative, this would considerably contribute to the application of conflict of laws, not only within but also beyond the region and certainly also in transboundary activities connected with China and its great plan.

Speaking of conflict of laws' strategic models, there are four options that are available. These are amplified ahead under two subheadings: quasi-collectivistic approaches and collectivistic approaches.

Quasi-collectivistic approaches

First, a harmonised individual approach is for all countries to apply the law of the forum, as this is likely to be adopted in Myanmar, Malaysia, the Philippines,

65 ASEAN Charter, art 9 <http://asean.org/asean/about-asean/overview/> accessed 25 December 2017.

66 ASEAN Political-Security Community Blueprint 2025, para 1.

67 ASEAN Economic Community Blueprint 2025, para 2.

68 ASEAN Socio-Cultural Community Blueprint 2025, para 1.

69 Wolfgang Wurmnest, 'Ordre Public (Public Policy)' in Stefan Leible (ed), *General Principles of European Private International Law* (Wolters Kluwer 2016), 305.

70 Respectively, Nartnirun Junngam, 'Public Policy in International Investment Law: The Confluence of the Three Unruly Horses' (2016) 51 *Texas International Law Journal* 45, 63–64; Ragne Piir, 'Application of the Public Policy Exception in the Context of International Contracts – The Rome I Regulation' (2015) 23 *Juridica International* 26, 30; Mills (n 36).

71 Wurmnest (n 69), 310.

and Thailand. Where limitation of action is classified internally in all countries as being within the wide-ranging scope of public policy, the law of the forum shall always be operative. Metaphorically, on the basis of this approach, a truck or a train journeying through China and ASEAN needs to be aware of which station among eleven countries it is going to make a stop at and to litigate therein.

Second, a harmonised individual approach is for all countries to apply the law of a foreign country, as it seems to be in Singapore and Vietnam. Where limitation of action is classified internally in all countries as being outside the wide-ranging scope of public policy, the foreign applicable law shall always be able to be operative. Metaphorically, on the basis of this approach, a truck or a train journeying through China and ASEAN need not be aware of which station among eleven countries it is going to make a stop at and to litigate therein, but it has to pay great attention to the applicable law.

Collectivistic approaches

Third, a regional approach is for all countries to mutually establish ASEAN conflict of law rules on prescription. This is where limitation of action is to be regarded as either being within or outside the wide-ranging sphere of public policy. Whether this approach can be achieved is a matter of regional consultation and consensus. Metaphorically, on the basis of this approach, a truck or a train journeying through China and ASEAN need not be aware much of which station it is going to make a stop at and to litigate therein, or to ascertain an applicable law, as there are only two main legal systems to consider – one is of China and another of ASEAN.

Fourth, a global approach is for all countries to altogether become members of an international convention, if there is any. This is where limitation of action is to be totally subject to an international legal framework. Whether this approach can be achieved requires a whole-of-region commitment. Metaphorically, on the basis of this approach, a truck or a train journeying through China and ASEAN need not be aware much of which station it is going to make a stop at and to litigate therein, or to ascertain an applicable law, as there are only two main legal systems to consider – one is of China and another of international law. The result would be even better if China joins such an international framework, so the truck and the train can be reassured that the law is substantially and consistency consolidated throughout the road and the rail network.

Selecting between the four options stated previously depends heavily upon the ASEAN public policy surrounding laws on prescriptions. Metaphorically speaking, the region has to identify the method that it is going to adopt to ensure that the law supports trade facilitation along the OBOR – individual, regional, or international. This question calls for an ASEAN way of consultation and consensus. To add to this call, consideration of the law related to public policy in the People's Republic of China may also be suggested. According to the Law of the People's Republic of China on the Laws Applicable to

Foreign-Related Civil Relations (LAL), public policy mechanism is one of its fundamental principles. This principle is prescribed under the term 'social and public interests'.[72] As a supplement to public policy, another section permits the direct application of Chinese mandatory rules.[73] For conflict of laws' issues on statute of limitations, the stand of China is positioned at the side of a civil law tradition. Limitation of action is categorised as substantive rather than procedural, hence being governed by the *lex causue* and not the *lex fori*.[74]

Conclusion

This chapter has attempted to trace the importance of regulatory regime on conflict of laws for ASEAN, and especially Thailand, in the context of OBOR. Uniting the ASEAN regional policy and reforming the public policy mechanism in conflict of laws is a key factor in resolving the conflict of laws throughout the Belt and the Road.

The law on public policy exception, whether international, regional, or national, significantly affects transnational private activities. For conflict of laws to be avoided and legal systems to be better harmonised, the first step is to mutually form policy goals and commitment among the countries along the common path. The second stage is to strengthen legal application throughout the pathway. Conflicts generated by conflict of law rules themselves must be taken into account and be minimised or eliminated. Special consideration should be given to their escape devices, so as to block up as many exit routes as possible. With regard to legal issues concerning public policy, the third step is for a region being a region, not a region being composed of a group of countries. Conflict of public policy related issues, such as prescription or limitation of actions, is, *inter alia*, a clear example. Should it be too difficult to resolve, other more complicated issues should be buried deep into the ground.

Contribution to the participation and sustained success of the OBOR would require a supportive legal regime with few escape routes and, importantly, a collectivistic approach to public policy in place of an individualistic one.

72 Art 5 which states: 'Where the application of a foreign law will be prejudicial to the social and public interest of the People's Republic of China ("PRC"), the PRC law shall be applied'. See also, Mo Zhang, 'Codified Choice of Law in China: Rules, Processes and Theoretic Underpinnings' (2011) 47 *North Carolina Journal of International Law and Commercial Regulation* 83, 105; Zhengxin Huo, 'An Imperfect Improvement: The New Conflict of Laws Act of the People's Republic of China' (2011) 60 *International and Comparative Law Quarterly* 1065, 1073; Guangjian Tu, 'China's New Conflicts Code: General Issues and Selected Topics' (2011) 59 *American Journal of Comparative Law* 563, 570.

73 Art 4 of the LAL which states: 'Where a mandatory provision of the law of the PRC exists with respect to a foreign-related civil relation, that mandatory provision shall be applied directly'.

74 Art 7 of the LAL which Prescribes That: 'Limitation Period Is Governed by the Law That Should Be Applicable to the Foreign-Related Civil Relation.' See also Zhang (n 72), 110; Tu (n 72), 571; generally, Yuanshi Bu (ed), *Chinese Civil Law* (C H Beck 2013), ch 3.

Collaboration between international, regional, and national affairs is a fundamental requirement; otherwise, no real common benefit could be reached nor sustained. In the ASEAN context, policy goals and commitment are quite well developed and well recognised across its members, although their actual operations in practice are doubtful. The ASEAN trade facilitation framework is a crucial factor in this collective pathway, but there is no concrete evidence showing a harmonious collaboration in terms of law and regulation. An individualistic approach seems to be the current trend. A call for a more collective manner in conflict of laws, including but not limited to the escape devices, like public policy exceptions particularly such as prescription or limitation of actions, needs to be established. In order to overcome the diversity and be an actual economic integration, it is perhaps the law, regulation, and policy of or among the ASEAN community that should bear equal weight to those of an ASEAN member. In an ASEAN country, the country's *lex fori* approach should, perhaps, be supplemented by the ASEAN's *lex fori* approach. This call certainly also directs towards Thailand and Thai conflict of law rules.

10 The "One Belt One Road" strategy – the role of private international law in combatting and strengthening anti-corruption standards transnationally

Thomas John, Rishi Gulati**

Introduction

China's "One Belt One Road" strategy, now referred to as the Belt and Road Initiative (hereinafter BRI), first announced by President Xi Jinping in September and October 2013, and developed further since, is an ambitious project by China that focuses on establishing a cohesive trade zone, including through collaboration among more than 60 nations spanning primarily Asia and Europe, Oceania and East Africa.

China's intent is to develop the region's, and indeed the world's, infrastructure, and to improve the economic well-being of millions of people by lifting them out of poverty.[1] But as several commentators have observed, the BRI also aims at asserting and strengthening China's position within world trade and affairs, and the initiative has been identified as an attempt to rebalance China's geostrategic position after the conclusion of the Western-centric trade pacts, the Trans-Pacific Partnership and Transatlantic Trade and Investment Partnership, often also identified as indicators of rising protectionist tendencies among Western powers.[2] It seems fair to say that the BRI is an expression of China's increasing global ambitions.

* The authors thank Ms Nishadee Perera for her valuable research assistance in the preparation of this chapter.

1 The National Development and Reform Commission, Ministry of Foreign Affairs, and Ministry of Commerce of the People's Republic of China, with State Council authorization, 'Full Text: Vision and Actions on Jointly Building Belt and Road' *CRIENGLISH.com* (2015) <http://english.cri.cn/12394/2015/03/29/2941s872030.htm> accessed 11 November 2017.

2 Rumi Aoyama, '"One Belt, One Road": China's New Global Strategy' (2016) 5 (2) *Journal of Contemporary East Asia Studies* 4–5; Ravi Boothalingam, 'The Silk Road as a Global Brand' (2016) 52(1) *China Report* 48–49; Geoff Wade, 'China's "One Belt, One Road" Initiative' (2017) *Australian Parliamentary Library Breifing Book* 4; Khanindra Ch. As, 'The Making of One Belt, One Road and Dilemmas in South Asia' (2017) 53 (2) *China Report* 126–127; Christine R. Guluzian, 'Making Inroads: China's New Silk Road Initiative' (2017) 37(1) *Cato Journal* 137–138; Andrew Sheng, 'OBOR and EuroAsia's New Great Game' (2017) 53(2) *China Report* 239–240; Sit Tsui et al., 'One Belt, One

With the BRI seeking to foster increased trade activities, it seems likely that strengthening anti-corruption frameworks will become a central issue. As Chinese banks (or Chinese-led multilateral development banks) provide, and are expected to provide, loans and other forms of funding for future infrastructure projects that are part of the BRI, checks and balances to prevent the misuse of funds, and a regulatory sanctioning of cross-border corruption cases, will require consideration.

Questions surrounding this issue are vexed and include what anti-corruption standards are to be put into place, who monitors compliance with such standards, what are the civil and criminal consequences of breaches of existing and future anti-corruption standards, and how can civil or regulatory sanctions be enforced across borders. These issues relate to jurisdiction and forum, applicable law and the recognition and enforcement of judgments as well as legal cooperation. It is thus opportune to ask whether and, if so, to what extent, private international law (PIL) can make a contribution in this field and specifically in the context of the BRI.

This chapter explores what contribution PIL may make to anti-corruption frameworks internationally and, with an emphasis on strengthening legal cooperation among States that participate in the BRI, proceeds on the basis that PIL not only can, but must, play a greater role as part of a global governance and regulatory framework that is not merely allocative, but regulates substance, including through robust (regulatory) enforcement regimes. However, as much of the detail surrounding the BRI is still unclear, the chapter proceeds to raise questions, rather than seeking to answer them in detail. It will do so by setting out some of the existing international provisions that apply in this space, and probe their effectiveness, in light of other relevant international instruments, such as the instruments of the Hague Conference on Private International Law (HCCH).

Legal cooperation in matters of corruption

In addition to questions around China's geopolitical motivations behind the BRI, the greatest concerns relate to potential corruption associated with BRI infrastructure projects.[3] Therefore, approaching PIL from the perspective of

---

Road – China's Strategy for a New Global Financial Order' (2017) 36 *Monthly Review*; Hong Yu, 'Motivation behind China's "One Belt, One Road" Initiatives and Establishment of the Asian Infrastructure Investment Bank' (2017) 26 (105) *Journal of Contemporary China* 355–358.

3 Spencer Sheehan, 'The Problem with China's One Belt, One Road Strategy' (*The Diplomat*, 24 March 2017) <https://thediplomat.com/2017/05/the-problem-with-chinas-one-belt-one-road-strategy/> accessed 10 November 2017; Xiaoqing et al., 'China's Silk Road Cuts Through Some of the World's Riskiest Countries' (*Bloomberg News*, 26 October 2017) <www.bloomberg.com/news/articles/2017-10-25/china-s-new-silk-road-runs-mostly-through-junk-rated-territory> accessed 1 November 2017; Chang Ping, 'One Belt, One Road, Total Corruption' (*Deutsche Welle* (translated by *China Change*)

legal cooperation in civil and commercial matters, which is often referred to as its fourth dimension or pillar, is critical. First, this chapter provides some brief remarks as to why the issue of corruption must be addressed and dealt with and second, considers strategies that may be developed and adopted to create and enhance legal cooperation in such matters. However, it is important to remain cognizant of the fact that, as the BRI is still in its infancy, any suggestions can constitute only a starting point. The issues raised here are constantly evolving, and much work will need to be done to translate the suggestions into practice.

The need to combat corruption in BRI-related projects

The corrosive effects of corruption are well known. In his Foreword to the United Nations Convention Against Corruption (hereinafter UNCAC), former UN Secretary-General Kofi Annan said:

> Corruption is an insidious plague that has a wide range of corrosive effects on societies. It undermines democracy and the rule of law, leads to violations of human rights, distorts markets, erodes the quality of life and allows organized crime, terrorism and other threats to human security to flourish . . . it is in the developing world that its effects are most destructive. Corruption hurts the poor disproportionately by diverting funds intended for development, undermining a Government's ability to provide basic services, feeding inequality and injustice and discouraging foreign aid and investment. Corruption is a key element in economic underperformance and a major obstacle to poverty alleviation and development.[4]

There appear to be two main reasons why the risk of corrupt activity, such as bribery, fraud, kickbacks and embezzlement, is particularly high in BRI-related projects. First, large infrastructure projects readily lend themselves to acts of corruption of various kinds. Second, as has been noted in several reports, the states where the BRI projects are carried out, or are intended to be carried out, are high risk when it comes to the potential of corrupt activity.

18 May 2017) <https://chinachange.org/2017/05/18/one-belt-one-road-total-corruption/> accessed 8 November 2017; Joshua Eisenman and Devin T. Stewart, 'China's New Silk Road Is Getting Muddy' (*Foreign Policy*, 9 January 2017) <http://foreignpolicy.com/2017/01/09/chinas-new-silk-road-is-getting-muddy/> accessed 13 December 2017; Alexandra Wage, 'Companies Engaging in China's Belt and Road Project Must Address Bribery Risks' (*Forbes*, 12 October 2017) <www.forbes.com/sites/alexandrawrage/2017/10/12/companies-engaging-in-chinas-belt-road-projects-must-address-bribery-risks/#72c1c534f52c> accessed 17 December 2017.

4 *United Nations Convention Against Corruption*, opened for signature 9 December 2003, 2349 UNTS 41 (entered into force 14 December 2005).

Such concerns are not mere hypothesis. In December 2017, China temporarily halted the release of funds for certain projects carried out under the China-Pakistan Economic Corridor (hereinafter CPEC).[5] CPEC is, with investments of up to US$50 billion, one of the most significant initiatives of BRI to date,[6] and the halt followed reports of corruption in Pakistan in relation to those particular projects.[7] China's reaction seems to be indicative of a broader nervousness around corruption related to the BRI. Moreover, it also seems key to a wider reticence to embrace the BRI despite the significant opportunities it may offer. As has been noted from a US perspective:

> [T]he greater challenge for U.S. businesses is that Chinese funding means Chinese rules. This is likely to be bad news for transparency. While we have seen China crackdown on corruption under Xi, efforts have been focused within China, reaching across borders only to nab Chinese citizens who have fled with their corrupt bounty. The Chinese enforcement agencies have never brought an action against a Chinese entity for bribery abroad in spite of rampant anecdotal evidence that many Chinese companies use bribery as a business strategy across Asia and Africa. That track record shows no signs of changing. Couple this apparent indifference to bribery beyond its borders with the fact that the 65 OBOR countries include some of the most notoriously corrupt in the world. Four OBOR countries are amongst the eight riskiest in the world according to the TRACE Matrix: Yemen, Cambodia, Myanmar and Syria. Most others (Pakistan, Vietnam, Uzbekistan, Iraq, Iran and others), fall in the bottom half.[8]

5 Nyshka Chandran, 'Pakistan Learns the Downside of Taking Infrastructure Money from China' (*CNBC*, 12 December 2017) <www.cnbc.com/2017/12/12/china-and-pakistan-infrastructure-spending-on-road-project-dries-up.html?view=story&%24DEVICE%24=native-android-mobile> accessed 17 December 2017; Press Trust of India, 'China Stops Funding CPEC Road Projects Over Graft Issue: Report' (*The Economic Times*, 5 December 2017) <https://economictimes.indiatimes.com/news/international/business/china-stops-funding-cpec-road-projects-over-graft-issue-report/articleshow/61929470.cms> accessed 17 December 2017.

6 *Ibid.*

7 Press Trust of India, 'China Stops Funds for China-Pak Economic Corridor Over Corruption: Report' (*NDTV*, 5 December 2017) <www.ndtv.com/world-news/china-stops-funds-for-china-pak-economic-corridor-over-corruption-report-1783849> accessed 19 December 2017.

8 Alexandra Wrage, 'One Belt, One Road, Many Bribes?' (*Forbes*, 23 May 2017) <www.forbes.com/sites/alexandrawrage/2017/05/23/one-belt-one-road-many-bribes/#550ae33503c2> accessed on 19 December 2017. Similar views were also expressed by Jörg Wuttke, President of the European Union Chamber of Commerce in China, who said: "I hope China is actually embracing the world and opening up to foreign trade instead of just reaching out". Risk analyst Andrew Gilholm said: "I don't think many people are buying the spin that this is all in the name of free trade and global prosperity". Siegfried O. Wolf, Director of Research at South Asia Democratic Forum in Brussels, was even more candid: "At present there is a lack of an effective platform for 'One Bridge, One Road' cooperation between Europe and China. If China is reluctant to build this bridge,

Its own nervousness, and the apparent widespread reticence to join the BRI, provides a strong justification for decisive steps to combat corruption. They will be paramount for China's intentions to succeed.

China has woken to this issue. Despite its own rather lackluster record in tackling cross-border corruption, in May 2017, China advocated for a so-called clean BRI, calling for a strengthening of "international counter-corruption cooperation so that the Belt and Road will be a road with high ethical standards".[9] First steps in this regard have been taken. For example, China's Central Commission for Discipline Inspection and Ministry of Supervision, together with the World Bank, held recently a symposium focusing on strengthen international cooperation for a "Clean Belt and Road".[10] However, the results of this symposium remain unclear. Therefore, while the intention of a clean BRI, and such first steps, are welcomed, they are embryonic to developing a systematic rules-based order that underpins a comprehensive anti-corruption regime featuring robust implementation measures.

An anti-corruption regime for BRI-related projects

Without a comprehensive anti-corruption regime, it seems at least arguable that the chances of China's intentions behind the BRI succeeding remain rather low. Starting with existing regimes, the following discussion identifies some of their strengths and weaknesses.

The existing anti-corruption regime – sufficient or lessons to be learnt?

In the preceding two or so decades, the international community has developed a fairly comprehensive regime on anti-corruption both at the global level as well as at regional levels.[11] To mention here are, perhaps first and foremost,

---

and is unwilling to move toward multilateral mechanisms and disregards the values of the European Union based on good governance, rule of law, human rights, and democracy, then European scepticism of 'One Belt, One Road' will continue": see these views contained at Chang Ping, 'One Belt, One Road, Total Corruption' *ChinaChange.org* (2017) <https://chinachange.org/2017/05/18/one-belt-one-road-total-corruption/> accessed 19 December 2017.

9 Alexandra Wrage, 'Companies Engaging in China's Belt and Road Projects Must Address Bribery Risks' (*Forbes*, 12 October 2017) <www.forbes.com/sites/alexandrawrage/2017/10/12/companies-engaging-in-chinas-belt-road-projects-must-address-bribery-risks/#53056bf24f52> accessed 19 December 2017.

10 *Ibid.*

11 The multilateral instruments to prevent and combat corruption, including, *inter alia*, the Inter-American Convention Against Corruption, adopted by the Organization of American States on 29 March 1996, the Convention on the Fight Against Corruption involving Officials of the European Communities or Officials of Member States of the European Union, adopted by the Council of the European Union on 26 May 1997, the Convention on Combating Bribery of Foreign Public Officials in International Business

the UNCAC, to which the world's major powers, including China, are a party, as well as the OECD Foreign Bribery Convention (hereinafter OECDC), and the Civil Law Convention on Corruption 2003 of the Council of Europe (hereinafter CLC). Plainly, these existing instruments can provide a starting point for developing an anti-corruption regime for BRI-related projects.

However, there are shortcomings. The geographical reach of some of the key conventions is comparably limited. While several Asian states are parties to the UNCAC,[12] Asia remains one of the very few regions without its own regional anti-corruption regime, and recalling that several of the states who have presently joined the BRI initiative are located in the Asian region, the pressing need especially for the full implementation of UNCAC is immediately apparent.[13] Moreover, these instruments focus predominantly on criminalising corrupt conduct. Examples include the prohibition on the bribery of foreign public officials in the context of international business transactions under the OECDC[14] and the criminalisation of both active and passive bribery under the UNCAC,[15] which also requires countries to criminalise other forms of corrupt activity, including embezzlement,[16] trading in influence[17] and the abuse of functions.[18]

This focus on criminalisation is not surprising. For a plentitude of reasons, including political expedience, rhetoric and gain, the international community has tended to focus on the "law and order" effect of the criminal aspects of anti-corruption. It goes without saying that this is an important key to the fight against anti-corruption. However, it is equally important to combat corruption through strong civil and regulatory measures that complement criminal ones. These measures remain understudied and poorly understood, and the focus of the remainder of this chapter is thus on the civil aspects of corruption.

Transactions, adopted by the Organisation for Economic Co-operation and Development on 21 November 1997, the Criminal Law Convention on Corruption, adopted by the Committee of Ministers of the Council of Europe on 27 January 1999, the Civil Law Convention on Corruption, adopted by the Committee of Ministers of the Council of Europe on 4 November 1999, and the African Union Convention on Preventing and Combating Corruption, adopted by the Heads of State and Government of the African Union on 12 July 2003.

12 There are 183 state parties, including BRI countries such as Pakistan, Bangladesh, Sri Lanka, Mongolia and Myanmar (amongst others).

13 Most Asian states are not members to the OECD Foreign Bribery Convention, see 'Cite A Website – Cite This for Me' (*Oecd.org*, 2017) <www.oecd.org/daf/anti-bribery/WGBRatificationStatus.pdf> accessed 31 December 2017.

14 *Convention on Combatting Bribery of Foreign Public Officials in International Business Transactions*, opened for signature on 17 December 1997, [1999] ATS 21 (entered into force 15 February 1999), Art 1, 3, and 8.

15 *Ibid* art 15 and 16.

16 *Ibid* art 17.

17 *Ibid* 18.

18 *Ibid* 19.

Combatting corruption through civil and regulatory measures

To date, a comprehensive framework that provides rules governing questions concerning jurisdiction, applicable law and the recognition and enforcement of foreign judgments in civil corruption cases has not yet been developed. However, there are a few international instruments that provide relatively detailed regulatory frameworks for legal cooperation in such cases.

The UNCAC contemplates forms of legal cooperation in relation to the civil aspects of anti-corruption but does so almost as an afterthought. Contrasting the language used to establish the cooperation obligations under the UNCAC in relation to criminal matters as opposed to civil cases is instructive. Relevantly, Article 43(1) of the UNCAC states:

> States Parties *shall cooperate* in criminal matters in accordance with articles 44 to 50 of this Convention. Where appropriate and consistent with their domestic legal system, States Parties *shall consider* assisting each other in investigations of and proceedings in civil and administrative matters relating to corruption.
>
> (emphasis added)

The use of "shall cooperate" in the criminal context plainly imposes a much more stringent obligation on states when compared with the language used in the civil context. However, the distinction is most unfortunate. If the fight against corruption is to succeed, complementary criminal and civil regimes that provide strong and robust anti-corruption measures are equally needed. Mandatory language for both would have been preferable.

The CLC goes further in this regard, constituting the first attempt to define common international rules in the field of civil law and corruption. When implemented, the instrument requires state parties to provide in their domestic law "for effective remedies for persons who have suffered damage as a result of acts of corruption, to enable them to defend their rights and interests, including the possibility of obtaining compensation for damage."[19] Moreover, should an act fall within the scope of the CLC, then the state parties must provide to a person who has suffered losses as a result of the alleged corruption a right to initiate civil proceedings to recover damages for any losses caused by that corrupt conduct,[20] including a right to initiate proceedings aiming to invalidate any contract created following corrupt conduct.[21] Importantly, corruption is defined relatively broadly to include both public and private sector bribery.[22]

19 CLC, art 1.

20 *Ibid* art 3; see also Art. 4 for the liability regime.

21 *Ibid* art 8 (2).

22 Art. 2 of the CLC states: "For the purpose of this Convention, 'corruption' means requesting, offering, giving or accepting, directly or indirectly, a bribe or any other undue

Relevantly, the CLC sets forth obligations aimed at growing a regime for international cooperation in civil proceedings in cases of corruption, with Article 13 requiring that the state parties to the instrument:

> [S]hall co-operate effectively [. . .], especially concerning the service of documents, obtaining evidence abroad, jurisdiction, recognition and enforcement of foreign judgments and litigation costs, in accordance with the provisions of relevant international instruments on international co-operation in civil and commercial matters to which they are Party, as well as with their internal law.

With this provision, the CLC provides important umbrella obligations to promote cooperation in this area. They can be enlivened through appropriate, already existing, domestic private international law and civil procedure regimes. They may also be implemented well and efficiently in the future, including through becoming contracting parties to important private international law instruments, including through those developed by the HCCH. In that sense, there can be no doubt that the CLC is an important evolutionary step, and indeed a starting point for developing a comprehensive regime for the BRI, with the added benefit that existing global instruments may tie such regimes into, and strengthen, the global fight against corruption. However, the CLC does leave several important questions *prima facie* unanswered.

The question of jurisdiction

While the CLC creates obligations to provide remedies and grant access to justice, it does itself provide for specific allocative rules in this regard. Broadly whether a court will take jurisdiction in a multi-jurisdictional case depends on criteria that most closely connect the case to a jurisdiction. These connecting factors may be based on subject matter (i.e. tort or contract), on party characteristics (i.e. presence or habitual residence) or party choice (i.e. implied or express). Where they are based on subject matter, the connectors vary depending on the characterisation of the issues at hand. For example, is an issue characterised as claim in tort, then the connector may require claimants to bring proceedings for compensation in the jurisdiction in which the damage occurred (i.e. *lex fora deliciti*). However, other connectors exist, and in light of a distinct paucity of internationally agreed connecting factors, significant uncertainty remains. The same can be said where an issue is characterised as contractual.[23] However, in such cases, courts may be guided by express or

advantage or prospect thereof, which distorts the proper performance of any duty or behaviour required of the recipient of the bribe, the undue advantage or the prospect thereof."

23 Importantly, this concerns contracts obtained through corruption as distinct from the agreement to bribe or engage in any other corruptive conduct. This type of agreement

implied forum choices. Further, where the parties to the contract are resident in at least two jurisdictions that are Contracting States to the Hague 2005 Choice of Court Agreement Convention, and have agreed to an express choice of court clause that designates a court located in a Contracting State to that Convention, their express choice may result in the chosen court assuming jurisdiction. However, unless this Convention does apply, there is simply no guarantee that party choice prevails, and that a court does not resort to different connecting factors to determine whether it has jurisdiction.

Moreover, as a result of such uncertainty, there seems to be an increased risk that multiple courts assume jurisdiction over a corruption case, resulting in parallel proceedings. The result is, at best, increased costs for the litigants and, at worst, conflicting judgments. This issue raises questions relating to *lis alibi pendens* and the declining of jurisdiction on *forum (non-) conveniens* grounds. Whereas especially the latter doctrine has been identified as particularly relevant in relation to corruption cases,[24] both are fraught with considerable complexity,[25] and previous attempts to provide international standards in this regard have failed.[26] Leaving for now to one side the issue of sovereignty and immunity, it seems apparent that the uncertainty surrounding jurisdiction in multi-jurisdictional corruption cases has the potential to undermine access to justice for those detrimentally affected by corruption.

The question of applicable law

Even if the respective jurisdiction to bring a claim in has been established, the question against which law the matter must be adjudged will remain

has been referred to as the primary contract, whereas the contract which is the result of the corruptive conduct is known as the secondary contract. Primary contracts are well recognised to be invalid and unenforceable, including by the CLC (Art. 8) and the UNCAC (Art. 34). The legal situation of secondary contracts is far less clear-cut. See Kramer, at 2.1.3.

24 The doctrine of *forum (non-) conveniens* would allow a (common law) court to inquire into the circumstances prevalent in another jurisdiction. Instructive here, Kramer, 3.3. It is worth noting that under the 2005 Hague Choice of Court Convention, a court not chosen may assume jurisdiction in a case where giving effect to the express agreement would result in a manifest injustice (Art. 6 c). According to the Explanatory Report to that instrument, this may include the situation where a party cannot expect a fair trial because there is corruption in the chosen court. T C Hart/M Dogauchi, Explanatory Report to the Convention of 30 June 2005 on Choice of Court Agreements, 61 (para 151), <https://assets.hcch.net/upload/expl37final.pdf> accessed 28 December 2017.

25 Instructive here, Xandra E. Kramer, 'Approaches to Jurisdiction and Foreign Judgments and the International Fight Against Corruption' in *International Law and the Fight Against Corruption*, Mededelingen van de Koninklijke Nederlandse Vereniging voor Internationaal Recht, Preadviezen 139 (Advisory Report for the Dutch Royal Society of International Law), (Asser Press 2012), 99–142, at 3.3.

26 As part of its Judgments Project, the HCCH will consider these issues through an Expert Group in due course. See specifically No. 13 of the Conclusions and Recommendations, as adopted by the HCCH's Council on General Affairs and Policy, held on 15–17 March 2016.

unanswered.[27] However, these questions are of significant importance as they, for example, will govern the application of mandatory domestic law as well as of public policy, including, arguably, any domestic rules concerning corruption.[28]

As is the case regarding jurisdiction, the question which law governs a relationship is ruled by connecting factors recognised in individual domestic jurisdictions. Broadly, prevailing connecting factors are usually based on a closest connection, leading to the application of the law, for example, of the forum, of the plaintiff's or of the defendant's jurisdiction, or even an altogether different one. However, the establishment of the correct connector is not an accurate science, and a significant level of uncertainty and unpredictability remains.

This level of uncertainty may be somewhat reduced where the parties agreed on a law that applies between them. Here, a court may take guidance from such choices, possibly being assisted by The Hague 2015 Choice of Law Principles in International Commercial Contracts (Principles), which, while non-binding, promotes party autonomy in international commercial transactions and may be used by courts when having to decide questions of applicable law in corruption matters. The Introduction to the Principles explains that the instrument can offer:

> I.20 [. . .] guidance as to how to approach questions concerning the validity and effects of a choice of law agreement, and resolve choice of law disputes within the prevailing legal framework (. . .). The Principles may be useful, in particular, for addressing novel situations.[29]

To what extent the instrument can offer such assistance in corruption matters requires further analysis. *Prima facie*, its operation may be limited. While increasingly accepted as an essential doctrine to promote commercial and other activity, party autonomy is not a global concept. States who do not accept this doctrine are unlikely to depart from this position on the basis of the Principles. Moreover, the Principles apply to applicable law agreements in multi-jurisdictional commercial contracts; tortious matters would not benefit in the same way, if at all. Finally, in many, if not all jurisdictions, the law surrounding corruption and related matters tends to be of a mandatory nature, thus overriding party autonomy, or a matter of public policy.[30] It appears that the instruments currently available to deal with questions concerning the law

27 As Fentiman and others have pointed out, the majority of litigation of financial disputes in international settings concern questions of jurisdiction and that, as soon as these questions have been determined, parties proceed to settlement. Disputes rarely result in a judicial decision. Richard Fentiman, *International Commercial Litigation* (2nd edn, Oxford University Press 2015), 9.

28 Here instructive, with further references, Kramer, *op. cit.*, at 2.1.3. Kramer, (n 25).

29 Paragraph I.20 to the Introduction to the Hague 2015 Principles on the Choice of Law in International Commercial Contracts.

30 Kramer (n 25).

applicable in multi-jurisdictional corruption matters are underdeveloped, with the resulting lack of clear rules leading to uncertainty and a significant lack of predictability of outcome.

The question of recognition and enforcement

The effective recognition and enforcement of a foreign judgment is crucial to ensuring the vindication of a litigant's rights and obligations as established by judicial process and renders litigation viable.[31] It also provides the end to litigation in the sense that the issues adjudged upon become estopped or *res judicata*, and cannot be re-litigated.

In relation to corruption cases, issues arise in relation to judgments either rendered in a corruption case, that is, in a case where, for example, the secondary contract was the result of corruptive conduct, or to judicial decisions fouled by corruption. Assuming that international jurisdiction can be established, grounds for the refusal to enforce such judgment may then apply. It appears that to date, no specific grounds based on corruption exist domestically or internationally; however, in their absence, existing grounds such as procedural fairness, fraud and, in particular, substantive and procedural public policy may become relevant. In relation to fraud, Article 9 d) of the Hague Choice of Court Agreement Convention should be mentioned. It provides a ground of refusal where a judgment, to which the instrument applies, was obtained by "fraud in connection with a matter of procedure". The Explanatory Report then explains further that this would include a party seeking to corrupt a judge, juror or witness.[32]

Moreover, in relation to public order, commentators have noticed that, despite it being a domestic concept, recent developments seem to indicate the rise of corruption as a transnational public policy matter.[33] However, and again leaving issues pertaining to sovereignty and immunity, which are equally relevant to one side, better guidance in this area would be desirable. This should include clear rules targeted at both, the scenario where the judgments concerns, for example, contract obtained through corruptive conduct, as well where the outcome of the judicial proceedings were tainted by corruption of the judicial process.

31 Fentiman (n 27).

32 T C Hart/M Dogauchi, Explanatory Report to the Convention of 30 June 2005 on Choice of Court Agreements, 71, para. 188 <https://assets.hcch.net/upload/expl37final.pdf> accessed 29 December 2017. The Article is thus complementary to Art. 6 c) discussed above, according to which a court may assume jurisdiction over a dispute on the basis that a fair hearing, including for corruption, is not possible in a foreign court. See FN [24] above.

33 See here Kramer, *op. cit.*, 4.3.1 Kramer (n 25), referring to the award in the *World Duty Free Comp Ltd v Republic of Kenya* [2006] ICSID, ARB/00/7 (ICSID) 159.

Other questions

There remains a cluster of questions, which can only be noted in this chapter, without, however, exploring them in much detail. As part of international civil procedure, these questions are crucial and fall squarely within the scope of legal cooperation. To mention here are, first, the CLC's silence on standing, leaving it unclear who precisely may have standing to bring a civil claim in a corruption case, and the related issue of joinder. This issue is of considerable practical importance as the category of individuals and persons potentially suffering damages as a result of corrupt activity may be indeed vast.

Moreover, the CLC does not address questions concerning the interaction between criminal and civil proceedings in circumstances in which proceedings of both nature are ongoing. It could be argued that from a point of procedural efficiencies, a combined hearing of criminal and civil cases, as known in jurisdictions of civil law tradition, should be promoted. However, where jurisdictions do not allow such combining, not only is there a significant increase in the complexities caused by parallel proceedings, but also several consequential issues need addressing, including, for example, whether the sharing of evidence between the civil and criminal proceedings should be allowed. In the absence of rules governing such sharing, parties are required to lead evidence separately in different fora. This can result not only in increased costs, but also in procedural uncertainty, as rulings on evidence in one forum may contradict rulings in the other proceedings.

With the CLC silent on these issues, and no other international instrument providing guidance in this regard, and the considerable practical importance of these issues, it seems paramount to develop and agree on strong and cogent international civil procedure rules that can provide the required certainty in corruption cases, while promoting procedural efficiency through frameworks that equally safeguard the parties' rights and protect the rule of law.

The question of sovereignty and immunity

The final question concerns lacunae in the CLC relating to the issue of jurisdiction and immunities. While Article 5 provides that:

> Each Party shall provide in its internal law for appropriate procedures for persons who have suffered damage as a result of an act of corruption by its public officials in the exercise of their functions to claim for compensation from the State or, in the case of a non-state Party, from that Party's appropriate authorities.

It remains unclear what these "appropriate procedures" may be. At the very least, it may be posited that the provision connotes procedures that would ensure state parties not invoking the rules around state immunity should civil proceedings be brought against either or both states and state officials, for losses suffered concerning conduct falling within the scope of the CLC (assuming jurisdiction can be otherwise established), and that any other interpretation would potentially be inconsistent with the object and purpose of the instrument. However, the Article's unfortunate equivocal language simply reflects the significant problems that exist where suit against state entities is contemplated, be it through the application of the rules on state immunity,[34] or of other concepts, including the act of state doctrine.[35]

Kramer recently pointed to this difficulty, usefully couching the issues in terms of international comity.[36] These issues are engaged where courts are asked to exercise civil jurisdiction over corruption cases involving States or State instrumentalities as a defendant, in which state immunity may be raised, or are required to adjudicate cases between private actors impugning an act of a state.[37]

In this context, it is also important to note that, while the trend has been that States have moved away from an application of the absolute immunity doctrine, so that no immunity may be claimed in relation to a state's commercial activity, some states, including crucially China, continue to follow the absolute immunity approach.[38] Assuming that the majority of corruption cases are likely to arise in the context of large-scale BRI infrastructure projects, where these projects are funded by Chinese-owned banks,[39] it is not difficult to foresee how a rather conservative approach to state immunity may result in a procedural bar to a court's jurisdiction, and with that to effective access to justice.

It is apparent that questions relating to sovereignty and immunity are particularly pertinent in the context of the BRI, and have the potential to stifle significantly effective access to justice. Existing international instruments do

34 The 2004 UN Convention on Immunities provides in Article 4, a "State enjoys immunity, in respect of itself and its property, from the jurisdiction of the courts of another State". States, including state institutions and officials, thus enjoy jurisdictional immunity, and cannot be obliged to appear before a foreign court, even where private international law rules provide the basis for international jurisdiction.

35 As Kramer explains: Interwoven with sovereignty and state immunity is the act of state doctrine, mostly adopted in common law countries, including the United Kingdom and the United States. It prohibits courts from inquiring into the validity of sovereign acts performed within the sovereign's territory.

36 See generally Kramer, *op. cit.*, 99–142. Kramer (n 25).

37 Article 4 of UNCAC entrenches these issues further.

38 *Democratic Republic of the Congo and Ors v FG Hemisphere Associates LLC* [2010] FACV 5, 6 & 7 (Court of Final Appeal).

39 As has been noted, the BRI strategy is an 'estimated $5 trillion plan, to be funded primarily by Chinese banks and China-led multilateral financial institutions' see, Alexandra Wrage, 'Companies Engaging in China's Belt and Road Projects Must Address Bribery Risks' (*Forbes*, 12 October 2017) <www.forbes.com/sites/alexandrawrage/2017/10/12/companies-engaging-in-chinas-belt-road-projects-must-address-bribery-risks/#53056bf24f52> accessed 19 December 2017; also note that funding is also expected from the Asia Infrastructure Development Bank (AIDB). Issues around the immunities of the AIDB also exist. Those matters are outside the scope of this chapter.

not provide sufficiently effective and clear rules, and, accordingly, resolving jurisdictional concerns in this regard needs close consideration.

Conclusion

As was stated at the outset, BRI is in its infancy. It is unwise to make conclusive proposals. At this early stage of its development, what can be said is that dealing with the civil aspects of anti-corruption is of a high priority because there is a link between corruption and commercial activity.

For persons who suffer loss as a result of corrupt activity, appropriate remedies and dispute resolution mechanisms consistent with international standards of due process and procedural fairness must be available to provide appropriate and effective access to justice.

The allocative and cooperative rules of private international law are key. Their ability to provide clear answers to questions of jurisdiction, applicable law and the recognition and enforcement of foreign judgments, as well as a number of crucial procedural issues, suggests that this area of law is ideally suited to provide a flexible and neutral mechanism to combat corruption. Kramer succinctly concluded:

> The reality today is that private law is an important instrument to effect policy objectives and to influence human behavior. In an era of globalisation and in the face of the reality of corruption, not only criminal law and public international law can make a stand; private law and private international law can play a role as well.

The BRI is a bold initiative cross-cutting many diverse jurisdictions. For the BRI to be successful, the initiative must address the risk of corruption. China has already indicated its desire for a clean BRI. To achieve this goal, the UNCAC and CLC may serve as inspiration and a primary building block for a clear and robust legal infrastructure that can complement their efforts in combatting corruption. Existing instruments developed and adopted by the HCCH further complement the emerging scaffolding with tested, strong, effective and globally operating frameworks that govern specific civil matters that can arise in the context of corruption. Clearly, all participating jurisdictions should become State Parties to the most relevant commercial, civil procedure and legal cooperation instruments of this organisation.

However, there remain real uncertainties and gaps that could present significant risks to the success of the BRI. Much more research in this regard is needed, yet it is suggested that it will become paramount to build upon the existing scaffolding that resolves these issues and provides answers to the questions raised in this chapter. Only if and when dedicated allocative and cooperative rules of private international law have been agreed upon, at a preferably global level, sound access to justice for those adversely affected by corrupt activity may become a reality, and the global fight against corruption enters a new era.

Part VI

Judgments and arbitral awards recognition

11 The role of Hong Kong in the dispute resolutions of One Belt One Road

King Fung Tsang

Introduction

Hong Kong is in a special position on the roadmap of China's One Belt One Road (OBOR) initiative.[1] First, Hong Kong is part of China, so it is not a partnering country in the initiative.[2] However, due to its status as a world financial centre, Hong Kong plays a significant role in the financing of OBOR projects.[3] Second, Hong Kong has its own legal system[4] that is well regarded for its independent judiciary,[5] highly skilled professionals and vast experience in handling China-related disputes.[6] Thus, Hong Kong has the infrastructure to be a dispute resolution centre for China-related litigations. Third, and most relevant to this chapter, it can be argued that Hong Kong, with its private international law rules, offers litigants advantages for resolving transaction disputes in OBOR projects. As will be seen from the discussions ahead, these advantages appear greater than what litigation in alternative fora can offer.

Since Hong Kong's return to China in 1997, Hong Kong and China have entered into multiple judicial assistance arrangements that have substantially

1 For the background and policy goals of the One Belt One Road initiative, see Chapter 1.

2 For a list of 67 Belt and Road countries and their general profile, see Chapter 1 and references therein.

3 The Hong Kong Government, 'The 2016 Policy Address (Extract)' *(Belt and Road Initiative)* <www.beltandroad.gov.hk/pa2016.html> accessed 1 November 2017, see paras 42–48.

4 Art.8 of The Basic Law of the Hong Kong Special Administrative Region of the People's Republic of China (Adopted at the Third Session of the Seventh National People's Congress on 4 April 1990 Promulgated by Order No.26 of the President of the People's Republic of China on 4 April 1990 Effective as of 1 July 1997) (hereinafter the 'Basic Law of the Hong Kong SAR').

5 Art.2, Basic Law of Hong Kong SAR. The Global Competitiveness Report of the World Economic Forum ranked Hong Kong's judicial independence at 13th place in the world. See World Economic Forum, 'The Global Competitiveness Report 2017–2018' <www3.weforum.org/docs/GCR2017-2018/05FullReport/TheGlobalCompetitivenessReport2017%E2%80%932018.pdf> accessed 1 November 2017, see in particular p. 141.

6 *Botanic Ltd v China National Oil Corp* [2008] HKEC 1424., [65].

facilitated dispute resolutions.[7] These include 'Arrangement on Reciprocal Recognition and Enforcement of Judgments in Civil and Commercial Matters by the Courts of the Mainland and of the Hong Kong Special Administrative Region Pursuant to Choice of Court Agreements between Parties Concerned' ('Enforcement Arrangement');[8] 'Arrangement for Mutual Service of Judicial Documents in Civil and Commercial Proceedings Between the Mainland and Hong Kong Courts' ('Service Arrangement'); and, most recently, 'Arrangement on Mutual Taking of Evidence in Civil and Commercial Matters Between the Courts of the Mainland and the Hong Kong Special Administrative Region' ('Evidence Arrangement'). Of all these arrangements, the Enforcement Arrangement is of particular importance. Enforcement of commercial judgments has long been a contentious area in dispute resolutions relating to China,[9] but the enforceability of Hong Kong judgments in China gives Hong Kong a unique advantage in being a dispute resolution centre for matters involving OBOR.

In this chapter, we will examine how Hong Kong positions itself to facilitate dispute resolution in the OBOR initiative according to the three major issues of private international law, namely enforcement, jurisdiction and choice of law. Emphasis will obviously be placed on the Enforcement Arrangement. Further, having regard to the recent developments in the principle of reciprocity under the Chinese civil procedural law,[10] it appears that even Hong Kong judgments falling outside the scope of the Enforcement Arrangement might now be enforceable in China on the basis of reciprocity. This reciprocity requirement will in turn demand consideration of the enforcement regime of Chinese judgments in Hong Kong, which is itself undergoing a phase of development.

In addition to the discussion on the enforcement of Hong Kong judgments in China, this chapter will examine aspects of the jurisdiction and choice of law of Hong Kong's private international law that will facilitate OBOR dispute resolution. Last, the impacts of the recent Evidence Arrangement will be analysed to complete the discussion. However, this chapter will not discuss arbitration, which involves rather different considerations and may be best reserved for a specific piece of research.[11]

7 To date, Hong Kong has entered into five legal assistance arrangements with Mainland China. See Department of Justice, The Government of the Hong Kong Special Administrative Region, 'Arrangements with the Mainland and the Macao SAR' <www.doj.gov.hk/eng/mainland/intracountry.html> accessed 1 November 2017.

8 For background of the Enforcement Arrangement, see Xianchu Zhang and Philip Smart, 'Development of Regional Conflict of Laws: On the Arrangement of Mutual Recognition and Enforcement of Judgments in Civil and Commercial Matters Between Mainland China and Hong Kong SAR' (2006) 36 *Hong Kong Law Journal* 553.

9 Michael J. Moser, *Dispute Resolution in China* (JurisNet 2012), 381.

10 King Fung Tsang, 'Enforcement of Foreign Commercial Judgments in China' (forthcoming) *Journal of Private International* Law.

11 For Hong Kong private international law rules on enforcement of foreign arbitral awards, see Alan Gibb, Richard Morris and King Fung Tsang, *An Introduction to the Conflict of Laws in Hong Kong* (LexisNexis 2017), 87–92.

Enforcement of Hong Kong judgments in China

Enforcement of foreign judgments in China is arguably the most important topic of all private international law issues as far as OBOR dispute resolution is concerned. Because the legal systems of both China and many of the OBOR countries are still developing,[12] it is expected that a substantial amount of litigation stemming from the OBOR projects will be conducted in a third country. It is likely that one of the litigants will be a Chinese party, as China is the leader of the OBOR initiative. Combining these two factors, it is foreseeable that the need for the enforcement of foreign judgments in China will arise repeatedly throughout the OBOR initiative. However, to date, enforcement of commercial judgments rendered by foreign courts in China remains rather difficult.[13] A foreign judgment against a Chinese party may have no value if it is not enforceable in China assuming that the Chinese party has no assets elsewhere. It is exactly against this background that dispute resolution in Hong Kong provides a significant advantage due to the higher enforceability of its judgments in China.

Enforcement arrangement

Conceptually, Hong Kong judgments are treated as foreign judgments as far as Chinese private international law is concerned.[14] Under Article 282 of the Chinese Civil Procedure Law,[15] a foreign judgment will be enforceable in China only if either (a) there is a treaty between China and the judgment-rendering country that provides for such enforcement; or (b) the principle of 'reciprocity' ('Hùhuì yuánzé') is satisfied. Of the 67 OBOR countries, only 22 have entered into an enforcement treaty with China.[16] In addition, there are very few reported cases of successful enforcement in China under these treaties.[17] Because Hong Kong is not itself a country, no enforcement treaty can be entered into between Hong Kong and China. However, the treaty-like Enforcement Arrangement was concluded in 2006. Under this Enforcement Arrangement, Hong Kong and China will mutually enforce money judgments in civil and commercial cases as long as the judgment was rendered by a court

12 China's rule of law, despite its rapid developments, is still perceived by foreign countries as a problem. China currently ranks 46th in the latest report of the World Economic Forum. See World Economic Forum (n 5), 91.

13 See, in general, Moser (n 9).

14 See Petition of Yuanqiao Investment Ltd for the Recognition of the Civil Judgment Rendered by Hong Kong Court, Fujian Quanzhou IPC, (2001) Quan Min Zi No 1.

15 Civil Procedure Law of the People's Republic of China (Adopted at the Fourth Session of the Seventh National People's Congress and promulgated by Order No.44 of the President of the People's Republic of China on 9 April 1991).

16 King Fung Tsang, 'Chinese Bilateral Judgment Enforcement Treaties' (2017) 40(1) *Loyola of Los Angeles International and Comparative Law Review* 1, 6–7.

17 A rare successful case reported recently is *Case regarding The Application of Fuligubohr Co., Ltd. for Recognition and Enforcement of Poland Court Judgment, (2013) Zhe Yong Min Que Zi No1,(Zhejiang Ningbo IPC., Mar. 12 2014).*

that has been designated in the agreement between the litigants to have exclusive jurisdiction on the matter, subject to limited exceptions.[18]

In 2008, Hong Kong passed the Mainland Judgment (Reciprocal Enforcement) Ordinance (Cap. 597) which gives effect to the terms of the Arrangement. On China's side, again in 2008 the Supreme People's Court ('SPC') promulgated the 'Interpretation by the Supreme People's Court on the Arrangement on Reciprocal Recognition and Enforcement of Judgments in Civil and Commercial Matters by the Courts of the Mainland and of the Hong Kong Special Administrative Region Pursuant to Choice of Court Agreements between Parties Concerned' ('SPC Interpretation').[19] The ensuing discussion focuses on the SPC Interpretation as it is more likely for parties from OBOR countries to pursue dispute resolution against Chinese parties in Hong Kong and seek enforcement in China rather than the other way around.

In order to bring a Hong Kong judgment under the regime of the SPC Interpretation, it must be within the scope of the Enforcement Arrangement.[20] This is limited to 'an enforceable final judgment requiring payment of money in a civil and commercial case pursuant to a choice of court agreement in writing'.[21] It does not include certain types of judgments that might otherwise be broadly regarded as commercial but does include those dealing with employment contracts[22] and bankruptcy.[23]

The most significant threshold in qualifying for the enforcement is the requirement on 'choice of court agreement'. Article 3 provides that a choice of court agreement is one where a Hong Kong court is 'expressly designated as the court having sole jurisdiction for resolving any dispute' arising from the relevant civil or commercial contracts. In other words, only an exclusive jurisdiction clause designating Hong Kong as having exclusive jurisdiction on the matter will suffice.

Assuming the Hong Kong judgment satisfies the jurisdictional requirement, it will generally be enforceable in China as if it is a domestic judgment[24] but subject to limited exceptions under Article 9. These include cases in which (a) the exclusive jurisdiction clause is invalid under Hong Kong law;[25] (b) the Hong Kong judgment has been wholly satisfied;[26] (c) the Chinese courts

18 Arts.1, 3 and 9 of the Enforcement Arrangement.

19 SPC, 'Arrangement of the Supreme People's Court Between the Mainland and the HKSAR on Reciprocal Recognition and Enforcement of the Decisions of Civil and Commercial Cases under Consensual Jurisdiction' (2008) 9.

20 Art.1 of the SPC Interpretation.

21 *Ibid.*

22 Art.3 of the SPC Interpretation.

23 Re the Application of NORSTAR to Recognize the Order of the Court of HKSAR, [2011] Min Si Ta Zi No 19.

24 Art.11 of the SPC Interpretation.

25 Art.9(1) of the SPC Interpretation.

26 Art.9(2) of the SPC Interpretation.

have exclusive jurisdiction over the matter;[27] (d) the judgment debtor did not appear in court, having not been given due notice of the trial;[28] (e) the judgment was obtained by fraud;[29] (f) a judgment on the same cause of action between the parties has been made by a Chinese court, or by a foreign court, or an arbitral award has been made by the arbitration body concerned in which the said judgment or award has already been recognised or enforced by the Chinese court where enforcement of the judgment is sought; and (g) the enforcement of the Hong Kong judgment in China is contrary to the social and public interests of China.[30]

Overall, the SPC Interpretation is designed and functions very much like most of the other enforcement treaties China has entered into.[31] They all follow the scope, exceptions and enforcement according to the domestic judgment pattern, even though the exact scope and particular exceptions vary.[32]

Since the SPC Interpretation came into effect, there have been at least four reported cases involving the use of the Interpretation to enforce a Hong Kong judgment.[33] For example, in *Bel Nickel Resources Ltd*,[34] a Hong Kong judgment creditor sought to enforce a Hong Kong judgment regarding a loan agreement against a Chinese judgment debtor in Quan Zhou City, Fujian, China, under the SPC Interpretation. The Quan Zhou City Intermediate People's Court held that there existed a jurisdiction clause in favour of Hong Kong.[35] The judgment, therefore, fell under the scope of the Enforcement Arrangement. Further, the judgment did not conform with the exceptions

27 Art.9(3) of the SPC Interpretation.
28 Art.9(4) of the SPC Interpretation.
29 Art.9(5) of the SPC Interpretation.
30 Art.9 of the SPC Interpretation.
31 Tsang (n 10).
32 Tsang (n 16), 12–30.
33 *The Application of Bel Nickel Resources Ltd., Quanzhou Tenglong Coal Co. Ltd. and Xiao Wenlong for Recognition and Enforcement of HongKong Court Judgment, (2015) Quan Min Ren Zi No76, (Fujian Quanzhou IPC., Feb. 29 2016); The Application of Zhuoyue Investment Co., Ltd. and Xiao Wenlong for Recognition and Enforcement of HongKong Court Judgment, (2016) Min 08 Ren Gang No1, (Fujian Longyan IPC., Dec.12 2016); The Application of Rainbow Dream Worldwide Corp. for Recognition and Enforcement of HongKong Court Judgment, (2017) E 27 Ren Gang No1, (Wuhan Maritime Court, Apr. 20 2017);The Application of Swift Surplus Holdings Limited and Top Vision Management Limited for Recognition and Enforcement of HongKong Court Judgment, (2014) Zhao Zhong Min Fa Er Chu Zi No1, (Guangdong Zhaoqing IPC., Jul. 16 2015).*
34 *The Application of Bel Nickel Resources Ltd., Quanzhou Tenglong Coal Co. Ltd. and Xiao Wenlong for Recognition and Enforcement of HongKong Court Judgment, (2015) Quan Min Ren Zi No76, (Fujian Quanzhou IPC., Feb. 29 2016)*
35 *Ibid.*, The court's interpretation of jurisdiction agreement is rather liberal. Article 3 of the SPC Interpretation requires that the jurisdiction agreement must designate Hong Kong court having sole jurisdiction over the contractual disputes. However, on the basis of the relevant clause disclosed in the Chinese judgment, it is not clear that the clause designates exclusive jurisdiction to the Hong Kong court ('Any dispute arising out of the contract shall be subject to the jurisdiction of the Hong Kong courts').

provided under Article 9. Accordingly, the Hong Kong judgment was enforceable under the Enforcement Agreement.

While reported cases on successful enforcement are limited, this may have more to do with the reporting system of China.[36] In addition, based on the author's empirical research on China's enforcement of judgments rendered by the courts of ten major jurisdictions, only Taiwan and Macau have had more successful enforcement cases in China than Hong Kong.[37] In any event, the successful enforcement experience of Hong Kong judgments under the Enforcement Arrangement serves as a positive sign of similar enforcement in the future. It is also expected that future cases will refine the enforcement regime under the SPC Interpretation. For example, these cases may be able to clarify articles that have not been discussed in previous cases such as the circumstances where social and public interests of China may be used as a ground for rejection.[38]

Although the Enforcement Arrangement will substantially facilitate the enforcement of Chinese judgments against defendants from OBOR countries in Hong Kong,[39] it is unlikely to have many such cases due to the limited presence of OBOR defendants in Hong Kong. It is, nonetheless, positive to have an additional route to facilitate dispute resolutions if such OBOR defendants actually have assets in Hong Kong. There has been only one case involving the enforcement of Chinese judgment in Hong Kong under the Mainland Judgment (Reciprocal Enforcement) Ordinance to date. In吳作程 v 梁儷,[40] the judgment debtor argued that the judgment rendered by the Shenzhen Intermediate People's Court should not be enforced in Hong Kong on the basis that it was not final despite the fact that the Shenzhen court had issued a certificate to that effect. The Hong Kong court held that the judgment was enforceable because the certificate from the Shenzhen court was statutorily presumed to be evidence of finality unless it was proved otherwise by the judgment debtor under s.6(2) of the Ordinance.[41] In this case, the judgment debtor had failed to prove such a case.[42] Accordingly, the Chinese judgment was enforceable under the Ordinance.

36 Prior to 2013 when the Supreme People's Court developed the official judgment database (China Judgement Online), there was no official judgment reporting system in China. See Supreme People's Court, 'Provisions of the Supreme People's Court on the Issuance of Judgments on the Internet by the People's Courts', Fa shi (2013) 26.

37 Tsang (n 10).

38 Art.9 of the SPC Interpretation.

39 Chinese judgment may not be enforceable in the OBOR countries. However, Hong Kong will enforce the Chinese judgment under Mainland Judgment (Reciprocal Enforcement) Ordinance against OBOR parties which have assets in Hong Kong.

40 [2016] HKEC 400.

41 *Ibid.* [21].

42 *Ibid.* [22].

While the case was regarded as the first and only case under the Ordinance,[43] most Chinese judgments to be enforced under the Ordinance do not go through litigation, as enforceable Chinese judgments are registered pursuant to s.5(2) of the Ordinance. According to the court records, between 5 March 2015 and 8 March 2017 there were 25 Chinese judgments registered successfully by the Hong Kong courts under the Ordinance.[44] This suggests that the Enforcement Arrangement between Hong Kong and China is running well.

Reciprocity

If a case does not fall within the scope of the Enforcement Arrangement (hereinafter 'non-arrangement judgment'), such as the case where there is no exclusive jurisdiction agreement, enforcement of a Hong Kong judgment in China can rely only on the principle of reciprocity under the aforementioned Article 282 of the Civil Procedure Law. However, there is no definition of reciprocity under Chinese law. Until recently, it was widely perceived that enforcement of a foreign judgment under reciprocity was impossible.[45] However, the Chinese courts have now taken steps towards developing this limb of enforcement. As will be seen ahead, this opens up the possibility of non-arrangement judgments to be enforced in China.

In *Kolmar Group AG v Sutex Group*,[46] the Nanking Intermediate People's Court enforced a Singaporean judgment under the principle of reciprocity in December 2016. Although the court did not give a definition of reciprocity, it regarded reciprocity as being established between China and Singapore by way of an enforcement of a Chinese judgment by a Singaporean court in 2014.[47] In contrast, prior to that 2014 enforcement of a Chinese judgment

43 See O'Melveny, 'Hong Kong Law Update: Registering a Mainland Judgment in Hong Kong' <www.omm.com/resources/alerts-and-publications/publications/registering-a-mainland-judgment-in-hong-kong/> accessed 1 November 2017, Kwok Kit Cheung, 'First Reported Case Under Mainland Judgments (Reciprocal Enforcement) Ordinance (Cap 597)' (*Deacons*, 9 March 2016) <www.deacons.com.hk/news-and-insights/publications/first-reported-case-under-mainland-judgments-(reciprocal-enforcement)-ordinance-(cap-597).html> accessed 1 November 2017.

44 Register of Mainland Judgment (for Mainland Judgment registered in Hong Kong under the Reciprocal Enforcement Ordinance).

45 See Moser (n 9), 401; see also Donald C. Clarke, 'The Enforcement of United States Court Judgments in China: A Research Note' *(GW Law Faculty Publications & Other Works. Paper 1067)* <http://scholarship.law.gwu.edu/cgi/viewcontent.cgi?article=2260&context=faculty_publications> accessed 1 November 2017 (regarding the difficulty of enforcing US judgments in China on reciprocity).

46 *Kolmar Group AG v Sutex Group*, Civil Case No 3, Nanjing Intermediate People's Court (9 December 2016).

47 *Giant Light Metal Technology (Kunshan) Co Ltd v Aksa Far East Pte Ltd* [2014] 2 SLR 545, 551.

in Singapore, Chinese courts had denied enforcement of Singaporean judgments in China for lack of reciprocity.[48] It is, therefore, suggested that a single successful prior enforcement of a Chinese judgment in the judgment-rendering country can establish reciprocity between China and the foreign country.[49]

If one looks at the situation before the *Kolmar* case was decided, this new standard of reciprocity can hardly be considered a coincidence. Back in 2015, the SPC issued the 'Several Opinions of the Supreme People's Court on Providing Judicial Services and Safeguards for the Construction of the "Belt and Road" by People's Courts'.[50] Among the suggestions made by the SPC for facilitating OBOR dispute resolution was the encouragement of Chinese courts to take the initiative to enforce judgments from OBOR countries so as to establish reciprocity.[51] Not only is Singapore an OBOR country, but also it is one of China's leading trade partners among all the OBOR countries.[52] While it can be noted that the *Kolmar* case does not fall into the context described in the SPC Policy because it was Singapore which had taken the initiative to enforce Chinese judgments first, the *Kolmar* case clearly reflects the willingness of the Chinese judiciary to make enforcement of OBOR country judgments easier by way of the reciprocity limb.

The status of the *Kolmar* case has subsequently been elevated by the SPC. The case was selected as one of the top ten model cases for the establishment of OBOR in May 2017.[53] Although China does not run a common law system and so does not follow the doctrine of *stare decisis*, cases decided or endorsed by the SPC are generally expected to be followed by Chinese courts.[54] The selection by the SPC has, therefore, cemented the *Kolmar* case as a correctly decided precedent and it now reflects the official view of the SPC.

In fact, this new standard seems to have been adopted by at least two high profile cases involving the enforcement of US judgments in China.[55] In both

48 *Sino-Environment Technology Group Limited (Singapore) v Thumb Environmental Technology Group (Fujian) Co., Ltd. (disputes over shareholder's contribution), (2014) Min Si Zhong Zi No20, (SPC., Jun. 11 2014).*

49 Tsang (n 10).

50 SPC, 'Several Opinions of the Supreme People's Court on Providing Judicial Services and Safeguards for the Construction of the "Belt and Road" by People's Courts' (2015) 9.

51 *Ibid.*, para. 6.

52 See National Bureau of Statistics of China, 'Total Value of Imports and Exports by Country (Region) of Origin/Destination' <http://data.stats.gov.cn/english/easyquery.htm?cn=C01> accessed 1 November 2017.

53 The Supreme People's Court of The People's Republic of China, 'Model Cases Regarding the Building of "One Belt and One Road"' <www.court.gov.cn/zixun-xiangqing-44722.html> accessed 1 November 2017 (in Chinese).

54 Hongyi Chen, *An Introduction to the Legal System of the People's Republic of China* (4th edn, LexisNexis 2011), 167.

55 *Liu Li v Tao Li and Tong Wu* (2015) Yue Wuhan Zhong Min Shang Wai Chu Zi No.00026, the Intermediate People's Court of Wuhan City, Hubei province, 30 June 2017 (enforcing a California on reciprocity); *Application of Matthew Yangli and Lei Fukang for Recognition and Enforcement of Judgement and Arbitration Award* (2015)

cases, the Chinese courts cited *Hubei Gezhouba Sanlian Industrial Co., Ltd. et. al. v Robinson Helicopter Co., Inc.*,[56] a 2009 California case that enforced a Chinese judgment rendered by the Hubei Higher Court to establish reciprocity.[57] Neither case, however, discussed the few occasions in which US courts had rejected enforcement of Chinese judgments in the past.[58] This indicates that a single successful prior enforcement of a Chinese judgment can satisfy the requirement of reciprocity even if there is also a negative enforcement record in the same country.[59]

How then does the *Kolmar* case affect the enforceability of the non-arrangement judgments in China? Prior to the *Kolmar* case, Hong Kong judgments were denied enforcement in China on the basis of a lack of reciprocity.[60] However, with the lower standard of reciprocity indicated by the *Kolmar* case, it is at least arguable that Hong Kong cases will now be enforced in China given the record of successful enforcement of Chinese judgments in Hong Kong in the past.

As mentioned previously, there has been a number of successful enforcements of Chinese judgments in Hong Kong under the Enforcement Arrangement. However, it is not clear whether successful enforcement under these arrangements or treaties will count towards reciprocity under the new standard. One argument against the use of such cases for reciprocity is that this will effectively widen the scope of the relevant enforcement arrangements or treaties beyond their original intention. In particular, most of these arrangements and treaties have specific conditions that are not otherwise specified under Article 282. Allowing cases under arrangements or treaties to be treated for the purpose of reciprocity could, therefore, make it easier to enforce a foreign judgment under reciprocity than the arrangement or treaty itself.

Even if these Enforcement Arrangement cases are not included in establishing reciprocity, there are still successful enforcements of Chinese judgments in Hong Kong under the common law rules for the establishment of reciprocity.[61] According to the common law rules on the enforcement of foreign judg-

Yu 15 Xie Wai Ren No.3, the Intermediate People's Court of Xinyang, Henan province, 5 August, 2017 (declining to rule on issue of reciprocity due to lack of subject matter jurisdiction).

56 *Hubei Gezhouba Sanlian Industrial v Robinson Helicopter Company*, 2009 WL 2190187 (C.D.Cal.).

57 *Ibid.*

58 *Ibid.*

59 Tsang (n 10).

60 *NKK(Japan) v Beijing Zhuangsheng, (2008) Gao Min Zhong Zi No.99, (Beijing HPC., Jul. 06 2009) The Application of Li Dengli Corp. for Recognition and Enforcement of HongKong High Court Judgment,(Fujian Xiamen IPC., Feb. 23 2000).*

61 See, for example, *First Laser Ltd v Fujian Enterprises (Holdings) Co Ltd* [2012] HKCFA 52; [2012] HKEC 946 (The Hong Kong Court of Final Appeal).

ments, a foreign judgment can be enforced in Hong Kong if the following conditions are satisfied:

1 The judgment rendering court has international jurisdiction;
2 The judgment is a money judgment that does not relate to taxes or penalties;
3 The judgment is final and conclusive; and
4 No jurisdiction grounds exist to deny the enforcement such as being contrary to natural justice and public policy of Hong Kong.[62]

While it is not the intention of this chapter to discuss Hong Kong common law rules of enforcement in detail, four points must be noted. First, Chinese judgments are treated as foreign judgments under Hong Kong conflict of laws rules. Second, these common law enforcement rules are basically identical to those adopted by Singapore, with both jurisdictions sharing the same root in English private international law. Thus, it is foreseeable that the enforcement of a Chinese judgment under the same rules will establish reciprocity between Hong Kong and China.

Third, there are, in fact, successful enforcements of Chinese judgments based on these rules. These include successful recognition of a Chinese commercial judgment in *First Laser Ltd v Fujian Enterprises (Holdings) Co Ltd*[63] and a Chinese family law judgment in *ML v YJ*.[64] Both were decided by the Court of Final Appeal, the highest court in Hong Kong. The enforcement of a Chinese money judgment was also successful in *Hung Fung Enterprises Holdings Ltd v The Agricultural Bank of China*.[65]

Fourth, although Hong Kong does have its fair share of unsuccessful Chinese judgment enforcements, it does not appear that these are by themselves fatal for the establishment of reciprocity as long as there are also successes. In addition, there have also been developments in recent cases that make such failed enforcements less likely in the future.

Historically, the most usual common law basis of rejection comes from the lack of finality of the Chinese judgments. Under Chinese law, a judgment rendered by a court is subject to supervision by the Procuratorate.[66] This judgment supervision system is foreign to common law jurisdictions and has acted as a bar on enforcing cases in Hong Kong. The leading case is *Chiyu Banking Corporation Limited v Chan Tin Kwun*.[67] In that case, a dispute over a guarantee was litigated in the Fujian Intermediate People's Court. The plaintiff

62 For detailed discussion on the common law enforcement regime, see Gibb, Morris and Tsang (n 11), Chapter 4.
63 *First Laser* (n 61).
64 [2010] HKEC 1924.
65 [2012] HKEC 870.
66 Art.200 of the Civil Procedure Law of the PRC.
67 [1996] 2 HKLR 395.

prevailed and obtained a judgment against the defendant which the plaintiff sought to enforce in Hong Kong. A subsequent appeal by the defendant to the Fujian Higher People's Court was dismissed. The judgment debtor then presented a petition to the Fujian People's Procuratorate for a retrial.[68] At the time of the enforcement proceedings in Hong Kong, the Fujian People's Procuratorate had presented a report to the Supreme People's Procuratorate that requested it to lodge a protest against the Fujian judgment.[69] The issue for the Hong Kong Court of First Instance was whether the Fujian judgment was final and conclusive under the common law rules. Cheung J. was of the opinion that the Fujian judgment was not final and conclusive, and stated:

> It is not final and unalterable in the court which pronounced it. It is liable to be altered by the intermediate court on a retrial if the Supreme People's Procuratorate lodges a protest in accordance with the Civil Procedure Law. If upon protest being made, rare though the circumstances may be, a Chinese court has to retry the case, then, clearly it retains the power to alter its own decision.
>
> (internal quotation omitted)[70]

Accordingly, the court suspended the enforcement proceedings for six months pending the decision of the Supreme People's Procuratorate.[71] Six subsequent Court of Appeal cases discussed the finality issue but none of them managed to settle it.[72] In *Lee Yau Wing v Lee Shui Kwan*,[73] the majority of the Court of Appeal argued that the issue revolved around whether a Chinese judgment lacked finality just by the existence of the judgment supervision in China or whether it depended on the actual circumstances of the case.[74] Having regard to the public interest of the issue, the Court of Appeal held that it could not be decided without going through a trial which would give the court a chance to hear evidence from expert witnesses.[75] The court even urged the Legal Aid Department to provide funding to the defendant of the case to appeal to the Court of Final Appeal in order to settle the matter.[76]

68 *Ibid.*
69 *Ibid.*
70 *Ibid.*, 399.
71 *Ibid.*, 400.
72 *Lee Yau Wing v Lee Shui Kwan* [2007] 2 HKLRD 749; 伍威對劉一萍 unrep., CACV 32/2009, [2009] CHKEC 261); *Tan Tay Cuan v Ng Chi Hung* unrep., HCA 5477/2000, [2001] HKLRD (Yrbk) 195; 林哲民對林志滔 unrep., HCA 9585/1999, [2003] CHKEC 325; 林哲民日昌電業公司訴張順連 unrep., CACV No 1046 of 2001, [2002] CHKEC 2367; and 林哲民經營之日昌電業公司對林志滔 (unrep., CACV No 354 of 2001, 18 December 2001).
73 *Lee Yau Wing* (n 72).
74 *Ibid.* [24].
75 *Ibid.* [27].
76 *Ibid.* [29].

Unfortunately, the Court of Final Appeal is yet to be given the opportunity to consider this issue.[77]

More recently, however, in *Bank of China Ltd v Yang Fan*,[78] To J. sitting at the Court of First Instance gave a very detailed review of the issue.[79] Having regard to the latest relevant provisions in the Civil Procedure Law,[80] he was of the opinion that the judgment supervision system should not be a bar to enforcement of Chinese judgments. In particular, Article 211 provides that the issue revolved around whether the court which has accepted the protest can make a decision on whether to retry the case within 30 days of receipt of the protest. Thus, the court now has an option not to re-try the case and if it decides against re-trial, it will be the end of the protest. He, therefore, compared the current judgment supervision system to an appellate system, though one that is initiated by a non-party.[81] Having said this, To J. was mindful that he was bound by the Court of Appeal's decision to reserve the settlement of this issue to a full trial.[82] In any event, the case suggests that Chinese judgments may be able to overcome the issue of finality in a Hong Kong court in the future. This will make reciprocity more firmly established between Hong Kong and China.

Comparatively, while the lower standard under the *Kolmar* case can theoretically benefit judgments from the courts of OBOR countries to enforce their judgments directly in China, it is suggested that they generally do not have the positive enforcement record that Hong Kong does.[83] In other words, enforcement of Hong Kong judgments is more certain due to this historical advantage.

In short, whether it occurs under the Enforcement Arrangement or reciprocity, it appears that Hong Kong judgments will generally be enforced in China, and this clearly motivates parties in commercial transactions under the OBOR initiative to choose Hong Kong as the place of dispute resolution.

Enforcement of foreign judgments in Hong Kong against Chinese parties

Hong Kong is a commercial hub of China and serves as the regional centre for a large number of Chinese companies. For example, plenty of Chinese companies are listed in the Hong Kong Stock Exchange. It is reported that 56% of

77 Although the CFA was faced with recognition of Chinese judgment in the *First Laser* case, there was no issue on finality, as the relevant Chinese judgment was rendered by the Supreme People's Court. See *First Laser* (n 61).

78 [2016] 3 HKLRD 7.

79 *Ibid.*

80 Arts. 200 and 211 of the Civil Procedure Law of the PRC.

81 *Yang Fan* (n 78) [53].

82 *Ibid.* [54].

83 Tsang (n 10).

the constituents of the Hang Sang Index are from China.[84] As such, Chinese companies have considerable assets in Hong Kong. If a foreign party in an OBOR-related matter has received a judgment from a foreign, non-Hong Kong court against a Chinese party, it may not need to seek enforcement of the foreign judgment in China if the Chinese party has assets in Hong Kong to satisfy the judgment provided that the said judgment is enforceable in Hong Kong. For example, if an OBOR project has been litigated in England and an English judgment was rendered against a Chinese party with substantial assets in Hong Kong, enforcement of such an English judgment in Hong Kong is another way Hong Kong can contribute to the dispute resolution environment of OBOR.

As mentioned earlier, foreign judgments are generally enforceable under common law rules. Unlike Chinese law, common law enforcement rules do not require reciprocity. Any foreign judgment that has satisfied the enforcement conditions previously discussed will be enforceable in Hong Kong.

In addition, if the judgment-rendering country in question is one of the countries covered by the Foreign Judgment (Reciprocal Enforcement) Ordinance (Cap. 319), enforcement will be sought thereunder. Generally, the enforcement conditions under the Ordinance are designed to replicate those under common law so, apart from certain limited aspects, the test for enforcement is the same.[85] However, if the foreign judgment comes under the Ordinance, it does have certain procedural advantages, such as being able to register as a judgment directly instead of having to go through litigation for the purpose of enforcement.[86] For the time being, 15 countries are covered by the Ordinance.[87]

Last, Hong Kong courts are also willing to assist the enforcement of foreign judgments by granting a *Mareva* injunction in appropriate cases pursuant to s.21(m) of the High Court Ordinance. In *Compania Sud Americana de Vapores SA v Hin Pro*,[88] the Court of Final Appeal upheld the grant of a *Mareva* injunction against the defendant who ignored an English anti-suit injunction that prohibited it from continuing its legal proceedings in China in breach of exclusive jurisdiction agreements.[89] Further, the Court of Final Appeal did not share the concern of the lower court in a case where the grant of the *Mareva* injunction would have the effect of asking the Hong Kong court 'to choose between the [English and Chinese] courts and to . . . arrogate to itself the decision how a foreign court should determine the matter'.[90]

84 Eric Lam and Yue Qiu, 'Hong Kong's Stock Market Tells the Story of China's Growing Dominance' (*Bloomberg*, 23 June 2017) <www.bloomberg.com/graphics/2017-hang-seng-index> accessed 1 November 2017.
85 Gibb, Morris and Tsang (n 11), 85.
86 Section 4 of the Foreign Judgments (Reciprocal Enforcement) Ordinance.
87 Foreign Judgment (Reciprocal Enforcement) Order, Cap 319A.
88 [2016] HKEC 2463.
89 *Ibid.*
90 *Ibid.* [25].

In this light, this case is also an indicator of the independence of the Hong Kong judiciary.

Jurisdiction

The previous discussion on enforcement of Hong Kong judgments in China will not be meaningful if it is difficult for Hong Kong courts to assume jurisdiction in the first place. Like most common law jurisdictions, jurisdiction can be established in Hong Kong even if the transaction has no substantial connection with Hong Kong.[91] This section will examine the advantages offered by Hong Kong jurisdictional rules.

Exclusive jurisdiction agreement

Because the Enforcement Arrangement is based on the existence of an exclusive jurisdiction agreement designating a Hong Kong court, it is important to note that Hong Kong courts will ordinarily exercise jurisdiction if there was a jurisdiction clause in the contract that designated such courts as having exclusive jurisdiction.[92] Only in rare cases will the courts decline the assumption of jurisdiction based on *forum non conveniens*, such as where the insistence of strict adherence to the exclusive jurisdiction agreement would risk exposing non-parties to serious prejudice.[93]

In addition, Hong Kong courts will be willing to enjoin a party who initiates legal proceedings in a foreign jurisdiction in breach of an exclusive jurisdiction clause designating Hong Kong courts.[94] In fact, unlike an anti-suit injunction that does not involve a breach of an exclusive jurisdiction clause, comity with other jurisdictions will not be a concern.[95] This is so even if the alternative forum is a Chinese forum.[96] This is once again a display of Hong Kong's judicial independence.

Non-exclusive jurisdiction agreement

Even if the jurisdiction clause which designates Hong Kong courts is non-exclusive (and, therefore, not falling within the scope of the Enforcement

91 Jurisdiction can be established by submission, service of writ within Hong Kong and service of writ outside Hong Kong with leave from Hong Kong court. Jurisdiction established under these bases, particularly the first two bases, may not guarantee substantial connections between the transaction and Hong Kong.

92 This reflects the common law position as enunciated in *Donohue v Armco Inc and Others* [2001] UKHL 64, [24].

93 *Ibid.* See also Lord Collins of Mapesbury and others (eds), *Dicey, Morris and Collins on the Conflict of Laws* (15th edn, Sweet & Maxwell 2012), para 12–152.

94 *Ibid.*

95 *Hin-Pro* (n 88), [57].

96 *Ibid.*

Arrangement), Hong Kong courts will treat such a clause the same as an exclusive jurisdiction clause in the *forum non conveniens* context if the legal proceedings have indeed been initiated in Hong Kong as stipulated under the clause. In *Noble Power Investments Ltd v Nissei Stomach Tokyo Co Ltd*,[97] Ma CHJC said:

> I see no difference in principle between an exclusive jurisdiction clause and a non-exclusive jurisdiction clause to the extent that in both situations, the parties have agreed, if they are sued in the named forum, to submit to it . . . In considering the effect of a non-exclusive jurisdiction clause, it is critical to recognize that there are differences in approach depending upon where proceedings have been instituted. Where proceedings are instituted in the named forum (to which the parties have agreed to submit), the party who seeks a stay or otherwise to contest the jurisdiction or appropriateness of that forum, has a very heavy burden to discharge, since that party has by definition agreed contractually to submit to the jurisdiction. In other words, he is seeking to avoid a forum to which he has, by contract, agreed to submit.[98]

Service in Hong Kong as of right

In cases where there is no jurisdiction agreement, proceedings may be initiated in Hong Kong by service of writ inside or outside Hong Kong. A service of writ within Hong Kong is a convenient way to establish jurisdiction of the Hong Kong courts against Chinese companies considering that many of them have branch offices in Hong Kong. This might be regarded as an exorbitant way to establish jurisdiction, and yet it gives undeniable advantages to the plaintiffs in establishing jurisdiction.

For OBOR-related litigations, it is expected that the Chinese defendants may seek to move the litigations to China by arguing *forum non conveniens* to gain the 'home court' advantage. With *forum non conveniens* being the exception rather than the norm, it is submitted that such actions are unlikely to succeed. This is supported by empirical evidence. In a recent survey by the author, only 13 of the 48 cases were successful in moving the litigation to China under the *forum non conveniens* principle.[99]

The low rate of success is due to the nature of the *forum non conveniens* principle. Even without a jurisdiction clause, *forum non conveniens* is still the exception rather than the norm. The general test for *forum non conveniens* is set out in the two-stage test provided by the House of Lords in *Spiliada*

97 [2008] HKEC 1087.

98 *Ibid.* [29]-[31].

99 King-Fung Tsang, 'China's Rule of Law through the Eyes of Private International Law in Common Law Jurisdictions' (forthcoming).

Maritime Corp v Cansulex Ltd.[100] In the first stage of the test, the defendant will need to satisfy the court that there exists 'another available forum which is clearly or distinctly more appropriate than the English forum'.[101] The court will usually consider a number of factors including but not limited to the availability of evidence,[102] enforceability of the foreign judgment and the applicable law.[103] If stage one is satisfied (i.e. there is a more appropriate forum), the Hong Kong court will generally decline to exercise the jurisdiction unless the plaintiff can prove in stage two of the test that he or she will lose 'legitimate personal and juridical advantages' by having the litigation in the alternative forum.[104] These advantages are not clearly defined, but factors considered by precedents include the lack of legal aid[105] and the action being statute-barred in the alternative forum.[106] However, on the basis of a recent survey by the author of previous Hong Kong *forum non conveniens* cases involving China as an alternative forum, general accusations of the corrupted legal system of China have not been successful.[107] This is largely because such attacks must be supported by cogent evidence.[108]

Service out of jurisdiction

Finally, if the Chinese defendant does not have a presence in Hong Kong, jurisdiction may be acquired by service of writ out of jurisdiction. This is a long-arm jurisdiction that is subject to the leave of the Hong Kong courts.[109]

100 [1987] AC 460. In Hong Kong, the test for *forum non conveniens* has been slightly adjusted into three stages by the Court of Appeal: '(I) Is it shown that "Hong Kong is not only not the natural or appropriate forum for the trial, but that there is another available forum which is clearly or distinctly more appropriate than Hong Kong". The evidential burden here is upon the applicant. . . (II) If the answer to (I) is yes, will a trial at this other forum deprive the plaintiff of any "legitimate personal or juridical advantages" . . . The evidential burden here lies upon the plaintiff. . . (III) If the answer to (II) is yes, a court has to balance the advantages of (I) against the disadvantages of (II) . . . Deprivation of one or more juridical advantages will not necessarily be fatal to the applicant provided that the court is satisfied that notwithstanding such loss "substantial justice will be done in the available appropriate forum" . . . Proof of this, which can fairly be called the ultimate burden of persuasion, rests upon the applicant for the stay'. *The Owners of the Cargo lately laden on board the Ship or Vessel "Adhiguna Meranti" v The Owners of Ships or Vessels "Adiguna Harapan" and Others* [1987] HKLA 904, [5]. Despite this adjusted test, it is submitted that it does not negate from the general tenor of *The Spiliada*.

101 *Ibid.*, 477.

102 *Yantai Wahua Poluurethanes Co Ltd v Pur Products Ltd* (unrep, HCA 930/2011).

103 *New Link Consultants Ltd v Air China* [2005] HKEC 815.

104 *The Abidin Daver* [1984] AC 398, 410.

105 *Lubbe v Cape Plc* [2000] 1 WLR 1545 (HL).

106 *Peregrine Fixed Income Limited v JP Morgan Chase Bank* [2005] 2 HKC 37.

107 Tsang (n 10).

108 *Gain Park Holdings v Eversino Investments* [2014] HKEC 1982.

109 Order 11 of the Rules of the High Court (Cap.4A).

The test for the granting of such leave is essentially the same as the two-stage test for *forum non conveniens* except that the burden of proof in stage one is borne by the plaintiff instead of the defendant in a service-out case.[110] The actual service of the writ in China will be effected by the Service Arrangement which was concluded in 1999 between Hong Kong and China. The arrangement greatly facilitates the assumption of jurisdiction by Hong Kong courts in such cases.

Choice of law

In order for OBOR disputes to be resolved in Hong Kong, the dispute may be governed by Chinese law, the law of the relevant OBOR country or a third country law. For large transactions, the governing law will generally be provided expressly in the relevant contracts. Hong Kong provides two distinctive advantages in handling choice of law issues in contract.

First, like England where Hong Kong's private international law has its roots, Hong Kong's choice of law rules generally respect party autonomy in their choice of governing law. In Hong Kong, the choice of law rule in contract is provided in *First Laser Ltd v Fujian Enterprises (Holdings) Co Ltd*.[111] Lord Collins restated the longstanding common law test as follows:

> The common law rule is that the law applicable to a contract is the system of law by which the parties intended the contract to be governed, or, where their intention is neither expressed nor to be inferred from the circumstances, the system of law with which the transaction has its closest and most real connection.[112]

Thus, the first stage of the rule is always to see whether the contract has expressly provided for a governing law. This choice by the party will be respected even though the system of law chosen has no connection with the transaction.[113] For example, an English law-governed contract between a Chinese party and a Polish party will be given effect by the Hong Kong court even if England has nothing to do with the transaction other than its law being chosen as the governing law.

Second, because Chinese law may well be the law chosen by the parties, Hong Kong courts are particularly adept in applying Chinese law. Chinese is one of the official legal languages of Hong Kong.[114] Plenty of legal practitioners and judges are highly proficient in both spoken and written Chinese. Historically, Hong Kong courts have handled plenty of Chinese-related matters

110 *Spiliada* (n 100).
111 First Laser (n 61).
112 *Ibid.* [53].
113 *Vita Food Products Inc v. Unus Shipping Co.* [1937] AC 500, 529.
114 Art.9 of the Basic Law of Hong Kong SAR.

and in particular applied Chinese law in those cases. In *Botanic Ltd v China National Oil Corp*,[115] the court highlighted Hong Kong courts' abilities in handling Chinese law:

> [i]n view of the ever increasing commercial relationship between Hong Kong and PRC, the Hong Kong Courts have on numerous occasions to deal with issues of PRC law, including some complicated ones. More literature on PRC law is now available. . . . More bilingual judges have received legal education on PRC law.[116]

The ability of Hong Kong courts in applying Chinese law is also a factor favouring Hong Kong as an appropriate forum for *forum non conveniens* cases involving China as the alternative court.[117]

Evidence arrangement

Hong Kong entered into the Evidence Arrangement with China on 9 December 2016.[118] As far as obtaining evidence in China is concerned, the Evidence Arrangement was implemented by a SPC Interpretation in 2017.[119] Prior to the arrangement, requests for evidence relating to Hong Kong litigations will need to be made through the Hong Kong and Macau Affairs Office to the SPC.[120] Under Article 2 of the Evidence Arrangement, evidence requests can now be made by the Administration Wing of the Chief Secretary for Administration's Office to the SPC directly. This is clearly much more direct and efficient[121] and will thereby make litigation on OBOR cases more convenient for the litigants in Hong Kong proceedings.

Conclusion

Despite not being an OBOR country, it is easy to see how Hong Kong can play an important role as facilitator in OBOR-related dispute resolutions due

115 *Botanic* (n 6).
116 *Ibid.* [65].
117 New Link (n 103).
118 The Government of the Hong Kong Special Administrative Region, 'Hong Kong signs arrangement with the Mainland on mutual assistance in taking of evidence in civil and commercial matters' (*Press Releases*, 29 December 2016) <www.info.gov.hk/gia/general/201612/29/P2016122900569.htm> accessed 1 November 2017.
119 The Supreme People's Court of China, 'Arrangement on Mutual Taking of Evidence in Civil and Commercial Matters Between the Courts of the Mainland and the Hong Kong Special Administrative Region' [2017] No 4.
120 Zhang Xianchu, Commentary on Arrangement on Mutual Taking of Evidence in Civil and Commercial Matters Between the Courts of the Mainland and the Hong Kong Special Administrative Region *(working paper)*
121 *Ibid.*

to the many advantages offered by its private international law rules. These advantages are most obvious in the Enforcement Arrangement with China as discussed earlier but can also be found in the generally commercial-friendly private international law rules which respect parties' choice of jurisdiction and governing law and that are inherent in the private international law of Hong Kong. As Lord Denning once said about the openness of English courts in dealing with foreign litigations, '[y]ou may call this "forum shopping" if you please, but if the forum is England, it is a good place to shop in, both for the quality of the goods and the speed of service'.[122] It is submitted that Hong Kong provides much the same good service and more to OBOR-related disputes. Equally important is the presence of an impartial judiciary that is capable of making a judicial decision that may conflict with the jurisdiction of the Chinese courts.[123] Although these features all seem to create disadvantages to Chinese parties, it is submitted that the success of the OBOR initiative rests on the existence of an impartial forum, and Hong Kong is uniquely positioned to fill that role. This will encourage the OBOR countries to have a long and fruitful cooperation with China in the future. Finally, it is expected that there will soon be another new arrangement on private international law between Hong Kong and China. According to the meeting record in 2016 between the SPC and the Secretary of Justice Office, the two jurisdictions have been discussing a new arrangement on the recognition and enforcement of non-arrangement judgments. When that arrangement materialises, Hong Kong's status as the undisputed dispute resolution center for OBOR will be further enhanced.

122 *The Atlantic Star* [1973] QB 364, 381–382.

123 The Supreme People's Court of China, 'Reflection and Prospect on the 20th Anniversary of Judicial Assistance Between Mainland and Hong Kong' <www.court.gov.cn/zixun-xiangqing-41642.html> accessed 1 November 2017.

12 The recognition of foreign judgments as a tool of economic integration

Views from Middle Eastern and Arab Gulf countries*

Béligh Elbalti

Introduction

The 'One Belt One Road' (OBOR) initiative, announced by China's President Xi Jinping in 2013, is considered as 'an ambitious connectivity project'.[1] Amongst the declared objectives is the promotion of economic prosperity by fostering economic cooperation between the countries along the OBOR route. The initiative would foster 'economic integration, free flow of goods and services [. . .] enhance trade, commerce, economic activity including promotion of people to people exchanges'.[2] Such a laudable objective would not be successfully achieved if legal protection and assistance were not secured. One of the major tools to guarantee legal protection is to ensure the REFJ rendered in one of the states along the Belt and Road in other partner states. However, the examination of the recognition and enforcement regimes[3] in some potential OBOR countries[4] reveals that the status quo is far from being satisfactory.

This chapter focuses on the judgments' recognition and enforcement regimes in the Middle Eastern and Arab Gulf countries that are potentially concerned with the initiative.[5] The Hong Kong Trade Development Council (HKTDC) indicates that 13 Arab countries are concerned with this initiative:

* Abbreviation: UAE = United Arab Emirates; LAS (AL) = League of Arab States (Arab League); ACC = Arab Cooperation Council; GCC = Gulf Cooperation Council; PIL = Private International Law; CCP = Code of Civil Procedure; CCCP = Code of Civil and Commercial Procedure; CCPE = Code of Civil Procedure and Enforcement; EA = Enforcement Act; EFJA = Enforcement of Foreign Judgments Act; EFCJA = Enforcement of Foreign Court Judgments Act; PCSC = Procedure Code of Sharia Courts; REFJ = Recognition and Enforcement of Foreign Judgments.

1 Nivedita Das Kundu, 'Introduction' in Bal Kishan and Nivedita Das Kundu (eds), *China's One Belt One Road – Initiative, Challenges and Prospects* (Vij Books India Pvt Ltd 2016), 1.

2 *Ibid.*

3 The notions of the 'recognition' and 'enforcement' will be used interchangeably here unless otherwise indicated.

4 See Chapter 1 of this book for the list of OBOR countries.

5 For the purpose of this chapter, Arab countries refer to the States forming the LAS excluding Islamic countries such as Iran or Turkey. In addition, focus will be placed on the

Bahrain, Egypt, Iraq, Jordan, Kuwait, Lebanon, Oman, Palestine, Qatar, Saudi Arabia, Syria, UAE and Yemen. By examining the law of these countries, this chapter aims to highlight the difficulties that may be encountered by foreign judgment holders if appropriate measures are not taken to ameliorate the status quo of the recognition practices in a number of OBOR states. This can be done by reforming national law in order to align it to internationally accepted standards for judgments recognition.[6] A similar result can be achieved by enhancing regional cooperation through establishing and/or adhering to multilateral instruments that guarantee the free movement of judgments among the potential OBOR countries.

In the following pages, this chapter will first present the sources of the recognition law in the Middle Eastern and Arab Gulf countries that are potentially concerned with the OBOR initiative (Part I). It will then briefly outline the conditions required in those countries for the REFJ (Part II) before highlighting certain conditions that the author considers particularly problematic and a source of legal uncertainty (Part III). Finally, the chapter will present general concluding remarks.

Sources of law

One of the characteristics of the Arab jurisdictions' law on the REFJ is the plurality of its sources. These can be international conventions, model laws or domestic legislation.

International conventions

A network of international conventions has been concluded by most of the Middle Eastern and Arab Gulf countries. While is possible to distinguish here between multilateral and bilateral conventions, an international convention has *ex lege* a priority of application over domestic law no matter whether it is multilateral or bilateral.[7]

Multilateral conventions

Multilateral conventions can be either worldwide conventions or regional conventions. With regard to worldwide conventions, only Kuwait has ratified

---

enforcement before national state courts to the exclusion of the international courts established in Dubai and Qatar.

6 See Béligh Elbalti, 'Spontaneous Harmonization and the Liberalization of the Recognition and Enforcement of Foreign Judgments' (2014) 16 *Japanese Yearbook of Private International Law* 264.

7 See the Egyptian CCP Art. 301. A similar provision can be found in the law of Bahrain (Art. 255 CCCP); Kuwait (Art. 203 CCCP); Oman (Art. 355 CCCP); Qatar (Art. 383 CCCP); Saudi Arabia (Art. 11 EA); Syria (Art. 313 CCP); UAE (Art. 238 CCP) and Yemen (Art. 497 CCPE).

the 1971 Hague Convention on the REFJ in Civil and Commercial Matters and its Supplementary Protocol.[8] However, some other potential OBOR Arab jurisdictions are parties to a number of conventions relating to certain international procedural matters that have an impact on the REFJ. For example, Egypt and Kuwait are parties to the 1965 Hague on the Service Abroad of Judicial and Extrajudicial Documents in Civil and Commercial Matters. Both Egypt and Lebanon are parties to the 1954 Hague Convention on Civil Procedure. Both Bahrain and Oman are parties to the 1961 Hague Convention Abolishing the Requirement of Legalisation for Foreign Public Documents [Apostile Convention]. And finally, Kuwait is also party to the 1970 Hague Convention on the Taking of Evidence Abroad in Civil and Commercial Matters.[9]

Many Arab countries are engaged in regional conventions concluded under the auspices of certain Arab regional organisations – the Convention of the Arab League on the Enforcement of Judgments and Arbitral Awards of 14 September 1952 (1952 AL Convention),[10] the Riyadh Arab Convention on Judicial Cooperation of 6 April 1983 (1983 Riyadh Convention),[11] the Convention on Legal and Judicial Co-operation between Egypt, Iraq, Yemen and Jordan of 16 June 1989 (1989 ACC Convention),[12] and the Convention on the Enforcement of Judgments, Letter Rogatory and Judicial Notice between the Member States of Arab Gulf Cooperation Council of 4–6 December 1995 (1995 GCC Convention).[13]

8 Status Table of these two instruments available <www.hcch.net/en/instruments/> accessed 13 October 2017.

9 On these conventions and their status table, see <www.hcch.net/> accessed 13 October 2017.

10 The contracting States are Jordan, Syria, Iraq, Saudi Arabia, Egypt, Yemen, Libya and Kuwait. Lebanon signed the convention but has not ratified it. The English text of the Convention is available at <www.aia-adr.com/#!blank/c10t5> accessed 13 October 2017; See Ezzeddine Abdallah, 'La convention de la Ligue Arabe sur l'exécution des jugements – Etude comparative du droit conventionnel comparé avec le droit interne' (1973) 138 *Collected Courses* 513. The 1952 convention was replaced by the 1983 Riyadh Convention but still in force in some contracting States that have not ratified the latter one.

11 The contracting States are Palestine, Iraq, Yemen, Sudan, Mauritania, Syria, Somalia, Tunisia, Jordan, Morocco, Libya, UAE, Oman, Bahrain, Saudi Arabia and Algeria. Egypt has recently joined the Convention. <www.refworld.org/docid/3ae6b38d8.html> accessed 13 October 2017; See Kilian Balz and Aouni Shahoud Almousa, 'The Recognition and Enforcement of Foreign Judgments and Foreign Awards Under the Riyadh Convention (1983) – Thirty Years of Arab Judicial Co-Operation' (2014) 4(2) *International Journal of Procedural Law* 273.

12 This Convention was concluded after the creation of the ACC in 1989 by Yemen, Iraq, Jordan and Egypt. However, this organisation disappeared in 1990 after Iraq's invasion of Kuwait, and the convention seems to be no longer applicable. The text of the Convention is available at <http://wiki.dorar-aliraq.net/iraqilaws/law/14886.html> (accessed 13 October 2017, in Arabic only).

13 The contracting States are Saudi Arabia, UAE, Qatar, Bahrain, Oman, and Kuwait. <www.aia-adr.com/#!blank/cu0h> accessed 13 October 2017; See Ahmad 'abd Al-Karim

Amongst these, only the 1952 AL Convention is a simple convention in the strict sense, that is, a convention that deals exclusively with the REFJ (and arbitral awards). The three others are conventions on judicial cooperation in the large sense (service, letter rogatory, etc.) including, *inter alia*, a chapter on the REFJ.

Bilateral conventions

Apart from the regional conventions, many Arab states have contracted bilateral conventions amongst themselves and with non-Arab countries. Some of the intra-Arab bilateral conventions were concluded despite the existence of the regional instruments. In addition, a number of Arab countries have concluded certain conventions with some other potential OBOR countries, including China.[14]

Model laws

Model law instruments drafted by the international organisations of the region also contain chapters on recognition and enforcement of foreign judgments. These are the LAS unified model law on civil procedure,[15] the GCC model convention on judicial cooperation,[16] the GCC uniform law on civil procedure[17] and the GCC uniform law on the enforcement of judicial decisions.[18]

A cursory comparative glance over these instruments reveals the high degree of similarity of the adopted solutions. While the extent of influence of

---

Salama, 'The System of Enforcement of Judicial Judgments Among the Cooperation Council of the Arab Gulf States According to the Council's Convention of 1995' (2001) 57 *Egyptian Review of International Law* 131 (in Arabic); Habib Mohd. Sharif Al Mulla, 'Conventions of Enforcement of Foreign Judgments in Arab States' (1999) 14 *Arab Law Quarterly* 33.

14 For example, The UAE has concluded bilateral conventions with China (2004); India (2000); Armenia (2003); Pakistan (2005). Egypt and Kuwait have also concluded bilateral conventions with China (respectively in 1994 and 2007).

15 Model law adopted in Algeria by the Order of the Council of the Arab Ministers of Justice No. 493 of 8 October 2003 (2003 LAS model law). In addition to a chapter on the enforcement of foreign judgments (Articles 654–659), this instrument contains also chapters dealing with international jurisdiction (Articles 20–25). <https://carjj.org/laws> accessed 13 October 2017, in Arabic only.

16 Model Convention on Legal and Judicial Cooperation, adopted by the Supreme Council in 21–22 December 2003 in Kuwait (Articles 29–37) (2003 GCC Model Convention).

17 Manama Document relating to Uniform Law on Civil Procedure adopted the Supreme Council in Muscat in 30–31 December 2001 (2001 GCC Model Law). This uniform law contains, in addition to chapter on the enforcement of foreign judgments (Articles 229–232), a chapter on international jurisdiction (Articles 20–24).

18 The Kuwait Document relating to uniform rules on the enforcement of judicial decisions of the GCC Member States adopted by the Supreme Council in Abu Dhabi on December 2010 (Articles 16–20) (2010 GCC Model Law). <www.gcc-sg.org/ar-sa/CognitiveSources/DigitalLibrary/Pages/Categorization.aspx> accessed 13 October 2017, in Arabic only.

the model laws upon domestic law reform is not yet known, the similarity of the national law on foreign judgments allows a presumption in favour of the presence of such influence.

Domestic legislation

All Arab countries have enacted domestic statutes on the enforcement of foreign judgments, and such regulatory regimes could be found within the code of civil procedure in many countries within this region.[19] Other countries have included provisions on the enforcement of foreign judgments in a special law usually called 'Enforcement Act'.[20] Finally, some other countries have enacted special legislation for the enforcement of foreign judgments.[21]

Conditions for the REFJ: an outline

The reader of the different Arab states' law would notice their high degree of similarity, sometimes extending to the form and structure of the rule. The conditions for the enforcement of foreign judgments in the Arab countries can be grouped into three categories. The first is the category of conditions that are expressly stated in the law of all Arab legislation discussed here. Belonging to this category are (1) the condition of finality, *res judicata* and enforceability of the foreign judgment;[22] (2) the jurisdiction of the foreign court and (3) public policy and (4) reciprocity.

The second is the category of conditions that are largely shared and expressly mentioned by the law of almost, but not, all Arab countries. This category includes (5) the condition of due service,[23] (6) the right of defence[24] and (6) conflicting judgments.[25]

19 Bahrain (CCCP Articles 252–255); Egypt (CCP Articles 296–301); Kuwait (CCP Articles 199–203); Lebanon (CCP Articles 1009–1024); Oman (CCCP Articles 352–355); Qatar (CCCP Articles 379–383); Syria (CCP Articles 308–313); UAE (CCP Articles 235–238); Yemen (CCPE Articles 491–497).

20 Palestine (EA, Articles 36–39) and Saudi Arabia (EA Act, Articles 11–14).

21 Iraq (EFCJ) and Jordan (EFJA).

22 It is usually provided that foreign judgments can be enforced if they have *res judicata* effect in accordance with the law of the rendering state.

23 The service would be regarded as properly effectuated if it is done in accordance with the law of the rendering State. The Egyptian Supreme Court [Judgment of 2 July 1964, 2 *Collection of Egyptian Supreme Court* 909] held that summon of proceedings via publication in a local newspaper was proper since such summons were valid under the law of the rendering State. See Jalila Sayed Ahmed, 'Enforcement of Foreign Judgments in some Arab Countries – Legal Provisions and Court Precedents: Focus on Bahrain' (1999) 14 *Arab Law Quarterly* 169, 174 for whom the appropriateness of the service is subject to the law of the rendering State to the extent that it does not conflict with public order considerations of the forum.

24 Expressly admitted in all Arab legislations except for Palestine.

25 Expressly admitted in all Arab legislations except for Iraq and Jordan. In Lebanon, the enforcement will also be refused if the same dispute is still pending before the Lebanese courts provided that the action was brought before them first (Article 1016).

The third is the category of conditions that are found only in the legislation of some Arab countries. This category includes (8) the condition of fraud,[26] (9) the control of the applicable law[27] and (10) the review of the merits.[28]

Due to their practical and theoretical importance, only three conditions will be examined here. These are (a) reciprocity, (b) the jurisdiction of the foreign court and (c) public policy.

The implication of certain recognition conditions on the free movement of judgments

Reciprocity

Although reciprocity is largely admitted in all Arab jurisdictions potentially concerned with the OBOR initiative,[29] its meaning and establishment method largely differ.

In a number of Arab jurisdictions, including Jordan and Lebanon, reciprocity is required as a condition that, if not satisfied, would lead to the refusal of the enforcement of the relevant foreign judgment. Here, reciprocity works as an additional requirement among others, the non-satisfaction of which will lead to denying the foreign judgment of its legal effects.[30] However, in some other Arab jurisdictions, reciprocity is understood to mean 'equal treatment',[31] in the sense that foreign judgments will be treated in the same way as the forum's judgments are (will be) treated in the rendering state. Put differently, the foreign judgment to be enforced will be *subject to the same conditions* required in the rendering state's law for the enforcement of the foreign judgments.[32] Accordingly, the enforcement of the foreign judgment

26 See Iraq (Article 8); Jordan (Article 7–4) and Oman (Article 352–1). In Lebanon, fraud justifies the review of the merits of the foreign judgment (Article 1015).

27 See Oman (Article 352–4).

28 A limited review of the merit is still admitted under certain circumstances in Lebanon (Article 1015).

29 Reciprocity is required in Bahrain (Article 252–1); Egypt (Article 296); Iraq (Article 11); Jordan (Article 7–2); Kuwait (Article 199); Lebanon (Article 1014–4); Oman (Article 352–1 and 358–2(e)); Palestine (Article 36–1); Qatar (Article 379); Saudi Arabia (Article 11–1); Syria (Article 306); UAE (Article 235–1); Yemen (Article 494–3). Reciprocity is also included in the 2003 LAS Model law (Article 654) the GCC Model Laws of 2001 (Article 229–1) and 2010 (Article 16–1).

30 See, for example, the Lebanese Supreme Court's decision No. 79 of 31 May 2007, *Al-Adl* 2008 (1) 186 note Marie-Claude Najm (in Arabic) in which the court considered that it is sufficient to prove that Lebanese courts can be enforced in the territory of the rendering State in order to establish reciprocity.

31 Ahmed (n 23), 170.

32 See Article 296 of the Egyptian CCP. Similar (or identical) provision can be found in the law of the following countries: Yemen, Bahrain, UAE, Qatar, Kuwait, Syria and Palestine. In a law reform made in 2007, the Kuwaiti legislature excepted from the reciprocity rule judgments rendered in favour of a Kuwaiti (natural or legal) person the enforcement of which is sought against the assets of another Kuwaiti (natural or legal) person.

will be subject to two sets of conditions: (1) the conditions that are ordinarily required by the recognising state for the enforcement of foreign judgments, and (2) the conditions that are available under the law of the rendering state and which have no equivalent under the law of the enforcing state.[33] Two major consequences can stem from such understanding of the reciprocity rule. First, if the courts of the foreign state refuse to enforce the forum's judgments, then judgments of the rendering state's judgment will be treated in the same way.[34] Second, if the law of the foreign state subjects the enforcement of foreign judgments to restrictive requirements that are not available in the law of the enforcing state, those restrictive requirements will be imported and applied to the enforcement of the judgment of that rendering state.[35] Among all Arab jurisdictions, only Oman has combined both meanings of reciprocity in two different provisions.[36]

In other countries, such as Iraq, a different solution seems to have been adopted. According to Art. 11 of the Iraqi EFCJA, 'This law applies to foreign judgments rendered by foreign courts *specifically named by Ordinances issued from time to time* [. . .]' (emphasis added). This means that the enforcement of foreign judgments in Iraq depends on the existence of a governmental declaration to be issued regularly whenever the Iraqi government concludes an international convention with a foreign country or is convinced that Iraqi judgments are enforceable abroad.[37] The Iraqi Supreme Court seems to have ruled in this sense. In a reported decision, the Court declared that EFCJA did not apply to the enforcement of a judgment rendered in Bahrain because there was no ordinance with regard to the enforcement of Bahraini judgments

33 See, for example, the Supreme Court of Dubai has interpreted this condition as to require that the conditions provided for in the rendering state should be similar or more lenient than those adopted in the UAE. Decision No. 17/2001 of 10 March 2001, Government of Dubai, Justice Department, Supreme Court, Technic Office, No. 12, 2001, 208.

34 In Bahrain, see Ahmed (n 23); in Egypt, Karim EL Chazli, 'Recognition and Enforcement of Foreign Judgments in Egypt' (2013/2014) 15 *YPIL* 387, 400; in UAE, Saloni Kantaria, 'The Enforcement of Foreign Judgments in the UAE and DIFC Courts' (2014) 28 *Arab Law Quarterly* 193, 199; in Syria, Jacques El-Hakim, 'Enforcement of Foreign Judgments and Arbitral Awards in Syria' (1990) 5 *Arab Law Quarterly* 137, 138.

35 For example, the enforcement of the foreign judgment would be, as a matter of reciprocity (equal treatment), subject to a control of the law applied by the rendering judge if such a control is required by the law of the rendering state.

36 See the Omani CCCP Article 352. In a 2006 decision, the Omani Supreme Court justified its refusal for enforcement of a German judgment by the fact that German standards of recognition are more restrictive than those required in Oman. Decision of 25 January 2006 reported in Nicolas Bremer, 'Seeking Recognition and Enforcement of Foreign Court Judgments and Arbitral Awards in the GCC Countries' (2017) 3 *McGill Journal of Disputr Resolution* 52.

37 The following Ordinances have so far been issued: No. 18/1929 (Italy); No. 9/1929 (Egypt); No. 5/1929 (Syria and Lebanon); No. 11/1929 (Palestine); No. 10/1930 (India); No. 29/1932 (Canada, Jamaica, Hong Kong, Malta, Nyasaland [actual Malawi] and Cyprus); No. 32/1952 (Jordan).

at that time.[38] The Supreme Court, in application of Article 11, decided that the enforcement regime of the EFCJA could be applied to the judgments of countries specified within the ordinance.[39]

The establishment of reciprocity also largely differs from one jurisdiction to another. For example, under Saudi law and as a matter of principle, foreign judgments can be enforced either on the basis of an international treaty or reciprocity.[40] Nonetheless, some argue that it is very unlikely that foreign judgments would be granted any effect in the Kingdom in the absence of an international treaty,[41] although other authors challenge this statement.[42] However, assuming that foreign judgments can be enforced on the basis of reciprocity, the chances to establish reciprocity would come close to null if the party seeking enforcement fails to present an 'official' statement to the effect that Saudi judgments will be enforced in that state.[43]

In other jurisdictions, such as Lebanon, it is sufficient to prove that the courts of the rendering state generally accept the enforcement of Lebanese judgments. The Lebanese Supreme Court even declared that the fact that the courts of the rendering states had refused to recognise a Lebanese judgment on the ground that the Lebanese judgment did not meet one of the enforcement conditions required by that state – such as public policy – was not in itself a reason to consider that reciprocity was not established.[44]

In any case, because many Arab jurisdictions do not follow the Saudi or the Iraqi examples,[45] it can be said that unless the foreign jurisdiction involved

38 Nowadays, both countries are contracting states of the 1983 Riyadh Convention.

39 Decision of the Federal Supreme Court No. 364 of 3 March 1987 [unpublished].

40 See the Saudi EA Article 11.

41 In this sense, see David M. Wells, 'Saudi Arabia' in Lawrence W. Newman (ed), *Enforcement of Money Judgments – Vol. III* (Juris 2011) (Rel. 17–2002).

42 See Hilmar Krüger, 'Saudi Arabia' in Juergen Basedow et al. (eds), *European Encyclopaedia of PIL – Vol. 3* (Edward Elgar 2017); Bremer (n 36), 57 and the references cited thereof.

43 In a decision rendered by the Grievance Board (Decision No. 97/C/3-1411[1990]), an English judgment was refused enforcement because the judgment creditor failed to prove with conclusive evidence that Saudi Courts' judgments were enforced in the United Kingdom. In this case, the submission of a certificate from an office belonging to the English Ministry of Justice stating that foreign judgments can be enforced in the United Kingdom, an opinion of a British legal advisor who worked as a lawyer in the United Kingdom and a copy of the English procedural rules were deemed insufficient to prove reciprocity. However, in a decision rendered in 2007, a sworn statement made by an American judge to the effect that Saudi judgments would be enforced in the District of Columbia submitted by the judgment creditor was deemed sufficient to establish reciprocity with the United States. Decision No. 78/D/F/20 of 2007 cited in Bremer (n 36) 57.

44 See the Lebanese Supreme Court's decision No. 79 of 31 May 2007 (n 30).

45 The Egyptian Supreme Court in its decision No. 1136 of 28 November 1990 [(1990) 41–2 *Egyptian Judicial Review* 818] declared that the establishment of legislative reciprocity was sufficient to allow the enforcement of a foreign judgment. In Jordan, a Kuwaiti judgment could be enforced because the Kuwaiti enforcement law allowed the

adheres to an unduly restrictive enforcement regime, foreign judgments are unlikely to be refused enforcement on the basis of reciprocity,[46] although the proof of reciprocity can be particularly problematic in certain jurisdictions.[47]

The jurisdiction of foreign courts

Different approaches

The jurisdictional requirement is also one of the common conditions to all potential OBOR Arab countries.[48] Again, despite the apparent uniformity, Arab jurisdictions do not follow a uniform approach to the standard by which the foreign court's jurisdiction should be examined. Three different approaches can be distinguished.

The first approach, which is followed in Syria, Oman, Lebanon and Kuwait, consists of reviewing the jurisdiction of the foreign rendering court according to that court's own law.[49] From a comparative perspective, this test, which is rarely used nowadays,[50] is considered as outdated and useless, as it suffices that the foreign court takes jurisdiction on any jurisdictional ground admitted in its law, no matter how exorbitant that jurisdictional ground is, for this requirement to be satisfied.[51] This is probably the reason why, under Lebanese law, although the jurisdiction of the foreign court is subject to its own law, it is expressly stated that jurisdiction based solely on the nationality of the

enforcement of foreign judgments in Kuwait (Supreme Court Judgment No. 294/74 of 1974).

46 See El Chazli (n 34), 400; El-Hakim (n 34), 138.

47 For example, in Qatar, a French judgment was refused enforcement on the basis of reciprocity because it was not proven that French courts would allow the enforcement of foreign judgments in general or Qatari judgments in particular. Court of Appeal No.76/1999 reported in Ahmad Anani, 'Qatar' in Lawrence W. Newman (n 41) *Vol. II* [Rel.28–2010]. See also the decision of the Dubai Supreme Court No. 269 of 26 February 2006 (refusal to enforce an English judgment), reported in Ramsey B. Jurdi, 'United Arab Emirates' in Lawrence W. Newman (n 41) [Rel.30–2011]. However, the Abu Dhabi Supreme Court accepted to enforce an Iranian judgment after stating that the judgment satisfied all the conditions required by the Emirati law including reciprocity despite the absence of treaty between both countries (Decision No. 935 of 29 November 2010).

48 Bahrain (Article 252–2); Egypt (Article 298–2) Iraq (Article 6–2); Jordan (Article 7–1, 7–2); Kuwait (Article 199–1); Lebanon (Article 1014–1); Oman (Article 352–1); Palestine (Article 37–2); Qatar (Article 380–1); Saudi Arabia (Article 11–1); Syria (Article 308–1); UAE (Articles 235–1, 235–2); Yemen (Articles 494–2, 494–4). It is also included in all international conventions and model laws mentioned *supra*.

49 See also the 2003 LAS model law (Art. 656-a) and the 1991 ACC Convention (Article 28–3).

50 See Pierre Mayer, 'Le phénomène de la Coordination des ordres juridiques étatiques en droit privé' (2007) 327 *Collected Courses* 303, 304.

51 See George A.L. Droz, 'Regards sur le droit international privé comparé' (1991) 229 *Collected Courses* 90, 91.

plaintiff is not acceptable.[52] The Supreme Court held the rule inapplicable to cases where national courts possess exclusive jurisdiction over the dispute, the foreign court's jurisdiction excluded on ground of public policy.[53]

With regard to the scope of this control, in some countries, it is considered that the control of the domestic territorial jurisdiction of the foreign court is unnecessary and, therefore, not relevant.[54] In other countries, however, both the international jurisdiction and the domestic jurisdiction of the foreign court should be controlled according to that foreign court's own law.[55]

The second approach, which is followed in Bahrain, Egypt, Palestine, Qatar, Saudi Arabia, UAE, Yemen and Jordan,[56] is to subject the jurisdiction of the foreign court to a double control. This control is based on a positive test and a negative test. According to the former, the jurisdiction of the rendering court will be first examined according to that court's own law. The foreign court will then be regarded as competent if its jurisdiction is justified by its own rules of jurisdiction. However, the meaning of this first test is not always clear. In some jurisdictions, it is understood as to include both the general (international) jurisdiction and the special (domestic) jurisdiction of the foreign court.[57] Accordingly, the foreign judgment will be refused enforcement if it appears that the rendering was not competent according to its internal rules of jurisdiction even when the enforcing courts was competent according to its rules of international jurisdiction.[58] In other jurisdictions, it is generally

52 See Marie-Claude Najm, 'Lebanon' in Juergen Basedow et al. (eds) (n 42).

53 See the Lebanese Supreme Court decision of 31 May 2007 (2007) *Al-Adl* 1702 (a case concerning the recognition of a foreign divorce of a religious marriage of a Lebanese spouses). For critics of the combination of and the confusion between exclusive jurisdiction and public policy, see Najm, *ibid.*

54 For Lebanon, see the Lebanese Supreme Court Decision No. 36 of 2 March 1999 reported in Sami Badi' Mansour, 'Abdah Jamil Ghadhoub and Nasri Antoine Diab, *PIL Part II* (Majd Edition 2009), 229 (in Arabic). For Oman, see Mahmud Lotfi Mahmud Abd Al-Aziz, *The Omani PIL* (University Book House 2015), 362 (in Arabic).

55 See Jacques El-Hakim, 'Syria' in Lawrence W. Newman (n 41) (Rel. 5–7/92 Pub.597). The same can be said for Kuwait. See Hasan Al-Hadawi, *Conflict of Laws and Its Principles in the Kuwaiti PIL* (2nd ed., Jami'at Al-Kuwait 1974), 244 (in Arabic). The same solution is admitted in the 1952 Arab Convention Art. 2(a). On this provision and its interpretation, see Abdallah (n 10), 557.

56 However, unlike other Arab jurisdictions of this group, the Jordanian law identifies certain cases in which the foreign court would be regarded as having jurisdiction (Art. 7–1(b) EFJA). Similar provision can be found in the GCC model law of 2001 (Art. 229–2(a)) and 2010 (Ar. 16–2(a)).

57 See, for example, Art. 7(1)a of the Jordanian EFJA. This article is not crystal clear as simply states that the foreign judgment to be enforced should have been rendered by a competent court *(mahkamah dhat wadhifah)*. This part was interpreted to mean the competence of the foreign courts according to is domestic subject matter and venue rules. See Hasan Al-Hadawi, *PIL* (7th ed., Dar Al-Thaqafah 2017), 265 (in Arabic); Ghaleb Ali Ad-Daoudi, *PIL – Conflict of Laws, Conflict of Jurisdictions, Enforcement of Foreign Judgments – Comparative Study* (2nd ed., Dar Al-Thaqafah 2013), 343–345 (in Arabic).

58 See Article 235–2(b) of the Emirati CCP.

admitted that only the international jurisdiction of the foreign court should be examined.[59] Such interpretation has been confirmed by certain court decisions, which made it clear that this control will be made according to the rules of international jurisdiction of the foreign court and not according to its domestic territorial rules.[60]

According to the negative test, the foreign court will be regarded as lacking international jurisdiction if the enforcing court claims jurisdiction according to its own rules of international jurisdiction. Therefore, the review will be made according to the law of state addressed in the sense that enforcing courts will examine whether they would have been competent had the dispute been brought before them. Put differently, the jurisdiction of the foreign court would be excluded if the dispute falls under the competence of the enforcing court. The problem is that it is not clear whether the jurisdiction conferred upon the enforcing court according to its rules of international jurisdiction will be *in all cases* exclusive of the indirect jurisdiction of the foreign court.[61] The Supreme Court of Egypt distinguished between exclusive and concurrent jurisdiction, declaring that only the former would deprive foreign courts their indirect jurisdiction.[62] However, the Court failed to specify the cases in which the jurisdiction of the Egyptian courts will be considered as exclusive[63] so that the question was left to the speculations of legal scholars. Indeed, for some authors, the foreign court would not be regarded as competent if the defendant had his domicile in the forum.[64] Others, contesting the exclusive/ordinary or concurrent jurisdiction distinction, explain that the jurisdiction of the foreign

59 For Saudi Arabia, see Muhamed Ben Ali Ben Muhamed Al-Qurni, *Foreign Enforcement Orders and Their Enforcement* (1st ed., Al-Manhal 2016), 127 (in Arabic). For Yemen, see Muhamed Abdallah Al-Mu'ayed, *PIL – General Theory of the Conflict of Laws and Conflict of Judicial Jurisdiction in Yamani Law* (Isdarat Jami'at Sanaa 2005), 200–201 (in Arabic). In Palestine, the situation seems to be nuanced, as the control of the domestic competence of the foreign court should, in principle, be excluded except for the domestic jurisdictional rules that affect the existence of the judgment itself. See Sayf Eddine Muhamed Al-Bal'awi, 'The International Effects of Judgments: Comparative Study' (2001) 5(2) *J. H. S.* 60, 98 (in Arabic).

60 See the Egyptian Supreme Court Decision No. 231 of 6 Mai 1969 (1969) 20–2 *Egyptian Jud. Rev.* 730.

61 This is particularly the case in UAE. See Bremer (n 36), 59. See also for Jordan, Ad-Daoudi (n 59), 345. For Yemen, see Al-Mu'ayed (n 61), 193. For Saudi Arabia, see Al-Qurni (n 61), 125. For detailed analyses of the law of some Arab countries, see Abdallah (n 10), 553.

62 Decision of the Egyptian Supreme Court of 28 November 1990 *supra* n 45. In the same sense, the Bahraini Supreme Court's decision No. 34 of 12 May 1991 reported in Ahmed (n 23), 171–172.

63 In its 1990 decision, the Supreme Court considered that jurisdiction of Egyptian courts in contractual matter based on the place of the performance did not exclude the jurisdiction of the foreign court based on the place of the conclusion.

64 For example, Hafidha As-Sayed Al-Haddad, *PIL – Book I* (Cairo 2002), 206.

court should be excluded whenever national courts are competent.[65] However, for others, the foreign court's jurisdiction may be admitted if it appears that there is a strong connection between the dispute and the foreign court.[66]

In any event, it seems uncontested in legal literature that the jurisdiction of the foreign court should be excluded when the subject matter of the dispute falls within the jurisdiction of the enforcing court. As a result, the jurisdictional requirement can become a serious hindrance to the enforcement of a substantial number of foreign judgments, knowing that the jurisdictional rules in certain countries are particularly broad.[67] It seems also to be in contradiction with another requirement that is largely admitted in most Arab jurisdictions: that is, a conflict with a prior judgment rendered in the forum. As it was rightly indicated, such interpretation renders the requirement of conflicting judgments redundant because such a conflict cannot arise if the recognition is not possible due to lack of jurisdiction of the foreign court.[68]

The third approach, followed in few Arab jurisdictions,[69] consists of providing for a list of criteria on the basis of which the jurisdiction of the foreign rendering court will be assessed. This is the case of the Iraqi EFCJA, which identifies the cases where the foreign court will be regarded as having jurisdiction.[70]

65 See Ezzeddine Abdallah, *PIL – Part II* (9th ed., Cairo 1986) 904 (in Arabic). In Yemen, one author – Al-Mu'ayed (n 61), 198 – criticised the concurrent/exclusive jurisdiction distinction arguing that the exclusion of the foreign court's jurisdiction should be made on the basis of public policy.

66 In this sense, Hashem Sadiq, *Conflict of International Judicial Jurisdiction* (Alexandria 2007), 276 (in Arabic).

67 For a comparative analysis, see Béligh Elbalti, 'Establishment of Filiation in Arab Countries: PIL Perspective' (forthcoming).

68 In this sense, Bremer (n 36), 43. It is based on the existence of a provision relating to conflicts of judgments that the Bahraini Supreme Court decided in 1991 that the foreign court can be regarded as competent even when the Bahraini Courts would be competent according to the Bahraini rules of international jurisdiction.

69 This is the case of Iraq and to a certain extent Jordan. The Jordanian approach can also be included in this group as well since Art. 7–1(b) of the Jordanian EFJA specifies a number of cases according to which the foreign court will not be regarded as competent. These are (1) the judgment-debtor did not carry his business within the jurisdiction of the foreign court, (2) absence of residency and (3) absence of voluntary appearance or submission.

70 These are (1) jurisdiction over actions relating to movable or immovable property situated in the foreign state, (2) jurisdiction in contractual matters when the contract is concluded in the foreign State or to be partially or totally performed there, (3) jurisdiction over acts which partially or totally happened in the foreign state, (4) jurisdiction based on the domicile of the judgment-debtor in the foreign state or based on the business carried there when the action was initiated, (5) jurisdiction by voluntary appearance of the judgment-debtor before the foreign court and (6) jurisdiction based on the agreement of the judgment-debtor.

Uncertainties with regard to the effects of choice of court agreements

As the rules explained previously clearly show, the jurisdiction of the foreign court depends much on whether the enforcing Arab court is not competent according to its rule of international jurisdiction. Such an understanding renders the jurisdiction of the foreign court residual to cases where the enforcing courts will or will not claim jurisdiction over the dispute. However, this is not all. In most of the potential OBOR Arab countries, the rules of international jurisdiction are considered imperative, that is, they cannot be derogated from by agreements of the parties. For example, under Emirati law, choice of court agreements are void.[71] The solution has been confirmed in the case law of a number of Arab jurisdictions.[72] Judgments delivered by courts under exclusive choice of court agreements are unenforceable in those countries.[73] Yet, in some other countries, such as Lebanon, it is agreed that in the absence of mandatory jurisdictional rules, the parties can freely designate as competent a foreign court otherwise not having jurisdiction.[74]

With regard to the effect of choice of court agreements, the recent developments in Egyptian law need to be highlighted. Under Egyptian law, even when they are not competent by application of the Egyptian rules of international jurisdiction, Egyptian courts may still assume jurisdiction if the parties have consented to their jurisdiction over them.[75] Accordingly, choice of court agreement will be considered as valid only if the parties confer jurisdiction to Egyptian courts. However, in a recent decision, the Supreme Court interpreted this provision as including not only the prorogative but also the derogative effect of the choice of court agreement.[76] This is definitely a positive

71 The Emirati CCP Article 24 states that 'any agreement contrary to the [rules of international jurisdiction] shall be void'.

72 See, for instance, the Iraqi Supreme Court's decision No. 880 of 27 June 1971 reported in Abbas Qasem Mahdi Al-Daquqi, *Case law: Notion, Status and Scope* (Al Manhal 2015) 118 (in Arabic); the Qatari Supreme Court's decision No. 226 of 25 December 2012; the Emirati Supreme Court's decision No. 747 of 17 July 2013; the Kuwaiti Supreme Court's decision No. 436 of 21 May 2007. Under Iraqi law, there seems to be a contradiction between the solution of the Iraqi Supreme Court and its implication on the reception of foreign judgments and the Art. 7(f) according to which the foreign court would be regarded as competent if the losing party had consented to the jurisdiction of the foreign court.

73 For the case of UAE, see Kantaria (n 34), 200.

74 See Pierre Gannagé, 'Liban – Droit International Privé' *JurisClasseur Notarial Répertoire* Fasc. 6 (2011 update), 5.

75 The Egyptian CCP Art. 32 clearly states that a non-competent Egyptian court can 'have jurisdiction to decide lawsuit [. . .] if the defendant impliedly or expressly accepts their jurisdiction'. Similar provision can be found in Bahrain (Art. 17 CCCP); Jordan (Art. 27(2) CCP); Kuwait (Art. 26 CCP); Oman (Art. 32 CCP); Palestine (Art. 29(1) CCCP); Saudi Arabia (Art. 28 PCSC); Syria (Art. 9 CCP); Yemen (Art. 81 CCEP).

76 The Supreme Court decision of 24 March 2014. For a comment in English, see Yehya Ikram Ibrahim Badr, 'Forum Selection Clauses in Egypt: A Review of the Egyptian Court of Cassation Recent Award' (2015) 5 *International Journal of Procedural Law* 259.

move that is in line with the general trend of acknowledging the possibility of the party to choose the place of their litigation. However, the restrictions imposed by the court, notably by imposing, *inter alia*, a connection between the chosen court and the dispute, may render the choice of the parties nugatory.[77] The new interpretation adopted by the Egyptian Supreme Court will definitely have certain implications for the practice of the REFJ, although this would depend on whether the validity of choice of court agreements will be upheld.

Public policy

Public policy is another requirement that is expressly stated in the enforcement law of all potential OBOR Arab countries.[78] This requirement can also become, in certain Arab jurisdictions, a serious hurdle against enforcement of foreign judgments. This is because the notion of fundamental morals and principles that the concept of public policy aims to protect includes also the body of Sharia rules. The respect of Sharia is even mandated by two regional conventions[79] and expressly mentioned in the law of some Arab jurisdictions.[80]

The problem with Sharia law as a component of public policy is that its respect should be absolute.[81] Sharia rules do not know the difference between domestic public policy and international public policy: certain Sharia rules, especially the 'uncontested' ones, may always be invoked to bar the enforcement of the foreign judgment.[82] As such, the application of Sharia rules becomes universal regardless of the connection between the dispute and the state addressed. The intervention of Sharia through the public policy concept can also be very surprising to Muslims. This is because interpretation of Sharia principles varies according to the Islamic schools and especially to the degree of the impact of Sharia on the society.

Public policy based on the respect of Sharia rules concerns both procedural as well as substantive matters. With regard to the former, the mere fact that

77 See the decision No. 9139/84 of 22 June 2015 in which the Supreme Court refused to enforce a choice of forum clause because there was no connection between the chosen courts and the dispute.

78 Bahrain (Article 252–4); Egypt (Article 298–4) Iraq (Article 6–4); Jordan (Article 7–6); Kuwait (Article 199–4); Lebanon (Article 1014–5); Oman (Article 352–4); Palestine (Article 36–1); Qatar (Article 380–4); Saudi Arabia (Article 11–4); Syria (Article 308–4); UAE (Article 235–5) and Yemen (Article 494–1).

79 Article 30 of the 1983 Riyadh Convention; Article 2 of the 1995 GCC Convention.

80 This is the Case of Yemen (Article 494–1). In Saudi Arabia, Art. 11(3) of the Implementing Regulation of the 2012 EA identifies public policy with sharia. In other countries, inclusion of sharia in the concept of public policy is self-evident, knowing that almost all Arab countries refer to Islam and/or sharia in their Constitutions.

81 Abdulrahman Yahia Baamir, *Shari'a Law in Commercial and Banking Arbitration: Law and Practice in Saudi Arabia* (Ashgate 2010), 77.

82 See in civil and commercial matters, Bremer (n 36). In the field of family law, see Maurits S. Berger, 'Conflicts Law and Public Policy in Egyptian Family Law: Islamic Law Through the Backdoor' (2002) 50 *American Journal of Comparative Law* 555.

a judgment was rendered by a non-Muslim judge against a Muslim party was considered sufficient for refusing the enforcement of the foreign judgment.[83] Testimony rules that are not Sharia-compliant can also be regarded as against 'Islamic public policy'.[84]

With regard to substantive public policy, although the impact of public policy and Sharia rules is more sensible in disputes relating to family matters, its influence in civil and commercial matters remains important. For example, as commonly known, usury is prohibited in Islam. Thus, foreign judgments awarding damages with interest would be refused enforcement if the principles of Sharia are strictly applied.[85] Moreover, determination of rights and duties arisen from transactions that are considered as non-Sharia compliant would not be recognised, and damages awarded on the occasion of a dispute relating to such transactions would not be enforced.[86]

In any case, reference to Sharia renders the enforcement of foreign judgments more complicated even among Arab jurisdictions despite the fact that they share common religious, historical and linguistic backgrounds. In addition, if the foreign rendering court interprets and applies a Sharia-based law in a way that is different from how that law is understood in the state where it belongs (e.g. by choosing a liberal interpretation), the risk is that the judgment would be reviewed as to its merits because Sharia law, at least officially, is not supposed to have many interpretations.[87]

Conclusion

As the foregoing demonstrates, the law of foreign judgments as it stands in many Arab jurisdictions is particularly restrictive. This is the result of the existence of a number of requirements that are likely to hinder considerably the potential reception of foreign judgments in those countries. In addition, the non-publication of court decisions and the insufficiency of serious scholarly writings renders the situation in those countries quite opaque and

83 See El Chazli (n 34), 406 (n 85) citing a judgment rendered by a Texan court but was refused enforcement because, *inter alia*, the judge was not Muslim. It is not sure, however, whether the treatment of judgments rendered in civil and commercial matters will be treated alike.

84 See Saad U. Rizwan, 'Foreseeable Issues and Hard Questions: The Implications of U.S. Courts Recognizing and Enforcing Foreign Arbitral Awards Applying Islamic Law under the New York Convention' (2013) 98 *Cornell Law Review* 493, 499.

85 For example, in the Saudi Arabian practice, foreign judgments awarding damages with interests are likely to be refused enforcement even when the judgment was rendered by another Arab court. See the Saudi Grievance Court Decision No. 19/28 of 1979 (enforcement of Bahraini judgment). However, in other Arab jurisdictions including Egypt and UAE, interests are admitted in domestic law.

86 For example, when the transaction concerns things declared impure by Islamic law (pork, wine, etc.).

87 On the excessive use of public policy entailing a comprehensive review of the merits, see Bremer (n 36), 42; Al Mulla (n 11), 41.

unpredictable. This unsatisfactory status quo is not in line with the objectives proclaimed by the OBOR initiative. Unfortunately, the situation is not limited to the Arab countries potentially concerned with the OBOR initiative. A similar situation can be found in other Asian countries concerned with the OBOR project, including China itself.[88]

There are two possible ways to improve the status quo. The first, and probably the most effective one, is that national legislature in those countries catch up with the emerging trend of the spontaneous harmonisation of the REFJ. This can be done through domestic law reform drawing guidance from internationally accepted standards for REFJ. Although effective, the implementation of this method requires much time and especially a perception of the need of and the benefits from adopting a liberal regime on judgments recognition. However, this is unfortunately not always the case.[89]

The second is by way of international instruments, namely conventions. Here again, the most effective way is to conclude a worldwide convention establishing a single regime for the enforcement of foreign judgments. For example, the states involved with the OBOR initiative can ratify the 2005 Hague Convention on Choice of Court Agreements, which secures the recognition of judgments rendered by a court having exercised jurisdiction on the basis of an exclusive choice of court agreement in certain matters.[90] In addition, OBOR states can also consider the ratification of the future Hague Convention on the REFJ in Civil and Commercial Matters which, if successfully elaborated, would have a broader scope of application.[91] States concerned with the OBOR initiative can also consider the preparation of a closed multilateral convention that would facilitate cooperation between all future OBOR countries. This initiative would have at least the advantage of securing the recognition of judgments rendered in the countries involved in the project. Finally, OBOR states can decide to secure the recognition of their judgments by concluding bilateral conventions. However, this solution is not preferable because it will lead to the creation of a huge network of bilateral conventions between different OBOR states with potential diverging and even conflicting solutions.

In any event, the methods of harmonisation of national legislation on the REFJ may differ, but the pursued objective remains the same: to implement

88 However, there seems to be some improvements, see Wenliang Zhang, 'Sino-Foreign Recognition and Enforcement Judgments: A Promising Follow-Suit Model?' (2017) 16 *Chinese Journal of International Law*.

89 Even the most recent codifications and reforms as adopted in Syria (2016), Saudi Arabia (2012), Algeria (2008), Palestine (2005), Oman and Yemen (2002) follow an outdated modal of legislation rending the reform attempt meaningless.

90 See <www.hcch.net/en/instruments/conventions/publications1/?dtid=1&cid=98> for an extensive bibliography.

91 An extensive bibliography on this project can be found at <https://assets.hcch.net/docs/bd35517f-09ea-47d6-95ad-865d2c162504.pdf> For a general idea on current developments of the project, see <>www.hcch.net/en/projects/legislative-projects/judgments>.

an effective regional integration through securing the free movement of judgments across the national borders. This is why the seriousness of the problems mentioned earlier should not be underestimated. Experience in Europe showed the key to success of any market integration initiative is to ensure judgments rendered in one country should be respected and honoured in other countries. It shows how the REFJ can be an effective tool to regional integration. Europe has shown the way; others can surely follow.

13 Recognition and enforcement of foreign arbitration awards, foreign court judgments and contracts of international carriage

Banu Bozkurt

Introduction

The Belt and Road Initiative (BRI), by far the largest economic partnership ever proposed, is intended as an economic causeway for nations that are situated on the land-based Silk Route and the Maritime Route. Driving the initiative, China announced the One Belt One Road (OBOR) partnership as part of the BRI, to be understood as a collection of networks between participant states that would generate increased economic activity and extensive movement of goods and commodities across nations. This grandiose proposition could, however, be exposed to multiple roadblocks as a result of the legal diversity amongst the participants, in particular with regard to key issues concerning the foundational element of international commerce – contracts and their enforcement. This diversity is, evidently, pertinent in the context of enforcement of a foreign judgment or an arbitral award in a contract for international carriage.

International carriage of goods involves more than one country, and is thus impacted by more than one national jurisdiction. Most contracts of international carriage specify the applicable law along with an arbitration or jurisdiction clause.

When concluding an international carriage agreement, the parties often overlook the possibility of the termination of the contract due to repudiation or frustration. A termination of the contract may then cause conflict, thus leading to litigation/arbitration and the result being subjected to enforcement action in a foreign jurisdiction.

As Turkey is one of the countries along the proposed OBOR route, this chapter, in the first part, discusses the legal regime on the recognition and exequatur of foreign arbitration awards under Turkish law. It commences by outlining the national law on recognition and enforcement of foreign awards, followed by a detailed analysis of the recognition and exequatur of foreign arbitration awards. The second part of the chapter is dedicated to the recognition and exequatur of foreign judgments and arbitration awards on contracts of international carriage, with special emphasis on the Tribunal of First Instance and the Supreme Court approach.

Arbitration, an alternative to the national jurisdiction, allows the parties to appoint their own judges (namely arbitrators), or nominate another institution to do so, for the resolution of their litigation.[1]

The appointment of the arbitration panel may have been made by agreement or by the insertion of an arbitration clause to the main contract. The arbitral award would require recognition through judicial proceedings and become executable by a judgment of recognition and exequatur of the national court.

Recognition proceedings have a declaratory effect and may give the effect either of conclusive evidence or definitive judgment.[2] Therefore, recognition might be made for the unilateral kind of awards (such as the kind of decisions that should be registered to the Trade Register), whereas an award that should be enforced would need an exequatur decision. The Turkish legal system does not stipulate the recognition procedure under separate articles; it is regulated by reference to the exequatur procedure's stipulations.

An exequatur judgment, unlike recognition, renders enforceability to the arbitration award. The exequatur gives the award the power of a national jurisdiction judgment and enforceability as a national jurisdiction judgment.[3]

On the other hand, recognition of a foreign award (or judgment), different from the exequatur, might be undertaken without any request. When a final and binding foreign award (or judgment) submitted to a Turkish court is accepted as conclusive evidence, the recognition would be realised *ipso jure*.[4]

The Turkish legal regime on the recognition and exequatur of a foreign arbitration award is sourced from the Turkish Code on International Private and Procedural Law (numbered 5718, 27.11.2007 – hereinafter IPPL) and the New York Convention on the Recognition and Enforcement of Foreign Arbitral Awards 1958 (hereinafter the New York Convention).

Secondary sources inform the absence of clarity with regard to the choice of application of these sources in the Turkish law. While some authors argue that the applicant party for the recognition and exequatur would have the right of choice between IPPL and the New York Convention wherein applicants may submit their demand to the national jurisdiction either on the basis of IPPL or the New York Convention, some others argue that an application of IPPL is allowed only for the awards that are outside the scope of application of the New York Convention.[5]

The analysis in this chapter is founded upon the stipulations of IPPL.

1 Aysel ÇELİKEL, *Milletlerarası Özel Hukuk* (International Private Law) (Beta Publishing 2012), 670–671; Ergin NOMER, *Devletler Hususi Hukuku* (International Private Law) (Beta Publishing 2015), 543–548; Ergin NOMER, *Nuray EKŞİ and Günseli ÖZTEKİN GELGEL, Milletlerarası Tahkim Hukuku* (Law of International Arbitration) (vol. 1, Beta Publishing 2016), 1–3.

2 Ergin NOMER, *Milletlerarası Usul Hukuku* (International Procedural Law) (Beta Publishing 2009), 145, 145–147, 554–555; NOMER, EKŞİ and GELGEL (n 1), 9–10.

3 NOMER (n 2), 147–148, 554–556.

4 NOMER (n 2), 506–507.

5 NOMER (n 2), 554; NOMER, EKŞİ and GELGEL (n 1), 10–15, 87–91.

Part I – Recognition and exequatur of foreign arbitration awards

Prerequisites

Arbitration agreement

The arbitration agreement or clause[6] clarifies how arbitration is conducted, and the parties to such an agreement accept that the dispute resolution will be transferred from the national jurisdiction authorities to the arbitration panel.

The creation and jurisdiction of the arbitration panel should be in accordance with the arbitration agreement, and the qualifications of the arbitrator(s) might also be specified by the arbitration agreement.[7]

The arbitration agreement should specify the dispute to be submitted to the arbitration tribunal.

Additionally, the arbitration agreement should bear its effects and consequences only on the parties of the agreement. In other words, the arbitration agreement, except in some circumstances, may not be dismissed against a third party who did not take part in the arbitration agreement.[8]

As a valid arbitration agreement is one of the preliminary conditions of the recognition and exequatur of a foreign arbitration award,[9] the validity of the arbitration agreement is assessed according to the jurisdiction identified as lending the governing law to it. If the parties failed to choose a governing law, the law of the siege of the panel would be applied regarding to determine the validity of the arbitration agreement.[10]

When an arbitration award is not in accordance with the law of the jurisdiction to be applied to the dispute, it could lead to a dismissal of the recognition and exequatur of the foreign arbitration award according to IPPL, as discussed in the following paragraphs.[11] Moreover, regarding the existence of the need for recognition and exequatur, a foreign law should be applied during the arbitration proceeding.[12]

6 Hereinafter, arbitration agreement will be used to mean arbitration clause as well.

7 On the constitution of the tribunal, Parties could either nominate the arbitrators or approach the arbitral institutions for the same. ÇELİKEL (n 1), 680–682; NOMER, EKŞİ and GELGEL (n 1) 2–3; NOMER (n 2), 2–3, 550–551.

8 Carriage of goods by sea constitutes one of the main exceptions to this irrevocability of the arbitration agreement to the third party rule. For further detail please see ÇELİKEL (n 1), 671.

9 Adnan DEYNEKLI, 'Türkiye'de Yabancı Hakem Kararlarının Tanınması Ve Tenfizinde Karşılaşılan Sorunlar' (Problems in the Recognition and Exequatur of the Foreign Arbitral Awards in Turkey) (V: 16, 2014) Dokuz Eylül University *Journal of the Faculty of Law*, 118–120; NOMER, EKŞİ and GELGEL (n 1), 72–76.

10 According to the Turkish legal system and the New York Convention, the arbitration agreement should be concluded in writing.

11 For further detail, please see Paragraph III/8.

12 For further detail, please see Paragraph III/2/a.

In the context of arbitrator appointments, non-conformity with the arbitration agreement also constitutes a reason for the dismissal of the recognition and exequatur of the foreign arbitration award according to IPPL.[13]

Preliminary conditions

FOREIGN ARBITRATION AWARD

Various criteria are used for the determination of the foreignness of an arbitration award. They include the citizenship of the parties, the place of the arbitration and the applicable law to the arbitration.[14]

Turkish law adopted a similar approach until the decision of the Turkish Supreme Court was taken in 1951.[15] The Supreme Court emphasised that the criterion for the determination of the foreignness element should be the applicable law of the arbitration. If the arbitration award is given under the national jurisdiction of a country other than Turkey, the arbitration award should be classified as foreign and a recognition or exequatur judgment from a Turkish Court is needed.[16] In other words, the foreignness of the arbitration award would be classified in accordance with the consent of the parties on the applicable law to the arbitration. In the absence of an express/implicit choice of the applicable law and being incapable of determination, the place of the arbitration might also be used as a complementary criterion.[17]

Turkey is a signatory to the New York Convention on Recognition and Enforcement of Foreign Arbitral Awards, 1958. However, Turkey made two reservations – it undertook to apply the New York Convention unless the award is granted in another signatory state, and the New York Convention shall apply to commercial conflicts only. The commercial character of the conflicts needed to be determined according to Turkish law. Academic scholarship is divided on the application of the New York Convention in Turkey. While one view is that the applicant party for the recognition or exequatur would have the right of choice between IPPL and the New York Convention, the other view states that the awards falling outside the scope of application of the New York Convention would be subjected to the application of IPPL.[18]

13 For further detail, please see Paragraph III/8.
14 For further detail, please see ÇELİKEL (n 1), 674–680; NOMER (n 2), 551–554; NOMER, EKŞİ and GELGEL (n 1), 3–9.
15 Supreme Court Assembly of Civil Chambers decision dated 7 November 1951 and numbered 126/109 "an arbitral award which is given under a foreign arbitral authority shall be considered as a foreign arbitral award".
16 For further detail and the critics on the Supreme Court decision and the application of the criterions, please see ÇELİKEL (n 1), 676–679; DEYNEKLİ (n 9), 107–109; NOMER (n 2), 552–553; NOMER, EKŞİ and GELGEL (n 1), 61–67.
17 ÇELİKEL (n 1), 679.
18 For further detail and discussions, please see NOMER (n 2), 554; NOMER, EKŞİ and GELGEL (n 1), 10–15, 87–91.

The Turkish International Arbitration Code (hereinafter IAC)[19] aims to regulate the terms and conditions of international arbitration awards that are granted in Turkey. Article 2 stipulates the conditions of the classification of the arbitration as foreign. Differing from IPPL and the Supreme Court 1951 decision, the IAC considers the citizenship or the corporate seat's place for the determination of the foreignness. Furthermore, IAC would be applicable to the foreign arbitration awards that were granted in Turkey. If a foreign arbitration award (determined as per Article 2) is granted in Turkey, IAC would be applied and the award would become directly applicable and enforceable with an approval of the civil court placed in the residence of the applicant party unless an application for declaration of nullity is pending. When IAC is applied, a foreign arbitration would be treated as a Turkish arbitration award and would not be subjected to the recognition and enforcement procedure.[20]

EXECUTABLE ARBITRATION AWARD

IPPL, in Article 60, stipulates that an award, for recognition and exequatur, should be final and binding on the parties.

The foreign arbitration award should be final and enforceable in accordance with the applicable law to the arbitration or (in the case of non-existence of such law) with the law of the place of arbitration. The Supreme Court underscored the importance of finality of the award, holding that the approval of the secretariat of the arbitration institution alone would not be enough for the enforceability of the award if the procedural law of the country of arbitration obliged the approval of the Court for the enforceability of such decision in the place of arbitration.[21] Parties would need to verify the finality and enforceability of the foreign arbitration award according to the law of the place of arbitration.

Article 60 gives also the possibility of the recognition or exequatur of an arbitration award that is binding only for the parties.[22] The Article could be explained as: if the foreign award became binding for the parties, the national court that is to decide for the recognition or exequatur would not need to verify if such award had also become final and enforceable according to the law of the place of arbitration.[23]

19 Numbered 4686 and dated 21.06.2001.

20 For further details, please see ÇELİKEL (n 1) 682–687; NOMER (n 2) 553; For further detail and discussions, please see NOMER (n 2) 554; NOMER, EKŞİ and GELGEL (n 1), 33–50.

21 For further detail and other examples of the Supreme Court decisions and discussions, please see ÇELİKEL (n 1), 690–691; DEYNEKLİ (n 9), 117–118; NOMER (n 2), 554–556; NOMER, EKŞİ and GELGEL (n 1), 67–69.

22 ÇELİKEL (n 1), 690–691; DEYNEKLİ (n 9), 117–118; For further detail and discussions, please see NOMER (n 2), 554; NOMER, EKŞİ and GELGEL (n 1), 67–69.

23 One other preliminary condition for the recognition and exequatur was the reciprocity. According to the old Code, the recognition and exequatur of a foreign arbitration award

Public order and existence of compulsory national legislation

Turkish courts hearing applications for recognition and exequatur of a foreign award review the arbitral proceedings alone and do not attempt to review the merits of the arbitration award.[24] Courts in Turkey, however, are allowed to consider the effect of the foreign arbitration award on Turkish public order.

The Supreme Court has attempted to delimit public order in its decisions. In cases where there are evident benefits for the economically powerful party and an economic weakness of the other party in the foreign arbitration award, the recognition and exequatur of this award should be dismissed by the judge according to the jurisprudences of the Supreme Court.[25] Incidence of abuse of rights could lead to application of public order and the judge could dismiss the application for recognition and exequatur.[26]

Moreover, the impartiality and neutrality of the arbitrators should also be treated under public order. Therefore, during the review of the foreign arbitration award, the judge should take into consideration the impact of the partiality of the arbitrators on the award. More concretely, in such a case, the judge should not dismiss the whole award's recognition or exequatur but should dismiss the part of the award that has been influenced by the partiality of the arbitrator(s).[27]

In addition, the arbitrariness approach of the arbitrator(s) by exceeding their discretionary power should also be examined under public order.[28]

Another aspect of the public order is to review the foreign arbitration award in light of the existing legal order. More concretely, the judge first should determine if the merits of the litigation fall into the scope of the arbitration; in other words, whether the merits of the case are arbitrable. The arbitrability of the merits would be determined according to Turkish legal order. Accordingly, all kind of commercial litigations fall within the scope of arbitration.[29]

---

could have been possible in case of the existence of a legal or actual reciprocity between Turkey and the country of the arbitration award. Therefore, the new IPPL removed the reciprocity condition that was really criticised during the years by Turkish doctrine. For critics and further detail, please see ÇELİKEL (n 1) 693; For further detail and discussions please see NOMER (n 2), 554; NOMER, EKŞİ and GELGEL (n 1), 10–15, 87–91.

24 For further detail and the interdiction of the "revision au fond", please see NOMER (n 2), 555–556.

25 For further detail and the jurisprudences, please see NOMER (n 2) 558–559; NOMER, EKŞİ and GELGEL (n 1), 73.

26 DEYNEKLİ (n 9), 121; NOMER (n 2), 558–559; NOMER, EKŞİ and GELGEL (n 1), 73–74.

27 DEYNEKLİ (n 9), 121; NOMER (n 2), 559–560; NOMER, EKŞİ and GELGEL (n 1), 73–74.

28 DEYNEKLİ (n 9), 121; NOMER (n 2), 560; NOMER, EKŞİ and GELGEL (n 1), 74.

29 For further detail and the scope of arbitration, please see DEYNEKLİ (n 9), 120–121; NOMER (n 2), 561; NOMER, EKŞİ and GELGEL (n 1), 75.

Last, the foreign arbitration award should not be in contradiction with Turkish courts' judgments. In other words, if the arbitration award contains express contradictory measures or solutions to Turkish courts' judgments, the judge should dismiss totally or partially the recognition or exequatur of such arbitration award.[30]

The rights of audience of the parties

Turkish law requires the judge to review the arbitral procedure related to due process rights of the parties, especially the right to be heard, during the procedural review of the arbitration award.

Due process rights include, first, a notice about the arbitration by the party initiating the process and shall include a request for the nomination of the arbitrator. Non-compliance could constitute a reason for the dismissal of the recognition and exequatur of the foreign arbitration award.[31]

Second, Turkish law places high importance on the right to defend and be represented at the arbitration. If a party not represented at the arbitration would not approve the acts and/or the arbitral award, it could be reason for the judge to partially or wholly dismiss the recognition and exequatur of the arbitration award.[32]

The burden of proof on the non-respect of the rights of audience would be on the contesting party.[33]

Court for the recognition and exequatur of arbitral awards

The party applying for the recognition and exequatur decision should approach the competent court. The second paragraph of Article 60 of IPPL stipulates that the application shall be presented to the civil court at the place of jurisdiction regulated in the arbitration agreement for the recognition and exequatur of the foreign arbitration award.

The civil court is nominated as the competent court for the recognition and exequatur. Because the review is intended to be procedural, according to some writers, general civil courts would have competence over every kind of award (concerning, for instance, commercial issues, issues on carriage etc.), whereas a few others, as well as the Supreme Court, are of the opinion that although the review would be procedural, the competent court should be a special civil court such as the Commercial Court, Specialised Court of Maritime (Admiralty) or Civil Court for Intellectual and Industrial Property Rights along with a general civil court. Although the Turkish courts' review

30 NOMER (n 2), 559.
31 DEYNEKLİ (n 9), 120; NOMER (n 2), 561; NOMER, EKŞİ and GELGEL (n 1), 75–76.
32 NOMER, EKŞİ and GELGEL (n 1), 75–76.
33 DEYNEKLİ (n 9), 120; NOMER, EKŞİ and GELGEL (n 1), 75–76.

would be procedural, the reviewing court is expected to be competent on the issues that formed the merits of the award, as these would form part of a challenge on violation of public order. For this reason, academic scholarship has been in favour of the recognition and exequatur of the foreign arbitration award being given by the Commercial Court, general civil court or specialised court in accordance with the merits of the litigation in the arbitral award.[34]

The competent jurisdiction is also stipulated in Article 60/2 of IPPL. Accordingly, the place agreed in the arbitration agreement and, in the absence of the agreement, the residence or the corporate seat of the non-prevailing party, would be the competent jurisdiction for the recognition and exequatur judgment. If the person or the entity does not have a registered address, a de facto residence or corporate seat's courts would have the jurisdiction competence. In the case of non-existence of either registered or de facto residence or corporate seat, the courts in the place of the attachable assets would have the jurisdiction competence for the recognition and exequatur of the foreign arbitration award.[35]

Procedural rules on the recognition and exequatur decision of the Turkish court

The procedure that should be followed by the Turkish court during the recognition and exequatur decision is not stipulated separately but regulated by reference to the articles on the recognition and exequatur of foreign arbitration awards and also by some jurisprudences of the Supreme Court.

Accordingly, the Supreme Court in some of its decisions argued, in light also of the New York Convention, that the costs to be paid for the recognition and exequatur of the foreign arbitration award would be the same as the approval of the Turkish arbitration award by the civil court, namely an application and, in some cases, the proportional decision and judgment fees.[36] Furthermore, if the plaintiff is a foreign person or entity, a deposit of an amount of security might be requested by the competent court. In other words, according to

34 It should be underlined here also that until the recent amendment of the Turkish Code of Procedure (hereinafter referred to as CP), it was accepted that the division between general Civil Court and Commercial Court was only a work basis division and not on competence. Since amendment, such division became competence sharing and thus required ex officio examination. See DEYNEKLİ (n 9), 110–112; NOMER, EKŞİ and GELGEL (n 1), 83–84.

35 If there is not any attachable asset, it is not possible to demand the exequatur of the foreign arbitration award. For further detail, please see DEYNEKLİ (n 9), 111–112; ÇELİKEL A, 691; NOMER, EKŞİ and GELGEL (n 1), 83–84. It should also be indicated here that the jurisdiction competence should not be examined ex officio according to Turkish procedural law; it should be submitted as preliminary objection by the defendant party.

36 See DEYNEKLİ (n 9), 113–114 for the discussion on Supreme Court jurisprudence.

Article 48 of IPPL, the court, in the case of non-existence of the reciprocity (legal or de facto), might oblige the foreign party to deposit an amount of security.[37]

Following the proceedings in the court, the respondent would have two weeks to respond, extendable by another two weeks. The court should conclude the case in two hearings after the preliminary hearing, and the two hearings shall be spaced in a month's time. However, if the merits of the case required a deviation from this procedure, the court is authorised to do so. Such cases are classified as urgent matters and are to be decided in simple proceedings.[38]

An application for exequatur should be accompanied by the original (or conformed) copy of the arbitration agreement and the award and their translations as per Article 61, IPPL.

The defendant(s) would have two possibilities for defence. They might either object to the arbitral award on the basis of the non-existence of the conditions of the recognition and exequatur or accept the award by arguing that he or she is performing or will perform his or her obligations arising from the award.[39]

Last, it should be underlined here that the Turkish court could procedurally examine the foreign arbitral award. The court cannot examine the judgments of the arbitration panel on the merits of the case; it should carry out its examination without consideration of the merits. This limitation of the court is called the interdiction of the "*revision au fond*".[40]

Conditions and consequences of the recognition and exequatur

REASONS FOR THE DISMISSAL

The Turkish court might either decide on the recognition and exequatur of the foreign arbitration award or dismiss the recognition and exequatur demand partially or wholly. Article 62 of IPPL states the conditions, the existence of which could lead the court to order dismissal of recognition and exequatur demand.

Non-existence of a valid arbitration agreement could be a reason for dismissal of an application for recognition. The existence and validity of the arbitration agreement should be examined separately from the main agreement.[41] According to the Supreme Court decision, an award granted by a tribunal that was not constituted in accordance with the arbitration agreement should

37 DEYNEKLİ (n 9), 114.
38 For further detail, please see DEYNEKLİ (n 9), 114–116.
39 DEYNEKLİ (n 9), 116; NOMER E, EKŞİ N, GELGEL ÖZTEKİN G, 84.
40 See DEYNEKLİ (n 9), 112–113; NOMER (n 2), 555; NOMER, EKŞİ and GELGEL (n 1), 83–86.
41 NOMER, EKŞİ and GELGEL (n 1), 72–73.

also be examined under the non-existence of the arbitration agreement.[42] This stipulation can be waived neither by the preparation or existence of the Terms of Reference nor by the decision of the arbitration panel on the existence of an arbitration agreement.[43] Validity of the arbitration agreement is not affected by the non-compliance of the stipulated alternative dispute resolution methods for resolution of the dispute, but it might constitute reason for dismissal on another basis such as excess of competence or breach of the agreed arbitration procedural rules.[44]

Non-conformity with the arbitration agreement regarding appointments to the tribunal or in the case of non-existence of such agreement or stipulation, non-conformity to the *lex arbitri* would be another reason for the dismissal.[45]

Interesting and unique to Turkish law is the ground of dismissal of the recognition application if the award is not in conformity with the public order, including immorality and lack of subject-matter arbitrability according to Turkish legal order.[46] Furthermore, the award could be denied recognition and exequatur if it relates to an issue other than the reference to the tribunal. Non-respect of the audience rights of the party (or parties) would also be a reason for dismissal.[47]

If the arbitration award is invalid according to the applicable law or in the case of non-existence of such law according to the place of the arbitration panel, this would also be a reason for the dismissal of the recognition and exequatur[48] demand.

Awards that lack finality and are neither enforceable nor binding for the parties could be denied recognition and exequatur. If the award is not legal and executable, it should not be recognised or enforced.[49]

CONSEQUENCES OF THE RECOGNITION AND EXEQUATUR

As the review of the Turkish court on the foreign arbitration award would be procedural, the Turkish court should recognise and declare enforceable the foreign award or dismiss wholly or partially the demand.

When the recognition and exequatur is granted, the award would have the effect of a Turkish court decision in accordance with Article 57 of IPPL and might be subjected to the enforcement proceeding with judgment.

Courts might partially approve and/or partially dismiss the demand. In such cases, the approved part would have the effect of a judgment, whereas

42 See NOMER (n 2), 556.
43 *Ibid.*, 557.
44 *Ibid.*, 555.
45 Paragraph III/1 and NOMER, EKŞİ and GELGEL (n 1), 61–67.
46 Paragraph III/3.
47 Paragraph III/4.
48 Paragraph III/1.
49 NOMER (n 2), 563.

the dismissed part would not become enforceable nor constitute definitive judgment/direct evidence.

International carriage and recognition and exequatur

Arbitration is a common dispute resolution practice in international carriage of goods. Parties to the contract of carriage agree on an arbitration agreement for the resolution of the disputes arising in the application of the carriage agreement.

Under the Turkish legal system, no special rules exist for the recognition and enforcement of foreign arbitration awards on the international carriage of goods. The competent court for the recognition and exequatur is the Commercial Court or Specialised Court of Maritime (in the case of involvement of maritime carriage), as this is classified as commercial affairs and commercial litigation according to Articles 3 and 4 of the Turkish Commercial Code (hereinafter referred to as TCC).[50]

Carriage of goods involves third parties to the enforcement of the contract. The contract of carriage would be concluded between the contractual carrier and shipper (or charterer). Therefore, in the enforcement of the contract, third parties (such as actual carrier, sub-carrier, employees, stevedores, freight forwarders, consignees) could be involved.[51] The main question in the arbitration (foreign or Turkish) would be the revocability of the arbitration agreement to these third parties of the agreement. Could the arbitration agreement be revocable to the third parties of the contract of carriage despite the existence of the doctrine of the privity of the contract under Turkish law?

The Turkish Supreme Court decided that the arbitration agreement incorporated into the charterparty might be revocable to the third party who would be the holder of the bill of lading. The court held that in the case of reference of the bill of lading to the charterparty (general reference or specific reference to the arbitration agreement), the arbitration agreement would become revocable to the holder of the bill of lading who might be a third party to the contract of carriage (as consignee, for instance).[52] The Supreme Court also accepted that the arbitration agreement concluded between the carrier and

50 According to Article 3, all affairs regulated in the TCC should be classified as commercial affair. The Article stipulates that such affairs regulated under TCC should be judged in Commercial Court.

51 See BOZKURT BOZABALI B, *Havayoluyla Yolcu Taşıma Sözleşmelerinde Taşıyanın Ölüm ve Cismani Zarardan Doğan Hukuki Sorumluluğu* (Legal Responsibility of the Air Carrier in Case of the Death and Bodily Injury of the Passenger) (Seçkin Publishing 2013), 27–34; SÖZER B, Havayoluyla Yük Taşıma Sözleşmesi (Contract of the Carriage of Goods by Air) (Vedat Publishing 2009), 53–54.

52 See EKŞİ N, *Milletlerarası Deniz Ticareti Alanında "Incorporation" Yoluyla Yapılan Tahkim Anlaşmaları* (Arbitration Agreement via Incorporation concluded in the field of International Maritime Commerce) (Beta Publishing 2010), 110–115.

the insurant (or insuree) would be revocable to the insurer as well under the principle of subrogation.[53]

Might such kind of arbitration agreement be revocable to the third parties of the contracts of carriage other than carriage by sea on the basis of the carriage documents (such as airway bill, railway bill or inland bill of lading)? Might the revocable character of the arbitration agreement to third parties in the contracts of carriage by sea on the basis of the negotiable instrument nature of the bill of lading be extendable to the other documents of carriage, even those that are not of a negotiable instrument nature? A perusal of the jurisprudence of the Supreme Court would help conclude that the revocability of the arbitration agreement to a third party is based on the signature of the third party to the bill of lading. As the Turkish law requires a written arbitration agreement, such condition could be fulfilled by the signature of the third party on the document containing express stipulation of the arbitration agreement or reference to the charterparty having an arbitration clause (or agreement). The signature of the third party on the document of carriage (whether negotiable or non-negotiable instrument) would render the arbitration agreement revocable to this third party even if the document has referred only to the main agreement containing the arbitration agreement. In conclusion, the arbitration agreement might be revocable to the third parties of every kind of contract of carriage if these parties have their signature on the documents of carriage containing an express stipulation or reference to the arbitration agreement.

Conclusion

The Turkish legal order, over the years, has evolved on its approach to the arbitration and the recognition and exequatur of arbitration awards.

Post-millennium, there has been an easing of the regulatory structure related to arbitration and the recognition and exequatur procedure, especially for foreign arbitration awards. With the growth of foreign trade, Turkey started to become an arbitration-friendly country.

The enforcement of IAC in 2001 and IPPL in 2007 helped position Turkey as an arbitration-friendly country, especially with the removal of the conditions of reciprocity in the recognition and exequatur in foreign arbitration awards.

The practices of arbitration started to grow, which also increased the number of recognition and exequatur demands in front of Turkish courts that started to favour the recognition and exequatur of foreign arbitration awards.

Last, but not least, in light of the explanations in the previous paragraphs, Turkey's practice in the recognition and exequatur of foreign arbitration awards might be classified as similar to the New York Convention, with slight

53 See KENDER R, *Türkiye'de Hususi Sigorta Hukuku*, (Law of Private Insurance in Turkey) XII (Levha Publishing 2015), 351–368. On the revocability and different views in the Turkish doctrine, please see EKŞİ N, 134–141.

differences on the basis of public order. Especially in cases of a foreign arbitration award being granted in Turkey, IAC that is derived from New York Convention would become applicable.

Part II – Recognition and exequatur of foreign court judgments and the contract of international carriage

Introduction

Besides the foreign arbitration awards, the foreign court's judgment needs to have a recognition and exequatur decision from a Turkish national court in order to become enforceable or revocable in the Turkish legal system.

Accordingly, the recognition and exequatur of the foreign court's judgment procedure is regulated similarly to the recognition and exequatur of a foreign arbitration award.[54]

The process of recognition and exequatur of the foreign court judgment is simpler, in comparison to that of the arbitral award.

According to Article 50 paragraph 1 of IPPL, the judgment should be foreign[55] and final (binding).

Such foreign judgment, whether civil or penal, should be given in order to solve a litigation arising from individual rights.[56]

The effect of the recognition and exequatur of the foreign judgment is similar – it would be considered as conclusive evidence and final; the foreign judgment is enforceable as a Turkish court judgment, as per the first paragraph of Article 57 of IPPL.

Last, it should be underlined here that the recognition and exequatur of the foreign judgment decision should be given on the basis of IPPL. If the merits of the foreign judgment fall within the scope of a bilateral or multilateral foreign agreement, the stipulations of IPPL would be applied as secondary legal source (namely, in case of the lacuna in the agreement).[57]

Terms and conditions of the recognition and exequatur of foreign court decisions

Reciprocity

Differently from the foreign arbitration award, reciprocity is the first condition for the exequatur of a foreign judgment. Before starting to explain reciprocity

54 Or vice versa as the recognition and exequatur of the foreign court judgments procedure is stipulated before the recognition and exequatur of foreign arbitration award in IPPL.
55 The principle of foreignness was discussed in Paragraph III/2/a of Sub-Chapter 1.
56 See NOMER (n 2), 501–503. Accordingly, the judgments on punitive damages could not be subjected to an exequatur demand because of their punitive (penal) nature.
57 See NOMER (n 2), 511–512.

in detail, it should be emphasised here that reciprocity would be looking only for the exequatur.[58]

Reciprocity is very controversial condition[59] on the exequatur proceeding. To determine reciprocity, national courts' judges inquire as to the existence of a bilateral or multilateral agreement between Turkey and the country-of-origin of the judgment.[60]

The Supreme Court accepted the existence of legal reciprocity if the foreign country's procedural legal order does not lay down reciprocity as a condition for the recognition and exequatur.[61] The possibility of exequatur according to foreign country's procedural legal order should also be verified.[62] Obstacles in the foreign country's legal order in relation to the judgment to be executed also need to be investigated. Specifically, such foreign legal system should not demonstrate legal obstacles for the exequatur of such judgment.

In the absence of a clear reciprocity agreement, de facto reciprocity could be verified in the application of the foreign courts' practices. A lasting non-recognition or refusal of exequatur of a Turkish court's judgment in a foreign country would be a reason for the refusal of a Turkish court of the exequatur on the basis of reciprocity. The lasting practice of refusal of recognition and exequatur of Turkish court judgments of the foreign courts should also be against the legal order of this country.[63]

Legal or de facto reciprocity should be verified according to the foreign court's legal order and not according to the national legal order of the parties of the litigation.[64]

Public order and existence of compulsory national legislation

Public order

Turkish courts should also take into consideration the impact of the foreign judgment on Turkish public order after the recognition and exequatur. Therefore, during the review of the compatibility of the foreign judgment with Turkish public order, the courts review the possible impact of the recognition and execution of this judgment on the order.[65]

Accordingly, an important impact of the foreign judgment's recognition and exequatur is on economic life, especially endangering the existence of an economically weak person or entity might be a reason for the refusal on the basis of public order.

58 *Ibid.*, 533–535.
59 *Ibid.*, 511–512.
60 *Ibid.*, 510–511.
61 Supreme Court 11th Circuit decision given at 06.11.1985; NOMER (n 2), 12–513.
62 See NOMER (n 2), 512.
63 *Ibid.*, 511.
64 *Ibid.*, 515–519.
65 This should also be assessed in the interdiction of the "revision au fond". See NOMER (n 2), 508, 519–521; Paragraph III/3 of Sub-Chapter 1.

Furthermore, the conformity of the basic procedural rules of Turkish law such as the existence of a foreign judgment given by a judge that should be recused would be taken into consideration under public order.[66]

In addition to this, the existence of the new reasons for the reopening of the case in the foreign country would also be a reason for the dismissal of recognition and exequatur demand.[67]

Therefore, Turkish courts may dismiss the recognition and exequatur demand only on the basis of the effects (in other words, consequences) of the recognition and exequatur on Turkish public order.[68]

Despite not being expressly stipulated in IPPL, the existence of a final and binding judgment of a Turkish court on the same merits, same subject and between the same parties of the foreign judgment, the recognition and exequatur demand should also be dismissed on the basis of public order.[69]

Existence of compulsory national legislation

According to Article 54/b of IPPL, if the merits of the case fall into the compulsory national competence of a Turkish court, the foreign court's judgment would not be recognised or executed.

The Turkish courts could verify if there exists national legislation on the merits of the case, rendering a Turkish court a compulsory competence.[70]

The Turkish courts could also examine the jurisdictional competence of the foreign court. If the foreign court gives its judgment without the existence of its point of attachment to the merits of the case or the parties, this would also constitute a reason for the dismissal of the recognition and exequatur demand.[71]

Therefore, this would be different from the competence and jurisdiction rights of the foreign court. The Turkish judge should examine the relation ship of the foreign court to the merits of the case or the parties. If, according to the rules of the conflict of laws of this foreign court, this court might be regarded as one of the competent national jurisdictions, then its judgment should be recognised and executed by a Turkish judge, or else the demand should be dismissed.

The rights of audience of the parties

Due process and the right of audience to the parties are important criteria for a decision on the exequatur of the foreign judgment.

66 See NOMER (n 2), 519–522.
67 *Ibid.*, 526.
68 *Ibid.*, 522–525.
69 *Ibid.*, 526.
70 Paragraph III/2 of the Sub-Chapter 1; NOMER (n 2), 513–515.
71 See NOMER (n 2), 525–526.

The party that alleged the denial of the right of audience would be the concerning party whose rights of audience are violated. In other words, the person (or entity) who could allege non-respect should not be one of the parties of the recognition and exequatur case but might only be a party interested in the consequences of this case.

Accordingly, Article 54/c, in stating briefly "the rights of audience", cites in detail the cases of non-respect of the rights of audience. They are:

- if the party has no notice of the proceedings as per the law of the foreign court; or
- if he or she is not represented in the proceeding; or
- in contradiction with the national law of the foreign court;
- if the foreign judgment is *ex parte.*

However, if a party has participated in the foreign court's proceeding, the absence of a due invitation would not constitute a reason for the dismissal of recognition and exequatur demand.[72]

A Turkish judge cannot take *suo motu* cognisance of the denial of audience rights of the parties in a foreign court's proceedings, within the application for recognition and exequatur. The judge can only act upon the application by a party during such proceedings.[73]

Objection possibilities of the defendant

Article 55 of IPPL stipulates the objection possibilities of the defendant.

Accordingly, the defendant would have three possibilities:

- object to the recognition and exequatur of the foreign court judgment on the basis of the non-existence of the conditions of recognition and exequatur; or
- accept the foreign judgment and ensure compliance; or
- will perform his or her obligations or the occurrence of an obstacle is preventing him or her from fulfilling these obligations.[74]

Article 55 also stipulates that the proceedings shall not be complex but a simple trial procedure.[75]

Procedural rules

The procedural rules on the recognition and exequatur are regulated under different Articles.

72 *Ibid.*, 526–527.
73 *Ibid.*, 527–528; Paragraph III/2/a of Sub-Chapter 2.
74 See NOMER (n 2), 531.
75 Paragraph III/6 of Sub-Chapter 1.

Article 51 stipulates that the competent courts for the recognition and exequatur of foreign judgments are civil courts. Therefore, as it was explained under the recognition and exequatur of foreign arbitration awards, here also a specialised court should be accepted as competent.[76]

The Turkish court hearing the exequatur should consider the circumstances at the time of the finalisation of the foreign judgment.[77]

Any party having legal interest in the recognition and exequatur of the foreign judgment may apply for recognition and exequatur even if they were not one of the parties of the foreign judgment in question.[78]

In the case of conformity of the foreign judgment to the conditions, a Turkish judge should decide on the recognition and exequatur of the judgment. The Turkish court does not have the right to examine the merits of the case; the judge should only procedurally review the judgment.[79] In accordance with the interdiction of the "*revision au fond*", the court may partially or wholly accept or dismiss the recognition and exequatur demand.[80]

Similar to the recognition and exequatur of foreign arbitration awards, Article 53 of IPPL stipulates that the applicant for the recognition and exequatur of the foreign court judgment should annex the original (or conformed copy) of the final and binding court judgment, a formal letter of the competent authorities authenticating that judgment and the translation, if required. It is not possible to submit a photocopy of these documents.[81]

Recognition and exequatur and international contract of carriage

The Turkish law does not have any special provisions with regard to the recognition and exequatur of foreign court judgments on the international contract of carriage. The earlier narrative on this issue also applies to contracts of international carriage.

An interested party could apply to the Commercial Court (as the carriage is a commercial affair) or Specialised Maritime Court (if the litigation is on the international carriage by sea) for the recognition and exequatur of the foreign court judgment.

Turkish courts apply the stipulations under IPPL especially with regard to existence of the conditions – reciprocity in the case of exequatur, public order, compulsory national competence and rights of the audience of the parties, decided upon in a simple trial procedure.

76 Here there exist also specific regulations of different Codes (such as the competence of the Family Court made in Article 4 of the Code numbered 4787). see NOMER (n 2), 505; paragraph III/5 of the Sub-Chapter 1.

77 See NOMER (n 2), 505.

78 *Ibid.*, 529.

79 The interdiction of "revision au fond" is also in force here. NOMER (n 2), 530–531.

80 See NOMER (n 2), 531–532.

81 *Ibid.*, 542.

Objections against recognition and exequatur could be founded upon the non-existence of the conditions of exequatur or fulfilment of obligations arising from the international carriage contract in due diligence or that an obstacle has occurred, preventing fulfilment of obligations. In hearing the parties' arguments for and against the exequatur, the Turkish courts would not examine the merits of the case – the stipulations of the contract of international carriage and the judgment are given on the basis of this contract by the foreign court.

Conclusion

Compared with recognition of foreign arbitration awards, Turkish law and courts seem reticent about recognition and exequatur of foreign judgments – the existence of reciprocity as one of the conditions of recognition and exequatur renders the Turkish legal system unfavourable for recognition and exequatur of foreign court judgments.

As a key jurisdiction in the geography that forms part of the OBOR initiative, Turkey could consider law reform, especially in the space of recognition and exequatur of foreign awards and judgments. It could help create increased economic value by reducing the transaction costs for international contracts, especially those arising from dispute resolution, through strengthening the legal regime related to foreign court/tribunal orders, interim as well as final, especially in the space of international contracts for carriage. This would require that Turkey consider law reform in the space of substantial as well as procedural law affecting contractual, maritime and carriage-related commercial laws as well as dispute resolution laws.

Conclusion

Tackling private international law issues for the success of the OBOR

Poomintr Sooksripaisarnkit, Sai Ramani Garimella

The editors chose in this book to address a much-neglected topic in discourses surrounding China's gigantic 'One Belt One Road' (OBOR) project – *private international law*. Readers who read this book up until this page would readily realise how fascinating this area of law is. With the OBOR project being driven in full speed by the Chinese government, this book presents a warning sign to the Chinese government that without private international law issues being consciously addressed, the OBOR project will not be sustainable.

Despite 67 countries involved in the OBOR plan, the editors observed that the Chinese government and the Supreme People's Court (SPC) still take 'inward'-looking attitude. Two developments within the People's Republic of China in support of the OBOR has come into focus. The first development is the plan to issue a 'judicial interpretation on the recognition and enforcement of foreign civil and commercial judgments' to clarify the concept of reciprocity to be applied in the Chinese courts.[1] In his chapter, Tsang discusses complexity surrounding the meaning of reciprocity within the context of the Chinese law. However, leaving aside problems concerning the law on the recognition and enforcement of foreign judgments in China, Elbalti reveals there are also problems and uncertainties concerning such laws in the Arab countries. He maintains further that uncertainties also exist among ASEAN countries participating in the OBOR project. Among ASEAN countries, there is much disparity among those countries which adopt the civil law legal system.[2] In Indonesia and in Thailand, there is not even a law on the recognition and enforcement of foreign judgments.[3] In her contribution, Bozkurt also reveals complications in the law of on the recognition and enforcement of foreign judgments in Turkey. There has been a suggestion that China has been active in the

1 'SPC Reveals New Belt & Road-Related Initiatives' <https://supremepeoplescourtmonitor.com/2017/10/07/spc-reveals-new-belt-road-related-initiatives/> (*Supreme People's Court Monitor*, 7 October 2017) accessed 29 January 2018.

2 Adeline Chong (ed), *Recognition and Enforcement of Foreign Judgments in Asia* (Asian Business Law Institute 2017), 3.

3 *Ibid.*, 4.

'Judgments Project' under the auspices of the Hague Conference on Private International Law.[4] However, whether the Judgments Project will come to fruition remains questionable. Even if the Judgments Project does materialise, the fact remains that it inevitably takes time for any international convention to be ratified and to come in force, and it is unlikely to come in time for the OBOR developments.

Another development from the SPC is an establishment of the dispute resolution forum specifically for the OBOR disputes.[5] The recent news is that this forum will come in a form of an international commercial court to be established with the headquarters in Beijing and with the court in Xi'an having jurisdiction over disputes involving the 'Silk Road Economic Belt' and the court in Shenzhen having jurisdiction over disputes involving the '21st-century Maritime Silk Road'. Illuminating such a plan, Yip reveals in her contribution experiences from the Singapore International Commercial Court, and such experiences are not without difficulties. Cross-border commercial litigations are always complex, and such disputes require well-versed and sophisticated judges. The Singapore International Commercial Court has drawn on expertise of international judges. It is yet to be seen whether the international commercial court to be established in China will involve international judges as well. The fact remains that today most complex commercial litigations are brought before courts in countries such as the United Kingdom or the United States or Singapore. It is unclear whether Chinese judges have required sophistication in handling complex commercial cases.

While courts are important in international litigations, the law the courts are to apply is equally important. Both Zeller and Garimella highlight the likely importance of the United Nations Convention on Contracts for the International Sale of Goods (Vienna, 1980) (CISG) in further enhance harmonisation among the OBOR countries. However, the CISG is an optional instrument, and it does not deal with all aspects of contractual issues involved in international trade. To this end, Zeller suggests the UNIDROIT Principles of International Commercial Contracts (latest updated version 2016) should be used to supplement the CISG. Similar to the CISG, the UNIDROIT Principles come into play only if the parties to the contract choose them. This brings into question the issue of party autonomy.

In his chapter, Sooksripaisarnkit highlights the fact that not all OBOR-participating countries recognise the concept of party autonomy in choice of law in contract. Even if the concept of party autonomy is recognised, as Chunchaemsai suggests in his chapter, the choice of law may not be given effect to if it is contradictory to the public policy of the forum. He points out that even just within the ASEAN countries different countries have different perception of what constitutes the public policy. It is suggested here that it is the case also in countries outside the ASEAN region.

4 'SPC Reveals New Belt & Road-Related Initiatives' (n 1).

5 *Ibid.*

With the project of enormous scale as the OBOR, the law concerning international trade becomes just a facet of it. John and Gulati point us to another facet – anti-corruption. This is significant, especially when large funds have become accessible for the building of infrastructures. They point out concerns from private international law perspective that the law to combat corruption is largely premature, and they encourage more researches into the field. This is in conjunction with the warning of some that, without careful control, the OBOR project may end up creating global financial problems.

Other facets relevant to the OBOR as Kunda discusses are competition and data protection. Indeed, these facets are significant, not only in the context of the EU. Not much discussion has been made in other parts of the world. Indeed, the laws on these aspects in some OBOR countries are currently inaccessible – due to languages or otherwise.

This echoes concerns Huo raises in his contribution. The law of many countries along the OBOR routes remain unknown and inaccessible due to language barriers, lack of systematic record keeping systems and different legal cultures. So even with the successful establishment of the international commercial court in China, difficulties in proving and applying the law of these countries remain inevitable. Indeed, the editors faced similar problems when they tried to invite contributors to this collection that locating relevant scholars in some of these countries happened to be an insurmountable task.

But the OBOR is not only about the courts in China. It involves the courts in 67 jurisdictions. Therefore, the synchronisation in terms of judicial procedure becomes another important matter. In this respect, Guo and Fu raise an important point concerning the prospect of the service of process by electronic means. However, as they realise, these 67 countries are not on the same page in terms of technological advancement. The synchronisation of judicial procedure, not only on the aspect of the service of process, becomes significant bearing in mind the procedural law is always the matter for the *lex fori* (law of the forum).

To some extent, discussions on the private international law issues pertaining to the OBOR undeniably overlap with the larger topic of harmonisation of private international law on the global level. However, attempts at unification at the global level involve all 195 countries of the world, unification at the OBOR level requires consensus of only 67 countries. However, as the editors and different contributors in this book repeatedly emphasise, seamless trade and cooperation cannot occur without a certain degree of harmonisation in terms of legal infrastructure. It is the editors' hope that this book presents, not the end, but the start of further academic discourses on the private international law issues involving the OBOR.

Index

www.ingramcontent.com/pod-product-compliance
Ingram Content Group UK Ltd.
Pitfield, Milton Keynes, MK11 3LW, UK
UKHW022002180926
475701UK00003B/155
9780367590444